RELAPSE AND RECOVERY IN ADDICTIONS

RELAPSE AND RECOVERY IN ADDICTIONS

RELAPSE AND RECOVERY
IN
ADDICTIONS

edited by

Frank M. Tims
Carl G. Leukefeld
Jerome J. Platt

Yale University Press/New Haven & London

Designed by Mary Valencia.
Set in Minion and Syntax types by Tseng Information Systems, Inc.
Printed in the United States of America.

Library of Congress Cataloging-in-Publication Data
Relapse and recovery in addictions / edited by Frank M. Tims, Carl G. Leukefeld, Jerome J. Platt.
p. cm.
Includes bibliographical references and index.
ISBN 0-300-08383-1 (alk. paper)
1. Substance abuse — Relapse — Prevention.   2. Substance abuse — Patients — Rehabilitation.
I. Tims, Frank M.   II. Leukefeld, Carl G.   III. Platt, Jerome J.
RC564. R4376   2001
616.86′0651 — dc21   00–043598

A catalogue record for this book is available from the British Library.

The paper in this book meets the guidelines for permanence and durability of the Committee on Production Guidelines for Book Longevity of the Council on Library Resources.

10   9   8   7   6   5   4   3   2   1

*Dedicated to the memory
of David Nurco,
scholar and friend*

CONTENTS

CONTRIBUTORS

ANGLIN, M. DOUGLAS, Ph.D., Professor-in-Residence, Director Drug Abuse Research Center, University of California–Los Angeles.

BROOME, KIRK M., Ph.D., Associate Research Scientist, Institute of Behavioral Research, Texas Christian University.

BROWN, BARRY S., Ph.D., Professor, Graduate Faculty, University of North Carolina at Wilmington.

BÜHRINGER, GERHARD, Ph.D., Director, IFT Institute for Therapy Research, Munich.

CIESLA, JAMES R., Ph.D., Assistant Professor, School of Allied Health Professions, Northern Illinois University.

CRADDOCK, S. GAIL, M.S., National Development and Research Institute.

DE LEON, GEORGE, Ph.D., Director, Center for Therapeutic Community Research; Research Professor of Psychiatry, New York University School of Medicine.

DEMATTEO, DAVID S., Law-Psychology Graduate Program, Allegheny University of the Health Sciences and Villanova University School of Law.

FARABEE, DAVID, Ph.D., Assistant Research Psychologist, University of California at Los Angeles Drug Abuse Research Center.

FESTINGER, DAVID S., Ph.D., Assistant Professor, Institute for Addictive Disorders, Allegheny University of the Health Sciences.

FLETCHER, BENNETT W., Ph.D., National Institute on Drug Abuse.

FLYNN, PATRICK M., Ph.D., National Development and Research Institute.

GLASS, DAVID J., J.D., Ph.D., Schnader, Harrison, Segal and Lewis, LLP.

GOSSOP, MICHAEL, Ph.D., Head of Research, Drug Dependence Unit, National Addiction Centre, Institute of Psychiatry, London.

GRELLA, CHRISTINE E., Ph.D., Associate Research Psychologist, Drug Abuse Research Center, University of California–Los Angeles.

HART, CARL, Ph.D., Research Fellow, College of Physicians and Surgeons, Columbia University; Division of Substance Abuse, New York State Psychiatric Institute.

HSER, YIH-ING, Ph.D., Adjunct Professor, Drug Abuse Research Center, University of California–Los Angeles.

HUBBARD, ROBERT L. Ph.D., Director, Institute for Community Based Research, National Development and Research Institute, Inc., Raleigh, N.C.

JOE, GEORGE W., Ed.D., Senior Research Scientist, Institute of Behavioral Research, Texas Christian University.

KANIA, EDYTA D., Graduate Assistant, School of Allied Health Professions, Northern Illinois University.

KAPLAN, CHARLES, Ph.D., Coordinator, Drug Use and Abuse Research, International Institute for Psychosocial and Socioecological Research, Netherlands.

KINLOCK, TIMOTHY W., Ph.D., Assistant Adjunct Professor, Division of Criminal Justice, Criminology and Social Policy, University of Baltimore; Research Associate, Friends Research Institute, Inc., Baltimore, Md.

KOSTEN, THOMAS R., M.D., Professor of Psychiatry, Yale University School of Medicine; Chief of Psychiatry, VA Connecticut Healthcare System.

LEUKEFELD, CARL G., D.S.W., Professor and Director, Center on Alcohol and Drug Research, Lexington, Kentucky.

LI, LI, Ph.D., Assistant Professor and Research Scientist, Substance Abuse Intervention Programs, School of Medicine, Wright State University.

LONGSHORE, DOUGLAS, Ph.D., Associate Research Sociologist, Drug Abuse Research Center, University of California–Los Angeles; RAND Drug Policy Research Center.

MARCZYK, GEOFFREY R., Law-Psychology Graduate Program, Allegheny University of the Health Sciences and Villanova University School of Law.

MARLOWE, DOUGLAS B., J.D., Ph.D., Senior Scientist, Treatment Research Institute of the University of Pennsylvania.

MCCANCE-KATZ, ELINORE F., M.D., Ph.D., Associate Professor of Psychiatry, Yale University School of Medicine, VA Connecticut Healthcare System.

MCCARTY, DENNIS, Ph.D., Human Services Research Professor, Heller Graduate School, Brandeis University.

MELNICK, GERALD, Ph.D., Principal Investigator, Center for Therapeutic Community Research.

MERIKLE, ELIZABETH P., Ph.D., Assistant Professor of Psychiatry, University of Pennsylvania.

MONTI, PETER M., Ph.D., Professor of Psychiatry and Human Behavior Career Research Scientist, Providence VA Medical Center and Center for Alcohol and Addiction Studies, Brown University.

NURCO, DAVID N., D.S.W., Research Professor, Department of Psychiatry, School of Medicine, University of Maryland at Baltimore.

PLATT, JEROME J., Ph.D., Professor of Psychiatry; Director, Institute for Addictive Disorders, MCP Hahnemann School of Medicine.

PRENDERGAST, MICHAEL L., Ph.D., Associate Research Historian, Drug Abuse Research Center, University of California–Los Angeles.

RAPP, RICHARD, C., M.S.W., Assistant Professor, Project Director, Substance Abuse Intervention Programs, School of Medicine, Wright State University.

ROHSENOW, DAMARIS J., Ph.D., Professor (Research) of Community Health, Providence VA Medical Center and Center for Alcohol and Addiction Studies, Brown University.

RUBENSTEIN, DAVID F., Psy.D., M.S.W., Clinical Assistant Professor, Institute for Addictive Disorders, Allegheny University of the Health Sciences.

SAHA, PRANJIT, M.S., Research Associate, Substance Abuse Intervention Program, School of Medicine, Wright State University.

SCHOTTENFELD, RICHARD, M.D., Professor of Psychiatry, Yale University School of Medicine.

SIEGAL, HARVEY A., Ph.D., Professor and Director, Substance Abuse Intervention Programs, School of Medicine, Wright State University.

SINHA, RAJITA, Ph.D., Assistant Professor and Clinical Director, Substance Abuse Treatment Unit, Department of Psychiatry, Yale University School of Medicine.

SIMPSON, D. DWAYNE, Ph.D., Professor of Psychology and Director, Institute of Behavioral Research, Texas Christian University.

SKALA, SHARON Y., M.S., Project Manager, School of Allied Health Professions, Northern Illinois University.

SPEAR, SHERILYNN F., Ph.D., Professor, School of Allied Health Professions, Northern Illinois University.

STEENROD, SHELLEY A., M.S.W., Research Assistant, Heller Graduate School, Brandeis University.

TIMS, FRANK M., Ph.D., Visiting Professor, Department of Psychiatry and Behavioral Medicine, University of South Florida.

TÜRK, DILEK, Junior Scientist, IFT Institute for Therapy Research, Munich.

WANIGARATNE, SHAMIL, Ph.D., Clinical Psychologist, Drug Dependence Unit, National Addiction Centre, Institute of Psychiatry, London.

I

*Understanding Relapse and Recovery
in Drug Abuse*

ONE

RELAPSE AND RECOVERY

Frank M. Tims, Carl G. Leukefeld, & Jerome J. Platt

INTRODUCTION

Understanding of relapse and processes underlying recovery are essential elements in both the science and treatment of addictions. In this volume, we have set out to review major scientific issues, research findings, and treatment insights relating to those processes. This volume was originally conceived as an opportunity to revise and update the National Institute on Drug Abuse (NIDA) research monograph *Relapse and Recovery in Drug Abuse* (Tims and Leukefeld 1986). The reader will see that this new effort goes beyond that limited goal. For one thing, the field has enlarged greatly in terms of our understanding of addiction, the development of treatments, and the structure of the treatment establishment. In just a little over a decade, the annual research budget for NIDA has increased severalfold, and funding of drug abuse research by other organizations has increased. Treatment research has been ambitious, and promising developments in medications to treat addictions, behavior therapies, and cognitive-behavioral approaches have emerged. Clarification of the natural history of alcoholism and drug abuse have made major contributions to knowledge. Our understanding of the significance of the financing, organization, availability, and delivery of treatment is being dramatically strengthened through health services research. Thus, the present work addresses issues of relapse and recovery at several levels and explores critical issues.

ADDICTION, ABUSE, AND DEPENDENCE

Historically, addiction referred to a physical phenomenon characterized by withdrawal, i.e., an abstinence syndrome, and the repeated behaviors to avoid withdrawal. Because the behaviors associated with obtaining and using the drug had consequences for others (e.g. victimization) and led to neglect of obligation to others, the term *addiction* came to have meaning as a short-hand for behavioral health disorders that involve the compulsive, continuing use of psychoactive substances in ways that are harmful to the user and/or innocent parties with whom the user comes in contact. Over time, psychiatrists and other professionals dealing with problems of drug addiction and dependence refined and operationalized concepts of abuse and dependence, defining them in terms of their commonalities. While such an approach does not resolve all serious conceptual problems, it has proven useful in developing a common schema for research and clinical practice. Abuse and dependence criteria are specified in terms of symptoms and problems of social functioning in the American Psychiatric Association's *Diagnostic and Statistical Manual of Mental Disorders,* 4th edition (DSM-IV).

Addiction in the broad sense has physical, psychological, and social aspects. It tends to be associated with social complications, risk of chronicity, and stigma. Political and economic considerations have had a considerable impact on provision of treatment. Leshner (1997) has characterized drug addiction is a "brain disease" with behavioral manifestations and social consequences. Drug use has immediate effects that "modify brain function in critical ways," and "prolonged drug use causes pervasive changes in brain function that persist long after the individual stops taking the drug." It is a chronic and relapsing disease. The brain disease model is based on neurobiological changes in vulnerable individuals, brought on by sustained use of the drug, in response to its effects on the brain. In addition to biological mechanisms, the role of conditioning has been repeatedly cited as central to understanding and managing addiction (Wikler 1973; Vaillant 1983; O'Brien et al. 1993). Conditioning models provide a theoretical convergence for explanation of craving and relapse. For example, the argument that drug users may be self-medicating emotional pain (Khantzian 1985) fits well with a general conditioning model. Addiction is not simple, and multiple problems must be addressed in dealing with it. It is not a single type, but rather it involves variation in neurobiology, comorbidities, conditioning, environmental cues, social context and contingencies of use, culture, and personal/social resources for recovery. The complexity of addiction and the pervasive role of conditioning argue against the notion that individuals can easily stop use.

RELAPSE AND RECOVERY

Our understanding of relapse and recovery has unfolded in evolutionary fashion. Early studies of treatment outcomes found return to regular narcotic use to be ubiquitous (see O'Donnell 1969), yet periods of abstinence, sometimes quite long, were noted. Others found that, with the passage of time, the percentage of these subjects voluntarily abstinent at follow-up increased (Duvall, Locke, and Brill 1963). Studies of long-term outcomes of treated opioid addicts have found substantial proportions to be abstinent a decade later (Vaillant 1966; Simpson and Sells 1990). Research on the natural history of alcoholism (e.g., Vaillant 1983, 1998), long-term outcomes of addiction treatment (Simpson and Sells 1990), and treatment career perspectives (Vaillant 1998; Anglin et al., this volume), as well as co-occurring psychiatric disorders (Rounsaville et al. 1982; Regier et al. 1990) have made it abundantly clear that subtypes exist among addicted persons, that the pattern and significance of outcomes may vary, and that multiple treatment strategies must be developed to address the needs of different populations.

Relapse is a persistent feature of addiction. In fact, relapse may be part of a learning process that leads ultimately to recovery. There are a number of conceptual and methodological problems in defining both relapse and recovery. These include the need for continuous measures of outcome, methods for assessing outcomes, the inclusion of non-drug-related criteria, and the impact of compliance or attrition on outcomes. Hubbard and Marsden (1986) noted that "the understanding of relapse to drug abuse is complicated by current drug abuse patterns that involve multiple use of a wide range of types of licit and illicit drugs, and many patterns of abuse. . . . A basic type of relapse is the posttreatment return to use of a specific drug (e.g. cocaine) that was used before treatment. A second type is the nonmedical use of a drug to substitute for a principal pretreatment drug. . . . A more comprehensive definition of relapse is the posttreatment resumption of the pretreatment pattern of drug use, or the development of new patterns of use." A similar but somewhat enlarged formulation is presented by Hubbard et al. in the present volume. They argue that "a full multidimensional definition of relapse should also include consideration of the type, extent, and timing of relapse," and they take into account the severity of patterns of use. It may be posttreatment resumption of a specific drug, nonmedical use of a drug to substitute for a principal pretreatment drug, resumption of the pretreatment pattern of drug use (e.g., multiple use of heroin, cocaine, marijuana, and alcohol) or the development of new patterns of use comparable to previous levels. Among a national sample of clients admitted to treatment in 1991–93, about two-thirds relapsed in the year after treatment, and over three-quarters of the relapses were within the first three months. Time to relapse was comparable to previous studies. Some 15% of those who relapsed were already using drugs at the time they left treatment.

Recovery is reflected in longer-term patterns of outcome. Its criteria and complexity may be related to the drug in question, the treatments available, and sources of social support. Twelve-step programs define recovery as a process that sustains itself by a consciousness that it never ends, and it must be constantly part of the awareness of a person "in recovery." Achieving and maintaining abstinence is the goal toward which all work, and the fellowship is a key source of social support (see chapter by Brown, Kinlock, and Nurco in this volume). Other formulations of recovery view periods of reduced, controlled use as part of recovery patterns. Babor, Cooney, and Lauerman (1986) defined recovery as "either the stabilization of abstinence, or the regular consumption of a substance without the negative consequences previously associated with drug use." Vaillant (1983; 1998) identified a subtype of (nonprogressive) problem drinker able to return to controlled, social drinking, though recovery for most alcoholics must be abstinence-oriented. In his work on opioid addicts, Simpson (1990a) argues that significant subgroups of addicts return to patterns of occasional use without relapsing to daily, compulsive use and becoming readdicted. So long as the use did not amount to readdiction, and the individual had adequate levels of social functioning, this could be viewed as a favorable outcome.

Winick's (1962) observation that some addicts may "mature out" of addiction has sometimes been put forward in attempts to explain cessation of drug use. Simpson (1990b) argues that "as others have suggested . . . quitting daily opioid use is not simply a direct result of getting older or 'maturing out' of addiction. We observed a wide variation in the total number of years spent addicted, and chronological age and years of addiction were both unrelated to whether individuals were still addicted at the time of follow-up." Simpson further states, "Few addicts maintained daily use throughout their entire addiction career. . . . Almost three-fourths of the sample reported one or more relapses."

RECOVERY AND TREATMENT MODELS

Though relapse rates are high, treatment plays an important role in recovery. The decision to enter treatment and to maintain abstinence or some other pattern of recovery is usually in response to some major event, such as physical illness or arrest, social pressure from family, friends, or employer, or legal pressure, such as parole supervision and threat of reincarceration. Individuals vary widely in their levels of functioning, needs, settings, resources, social supports and degrees of pressure from significant others, and access to health and social services. The choice of treatments will vary based on both personal circumstances and availability. The role of different treatments and treatment adjuncts is reviewed in this book, along with the factors that influence response to treatment. In addition to examining research conducted mainly in the United States, the chapter by Buhringer et al. highlights work with a similar focus in Europe.

Treatment models vary in their underlying assumptions about the nature of the disorder, the client (or patient), and strategies for managing the course of treatment and recovery. Consideration of substance abuse as a chronic, relapsing disease introduces the expectation that relapse is a normal part of the natural history of the disease, and that prevention of relapse is a key element in recovery. The reasonable expectation that treatment will be associated with significant improvements and longer periods of abstinence, with fewer relapses, has been suggested by McLellan et al. (1997). Thus, an argument for criteria of treatment success is set forth that the disease is managed, not cured. However, one could consider "management" of chronic disease in a social context, such that an array of services, aids to self-management, and mechanisms of social control operate, though imperfectly, to direct and constrain behavior. Such interventions as case management and linkages between social agencies and treatment can help overcome fragmentation of services and limited treatment access.

The commitment to abstinence is a major theme in treatment. Abstinence is defined as essential to recovery, despite unspecified allowances for slips, in several models of treatment for cocaine and other stimulant abusers (Platt 1997). An example is Millman's (1988) definition of his third phase of treatment as "long term treatment," which includes maintaining a commitment to abstinence, avoiding renewed denial and overconfidence, and participation in self-help groups. This view is widely accepted in the substance abuse field. Because there is, at present, no substitution (or antagonist) therapy

available for cocaine abusers, as there is for opioid addicts, abstinence strategies are especially important. McAuliffe et al. (1990–91) call for maintaining
a "wall" against relapse triggers and supplies and point out that extinguishing the conditioned responses of addiction calls for continuing commitment
to abstinence, within a community of recovering persons. Functioning in the
larger society calls for developing a "commitment response" to drug stimuli,
which can bind the individual to an appropriate course of action and resolve
ambivalence.

Most individuals experience shifts in emotional states as part of everyday
life and deal with them in a variety of ways. Many substance abusers may
experience emotions more profoundly, whether as a consequence of drug
effects, withdrawal, co-occurring psychopathology, or greater exposure to
stressors in addict lifestyles. The role of emotional states and craving has
been addressed repeatedly in development of treatment models, in achieving
and maintaining abstinence. As Festinger et al. (in this volume) make clear,
the management of substance abuse and dependence includes coping with
emotional states and craving that can precipitate relapse. Emotional states
may be intertwined with craving, with conditioning enhanced by relief of
emotional distress or of craving (or both) by the substance abused. Intense
craving, even in abstinent persons, may be triggered by cues associated with
prior substance use. Such cues may include shifts in internal mood states, as
well as the presence of persons, locations, and paraphernalia associated with
prior use. Attempts to eliminate or reduce craving have included behavioral
approaches, as well as pharmacotherapies. Learning to cope with craving is
an essential part of maintaining abstinence. Strategies to reduce craving and
arousal (Childress et al. 1993) include avoiding stimuli that induce craving
and learning other responses to craving than substance use.

In their chapter "Relapse Among Cocaine Abusers," Rohsenow and Monti
examine relapse from the perspective of social learning theory. Social learning theory has been shown to be useful in developing effective interventions
to assist in achieving and maintaining drug abstinence. Examples cited by
Rohsenow and Monti are contingency management, aversive counterconditioning, relapse prevention training, cocaine specific coping skills training,
and use of pharmacological agents (such as disulfiram) to reduce the conditioning effect of cocaine by preventing its use in conjunction with alcohol.
Cue exposure with response prevention treatment (CET) was found to be
promising, but requires further development. In addition to recommending
further development of behavior therapies and application of motivational

enhancement approaches, Rohsenow and Monti point to the possible development of medications to reduce the likelihood of relapse, and the integrated study of multiple addictions.

The chapter by Hart et al. provides an overview of available pharmacological strategies for preventing relapse to alcohol, opiates, tobacco, and cocaine. Of these four categories of abused drugs, effective pharmacotherapies are available for all but cocaine, though a large body of research to discover agents useful in controlling craving for cocaine, associated complications, or blocking its effects dates back well over a decade. Although pharmacotherapies rely on regular administration of a substance, each requires psychosocial components for treatment to be effective over time. The function of the pharmacological agent is to control some facet of the addictive drug's effects, whether it be short-term relief of adverse consequences of toxicity or withdrawal, relief over time of felt need to use the abused drug (drug substitution), blocking of drug effects through administration of antagonists, or providing aversive consequences for use of the drug. Whatever the choice of pharmacotherapies, relapse prevention requires psychosocial treatments and a recovery model appropriate to the client.

A persistent problem in methadone clients is their use of other drugs, particularly stimulants, while in treatment (Condelli et al. 1991). In their chapter of this book, Broome, Simpson, and Joe report findings from their follow-up study of 711 methadone clients to examine their return to drug use, particularly heroin and cocaine. They defined relapse in terms of pretreatment to posttreatment use, drugs used, and frequency of use. Resumed use of the same drug and shifting to a new drug (substitution) are qualitatively different aspects of returning to use. Likewise, posttreatment use that is significantly less frequent than pretreatment use may be considered a step toward recovery. In this study, one-third (36%) had been frequent cocaine users pretreatment, 33% had used cocaine less than weekly, and 31% did not use cocaine. The frequent cocaine users dropped out of treatment earlier, and had poorer outcomes. All three groups had about the same level of relapse to daily opioid use (ranging from 53% to 56%) at follow-up. However, 59% of the pretreatment heavy cocaine users had daily posttreatment cocaine use, compared to 39% of pretreatment less-than-weekly cocaine users and 25% of those who did not use cocaine pretreatment. The authors recommend that methadone treatment providers add treatment enhancements to address cocaine use.

MOTIVATION, COERCION, AND SUBSTANCE ABUSE TREATMENT CAREERS

The role of motivation and readiness for treatment and change have been examined in recent years (e.g., see Simpson and Joe 1993; De Leon et al. 1994). The ambivalence evident in many clients raises questions regarding the extent to which they are simply responding to external pressures, or whether they are ready for changes. Our ability to assess their underlying motivation and its stability is important because that relates directly to retention in treatment and, ultimately, to the progress of patients' recovery. De Leon, Melnick, and Tims (this volume) address the role of motivation and readiness, as well as conceptual models of stages of change. Motivation as a broad, multidimensional construct referring to cognitions and perceptions of the individual's need for and readiness to change has been empirically demonstrated. Motivational factors themselves do not directly result in recovery, but they function to engage the individual in treatment or other interventions that lead to recovery. Although motivational factors are essential to recovery, their contribution is limited by the complexity of the recovery process itself. The authors explore interventions that may enhance motivation. Studies indicate that focusing on components of motivation can result in positive outcomes by increasing the client's acceptance of treatment and improving retention in programs.

Motivation may have aspects that are internal (e.g., desires) and external (e.g. coercion, social pressures). Marlowe et al. (this volume) consider the efficacy of coercion in substance abuse treatment and relapse prevention. Research has shown that clients under legal pressure stay in treatment longer than (and have outcomes as good as) clients entering treatment voluntarily, though some studies have found non-mandated clients to do better than mandated ones. The authors question the relative severity of mandated and non-mandated clients, with implications for treatment outcomes.

ADDICTION AND TREATMENT CAREERS

Given the complexity and variability in the lives of addicts, recovery can best be understood in the context of longitudinal studies of the natural history of addiction. Treatment careers are an integral part of addiction careers, given the tendency of treatment populations to have multiple treatment episodes (Simpson and Sells 1990). Anglin et al. (1997) point to a heterogeneity of addiction careers, with opiate addicts more likely to have longer treatment histories (owing in large part to the widespread availability of outpatient methadone maintenance in the past two decades), while those primarily addicted to alcohol and cocaine have more of a tendency to use shorter-term treatments. Anglin et al., (this volume) examine the factors related to treatment careers among opioid addicts, with special emphasis on the California Civil Addict Program (CAP) and the influence of treatment policy on the duration of addiction careers. In addition, they examine longitudinal data on cocaine addicts experiencing different treatment modalities. Among their observations are that daily narcotic use among CAP subjects escalated soon after initiation of use and remained relatively high until about age 30, when it began to decline, due in part to methadone maintenance enrollment after it became available in California. The policy implications they draw include provision of treatment much earlier in patients' addiction careers. The authors argue for treatments that address the needs of different addict subgroups. For the truly recalcitrant, they recommend developing and applying program options, including those provided through the criminal justice system.

SPECIAL RISK GROUPS:
ADOLESCENTS AND THE DUALLY DIAGNOSED

Addiction at an early age poses both health and developmental problems, and creates a host of dilemmas for clinicians and researchers. In their chapter, Spear, Ciesla, Skala, and Kania review issues of relapse and recovery as they pertain to adolescents, and treatment needs of this risk population. Drug use patterns may be highly variable, mixed, and episodic among adolescents. Conceptualizing and measuring drug use among adolescents affects the perceived level of treatment success. Most drug involvement among adolescents involves marijuana and/or alcohol and may be episodic — thus the baseline may include both occasional and regular users. In addition, adolescents entering treatment may be doing so after a period of supervision, either in a controlled environment or through court supervision. Ineffective treatments may show reduction in use due to contextual factors, while effective treatments may not appear to reduce substance use as much as is really the case, because of artificially low baselines. Thus, care must be taken in baseline assessments.

Because they are in the early phase of substance abuse careers, the opportunity to intervene entails greater long-term benefits to the child and to society. Intervention with this population must provide adequate services, which recognize that the problem is "not just drugs or alcohol." At moderate to high levels of severity, there may be health and cognitive developmental issues to be addressed. Histories of physical and sexual abuse and family dysfunction may be present. Psychiatric comorbidity is increasingly common among both adolescent and adult admissions to treatment, and research has not adequately established the relation between specific comorbid conditions and treatment outcome. The authors recommend research focusing on approaches to sustaining recovery that specifically targets adolescents, recognizes heterogeneity within adolescent treatment populations, and measures posttreatment drug use in ways that take into account different levels and patterns of use.

Dually diagnosed patients present greater risk of relapse in substance abuse treatment. The problem is complicated by the fact that subtypes of mental disorders may require differing approaches. Sinha and Schottenfeld, in their chapter, consider the diagnostic and prognostic significance of co-occurring psychiatric disorders among substance abusers and present an integrated approach to treating substance abuse in the presence of mental disorders. Their approach recognizes heterogeneity (i.e., dual diagnosis involving psychotic disorders, and dual diagnosis with nonpsychotic axis I and axis II disorders) and the differing treatment needs of subtypes. For those with psychotic illness, a level of care determination is made and a treatment plan developed. Psychotic symptoms may be aggravated by substance abuse, and thus drug abstinence, along with appropriate medications, may significantly reduce psychiatric symptoms. Medications compliance is a key concern here. Harm reduction approaches may be indicated for some patients who have difficulty maintaining abstinence.

TREATMENT PROVISION, COORDINATION OF SERVICES, AND SELF-HELP GROUPS

Services may be delivered in a variety of environments, and they involve an assortment of providers. Recovery spans a long period, encompassing periods of treatment on an acute care basis, longer-term rehabilitation programs, and reliance on support in the form of social networks and self-help groups. The two-tiered substance abuse treatment "system" was described by Gerstein and Harwood (1991) as consisting of one sector paid by public funds and another supported by private insurance. Within the public tier, the treatment system and the criminal justice system intersect, either through self-contained facilities or linkages. Such linkages, properly implemented, can overcome the tendency for a brief episode of treatment to be the only intervention provided, and instead provide the continuum of care that will promote recovery. In addition, fragmentation of the service system in both public and private sector programs tends to limit access to a continuum of care that is necessary to treat substance abuse effectively and prevent relapse. The issue is complicated by the introduction of managed care into the health care system generally, and the question of how it affects access to, utilization of, and effectiveness of substance abuse and related care must be addressed. In addition, the reality that much of substance abuse treatment takes place in the criminal justice system requires serious consideration of this system as a provider in the overall context of addictions recovery.

The fragmentation of services has been problematic for substance abuse treatment providers. The generally limited resources and skills of many substance abuse clients, especially those in the criminal justice system, the dually diagnosed, and the homeless, make access to and coordination of needed services difficult. Case management approaches are used to enhance service coordination, promote retention of clients in treatment, provide coordination between substance abuse providers and such other agencies as courts, reduce barriers to treatment, orient clients to the treatment system, monitor progress of clients, and provide advocacy for clients. Siegal, Rapp, and Saha, in this volume, present a conceptual overview of case management, models of case management, and research findings on use of case management with differing treatment populations to enhance outcomes. The relation of case management to improved outcomes is examined, and observations are offered regarding the potential of case management for more effective treatment.

Given the prominence of substance abuse and dependence among prison and jail populations, the need and opportunity for treatment are clear. The question of external vs. internal (i.e., compulsory vs. voluntary) motivation is addressed in the chapter by Farabee and Leukefeld, in terms of feasibility, efficacy, and ethics, with a key question being how much convergence exists between the goals of treatment and corrections. In the 1970s, availability of such treatment was limited, with only about one-quarter of jails and about half of state prisons having any provision of treatment (Tims and Leukefeld 1992). Since that period, increased state and federal resources have been made available, and research has addressed both development of models and outcomes for corrections-based treatment. The tendency for high drug use years to also be high street crime years suggests that intervention during periods of incarceration could reduce both. Thus, from both perspectives of crime control and public health, one available strategy is a combination of enhancing motivation for voluntary participation (through therapies) and compulsory treatment, such that addicts are given maximum help in avoiding relapse during their most vulnerable years. In addition to providing such treatment during periods of incarceration, courts have other leverage over offenders, such as drug courts, diversion, and probation and parole stipulations. Among those at greatest risk of drug-related harm, combinations of internal motivation, external motivation, and harm reduction approaches may provide the greatest social gain.

In their chapter, McCarty and Steenrod set out a very cogent set of answers to the provocative question, "Is managed care compatible with relapse prevention?" Although managed care has reduced a great deal of unnecessary and costly hospital detoxification, in favor of less costly outpatient clinics, managed care has not realized its potential to reduce high utilization by promoting aftercare and preventing relapse. The authors state that managed care and relapse prevention are compatible if care is managed to promote recovery and inhibit relapse. The authors present the Massachussets Medicaid mental health carve-out as a case study in how managed behavioral health care actually increased admissions to treatment services in non-hospital settings, coupled with a decline in utilization of more costly hospital detoxification units. In the carve-out, support is provided for a strong continuum of outpatient care, though specialized services to prevent or arrest relapse are not evident. The potential for effective managed care strategies, including case management, is evident as part of a suggested overall improvement. The authors point to the need to change the view of policy makers that substance abuse is an episodic disorder rather than an illness that requires chronic care strategies.

The role of self-help groups in preventing relapse (Brown, Kinlock, and Nurco, this volume) has long been a subject of interest in the treatment research community. The potential of self-help groups is implicitly recognized by treatment and correctional agencies, as the large number of referrals to AA, NA, and other groups attest. The twelve-step philosophy has been incorporated into formal treatment programs, and AA or NA participation is set forth in treatment and aftercare plans. The widespread use of recovering staff, many of whom are active AA or NA members (there is no formal membership, but rather a fellowship) in treatment programs creates a web of influence for these self-help movements' philosophies. The emphasis on abstinence and mutual peer support, as well as the disease concept of alcoholism or addiction, is an ideological set that appears to work for many. What is missing in self-help organizations is a body of research on effectiveness of self-help groups. One constraint is the AA/NA emphasis on anonymity, which renders longitudinal study of its members difficult. Participation in self-help groups during aftercare is one aspect of treatment that can be studied and effectiveness assessed. The use of self-help groups to enhance the duration and intensity of treatment, and to extend the periods of abstinence, holds clear promise, but remains to be documented through systematic research.

CONCLUSION

Drug abuse and dependence are a complex, multidimensional problem, and the path to recovery may be highly variable. The weight of the evidence is that treatments do effectively reduce relapse and promote recovery. It is essential that we understand the role of social influences, motivation, and the organization and effective provision of services in support of recovery. In addition to medications, a broad array of social resources is available to us. These include heightened public awareness of addiction problems, opportunities to intervene earlier with health services, provision of services to those in the criminal justice system, use of social and legal pressures to reduce relapse and move addicts toward recovery, use of a growing knowledge base to improve treatment, provision of more comprehensive and targeted treatments, and use of aftercare and self-help to enhance outcomes. When relapse prevention fails, especially among the dually diagnosed, appropriate harm reduction strategies must be considered. The chapters that follow provide in-depth examination of these issues and approaches.

References

Anglin, M. D., Hser, Y. I., and Grella, C. E. (1997). Drug addiction and treatment careers among clients in the Drug Abuse Treatment Outcome Study (DATOS). *Psychology of Addictive Behaviors* 11 (4): 308–323.

Babor, T. F., Cooney, N. F., and Lauerman, R. J. (1986). The drug dependence syndrome as an organizing principle in the explanation and prediction of relapse. In Tims, F. M., and Leukefeld, C. G., *Relapse and Recovery in Drug Abuse.* NIDA Research Monograph 72, Washington, D.C.: U.S. Govt. Printing Office, pp. 20–35.

Childress, A. R., Hole, A. V., Ehrman, R. N., Robbins, S. J., McLellan, A. T., and O'Brien, C. P. (1993). Cue reactivity and cue reactivity interventions in drug dependence. In Onken, L. S., Blaine, J. D., and Boren, J. J., eds., *Behavioral Treatments for Drug Abuse and Dependence,* NIDA Research Monograph 137. Rockville, Md.: National Institutes of Health.

Condelli, W. G., Fairbank, J. A., Dennis, M. L., and Rachal, J. V. (1991). Cocaine use by clients in methadone programs: Significance, scope, and behavioral interventions. *Journal of Substance Abuse Treatment* 8:203–212.

De Leon, G., Melnick, G., Kressel, D., and Jainchill, N. (1994). Circumstance, motivation, readiness, and suitability (the CMRS scales): Predicting retention in therapeutic community treatment. *American Journal of Drug and Alcohol Abuse* 20(4): 495–515.

Duvall, H. J., Locke, B. Z., and Brill, L. (1963). Follow-up study of narcotic drug addicts five years after hospitalization. *Public Health Reports* 78:185–193.

Gerstein, D. R., and Harwood, H. J. (1990). Treating drug problems, vol. 1. Washington, D.C.: National Academy Press.

Hubbard, R. L., and Marsden, M. E. (1986). Relapse to use of heroin, cocaine, and other drugs in the first year after treatment. In Tims, F. M., and Leukefeld, C. G., *Relapse and Recovery in Drug Abuse.* NIDA Research Monograph 72, Washington, D.C.: U.S. Govt. Printing Office, pp. 157–166.

Khantzian, E. J. (1985). The self-medication hypothesis of addictive disorders: Focus on heroin and cocaine dependence. *American Journal of Psychiatry* 142(11):1259–1264.

Leshner, A. I. (1997). Addiction is a brain disease, and it matters. *Science* 278:45–47.

McAuliffe, W. E., Albert, J., Cordill-London, G., and McGarraghy, T. K. (1990–91). Contributions to a social conditioning model of cocaine recovery. *International Journal of the Addictions* 25(9A and 10A): 1141–77, 1990–91.

Millman, R. B. (1988). Evaluation and clinical management of cocaine abusers. *Journal of Clinical Psychiatry* 49 (suppl.2):27–33.

McLellan, A. T., Woody, G. E., Metzger, D., McKay, J., Durell, J., Alterman, A. I., and O'Brien, C. P. (1997). Evaluating the effectiveness of addiction treatment: Reasonable expectations, appropriate comparisons. In Egertson, J. A., Fox, D. M., and Leshner, A. I., *Treating Drug Abusers Effectively.* Malden, Mass.: Blackwell, pp. 7–40.

O'Brien, C. P., Childress, A. R., McLellan, A. T., and Ehrman, R. (1993). Developing treatments that address classical conditioning. In Tims, F. M., and Leukefeld, C. G. (eds.), *Cocaine Treatment: Research and Clinical Perspectives.* NIDA Research Monograph 135. Rockville, Md.: National Institutes of Health, pp. 71–91.

O'Donnell, J. A. (1969). *Narcotic Addicts in Kentucky.* Washington, D.C.: U.S. Govt. Printing Office.

Platt, J. J. (1997). *Cocaine Addiction: Theory, Research, and Treatment.* Cambridge, Mass.: Harvard University Press.

Regier, D. A., Farmer, M. E., Rae, D. S., Locke, B., Keith, S. J., Judd, L. L., and Goodwin, F. K. (1990). Comorbidity of mental disorders with alcohol and other drug abuse: Results from the Epidemiological Catchment Area study. *JAMA* 264:2511–2519.

Rounsaville, B. J., Weissman, M. M., Kleber, H., and Wilber, C. (1982). Heterogeneity of psychiatric diagnosis in treated opiate addicts. *Archives of General Psychiatry* 39:161–166.

Simpson, D. D., and Joe, G. W. (1993). Motivation as a predictor of early dropout from drug abuse treatment. *Psychotherapy* 30(2):357–68.

Simpson, D. D., and Sells, S. B. (1990). *Opioid addiction and treatment: A 12-year follow-up*. Malabar, Fl.: Krieger.

Simpson, D. D. (1990a). Longitudinal outcome patterns. Chapter 3 in Simpson, D. D., and Sells, S. B. (1990), *Opioid Addiction and Treatment: A 12-Year Follow Up*. Malabar, Fla.: Krieger (pp. 55–71).

Simpson, D. D. (1990b). Final comments. Chapter 13 in Simpson, D. D., and Sells, S. B. (1990), *Opioid Addiction and Treatment: A 12-Year Follow Up*. Malabar, Fla.: Krieger (pp. 239–252).

Tims, F. M., and Leukefeld, C. G., eds. (1986). *Relapse and Recovery in Drug Abuse*. NIDA Research Monograph 72. Washington, D.C.: U.S. Govt. Printing Office.

Tims, F. M., and Leukefeld, C. G. (1992). The challenge of drug abuse treatment in prisons and jails. In Leukefeld, C. G., and Tims, F. M. (eds.). *Drug Abuse Treatment in Prisons and Jails*. NIDA Research Monograph 118. Washington, D.C.: U.S. Govt. Printing Office (pp. 1–7).

Vaillant, G. E. (1966). A twelve year follow-up of New York City addicts: I. The relation of treatment to outcome. *American Journal of Psychiatry* 122:727–737.

Vaillant, G. E. (1983). *The Natural History of Alcoholism*. Cambridge, Mass.: Harvard University Press.

Vaillant, G. E. (1998). Natural history of addiction and pathways to recovery. In Graham, A. W., Schultz, T. K., and Wilford, B. B., *Principles of Addiction Medicine* (2d ed.). Chevy Chase, Md.: American Society of Addiction Medicine, 295–308.

Wikler, A. (1973). Dynamics of drug dependence: Implications of a conditioning theory for research and treatment. *Archives of General Psychiatry* 28:611–616.

Winick, C. (1962). Maturing out of narcotic addiction. *Bulletin on Narcotics* 14:1–7.

TWO

DRUG TREATMENT CAREERS: CONCEPTUAL OVERVIEW AND CLINICAL, RESEARCH, AND POLICY APPLICATIONS

M. Douglas Anglin, Yih-Ing Hser, Christine E. Grella, Douglas Longshore, & Michael L. Prendergast

To obtain knowledge necessary for improving program practices and for informing policy makers, researchers have increasingly focused on drug use, its consequences, and its treatment from the perspective of the natural history of a person's life, contextually embedded in social conditions and recording major life events and transitions among them that are meaningful to the subject (Hser, Anglin, & Powers, 1993; Hser, Anglin, Grella, Longshore, & Prendergast, 1997; Tims & Ludford, 1984; Vaillant, 1966). Numerous natural history studies conducted over the past thirty years have examined both the course of drug use and its treatment. This research has demonstrated that, once initiated, drug use often escalates to more severe levels, with repeated cycles of cessation and relapse occurring over extended periods. This process has been characterized as a "drug use career," "dependence career," or "addiction career" (Frykholm, 1985; Hser et al., 1993; Maddux & Desmond, 1981; McGlothlin, Anglin, & Wilson, 1977; Simpson & Sells, 1982; Stephens, 1991). The similar process by which many drug users engage in cycles of treatment, abstinence, and relapse, however — essentially a "treatment career" (Hser et al., 1997; Senay, 1984) — has been studied less frequently. Such careers vary widely in length, patterns, and ultimate outcomes among drug users. Examinations of career patterns can help to identify and understand policy-relevant factors influencing drug use and its treatment over time and lead to improved interventions for reducing drug use and its consequences.

This chapter describes the treatment career perspective as a conceptual framework useful for consolidating research findings and suggesting research directions that have important policy implications. It presents findings of re-search by the UCLA Drug Abuse Research Center (DARC) as examples of the products of empirical applications of the concept and discusses related clinical, research, and policy questions.

DRUG TREATMENT CAREERS

Examining the effects of multiple, successive, and cumulative treatment epi-sodes over the course of a dependence career contrasts with the usual focus on single-treatment episodes used in conventional outcome evaluations. Al-though some individuals maintain long-term abstinence after a single treat-ment episode, others require multiple treatment episodes to produce sus-tained behavioral changes. Some may even require lifetime intervention to maintain their recovery or to minimize their drug use and its associated so-cial and personal consequences. Policy makers, practitioners, and research-ers concerned about drug treatment effectiveness have been disappointed by the small and often short-lived effects of most treatment approaches when examined in terms of a single episode (Anglin & Hser, 1990; Nurco, Balter, & Kinlock, 1994; Vaillant, 1988). Although such studies have consistently dem-onstrated that the duration of treatment is positively related to favorable out-comes, many drug users either do not access treatment or, if admitted, do not stay in treatment for sufficient time to accrue the potential benefit that single-episode treatment can produce. Moreover, research on addiction and criminal patterns has shown that those drug users who do utilize treatment typically delay entry until they are well established in a lifestyle committed to drug use and criminal activity (Stephens, 1991).

Even when drug users are successful at accessing treatment, the typical protocol experienced by most drug users is characterized by a low "dosage" of treatment, delivered in short-term episodes and rarely providing the full array of services needed to intervene with the multiple problems of this popu-lation (Etheridge, Craddock, Dunteman, & Hubbard, 1995; McLellan et al., 1996; McLellan & Weisner, 1996). These limitations help to explain why treat-ment, particularly when viewed as a single episode, is so frequently unable to provide significant, lasting improvements in clients with histories of long-term drug use. Unfortunately, a focus on treatment as a single-episode inter-vention is one that politicians, policy makers, and the public commonly hold when assessing the overall value of drug treatment. Too often, the conclu-sion is that drug users are unredeemable, rather than that policy attention needs to focus on improving treatment in ways that realistically address drug dependence as a chronic condition.

In contrast, studying treatment careers may more productively determine the different patterns of clients' treatment outcomes over time. Successive treatment admissions have been found to be associated with beneficial outcomes regarding drug use, alcohol use, employment, and criminality (Khalsa, Paredes, Anglin, Potepan, & Potter, 1993; Powers & Anglin, 1993; 1997; Simpson & Savage, 1980a, 1980b). Most importantly, a treatment career perspective provides an organizing framework for understanding the diverse results of previous research studies on treatment effectiveness and for synthesizing the wide range of factors that influence treatment access, entry, processes, and outcomes. As a policy tool, the treatment career approach can identify factors associated with the continuation or cessation of drug use over time; the longitudinal relations among drug use, criminal behavior, and drug treatment; the related social and economic costs; and the relative benefits of alternate intervention strategies.

A treatment career approach encompasses the complexity of diverse consumption patterns and related behaviors, especially those dynamic phenomena that influence recovery from drug dependence (Simpson, Joe, & Lehman, 1986; Vaillant, 1988). Previous research has identified initiation, maintenance, relapse, and termination as important stages in the addiction careers of opiate users (Simpson & Sells, 1990; Hser, Yamaguchi, Anglin, & Chen, 1995). Addiction careers can be analyzed in terms of onset, persistence, severity, and desistance. One important application of a career perspective moved beyond these simple descriptive dimensions to develop a career typology. Simpson and Savage (1980a, 1980b) sorted users by patterns of subsequent treatment over a period of four years after an index episode. Their typology included no treatment in the four posttreatment years, quick reentry (a new episode until the fourth year), and persistent treatment (participation in treatment in all four years). Determining those characteristics of users and programs that promote long-term abstinence after a single episode of treatment (a subset of cases receiving no further treatment after the index episode) can suggest improvements to interventions and existing treatment protocols in order to optimize clients' potential for recovery.

A treatment career approach draws upon other areas in which "career" has been applied as a theoretical construct, like studies of criminal careers, where researchers seek to analyze the development, maintenance, cessation, and resumption of criminal activity over the life course. In this application, the career perspective has been useful for identifying external factors that reduce the intensity or foster the early termination of criminal careers. In particular, individuals with particular career parameters can be selectively identified for specific criminal justice interventions. The drug treatment career is similar to the criminal career in that considerable stigma is associated with drug use and treatment participation (Cunningham et al., 1993). As a result, the initiation and development of a treatment career has to overcome many personal and social barriers. The treatment career is distinguished from the criminal career, however, in that drug users may choose to participate in treatment, whereas offenders are frequently remanded to interventions determined by others.

As a dynamic concept, treatment careers need to be examined within the context of the ever-evolving treatment service system ecology. Individual user characteristics make up only one aspect of how treatment is accessed and utilized. Program and system issues like accessibility and adequacy of services provided, client eligibility, and program financing are also important in the emergence and development of treatment careers (Hser et al., 1997). Only recently has research focused more intensely on program- and system-level influences on treatment outcomes (Gerstein & Harwood, 1990; Mechanic et al., 1995). Such attention has been partly driven by findings from treatment outcome studies indicating that client factors only weakly predict postdischarge relapse or abstinence. In addition, greater emphasis is being placed on health services research, particularly on the benefits and cost effectiveness of service elements and clinical protocols. Thus, social policy, service system characteristics, and program service arrays must all be assessed for their contribution to engagement and retention of users and to the typical levels of improvement produced during and after single and multiple treatment episodes.

DARC RESEARCH INVOLVING THE CAREER APPROACH

The concept of treatment careers has evolved over the past twenty years through work by DARC and other researchers in the field of drug use and treatment. (A comprehensive review of the relevant literature can be found in Hser et al., 1997.) After a brief overview of the historical development of the treatment career perspective as it emerged from DARC research studies, we provide examples of empirical findings and discuss their implications.

HISTORICAL OVERVIEW AND THE NATURAL HISTORY APPROACH

Starting in the early 1970s, UCLA drug abuse researchers initiated a series of evaluation studies using the natural history approach that had been developed by Nurco (Nurco et al., 1975) and Vaillant (1966). The development and application of the natural history approach to collecting data from drug users laid the methodological foundation for DARC's treatment career research. In brief, the UCLA Natural History Interview provides a view of each person's life from first drug use to the time of interview and allows chronological analysis of changes in behaviors and activities within various psychosocial domains over a person's lifetime. The initial DARC studies primarily concerned evaluation of the outcomes of the California Civil Addict Program (CAP) for the civil commitment of addicted offenders. These research efforts are described in articles by McGlothlin, Anglin, and Wilson (1975–76; 1977; 1978) that reviewed client characteristics at intake, behavior during the program, and the discharge and postprogram status of CAP participants. Results showed that success (defined as completion of the program and satisfactory discharge from parole) was achieved by fewer than 25% of these addicted offenders and was related to ethnicity, with whites showing higher rates of success than Mexican Americans, whose rates were in turn better than those of African Americans.

Assessing treatment effectiveness by using such crude endpoint measures, however, masked much of the behavioral and social benefits of the program. This realization prompted a reassessment of many of the measures and techniques previously used in similar investigations, with the intent to find sensitive approaches to assess important dynamic aspects of the behaviors of addicts before, during, and after the intervention. Thus, DARC researchers began to address the limits of the prevailing evaluation methodologies and attempted to "extend beyond the rigid and narrowly defined success rate" to more precise measures of outcomes that led to better long-term understanding of "what benefits are derived by the individual and society during the lengthy period of commitment, regardless of any lasting cure of addiction that may or may not be achieved" (McGlothlin et al., 1975–76, p. 176).

Collecting natural history data allows the addiction, criminal, and treatment career parameters, like participation in drug use or treatment; frequency of use or service utilization; type of drug used or treatment received; length of, intensity of, and the related perceptions about use and treatment to be established for any specified time period and for subgroups of users. These patterns of use, treatment, and related behavior can then be displayed as time-series data to show changes over time for specific groups in specific domains, as was done in a further investigation of the CAP sample, resulting in a comprehensive and dynamic depiction of the addiction, criminal, and treatment careers of the subjects. A ten-year follow-up study (McGlothlin et al., 1977), funded by the National Institute on Drug Abuse, used a retrospective longitudinal design that employed the Natural History Interview and assessed the impact of CAP and subsequent treatment episodes on drug use, crime, and employment during the decade after program admission. The CAP evaluation study concluded that the CAP inpatient interventions and the associated community-based legal supervision produced favorable results primarily through moderating rather than eliminating narcotics use.

An example of the natural history of narcotics addiction in terms of the CAP sample's annual status in several important domains (e.g., narcotics use, incarceration, treatment participation) is shown in figure 2.1 (Anglin et al., 1988). This longitudinal display of behavioral status in these domains highlights several policy-relevant relations. First, data from this offender sample indicate that, once initiated, use progressed to dependence fairly rapidly. Although initiation into narcotics (heroin) use appeared as early as age 17 (year 1956), by age 22 (year 1961) periods of occasional use had dropped dramatically as daily use became common. Entry into the CAP occurred in 1963/64 and continued until 1968/69. The percentage of the sample who were engaged in daily narcotics use remained relatively high to about age 30 (year 1970) and decreased thereafter, in part due to the subjects' increasing participation in methadone maintenance treatment. After age 32 (year 1972), daily use periods remained stable for the entire length of follow-up, to an average age of 47 years. As is typical of the criminal career, incarceration rates were highest between ages 20 and 30, decreasing thereafter to a relatively stable equilibrium by age 36 (year 1976).

The policy implications suggested by these data include the need for intervention through the provision of drug abuse treatment much earlier in the addiction career; such intervention is possibly most effective when linked to criminal justice system supervision, which was so evident in the earlier period of this sample's natural history. Moreover, given the persistence of daily use into the late 40s for many addicts, treatment and other interventions for narcotic-dependent individuals must be planned for the very long term.

Since the original CAP evaluation, additional research findings, presented below, have accumulated to demonstrate that a career approach is useful for understanding addiction, criminal behavior, and drug treatment participation (Anglin & Perrochet, 1998). Specifically, the career perspective allows (1) identification and description of career parameters (e.g., participation, frequency, type of treatment, career length, intensity, and perceptions and attitudes), associated correlates (e.g., demographics, critical life events, psychosocial status), and differences among groups in these parameters; (2) explanation of relations between addiction and treatment careers over time

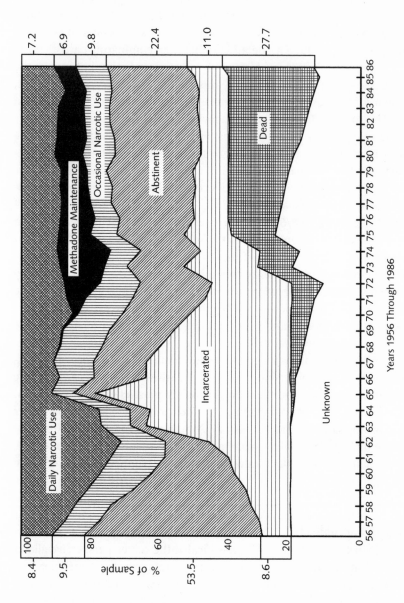

Fig. 2.1. The natural history of narcotics addiction. (N = 581)

and how they evolve; (3) prediction of treatment career development and transition (e.g., treatment seeking, utilization, engagement, retention, and outcomes) based on prior career characteristics and patterns; and (4) recommendations for more effective treatment strategies and policy development (Hser et al., 1997). Empirical examples of the career approach particularly relevant to policy making are presented in the following sections.

THE EFFECTS OF TREATMENT PARTICIPATION ON ADDICTION CAREERS

In a continuation of the outcome evaluation of the Civil Addict Program, successive follow-up studies revealed that some subjects were later admitted to methadone maintenance programs when that treatment modality became increasingly available in California after 1969, as seen in figure 2.1. Subjects who were interviewed in 1974–75 were divided into three subsamples according to their reported addicted use of narcotics in the three years prior to the follow-up interview (McGlothlin et al., 1977). Figure 2.2 illustrates the patterns of daily narcotics use among the three subsamples identified according to narcotics use and treatment status at the time of the interview, which occurred about twelve years after admission to CAP.

The group labeled Inactive (40% of the overall sample) consisted of subjects who steadily reduced narcotics use during the approximately six-year commitment period and did not resume addicted use following discharge from CAP; they could be considered to have achieved personal control of their recovery and to have "matured out" of addiction (Winick, 1962). The Active subjects (representing 30% of the sample) were chronic addicts for whom the highly structured program resulted in an average reduction in narcotics use of about 10% during the commitment period, but who resumed high levels of addicted use after discharge. The Subsequent Methadone subjects (also 30% of the sample) showed a 25% reduction in daily use during the structured and monitored commitment period, but resumed addicted use after CAP discharge, returning to levels of daily use similar to those reported during the precommitment years (years 14 through 10 of figure 2.2). These addicts apparently realized their need for further treatment and chose to reenter treatment, this time involving methadone maintenance. On entry to this modality, immediate and dramatic reductions in daily narcotics use were sustained during the three years of follow-up. Because of the availability of two types of treatment, widely separated in time, and their notable effects on addict behavior, this study exemplifies the importance of viewing the full addiction career rather than looking only at "snapshot" points in time. The varying addiction career patterns as they were related to treatment career

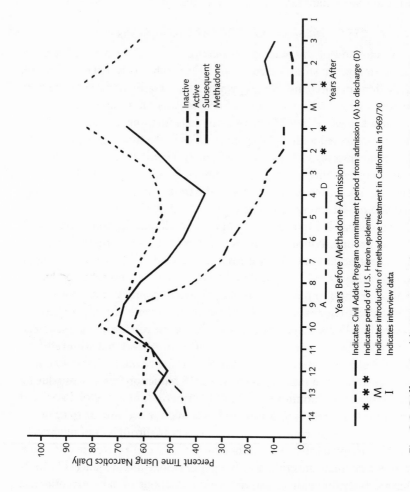

Fig. 2.2. Different addiction careers by treatment participation. (N = 425)

histories (presented in figure 2.2) demonstrates the different impacts of two treatment modalities on narcotics use. These findings suggest the importance of maintaining a treatment system with diverse components, both drug free and pharmacotherapy assisted, to meet the needs of different addict subgroups. Moreover, program options for the truly recalcitrant addict (here, making up the Active group) must be developed and applied, most likely through the criminal justice system. Providing such alternatives to meet the needs of this diverse population would likely in the long-term produce better outcomes for drug abuse treatment overall.

EFFECTS OF COMBINATIONS OF DIFFERENT MODALITIES

Although earlier UCLA career-based studies focused primarily on treatment for heroin addiction, a later evaluation of cocaine treatment using a career approach also demonstrated that treatment outcomes vary over time according to different patterns of treatment utilization. The relative effectiveness of the most commonly accessed cocaine treatment modalities was assessed, separately and in various combinations, for a representative sample of cocaine abusers presenting at the West Los Angeles Veterans Affairs Medical Center (Khalsa, Paredes, & Anglin, 1993; Khalsa et al., 1993). Four groups were defined based on their patterns and levels of involvement with formal and informal treatment during the follow-up period. In terms of continued abstinence, the greatest success at two-year follow-up was achieved by 30% of clients whose treatment consisted of an initial 21-day inpatient period, an outpatient follow-up regimen (individual and group counseling), and continued involvement in self-help groups throughout most of the follow-up period. By contrast, only 15% of clients whose treatment consisted solely of a single 21-day inpatient episode were abstinent throughout the follow-up period. Prosocial behavior (employment and stable interpersonal relationships) also improved most for the group that received a continuum of care (inpatient, outpatient, self-help). Figure 2.3 demonstrates how the level of severe cocaine use was considerably reduced for all subjects in the 24-month follow-up period compared to the 12-month period before treatment entry. As with abstinence, improvement was greater and more stable over time for the group with the higher participation in treatment. Over time, improvement was most dramatic for those with multiple episodes of residential treatment. Thus, a treatment career approach demonstrates that different patterns and sequences of treatment may produce different long-term treatment outcomes. These findings suggest that clinical practice policies that provide appropriately sequenced continuity of care and encourage clients to participate

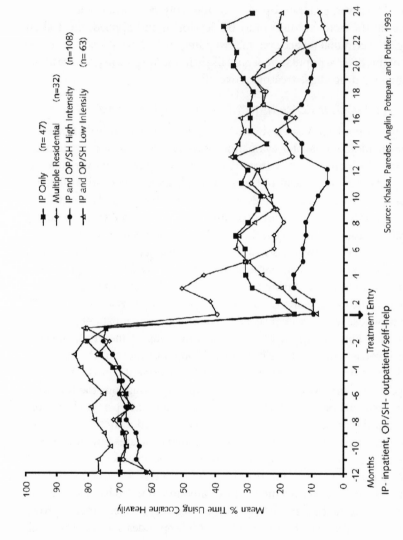

Fig. 2.3. Effects of different treatment modality combinations on severe levels of cocaine use. (N = 250)

Source: Khalsa, Paredes, Anglin, Potepan, and Potter, 1993.

in such care will likely result in improved behavioral outcomes compared with single-episode treatment approaches.

EFFECTS OF MULTIPLE TREATMENT EPISODES

Many people with drug dependence have multiple, separate treatment experiences, often involving the same modality but without a planned continuity of care. In this regard, the possibility of incremental gains from up to five episodes of methadone maintenance treatment was examined by Powers and Anglin (1993). The most notable findings included: (1) a dramatic reduction in daily narcotics use was achieved during each treatment episode, (2) the percentage of time engaged in daily narcotics use between periods of treatment, although high, remained less than that observed before initial treatment, and (3) many addicts returned for additional episodes of treatment because of relapse. In this analysis, no cumulative effects of treatment across episodes of methadone maintenance treatment were seen in the total sample.

A subsequent study (Powers & Anglin, 1998) disaggregated the sample into subgroups and examined their behavior over their first two periods of methadone maintenance treatment. Based on narcotics use patterns during on- and off-methadone periods, three groups of clients — Stabilized, Cumulative, and Deteriorating — were defined (see figure 2.4). In terms of daily narcotics use, the behavioral performance of the Stabilized addicts was promising. Although they did not demonstrate any noteworthy improvements from the first to the second treatment periods, these addicts showed no periods of addicted use while participating in treatment. This finding supports the idea that engaging long-term heroin addicts in methadone treatment reduces the overall impacts of their drug use on society. The policy implication of this finding is particularly notable because more than half of the sample were in the Stabilized group.

The Cumulative group demonstrated overall improvement in their various drug-related behaviors from the first to the second episode of treatment, suggesting that some addicts can achieve greater control of their drug use and other related behaviors over multiple episodes of treatment. Finally, the Deteriorating group, whose behavior worsened from the first to the second episode of treatment, can be characterized as more involved in drug dealing and property crime; they displayed few lasting signs of behavioral improvement due to methadone treatment participation. Addicts similar to members of this group should receive additional services to reduce their antisocial behav-

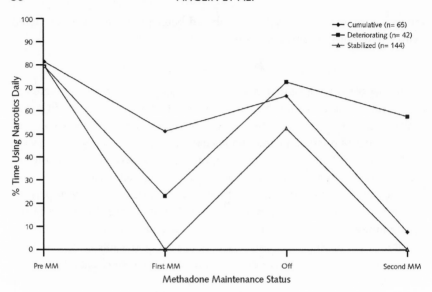

Fig. 2.4. Effects of multiple methadone maintenance treatment episodes on narcotics use. (N = 251)

iors, including greater concurrent monitoring by the criminal justice system. Although this analysis disaggregated treatment clients by level and pattern of daily use, other groupings are possible (e.g., psychiatric functioning) that may also be examined for differential successive and cumulative treatment effects.

IMPACTS OF PROGRAM POLICY AND SYSTEM CHANGES

DARC's career-based research showed that changes in treatment program policy and in public funding for drug treatment can profoundly affect the availability, utilization, and effects of treatment and thus can modify the course of individual addiction and treatment careers. One study examined the effects of program policies on retention and drug use outcomes among clients in three methadone maintenance programs (McGlothlin & Anglin, 1981b). Program A generally used a high-dose blockade level of methadone and employed a flexible policy regarding client behaviors. There was no firm date at which clients were expected to terminate treatment, and, except for cases involving violence, involuntary terminations for program violations were used only as a last resort after a series of client probationary periods. Program B subscribed to a policy where the maximum methadone dose for most patients was 80 mg. Program B was also flexible with respect to involuntary terminations, and there was no firm expectation with respect to a maximum time in the program. Program C, however, set the maximum dose for clients at 50 mg. In addition to the low-dose regimen, the program also imposed a fairly strict policy of termination for program violations, as well as an expected graduation after two years of maintenance treatment. In summary, during most of the time under consideration in the study, programs A and B followed a relatively high-dose, long-retention policy, while program C maintained a low-dose regimen with a relatively strict policy of termination for program violations.

Figure 2.5 shows the time to relapse to daily narcotics use after entry to methadone treatment of the three program samples for five years after admission. Although not shown, time to relapse tended to correspond directly to the time retained in methadone treatment. Program A shows the best performance, program B the second best, and program C the worst. The results of this long-term follow-up are remarkably consistent in showing that the two methadone maintenance treatment programs that used a high-dose, long-retention policy produced better results than did the third program utilizing low doses and a fairly strict policy of involuntary discharges for program violations. To a considerable degree, these benefits were due to the longer duration of time spent in maintenance treatment, but the advantage persisted to the time of interview some five years after admission.

Although these findings represent outcomes for programs established in California during the early 1970s, it is clear that the lack of standard operating policies across the state contributed to clinical practices in some programs that seriously attenuated the potential benefits of treatment for clients. Only recently have federal agencies established a minimum dose recommendation of 60 mg for most maintenance clients (Schuster, 1989) or provided standards for effective methadone maintenance treatment (Center for Substance Abuse Treatment, 1993). When considered from a natural history and treatment careers perspective, these findings suggest that effective program strategies can be identified and implemented to improve treatment outcomes.

Moving beyond program-level analysis to the level of the treatment system, funding policies in many states have decreased the availability of publicly funded methadone maintenance treatment in the past two decades. The consequences of this policy shift have been a reduction in the overall availability of subsidized methadone maintenance slots, disruptions in continuity of treatment for fee-for-service clients who are periodically unable to meet payment schedules, and a "revolving-door" use of repeated admissions to

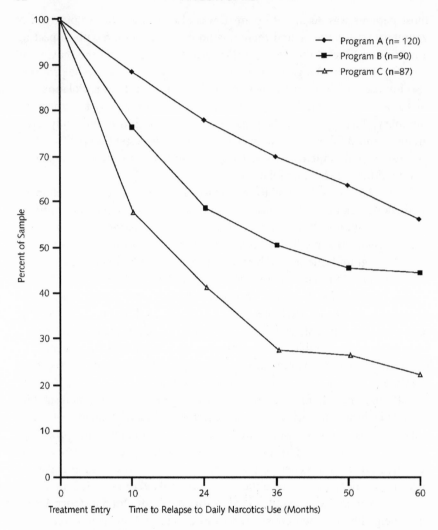

Fig. 2.5. Impact of program policies on time to relapse. (N = 297)

publicly subsidized methadone detoxification programs (Knight et al., 1996; McGlothlin & Anglin, 1981a; Rosenbaum, Irwin, & Murphy, 1988). When low-cost, publicly funded methadone treatment is unavailable, many addicts increase their levels of drug use, crime, and HIV risk behaviors (Rosenbaum et al., 1996). Reducing public funding for methadone maintenance, thereby reducing access to treatment, has been shown to dramatically alter the addiction and treatment careers of opiate addicts. For example, in a two-year

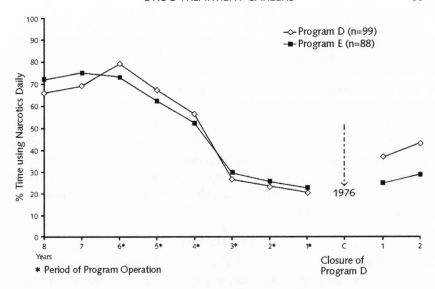

Fig. 2.6. Impact of system-level policy changes on addiction careers. (N = 187)

follow-up study of 99 clients who were enrolled in the only methadone clinic (program D) in a rural California county, which was defunded and closed by county officials, only 11 transferred to another form of treatment. More than one-half (54%) of the terminated clients resumed addicted-level use of heroin, and their arrest and incarceration rates were approximately double those of a comparison sample of clients from another clinic (program E) within a similar nonurban locale and with clients of comparable sociodemographic characteristics. Many of the clients involuntarily terminated from program D immediately relapsed to their previous levels of daily heroin use. Moreover, the terminated clients were less likely to be employed, more likely to deal drugs, and more likely to receive income from property crime compared to clients in program E (McGlothlin & Anglin, 1981a). Figure 2.6 illustrates the steady decreases in daily use for clients in Programs D and E in the years before the time of closure as increasing numbers of addicts elected to enter methadone treatment. After the closure of program D, a significant increase occurred in daily narcotics use by the clients terminated from the program.

DARC also conducted a follow-up study of more than 300 clients who were terminated from publicly subsidized methadone maintenance programs in San Diego, California. County officials, however, allowed client-paid fee-for-

service private methadone maintenance programs to be established by community providers. Results showed that clients who were unable or unwilling
to transfer into a private program were more likely at follow-up to be involved in criminal activity, particularly drug-related crime; to have contact
with the criminal justice system, including arrests, incarceration, and legal
supervision; and to use illicit drugs more frequently than were individuals
who continued their treatment without interruption by transferring to private methadone maintenance programs (Anglin, Speckart, Booth, & Ryan,
1989). Through tracking the addiction and treatment careers of heroin addicts, these studies have revealed the significant effects that program policies
and changes in service availability or public funding for treatment can have
on treatment outcomes.

DISCUSSION

In summary, although the empirical evidence of the effects and correlates
of successive and cumulative treatment episodes remains sparse, available
research findings have been encouraging. Research on program and system
effects on outcomes are only now being undertaken, but emerging findings
are likely to complement those reported above. The relations of program
and policy factors with treatment careers need to be examined in order to
support the development of more efficient and effective intervention strategies. For example, calculations of the cost benefits of drug treatment generally rely on the during-treatment and short-term posttreatment effects of a
single episode of treatment, but doing so is likely to underestimate the long-
term benefits of treatment (Hser & Anglin, 1991). Including relevant treatment career parameters (e.g., number, type, duration, and outcomes from
successive treatment episodes) within the estimation methodology will provide a more complete assessment of treatment costs and benefits. Furthermore, programs that use intake assessments that collect information on the
client's past treatment experiences will be in a better position to develop
treatment goals and plan activities that are suitable to clients with differing
career characteristics. Thus, a treatment career perspective can assist in designing and evaluating specific strategies and interventions within programs
or treatment systems; for example, treatment-experienced and treatment-
naive clients may require different intervention strategies to enhance their
motivation to engage in treatment and to sustain abstinence after treatment.

   As health policy adapts to a period of general transition, the past and current changes in the drug treatment service delivery system have had, and
will continue to have, substantial impact on treatment careers and outcomes.

If outcomes are not to be adversely affected under managed care and other emerging health care practices, the impacts of such changes on addiction and treatment careers need to be carefully researched.

This paper has argued for the utility of the career concept in understanding the effects of policy and program practice on treatment outcomes and in suggesting modifications to improve policy and treatment. Although the treatment career approach is in an early stage and needs to be more fully developed with theoretical rigor and research applications, its benefit is significant on matters relevant to drug policy, as indicated by the earlier discussions of empirical findings. Such findings provide a rationale and justification for the application of a treatment career perspective to future treatment evaluation. Results from such analyses will further our understanding of the addiction and treatment career patterns of individuals at treatment entry and the relation of career characteristics and treatment outcomes, particularly within the context of ongoing changes in client service needs and treatment program characteristics (Hubbard et al., 1997).

Acknowledgments

Preparation of this manuscript was supported by grant P50-DA07699 from the National Institute on Drug Abuse (NIDA). Drs. Hser and Anglin are also supported by NIDA Research Scientist Development Awards (K02-DA00139 and K02-DA00146, respectively). The authors wish to thank staff at the UCLA Drug Abuse Research Center for assisting in data analyses and manuscript preparation.

References

Anglin, M. D., & Hser, Y.-I. (1990). Treatment of drug abuse. In M. Tonry & J. Q. Wilson, eds. *Drugs and Crime* (393–458). Chicago: University of Chicago Press.

Anglin, M. D., Hser, Y.-I., Booth, M., Speckart, G. R., McCarthy, W. J., Ryan, T., & Powers, K. (1988). *The Natural History of Narcotic Addition: A 25-Year Follow-Up* (NIDA Grant R01 DA 03425). University of California Los Angeles, Drug Abuse Research Center.

Anglin, M. D., Hser, Y.-I., & Grella, C. E. (1997). Drug addiction and treatment careers among clients in DATOS. *Psychology of Addictive Behavior, 11*(4), 308–323.

Anglin, M. D., & McGlothlin, W. H. (1985). Methadone maintenance in California: A decade's experience. In L. Brill, & C. Winick, eds., *The Yearbook of Substance Use and Abuse* (219–280). New York: Human Sciences Press.

Anglin, M. D., & Perrochet, B. (1998). Drug use and crime: A historical review of research conducted by the UCLA Drug Abuse Research Center. *Substance Use and Misuse, 33*(9), 1871–1914.

Anglin, M. D., Speckart, G. R., Booth, M. W., & Ryan, T. M. (1989). Consequences and costs of shutting off methadone. *Addictive Behaviors, 14,* 307–326.

Besteman, K. J. (1992). Federal leadership in building the national drug treatment system. In D. R. Gerstein & H. J. Harwood, eds., *Treating Drug Problems,* vol. 2, (63–88). Washington, D.C.: National Academy Press.

Center for Substance Abuse Treatment (1993). *State methadone treatment guidelines.* Treatment Improvement Protocol No. 1. (SMA) 93-1991. Rockville, Md.: Author.

Cunningham, J. A., Sobell, L. C., Sobell, M. B., Agrawal, S., & Toneatto, T. (1993). Barriers to treatment: Why alcohol and drug abusers delay or never seek treatment. *Addictive Behaviors, 18*(3), 347–353.

Etheridge, R. M., Craddock, S. G., Dunteman, G. H., & Hubbard, R. L. (1995). Treatment services in two national studies of community-based drug abuse treatment programs. *Journal of Substance Abuse, 7,* 9–26.

Frykholm, B. (1985). The drug career. *Journal of Drug Issues 15,* 333–346.

Gerstein, D. R., & Harwood, H. J. (eds.). (1990). *Treating drug problems, Vol. 1: A study of the evolution, effectiveness, and financing of public and private drug treatment systems.* Washington, D.C.: National Academy Press.

Gerstein, D. R., Harwood, H. J., & Suter, N. (1994). *Evaluating Recovery Services: The California Drug and Alcohol Treatment Assessment (CALDATA)* (General Report). Fairfax, Va.: National Opinion Research Center.

Haaga, J., & McGlynn, E. (1993). *The Drug Abuse Treatment System: Prospects for Reform* (RAND, MR-226). Santa Monica, Calif.: Drug Policy Research Center.

Hser, Y., & Anglin, M. D. (1991). Cost-effectiveness of drug abuse treatment: Relevant issues and alternative longitudinal modeling approaches. In W. S. Cartwright and J. M. Kaple, eds., *Economic Costs, Cost Effectiveness, Financing, and Community-Based Drug Treatment* (NIDA Monograph #113, pp. 67–93). Rockville, Md.: National Institute on Drug Abuse.

Hser, Y.-I., Anglin, M. D., Grella, C., Longshore, D., & Prendergast, M. (1997). Drug treatment careers: A conceptual framework and existing research findings. *Journal of Substance Abuse Treatment, 14*(3), 1–16.

Hser, Y.-I., Anglin, M. D., & Powers, K. (1993). A 24-year follow-up of California narcotics addicts. *Archives of General Psychiatry, 50,* 577–584.

Hser, Y.-I., Yamaguchi, K., Anglin, M. D., & Chen, J. (1995). Effects of interventions on relapse to narcotics addition. *Evaluation Review, 19,* 123–140.

Hubbard, R. L., Craddock, S. G., Flynn, P. M., Anderson, J., & Etheridge, R. M. (1997). Overview of 1-year follow-up treatment outcomes in the Drug Abuse Treatment Outcome Study (DATOS). *Psychology of Addictive Behavior, 1*(4), 261–278.

Khalsa, M. E., Paredes, A., & Anglin, M. D. (1993). Cocaine dependence: Behavioral dimensions and patterns of progression. *American Journal on Addictions, 2,* 330–345.

Khalsa, M. E., Paredes, A., Anglin, M. D., Potepan, P., & Potter, C. (1993). Combinations of treatment modalities and therapeutic outcome for cocaine dependence. In F. M. Tims and C. G. Leukefeld, eds., *Cocaine Treatment: Research and Clinical Perspectives*, NIDA Monograph Series 135, pp. 237–259. Rockville, Md.: National Institute on Drug Abuse.

Knight, K. R., Rosenbaum, M., Kelley, M. S., Irwin, J., Washburn, A., & Wenger, L. (1996). Defunding the poor: The impact of lost access to subsidized methadone maintenance treatment on women injection drug users. *Journal of Drug Issues, 26,* 923–942.

Maddux, J. F., & Desmond, D. P. (1981). *Careers of Opioid Users.* New York: Praeger.

McGlothlin, W. H., & Anglin, M. D. (1981a). Shutting off methadone: Costs and benefits. *Archives of General Psychiatry, 38,* 885–892.

McGlothlin, W. H., & Anglin, M. D. (1981b). Long-term follow-up of clients of high- and low-dose methadone programs. *Archives of General Psychiatry, 38,* 1055–1063.

McGlothlin, W. H., Anglin, M., D., & Wilson, B. D. (1975–76). Outcome of the California civil addict commitments: 1961–1972. *Drug and Alcohol Dependence, 1,* 165–181.

McGlothlin, W. H., Anglin, M. D., & Wilson, B. D. (1977). An evaluation of the California Civil Addict Program. *NIDA Services Research Monograph Series.* DHEW Publication No. (ADM 78-558). Washington, D.C.: U.S. Government Printing Office.

McGlothlin, W. H., Anglin, M. D., & Wilson, B. D. (1978). Narcotic addiction and crime. *Criminology: An Interdisciplinary Journal, 16,* 293–315.

McLellan, A. T., & Weisner, C. (1996). Achieving the public health and safety potential of substance abuse treatments: Implications for patient referral, treatment "matching," and outcome evaluation. In W. K. Bickel and R. J. DeGrandpre, eds., *Drug Policy and Human Nature: Psychological Perspectives on the Prevention, Management, and Treatment of Illicit Drug Abuse.* New York: Plenum. 153–157.

McLellan, A. T., Woody, G. E., Metzger, D., McKay, J., Durrell, J., Alterman, A. I., O'Brien, C. P. (1996). Evaluating the effectiveness of addiction treatments: Reasonable expectations appropriate comparisons. *Milbank Quarterly, 74,* 51–85.

Mechanic, D., Schlesinger, M., & McAlpine, D. D. (1995). Management of mental health and substance abuse services: State of the art and early results. *Milbank Quarterly, 73*(1), 19–55.

Musto, D. F. (1987). *The American Disease: Origins of Narcotic Control* (2d ed.). New York: Oxford University Press.

Nurco, D. N., Balter, M. B., & Kinlock, T. (1994). Vulnerability to narcotic addiction: Preliminary findings. *Journal of Drug Issues, 24,* 293–314.

Nurco, D. N., Bonito, A. J., Lerner, M., & Balter, M. B. (1975). Studying addicts over time: Methodology and preliminary findings. *American Journal of Drug & Alcohol Abuse, 2,* 107–121.

Powers, K. I., & Anglin, M. D. (1993). Cumulative versus stabilizing effects of methadone maintenance: A quasi-experimental study using longitudinal self-report data.
Evaluation Review, 17, 243–270.

Powers, K. I., & Anglin, M. D. (1998). A differential assessment of the cumulative versus
stabilizing effect of methadone maintenance treatment. *Evaluation Review, 22*(2),
175–206.

Rosenbaum, M., Irwin, J., & Murphy, S. (1988). De facto destabilization as policy: The
impact of short-term methadone maintenance. *Contemporary Drug Problems, 15,*
491–517.

Rosenbaum, M., Washburn, A., Knight, K., Kelley, M., & Irwin, J. (1996). Treatment as
harm reduction, defunding as harm maximization: The case of methadone maintenance. *Journal of Psychoactive Drugs, 28*(3), 241–249.

Savage, L. J., & Simpson, D. D. (1981). Drug use and crime during a four-year posttreatment follow-up. *American Journal of Drug & Alcohol Abuse, 8,* 1–16.

Schlesinger, M., & Dorwart, R. A. (1992). Falling between the cracks: Failing national
strategies for the treatment of substance abuse. *Daedalus, 121,* 195–237.

Schuster, C. R. (1989). Methadone maintenance: An adequate dose is vital in checking
the spread of AIDS. *NIDA Notes* 4(3), 3, 33.

Senay, E. (1984). Clinical implications of drug abuse treatment outcome research. In
Tims, F. M. and Ludford, J.P., eds., *Drug Abuse Treatment Evaluation.* Rockville, Md.:
National Institute on Drug Abuse. 139–150.

Simpson, D. D., Joe, G. W., & Bracy, S. A. (1982). Six-year follow-up of opioid addicts
after admission to treatment. *Archives of General Psychiatry, 39,* 1318–1323.

Simpson, D. D., Joe, G. W., & Lehman, W. E. (1986). *Addiction Careers: Summary of
Studies Based on the DARP 12-Year Follow-Up.* NIDA Treatment Research Report
(ADM 86) Rockville, Md.: National Institute on Drug Abuse.

Simpson, D. D., & Savage, L. J. (1980a). Drug abuse treatment readmissions and outcomes: Three-year follow-up of DARP patients. *Archives of General Psychiatry, 37,*
896–901.

Simpson, D. D., & Savage, L. J. (1980b). Treatment re-entry and outcomes of opioid
addicts during a four-year follow-up after drug abuse treatment in the United States.
Bulletin on Narcotics, 32, 1–9.

Simpson, D. D., & Sells, S. B. (1982). Effectiveness of treatment for drug abuse: An
overview of the DARP research program. *Advances in Alcohol & Substance Abuse, 2,*
7–29.

Simpson, D. D., & Sells, S. B., eds. (1990). *Opioid Addiction and Treatment: A 12-Year
Follow-Up.* Malabar, Fla.: Krieger.

Stephens, R. C. (1991). *The Street Addict Role: A Theory of Heroin Addiction.* Albany:
State University of New York Press.

Tims, F. M., & Ludford, J. P. (1984). *Drug Abuse Treatment Evaluation: Strategies, Progress, and Prospects.* NIDA Treatment Research Report (ADM 84-1349). Rockville, Md.: National Institute on Drug Abuse.

Vaillant, G. E. (1966). A 12-year follow-up of New York narcotic addicts: III. Some social and psychiatric characteristics. *Archives of General Psychiatry, 15,* 599–609.

Vaillant, G. E. (1988). What can long-term follow-up teach us about relapse and prevention of relapse in addiction? *British Journal of Addiction, 83,* 1147–1157.

Wellisch, J., Prendergast, M. L., & Anglin, M. D. (1995). Toward a drug abuse treatment system. *Journal of Drug Issues, 25,* 759–782.

Winick, C. (1962). Maturing out of narcotic addiction. *Bulletin on Narcotics, 9,* 174–186.

THREE

RECOVERY AND THE CRIMINAL JUSTICE SYSTEM

David Farabee & Carl G. Leukefeld

Although every arrested drug dealer is almost immediately replaced by another drug dealer, the successful rehabilitation of chronic drug users can result in actual decrements in the illicit drug market (Boyum and Kleiman, 1995). Reduced substance use is also associated with lower rates of criminal activity (Nurco et al., 1988), increased employment (Simpson & Sells, 1982), and reduced health care costs (Harwood et al., 1988; Rice et al., 1990). Indeed, the potential impact of substance abuse treatment for criminal offenders reaches well beyond the individual user, as do the financial and social costs of not providing treatment.

In this chapter, we examine the growing role of the criminal justice system as a provider of substance abuse treatment. We also explore the compatibility of treatment and correctional goals, ethical implications of legal coercion, and selected research areas most likely to enhance the efficacy of compulsory treatment.

DEFINITIONS

COMPULSORY TREATMENT

The criminal justice system dominates the substance abuse treatment referral process in the United States. According to recent data, the criminal justice system is responsible for 40 to 50% of referrals to community-based treatment programs (Maxwell, 1996; Price & D'Aunno, 1992; Spiegelman, 1984; Weisner, 1987). These referrals are made through direct civil commitment or through a less formal process of legal coercion. Civil commitment is a procedure by which persons identified as mentally ill or as having substance use problems can be involuntarily committed for treatment. Compulsory treatment, however, refers to a broader class of referral mechanisms that, in addition to civil commitment, include pretrial diversion and treatment as a condition of probation or parole. In most cases, the substance abuser is given the option to enter treatment in exchange for a reduction in sentence length or level of supervision.

We use the term *compulsory treatment* to include directly or indirectly applied legal coercion for an individual to enter substance abuse treatment. Compulsory treatment, however, does not necessarily mean that the client is entering treatment involuntarily. The importance of this distinction is evidenced in studies, primarily found in the psychiatric literature, that show the majority of patients whose official records indicated that they entered treatment voluntarily actually were under some form of official custody and were under the threat of involuntary commitment if they failed to enter treatment "voluntarily" (Gilboy & Schmidt, 1971). Conversely, other studies have indicated that clients entering mental health treatment under involuntary status are not necessarily involuntary. For example, one study of committed psychiatric patients revealed that approximately one-half did not know their commitment status, and among those who said that they were denied the opportunity to enter voluntarily, approximately one-half said that they would have chosen to enter voluntarily if given the choice (Toews et al., 1984).

RECOVERY: DIMENSION AND DEGREE

The past thirty years of drug treatment research revealed some interesting similarities among treated drug abusers' relapse rates. According to one study (Hunt, Barnett, & Branch, 1971), approximately two-thirds of all relapses occur within three months after discharge. This study was particularly interesting because it demonstrated similar relapse curves for heroin, tobacco, and alcohol users. Using data from the Drug Abuse Reporting Program (DARP) evaluation, Simpson and Sells (1982) reported that, although the likelihood of relapse increases over time, the rate begins to stabilize approximately three to six months after discharge. This temporal pattern of relapse was also demonstrated in the Treatment Outcome Prospective Study (TOPS) data for those remaining in treatment for at least three months (Hubbard et al., 1989).

When defining criteria for "unsuccessful outcomes," it is important to distinguish between a brief "lapse" in abstinence and total relapse. Overly stringent criteria (e.g., any use at all) may result in a conservative assessment of treatment effectiveness. In fact, one study of treated opiate abusers found that, although 72% had used, or lapsed, within six weeks following discharge, 47% reported being abstinent by the end of six months (Gossop, Green, Phillips, & Bradley, 1987). If data were reported only for the first measure, the ultimate (or at least more distal) impact of treatment would have gone undetected. Return to regular use (e.g., in the DARP study this was defined as using opioids five or more days a week for at least a month) is a more useful indicator of treatment effectiveness than temporary or episodic resumption of drug use.

Finally, because drug use appears to enhance rates of criminal behavior rather than initiate it directly (Nurco et al., 1988), it is important to assess criminal recidivism outcomes by degree. Although there is evidence that substance abuse treatment can reduce rates of criminal activity, it is unlikely that the reduction or cessation of substance use will produce a commensurate decrease in other criminal behaviors that preexisted the substance use (Office of Justice Programs, 1988).

HISTORY AND PAST WORK

The roots of community drug abuse treatment in the United States can be traced through legislation that established the community mental health movement in the late 1960s and the early 1970s (Leukefeld, Matthews, & Clayton, 1992). The community mental health legislation as amended provided staffing for drug and alcohol treatment services. In addition, drug treatment can be traced through the criminal justice system. These criminal justice roots create a natural tension for many mental health providers, which to a large extent focus on issues related to conceptualizing and approaching treatment and control.

These criminal justice roots include two U.S. Public Health Service (PHS) hospitals for the treatment of narcotic addicts that were opened in 1935 in Lexington, Kentucky, and in 1938 in Fort Worth, Texas. These facilities began as narcotic farms, became hospitals, and are now part of the Federal Bureau of Prisons. They also include, at the federal level, the 1966 NARA (Narcotic Addict Rehabilitation Act) program, which provided civil commitment for narcotic addicts sentenced to a correctional Federal Bureau of Prisons facility under Title II of the NARA and civilly committed to the Surgeon General of the United States Public Health Service (PHS) under Titles I and III. The PHS also initiated community-based drug abuse treatment programs through federal grants that included community mental health centers and became the foundation for the existing U.S. drug and alcohol treatment system.

Aftercare drug treatment for persons involved in correctional facilities grew as part of the TASC (Treatment Alternatives to Street Crime) program, which began in the early 1970s. Although TASC has expanded to more than two hundred communities, it still provides the same types of services, including case management and identifying criminal justice clients for community drug abuse treatment as well as bridging bureaucratic regulations and impediments between providers and the criminal justice system. In addition, many of the first drug abuse studies used prisoner subjects at the Addiction Research Center (ARC), which is now the Federal Medical Center in Lexington, Kentucky. In fact, many seasoned drug abuse treatment researchers and clinicians can trace their roots or their mentor's roots to the Lexington Hospital or to the Lexington ARC, which is now located in Baltimore.

CONCEPTUAL ISSUES

Several issues emerge when criminal justice treatment is discussed. These issues include (1) the contrasting goals of treatment and correctional control, (2) ethical issues of coerced treatment participation, (3) the extent to which offender treatment is cost-effective, and (4) the roles of external versus internal motivation for behavior change.

TREATMENT VERSUS CONTROL

Conceptualizing treatment and control continues to be an issue for understanding the criminally involved drug abuser, and for the drug abuser in general. In fact, many individuals with whom we have talked place treatment and control along one continuum, with treatment at one end and control at the other end (see figure 3.1). Control is defined as incorporating authority derived from criminal justice sanctions—the status of probation, parole, or mandatory release. One way to clarify the definition of control used here is to call it criminal justice control, program control, or restrictiveness. Put another way, criminal justice system professionals are perceived to be "bad guys"—responsible for control and punishment, while on the other end of the continuum, treatment providers are described, and frequently see themselves, as "good guys" who provide treatment and focus on patient change in values, attitudes, and behaviors. Treatment intensity could be used in this instance to more fully conceptualize drug abuse treatment.

Within this framework, a therapeutic intervention is usually discussed in terms of its degree of control and is placed on such an imaginary continuum without considering the level of intensity. In other words, activities and programs are labeled as therapeutic or controlling, something that clients con-

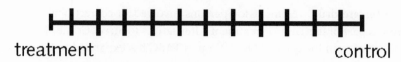

Fig. 3.1. Drug abuse intervention continuum.

tinually do as part of "navigating" a personally disruptive system. In fact, most therapists as well as criminal justice practitioners consider the goals of the criminal justice system and treatment system to be quite different. Many treatment providers point to the fact that authority derived from the criminal justice system is disruptive to the therapeutic process and that these systems come into contact with certain clients.

There are different ways to look at the issue of treatment and control (Leukefeld, Matthew, & Clayton, 1992; Leukefeld, Gallego, & Farabee, 1997). One way is to suggest that they are two distinct but very related concepts. Thus, they can represent two associated but different continua: (1) treatment represented as the degree of treatment from high to low and (2) control presented as the degree of control from high to low. For example, high control could include drug testing, intense probation, parole supervision, or house arrest. Low control would not incorporate drug testing and criminal justice status. These treatment and control concepts can be related on perpendicular axes, as in figure 3.2. The treatment/control continuum can represent degrees and combinations of treatment and control within the four broad areas represented in figure 3.2.

For example, a therapeutic community would be located in the upper right quadrant. This means that a therapeutic community, the most frequent treatment referral choice of most judges and consequently the criminal justice system, is very high in control and very high in the provision of treatment. On the other hand, outpatient counseling, the most often provided treatment in the United States for about 60% of people receiving drug treatment, would fall into the lower left quadrant, with less treatment exposure and less control. Additional control through probation or parole status would increase the level of both control and treatment for outpatients and, depending on the levels of contact, urine screens, and treatment engagement, would move from the lower left quadrant to higher treatment and higher control within that quadrant. One implication of this model is that specific combinations of treatment intensity and control can potentially be identified that are most effective and lead to more favorable outcomes for interventions.

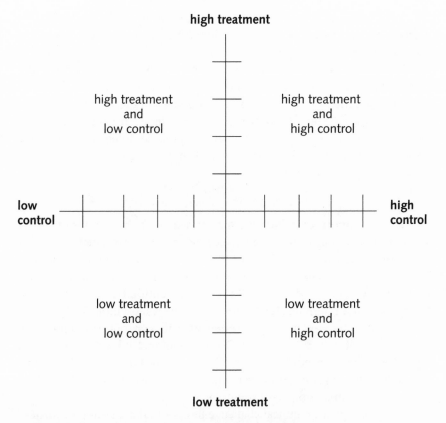

Fig. 3.2. Drug abuse treatment as a control model.

It appears that the most commonly used interventions for the drug-abusing offender should be more intense community treatment interventions. However, along with that need is the realization that these interventions (like residential treatment) are the most expensive and the most limited community treatments available. Thus, even though the most intense treatment possible should be provided for the drug-abusing offender, availability and cost considerations limit high-intensity treatment for drug-abusing offenders who are receiving community treatment.

This model also points to some interesting research possibilities. These research considerations suggest that treatment intensity could be taken into account when treatment efficacy is examined. Thus, it might be hypothesized that the level of treatment intensity would be associated with successful treatment outcomes. Little is empirically known, however, about the relation of treatment intensity for the drug-abusing offender and treatment placement with controlled and randomized studies.

This model clearly does not represent the final model for describing the treatment and control relation and is not precise, but it could be helpful in providing a framework for describing and understanding the interrelationship of drug treatment and control. Finally, this model has the potential for measuring programs and explaining overall program intensity, which may be important in unraveling the components of treatment interventions and for improving drug treatment.

THE ETHICS OF MANDATING TREATMENT

The ethical support for mandating substance abuse treatment for offenders is predicated on the belief that substance use causes or perpetuates criminal behavior. In actuality, there is very little support for the argument that substance use *directly* causes other forms of criminality. In fact, most inmates who reported current drug use did not begin until after their first arrest (Office of Justice Programs, 1988). However, there is substantial evidence that the onset of, or increase in, drug use often intensifies rates of criminal activity (Ball, Rosen, Flueck, & Nurco, 1981; Nurco, Hanlon, Kinlock, & Duszynski, 1988), relative to preaddiction levels. Consequently, there can be both ethical and pragmatic justification for mandating treatment for offenders whose substance use impacts others through their own criminality.

Perhaps the greatest ethical challenge lies not in the question of *whether* treatment should be mandated, but *how,* and for *whom,* it should be provided. When considering the question of *how,* two principles from Andrew Thompson's (1990) ethical guidelines for psychotherapy—autonomy and fidelity—can provide guidance. Autonomy requires that the therapist create an environment in which the client is free to actively collaborate in his or her own treatment. The clinician must also provide the least restrictive form of treatment necessary and limit any coercive elements of the program as quickly as possible. The principle of fidelity requires the therapist to work primarily for the good of the client and to avoid any dual responsibilities that may potentially compromise the therapeutic relationship.

The principle of autonomy can be maintained in the criminal justice setting. The key is to distinguish between the lost autonomy resulting from criminal justice supervision and the *additional* autonomy lost in treatment. Offenders are not brought into the criminal justice system because they need treatment; they are in the criminal justice system because they have broken the law. The ethical responsibility of the therapist operating within this context is to provide the maximum amount of autonomy allowable within the correctional environment.

Maintaining fidelity in the therapist/client relationship requires vigilance on the part of the therapist with some concessions by the corrections administration. A clinician must establish clear-cut policies regarding his or her obligations to the client and to the criminal justice system. The counselor must decide to what extent the counselor/client relationship should remain confidential and also under what conditions the counselor should report the client's infraction(s) (e.g., ongoing substance use in the facility) to the corrections staff. Regardless of how these questions are answered, they must be decided upon and communicated in writing to the client prior to treatment.

Existing federal guidelines for confidentiality (42 C.F.R., 2.12) require that any information obtained on an offender receiving substance abuse treatment is protected by law. The period of protection begins at the time of the initial assessment or screen and continues throughout treatment and after discharge. The disclosure of information without consent is limited to medical emergencies, program evaluations, and treatment planning. *Any* information obtained from a client can be released after the client has signed a proper consent form (outlined in section 2.31), however.

Because many substance abuse treatment programs operate at capacity, another ethical question arises concerning which offenders should receive treatment. It has been our experience that these decisions are typically made on the basis of availability, regardless of substance use severity, prognosis, or drug-crime relation. As the increasing proportion of drug-involved offenders entering the criminal justice system outpaces the development of new programs, however, there is a growing tendency to prioritize clients who appear to be most likely to benefit from treatment.

According to a panel of experts commissioned by the Center for Substance Abuse Treatment (CSAT, 1994), substance-abusing clients in the criminal justice system can be grouped into four major categories: (1) young offenders who have recently begun abusing substances and have not yet experienced any serious consequences of that behavior; (2) offenders who have abused substances for five or more years, have experienced some negative consequences of their substance abuse, but have not yet "hit bottom"; (3) offenders whose substance abuse has resulted in a personal crisis like losing a job, going to jail, or the loss of an important personal relationship; and (4) career criminals who abuse substances. The CSAT panel recommended that treatment priority should be given to offenders in the first and third groups: young substance abusers who have used for a short period of time, and substance abusers who have experienced some kind of major negative consequence of their substance use and, therefore, would be most willing to change their behavior.

REDUCTIONS IN RELATED COSTS (CRIME, HIV, OTHER HEALTH ISSUES)

Researchers have documented the high costs of drug abuse to the taxpayer and to society (Harwood et al., 1988; Rice et al., 1990). These costs are particularly dramatic for drug-abusing offenders whose criminal activity, criminal justice costs, usually poor health status, and use of expensive public health services put heavy burdens on the taxpayer and society. The current impetus for renewed interest in drug abuse treatment in corrections comes from the desire to reduce the burgeoning costs of criminal justice services and the cost of health care associated with rapidly increasing numbers of incarcerated chronic drug users with related acute health conditions (Inciardi & Martin, 1993). Only a few studies have addressed the cost-effectiveness issue, however (Apsler & Harding, 1991; Harwood et al., 1984; Hubbard et al., 1989). Hubbard and his colleagues reported that the 41 programs they studied were cost-effective in reducing the costs of crime well below treatment costs. However, this study has been criticized by Apsler (1991) for not having control or comparison groups, relying solely on self-reports of drug use and crime, and not having enough individual level impact data.

Recently, the CALDATA study reported on the cost-effectiveness of publicly supported treatment programs in California (California Department of Drug and Alcohol Programs, 1994). This 1992 California survey was a representative sample of the 150,000 persons receiving treatment in California, including those in criminal justice settings. Although there are some problems with sample representativeness, the CALDATA study reported an eighteen-month savings from treatment of $1.5 billion, with the largest savings coming from reduction in crime, followed by significant reductions in health care costs including emergency room admissions, which declined by one-third.

INTERNAL AND EXTERNAL MOTIVATION AND RELAPSE

Results from the Treatment Outcome Prospective Study (TOPS), a national evaluation of substance abuse treatment effectiveness, indicated not only significant reductions in substance use among clients remaining in treatment three months or more but also reductions in criminal recidivism — especially during treatment. Long-term outcomes, particularly criminal recidivism rates, for this population have not been as impressive (Gerstein & Harwood, 1990). Leukefeld and Tims (1988, 243) have suggested that:

Recovery from drug abuse is an interactional phenomenon involving . . . client factors with nontreatment factors, such as social climate, as well as treatment itself. . . . Client factors include . . . external pressure and internal pressure. Legal referrals belong in the external pressure category. A stable recovery cannot be maintained by external (legal) pressures only; motivation and commitment must come from internal pressure. The role of external pressure from this point of view is to influence a person to enter treatment.

Although it has been demonstrated that clients referred to treatment through the criminal justice system remain in treatment longer than those not referred through the criminal justice system (Collins & Allison, 1983; Leukefeld, 1978), the long-term implications of external versus internal motivation as they relate to treatment outcomes are still unclear. One study comparing voluntary and criminal justice–referred substance abuse clients entering treatment showed both groups to be almost identical on a battery of psychosocial measures, with the primary difference being significantly lower self-assessments of drug problems, desire for help, and readiness for treatment reported by those who had been legally referred (Farabee, Nelson, & Spence, 1993). Involuntary clients are also more likely to claim that their substance use is purely recreational and does not pose a problem for their lives (Schottenfeld, 1989). In summary, a large proportion of clients currently entering community-based treatment are referred by the criminal justice system, have treatment needs similar to those of their voluntary counterparts, but appear to lack the internal motivation to readily engage themselves in the treatment process.

The increased application of external sources of motivation for treatment may result in misleading short-term treatment outcomes. Some of the most sophisticated research literature in the area of motivation (as it relates to behavior change) is related to smoking cessation. For example, Curry et al. (1991) found that clients in a self-help smoking cessation program who were given financial incentives (external motivators) were more likely than clients who were given personalized feedback (intrinsic motivator) to use the program study materials but less likely to maintain abstinence. In fact, clients in the external motivation group had an abstinence rate of approximately one-half that of the clients in the intrinsic motivation condition. There is also evidence that clients who attribute their smoking cessation to external factors (e.g., the treatment program, the physician, etc.) are less likely than those who view themselves as responsible to maintain long-term abstinence. Although clients who were randomly assigned to a treatment program with an external motivation focus were more likely than clients in an intrinsic self-help group to quit smoking initially, clients in the intrinsically oriented group were more likely to maintain their abstinence (Harackiewicz, Sansone, Blair, Epstein, & Manderlink, 1987).

This study and others demonstrated that external motivators can reduce intrinsic motivation in a number of settings, and for many different populations studies suggest that this is a common psychological phenomenon (Deci & Ryan, 1985; Jordan, 1986). Furthermore, it has been demonstrated that the dynamics of relapse and recovery for tobacco and alcohol use are quite similar to those of heroin (Hunt, Barnett, & Branch, 1971).

According to Miller (1989), a client entering treatment prior to recognizing his or her substance use as being problematic is unlikely to be open to therapeutic intervention. In this early stage, a client is most likely to benefit from nondirective feedback and information to help raise awareness of the problem. Direct challenges to the client are perceived as aversive and typically disrupt therapeutic progress. Over time, these clients tend to shift between acknowledging and denying that they have a substance use problem. Again, direct challenges by a counselor may serve only to shift the client's perception back to denial. However, more direct recommendations toward taking action can be made during the client's ephemeral phases of problem recognition. Thus, both external and internal motivation play important roles in the treatment process and relapse. Failure to address both types of motivation, it would seem, will result in inferior treatment participation and less favorable outcomes than if these motivational sources are treated as complementary.

CURRENT STATUS

Drug use prevalence remains high among offender populations. According to the Drug Use Forecasting System (DUF, 1996), which reports the results of drug tests on incoming arrestees in 23 cities nationwide, 51 to 83% of male arrestees tested positive for at least one illicit drug during 1995, most commonly marijuana or cocaine. Among female arrestees, rates ranged from 41 to 84% during this period.

Among the state prison systems, tougher drug policies and mandatory sentencing requirements have led to a disproportionate increase in the number of inmates who use illicit drugs. In fact, the number of adults arrested for a drug offense increased by 108% between 1980 and 1992 (Bureau of Justice Statistics, 1993). According to a survey of U.S. state and federal prison populations, approximately 80% of the inmates reported having used illicit drugs at least once, 50% reported having used in the month prior to incarceration, and 25% of the inmates had injected drugs (most commonly heroin, cocaine, or both) for nonmedical purposes at least once in their lives (Bureau of Justice Statistics, 1993).

The most recent data from the Bureau of Justice Statistics (1997) documents a 478% increase between 1985 and 1995 in the number of state prisoners sentenced for drug offenses. Among African American inmates, the rate of increase was 707%. Although not all drug offenders can be assumed to be drug abusers, the dramatic increase in drug sentences over the past decade suggests that an overall culture of drug use and drug sales remains pervasive among the nation's state and federal criminal justice populations.

Because of the high rates of medical indigence among offenders (Farabee, 1995), many inmates receive their first exposure to drug treatment while in the criminal justice system (Leukefeld & Tims, 1988). The types and levels of treatment vary substantially between facilities, however, ranging from weekly drug education groups to nine- to twelve-month therapeutic communities. Prior research demonstrates that criminal justice–based treatment programs must be intensive (i.e., occupy 40–70% of the offenders' time) and must last for three to nine months (Gendreau, 1996; Wexler, Falkin, Lipton, & Rosenblum, 1992). Such programs can be as functionally cumbersome as they are costly, given that offender clients are often housed separately from the general prison population. Obviously, moving beyond nominal programming and providing effective treatment throughout the state and federal criminal justice systems is an enormous task. Less obvious are the long-term costs associated with underfunded and perfunctory offender treatment programs.

Offenders are also at higher risk for acquiring human immunodeficiency virus (HIV) relative to the general population. In 1993, 2.4% of federal and state prison inmates were known to be infected with HIV; slightly lower rates (1.8%) were found among jail inmates. Prevalence varies decidedly by region and gender, with the highest rates found among prisoners in the Northeast (7.4%) and among females (4.2% of females versus 2.5% of males) (Brien, 1995). Within the criminal justice system, a person's exposure to HIV prevention information and intervention decreases with the offender's level of supervision with jail as the least restrictive level of supervision and prison as the most restrictive. In fact, according to Hammett et al. (1995), jails were less likely than prisons to offer instructor-led education (62% versus 75%), peer education groups (7% versus 35%), HIV prevention counseling (69% versus 86%), videos (66% versus 88%), or written materials (72% versus 94%). A recent study of out-of-treatment drug users conducted by Farabee et al. (1997) demonstrated that drug users with any criminal justice involvement were no more likely than non-criminal justice–involved drug users to have ever been exposed to HIV prevention programs. The same study also indicated that the criminal justice–involved drug users were generally at higher risk of acquiring HIV than their non-criminal justice–involved counterparts, particularly through trading sex for money or drugs.

RECOMMENDATIONS AND CONCLUSIONS

Despite persistently high rates of substance abuse throughout the criminal justice population, the link between the public health and correctional systems remains inadequate (Wellisch et al., 1995). Furthermore, because the term *substance abuse treatment* refers to an array of services, the proportion of drug-using offenders who actually receive effective treatment programming is likely to fall below any survey-based estimates. Evaluation research continues to emphasize treatment outcomes over defining the components of the treatment process (e.g., community outreach strategies, qualities of the counselor-client relationship, therapeutic engagement, etc.) that facilitate positive change. Future research on treatment process and dynamics is essential for advancing the field of substance-abuse treatment (Simpson, 1995).

One of the primary philosophical barriers to implementing treatment programs more aggressively within the criminal justice system is the sustained perception that correctional and treatment goals cannot be addressed simultaneously. We maintain that treatment and control can serve complementary functions and are not mutually exclusive. Indeed, specific combinations of treatment intensity and control can potentially be identified that are most effective and lead to favorable outcomes for interventions. Some empirical work has already been conducted that suggests that high coercion and control appear to be most effective for older, long-term drug users (primarily opiate users) in outpatient settings (Salmon, 1982), but this potentially fruitful area of research has yet to be addressed systematically. Furthermore, because the amount of time a client spends in treatment has emerged repeatedly in the literature as a significant predictor of positive treatment outcomes (Hubbard et al., 1989; Wexler et al., 1992), any approach that increases the amount of time a client remains in treatment is also likely to be associated with superior treatment outcomes. Accordingly, legally coerced clients often do as well as or even better than clients entering treatment voluntarily (Anglin & Hser, 1990).

But establishing *long-term* changes in substance abuse also requires internal motivation for change. Most of the criminal justice treatment motivation research has focused on external motivation. Unfortunately, this emphasis has limited our understanding of internal motivation, though there is strong support for the role of internal motivation as a predictor of program retention and positive treatment outcomes. For example, Simpson, Joe, and Rowan-Szal (1997) report that a client's internal motivation for change at the time of program admission significantly predicted long-term posttreatment outcomes.

FUTURE DIRECTIONS

The future of substance abuse treatment in criminal justice settings depends largely on the extent to which policy is informed by research. Martinson's (1974) conclusion that "nothing works," although later rescinded, initiated a dramatic shift in correctional philosophy from rehabilitation to punishment and incapacitation. Over the past decade, however, there has been renewed interest in offender rehabilitation and compulsory treatment. There is now a growing acceptance of legal coercion, and external pressure in general, as a legitimate form of treatment motivation. It is crucial that the coercive nature of criminal justice referrals is matched by equally earnest efforts to enhance offenders' internal motivation during the early phases of treatment (Farabee, Simpson, Dansereau, & Knight, 1995).

PRIVATIZATION AND TREATMENT SERVICES

Although it is too early to determine the impact of the privatization of corrections, this shift will undoubtedly affect the provision of substance abuse treatment for offenders. Most commonly, private corporations receive contracts for the purpose of prison or jail construction. This role has remained relatively uncontested, given that the average age of U.S. correctional facilities is fast approaching ninety years (Kenyon, 1986). Over the past decade, however, private corrections corporations are also assuming operational roles. Although less than 5% of inmates are remanded to privately run institutions (Johnson & Ross, 1990), the trend for such services has grown rapidly over the past twenty years, and the debate over the legal, ethical, and economic consequences of privatization has intensified. Furthermore, given that the federal prison system and the majority of state systems reported operating at or above capacity by the end of 1996 (Bureau of Justice Statistics, 1997), it is likely that private construction and management of prisons will continue.

Evaluation research comparing the quality of private and public correctional facilities and programs is limited. In one study that compared the quality of a broad range of services of one private, one state, and one federal prison for women, the private facility outperformed the public facilities in virtually all of the dimensions assessed, including staffing, facility design, and security. The level of care that included medical and mental health services was the only category, however, in which the private facility received a lower rating than the state-run facility (Logan, 1992).

Because the results of the above study were based on only one facility in each condition (private, state, and federal), it is premature to generalize these findings to all public and private correctional facilities. The finding that medical and psychological services are somehow compromised in the private for-profit prison offers a cautionary note to policy makers. Specifically, the provision of *peripheral* rehabilitative services must not fall victim to cost-cutting measures that are inherent, and often appropriate, in other private sector industries.

ASSESSMENT: CRIMINAL ADDICT/ADDICTED CRIMINAL

The correspondence between criminality and drug use varies considerably and, in some cases, does not appear to exist at all (Nurco, Ball, Schaffer, & Hanlon, 1985). Given the mandate of the criminal justice system, it seems logical that priority be given to providing treatment to drug offenders whose drug use and criminality are most directly linked. The need to distinguish the addicted offender from the offender addict is underscored by the limited number of treatment slots allocated for this population. In fact, less than one-third of the nation's jails provide drug abuse treatment to their inmates (Peters, May, & Kearns, 1992). Within prison, as well, most inmates who could benefit from treatment do not receive sufficient treatment while they are incarcerated (Falkin, Prendergast, & Anglin, 1994). Thus, given the limited availability of treatment for offenders, prioritization of treatment candidates should be determined in accordance with the primary rehabilitative goal of the criminal justice system: the reduction of crime.

Although a host of screens and assessments have been developed to identify substance use severity and treatment need (see Center for Substance Abuse Treatment, 1994), we are not aware of assessment instruments designed to measure the extent to which an offender's criminality is "dominated" by his or her substance abuse.

THE ROLES OF INTERNAL AND EXTERNAL MOTIVATION

Finally, as we have described above, there is a crucial need to develop new strategies to personalize consequences of drug use, crime, and HIV-risky behavior for the increasing number of clients entering treatment under criminal justice pressure. High pretreatment motivation for change is predictive of twofold increases in the likelihood of positive outcomes for substance use and criminality (Simpson, Joe, & Rowan-Szal, 1997). It is increasingly clear that external motivators like criminal justice pressure are rarely sufficient to produce lasting change. Given that intrinsic motivation for change is the primary distinction between voluntary and criminal justice–referred substance abuse treatment clients (Farabee, Nelson, & Spence, 1993), we must not forget that, ultimately, it is the offender who decides upon the outcome. Further empirical work is needed to inform clinicians on the most effective means for enhancing internal motivation for substance-abusing offenders mandated to treatment.

In summary, there are a number of issues that can enhance recovery. Overall, the criminal justice system can provide an effective setting to identify, assess, and refer substance abusers to treatment. Moreover, once a client is referred to treatment, the auspices of the criminal justice system significantly improve retention rates and subsequent drug use and criminality outcomes. Improving upon this system, however, requires further development of strategies to enhance internal motivation for change within an externally coercive environment.

References

Anglin, M. D., & Hser, Y. (1990). Treatment of drug abuse. In M.H. Tonry and J. Wilson (eds.), *Drugs and Crime*, vol. 13, 393–460 of *Crime and Justice: A Review of Research*. Chicago: University of Chicago Press.

Apsler, R. (1991). Evaluating the cost-effectiveness of drug abuse treatment. In W. S. Cartwright and J. M. Kaple (eds.), *Economic Costs, Cost Effectiveness, Financing, and Community-Based Drug Treatment*. Washington, D.C.: U.S. Government Press.

Apsler, R., & Harding, W. M. (1991). Cost-effectiveness analysis of drug abuse treatment: Current status and recommendations for future research. In *Drug Abuse Services Research Series*, No. 1: *Background Papers on Drug Abuse Financing and Services Approach*. National Institute on Drug Abuse. Washington, D.C.: U.S. Government Press.

Ball, J. C., Rosen, L., Flueck, J.A., & Nurco, D. (1981). The criminality of heroin addicts: When addicted and when off opiates. In J. A. Inciardi (ed.), *Drugs-Crime Connection,* 39-65. Beverly Hills: Sage.

Boyum, D., & Kleiman, M. A. (1995). Alcohol and other drugs. In J. Q. Wilson and J. Petersilia (eds.), *Crime.* San Francisco, Calif.: ICS Press.

Brien, P. M. (1995). *HIV in Prisons and Jails, 1993.* Washington, D.C.: U.S. Department of Justice, Bureau of Justice Statistics. Report NCJ-152765.

Bureau of Justice Statistics (1993). *Survey of State Prison Inmates 1991.* Rockville, Md. Report NCJ-136949.

Bureau of Justice Statistics (1997). *Prisoners in 1996.* Washington, D.C.: U.S. Department of Justice, Report NCJ-164619.

California Department of Alcohol and Drug Programs (1994). *Evaluating recovery services: The California drug and alcohol treatment assessment.* Sacramento, Calif.: Author.

Center for Substance Abuse Treatment (1994). *Screening and Assessment for Alcohol and Other Drug Abuse Among Adults in the Criminal Justice System.* DHHS Publication No. (SMA) 94-2076, pp. 37-38.

Collins, J. J., & Allison, M. (1983). Legal coercion and retention in drug abuse treatment. *Hospital and Community Psychiatry, 34,* 1145-1149.

Curry, S. J., Wagner, E., & Grothaus, L. C. (1991). Evaluation of intrinsic and extrinsic motivation interventions with a self-help smoking cessation program. *Journal of Consulting and Clinical Psychology, 59,* 318-324.

Deci, E. L., & Ryan, R. (1985). *Intrinsic Motivation and Self-Determination in Human Behavior.* New York: Plenum.

Drug Use Forecasting (1996). *Annual Report on Adult and Juvenile Arrestees.* Washington, D.C.: National Institute of Justice.

Falkin, G. P., Prendergast, M., Anglin, M. D. (1994). Drug treatment in the criminal justice system. *Federal Probation, 58,* 31-36.

Farabee, D. (1995). *Substance Use Among Male Inmates Entering the Texas Department of Criminal Justice-Institutional Division, 1993.* (Austin, Tex.: Texas Commission of Alcohol and Drug Abuse).

Farabee, D., & Leukefeld, C. G. (1999). Opportunities for AIDS prevention in a rural state in criminal justice and drug treatment settings. *Substance Use and Misuse, 34,* 617-631.

Farabee, D., Nelson, R., & Spence, R. (1993). Psychosocial profiles of criminal justice- and noncriminal justice-referred substance abusers in treatment. *Criminal Justice and Behavior, 20,* 336-346.

Farabee, D., Simpson, D. D., Dansereau, D. F., & Knight, K. (1995). Cognitive inductions into treatment among drug users on probation. *Journal of Drug Issues, 25,* 669-682.

Gendreau, P. (1996). The principles of effective intervention with offenders. In A. T. Harland (ed.), *Choosing Correctional Options that Work.* Thousand Oaks, Calif.: Sage.

Gendreau, P., Little, T., & Goggin, C. (1996). A meta-analysis of the predictors of adult offender recidivism: What works. *Criminology, 34,* 575–597.

Gerstein, D. R., & Harwood, H. J. (eds.), (1990). *Treating drug problems,* vol. 1, Washington, D.C.: National Academy Press.

Gilboy, J., & Schmidt, J. (1971). "Voluntary" hospitalization of the mentally ill. *Northwestern University Law Review, 66,* 429–453.

Gossop, M., Green, L., Phillips, G., & Bradley, B. (1987). What happens to opiate addicts immediately after treatment: A prospective follow-up study. *British Medical Journal, 294,* 1377–1380.

Hammett, T. M., Widom, R., Epstein, J., Gross, Sifre, S., & Enos, T. (1995). *1994 Update: HIV/AIDS and STDs in Correctional Facilities.* Washington, D.C.: U.S. National Institute of Justice.

Harackiewicz, J. M., Sansone, C., Blair, L. W., Epstein, J. A., & Manderlink, G. (1987). Attributional processes in behavior change and maintenance of smoking cessation and continued abstinence. *Journal of Consulting and Clinical Psychology, 55,* 372–378.

Harwood, H. A., Hubbard, R. L., Collins, J. J., & Rachal, J. V. (1988). The costs of crime and the benefits of drug abuse treatment. In C. G. Leukefeld and F. M. Tims (eds.), *Compulsory Treatment of Drug Abuse: Research and Clinical Practice.* NIDA Monograph No. 86. Washington, D.C.: U.S. Government Press.

Harwood, H. J., Napolitano, D. M., Kristiansen, P., & Collins, J. J. (1984). *Economic Costs to Society of Alcohol and Drug Abuse and Mental Illness.* Research Triangle, N.C.: Research Triangle Institute.

Hubbard, R. L., Marsden, M. E., Rachal, J. V., Harwood, H. J., Cavanaugh, E. R., & Ginzburg, H. M. (1989). *Drug Abuse Treatment: A National Study of Effectiveness.* Chapel Hill, N.C.: Univ. of North Carolina Press.

Hunt, W. A., Barnett, L. W., & Branch, L. G. (1971). Relapse rates in addiction programs. *Journal of Clinical Psychology, 27:* 455–456.

Inciardi, J. A., & Martin, S. S. (1993). Drug abuse treatment in criminal justice settings. *Journal of Drug Issues, 23,* 1–6.

Johnson, B. R., & Ross, P. P. (1990). The privatization of correctional management: A review. *Journal of Criminal Justice, 18,* 351–358.

Jordan, P. C. (1986). Effects of an extrinsic reward on intrinsic motivation: A field experiment. *Academy of Management Journal, 29,* 405–412.

Kenyon, R. C. (1986). Constructing for security. *Correct Today, 48,* 78–82.

Leukefeld, C. G. (1978). A comparison of voluntary and involuntary admissions to treatment for addiction. In A. Schecter, H. Alkine, and E. Kaufman (eds.), *Critical Concern in the Field of Drug Abuse.* New York: Marcel Decker, pp. 260–264.

Leukefeld, C. G., Gallego, M. A., & Farabee, D. (1997). Drugs, crime, and HIV. *Substance Use & Misuse, 32* (6), 749–756.

Leukefeld, C. G., Matthews, T., & Clayton, R. (1992). Treating the drug-abusing offender. *Journal of Mental Health Administration, 19,* 76–82.

Leukefeld, C. G., & Tims, F. M. (1988). Compulsory treatment: A review of findings. In C. G. Leukefeld & F. M. Tims (eds.), *Compulsory Treatment of Drug Abuse: Research and Clinical Practice.* (NIDA Monograph No. 86, DHHS Publication No. ADM 89-1578, pp. 236–249), Washington, D.C.: U.S. Government Press.

Logan, C. H. (1992). Well kept: Comparing quality of confinement in private and public prisons. *Journal of Criminal Law and Criminology, 83* (3), 577–613.

Martinson, R. (1974). What works?—Questions and answers about prison reform, *Public Interest, 35,* 22–54.

Maxwell, J. C. (1996). Substance abuse trends in Texas, December 1995. *TCADA Research Briefs.* Austin, Tex.: Texas Commission on Drug and Alcohol Abuse.

Miller, W. R. (1989). Increasing motivation for change. In R. K. Hester & W. R. Miller (eds.), *Handbook of alcoholism treatment approaches.* New York: Pergamon Press, pp. 67–80.

Nurco, D. N., Ball, J. C., Schaffer, J. W., and Hanlon, T. E. (1985). The criminality of narcotic addicts. *Journal of Nervous Mental Disease, 173,* 94–102.

Nurco, D. N., Hanlon, T. E., Kinlock, T. W., & Duszynski, K. R. (1988). Differential criminal patterns of narcotic addicts over an addiction career. *Criminology, 26,* 407–423.

Office of Justice Programs (1988). *Drug Use and Crime.* Washington, D.C.: Department of Justice.

Peters, R. H., May, R. L., & Kearns, W. D. (1992). Drug treatment in jails: Results of a nationwide survey. *Journal of Criminal Justice, 20* (4), 283–295.

Price, R. H., & D'Aunno, T. (1992). *NIDA III Respondent Report Drug Abuse Treatment System Survey: A National Study of the Outpatient Drug-Free and Methadone Treatment System, 1988–1990 Results.* Ann Arbor: University of Michigan, Institute for Social Research.

Rice, D. P., Kelman, S., Miller, L. S. & Dunmeyer, S. (1990). *The Economic Costs of Alcohol and Drug Abuse and Mental Illness: 1985.* San Francisco, Calif.: Institute for Health and Aging.

Salmon, R. (1982). The role of coercion in rehabilitation of drug users. *Journal of Offender Counseling, Services, and Rehabilitation, 6,* 59–70.

Schottenfeld, R. S. (1989). Involuntary treatment of substance abuse disorders: Impediments to success. *Psychiatry, 52,* 164–176.

Simpson, D. D. (1995). Issues in treatment process and services research. *International Journal of the Addictions, 30* (7), 875–879.

Simpson, D. D., Joe, G. W., & Rowan-Szal, G. A. (1997). Drug abuse treatment retention and process effects on follow-up outcomes. *Drug and Alcohol Dependence, 47,* 227–235.

Simpson, D. D., & Sells, S. (1982). Effectiveness of treatment for drug abuse: An overview of the DARP research program. *Adv. Alcohol Subst. Abuse, 2,* 7–29.

Spiegelman, R. (1984). *Alcohol Treatment and Social Control: Contradiction in Strategies for California's Skid Rows.* Presented at a meeting of the International Group for Comparative Alcohol Studies, Stockholm, October 23–27.

Thompson, A. (1990). *Guide to the Ethical Practice of Psychotherapy.* New York: John Wiley & Sons.

Toews, J., el-Geubaly, N., Leckie, A., & Harper, D. (1984). Patients' attitudes at the time of their commitment. *Canadian Journal of Psychiatry, 29,* 590–595.

Weisner, C. M. (1987). The social ecology of alcohol treatment in the United States. *Recent Developments in Alcoholism, 5,* 203–243.

Wellisch, J., Prendergast, M. L., & Anglin, M. D. (1995). Toward a drug abuse treatment system. *Journal of Drug Issues, 25,* 759–782.

Wexler, H. K., Falkin, G. P., Lipton, D. S., & Rosenblum, A. B. (1992). Outcome evaluation of a prison therapeutic community for substance abuse treatment. In C. G. Leukefeld and F. M. Tims (eds.), *Drug Abuse Treatment in Prisons and Jails* (NIDA Monograph No. 118, DHHS pub no. [ADM]92-1884).

FOUR

EUROPEAN PERSPECTIVES ON RELAPSE AND RELAPSE PREVENTION

Gerhard Bühringer, Michael Gossop, Dilek Türk,
Shamil Wanigaratne, & Charles Kaplan

INTRODUCTION

For many years the issues of relapse and relapse prevention were neglected in European clinical practice as well as in research into the course of addictive behaviours or treatment outcome. Despite the knowledge about high relapse rates learned from early follow-up studies (e.g., Polich, Armor & Braiker, 1980; Vaillant, 1983; Hubbard, Rachal, Craddock, & Cavanaugh, 1984) little attention was directed toward relapse issues by treatment providers. Thus, patients were not made aware of the significance of relapse risk, and treatment did not include strategies for successfully dealing with the problem of relapse.

Litman and her colleagues in London in the 1970s conducted some of the earliest work to address specifically the problem of relapse (Litman et al., 1977, 1979). Their work helped to identify and legitimize relapse as an important problem in itself and to establish some of the key concepts for understanding relapse. Marlatt and Gordon's (1995) work somewhat overshadowed their work, however, especially in their book on relapse prevention (Marlatt & Gordon, 1985), which is widely regarded as a landmark in this field.

Marlatt's work stimulated a large amount of theoretical and empirical work on relapse both in the United States and in Europe. Early examples are comprehensive works edited by Körkel (1988), Watzl and Cohen (1989) in Germany, and Gossop (1989) in Great Britain. Since then many single-site and some multisite studies as well as meta-analyses have been published in Europe in the field of alcohol and drug dependence by European researchers who used a variety of pharmacological and psychosocial interventions. These studies have included analyses of relapse prevention, and some of this work was published in Germany, e.g., by Körkel, Lauer & Scheller (1995).

It is difficult to judge the extent to which there is something uniquely "European" in the work on relapse and recovery. We have reviewed material that has been developed and published in Europe, but it is not surprising that work from North America has greatly influenced our thinking. In the sections that follow, we review European work in terms of conceptual issues — understanding of lapses and relapses, elucidating the processes involved, models for the onset of relapse, and concepts useful for relapse prevention programs. Our review of empirical data includes consideration of relapse rates, empirical findings regarding risk and protective factors for relapses, and studies of outcomes of relapse prevention programs.

We conducted both computerized and manual searches of journals and other sources, using Addiction Abstracts and Medline, as well as major journals containing articles by European researchers. Keywords searched for included "relapse," "relapse prevention," "alcohol treatment," and "opioid treatment." We examined literature going back to 1990, and we limited our search to articles with titles and summaries in English. This clearly resulted in overrepresentation of northern European countries, especially Great Britain, the Scandinavian countries, the Netherlands, and Germany, which are traditionally more oriented to the North American scientific tradition. Therefore, this review cannot be said to be representative of Europe, but rather predominantly represents the English language–oriented research community in Europe.

CONCEPTUAL ISSUES

The recognition of the commonality between different addictive behaviours was one of the conceptual developments that occurred in European addictions research in the 1980s and 1990s. (Brownell et al., 1986; Donovan & Marlatt, 1993; Gossop, 1987; Peele, 1985). Another was the shift in treatment emphasis to intervene to enhance maintenance of change. In Europe, Gloria Litman and her colleagues in London (Litman et al., 1977; Litman et al., 1979; Litman et al., 1983) did the pioneering theoretical work in this area.

The cognitive-behavioural model and interventions developed by Marlatt and his colleagues attempted to integrate theoretical perspectives and diverse treatment approaches (Marlatt & Gordon, 1980; Marlatt, 1982; Marlatt & George, 1984; Marlatt & Gordon, 1985). Conceptually, this has been seen as an integration of elements of classical and operant conditioning, social learning theory, social psychology, cognitive psychology, and Buddhist philosophy.

A key concept of the cognitive-behavioural relapse prevention model in Europe as elsewhere is that of *high-risk situations;* these are defined as situations or mood states and they are likely to have previously been associated with relapse for the individual. Common high-risk situations include negative mood states, social pressure, social networks, interpersonal conflicts, negative physical states, and some positive emotional states (Litman et al., 1983; Gossop et al., 1990; Unnithan et al., 1992).

The validity of the concept of high-risk situations has been questioned (Sutton, 1993). In what has been termed the base rate problem, the relative frequency of an occurrence of a high-risk situation that is needed to produce a lapse is also questioned. For example, someone trying to maintain habit change may frequently experience negative mood states, but each occurrence may not produce a lapse. When and what is required for it to become risky is questioned.

Relapse prevention work has been particularly valuable in drawing explicit attention to issues concerning the longer-term maintenance of change. Relapse prevention requires the development of *specific coping strategies* to deal with high-risk situations like skills training and more *global coping strategies* that would address issues of lifestyle imbalance and covert antecedents of relapse. A good relapse prevention programme would include all the above elements and instill in an individual a sense of preparedness and confidence similar to that of individuals who have undergone a good programme of "fire training" or "fire drill" (Wanigaratne et al., 1990). The notion of *lifestyle imbalance* is an interesting feature of the model but has received relatively little explication, though on a related theme, Orford's (1985) work has pointed to the central and important role played by ambivalence in the addictive behaviours.

There has been some controversy regarding the use of the term *relapse* in the area of addictive behaviours (Grabowski, 1986; Saunders & Allsop, 1989). The term has been criticised because of its connotations of a disease model. Within the United States, this has been related to the treatment context. The dominant model in the field of addiction at the time the model was introduced, and to some extent at present in America, is the disease model with an accompanying twelve-step philosophy of treatment. Launching a radically alternative model within this context would have been problematic. Using the term *relapse prevention,* with its disease connotations, to introduce a radically new set of concepts is equivalent to the use of a "Trojan horse" (Marlatt,

1995). In many respects, the term *relapse management* would be a more appropriate, if less catchy, term. The term *relapse prevention* has certainly been seen as problematic when applying the model to areas other than substance misuse — for example, maintenance of behavioural changes like adoption of safer sex. The accusation of "pathologising" normal behaviours is hard to refute.

The terminology and jargon contained within the relapse prevention approach have become part of the language of clinical settings and, used without much reflection, may impede effective interventions because they may undermine the credibility of the message.

The Marlatt and Gordon (1985) model has been criticised on a number of grounds. The failure to place adequate emphasis on craving and the physical aspects of addictions like withdrawal experience is one of criticism (Heather and Stallard, 1989). Cognitive formulations within the model like positive outcome expectancies of the substance or addictive behaviour are not seen as adequate to explain the power of conditioned craving in the relapse process. Heather and Stallard (1989) argue that positive outcome expectancies are a separate phenomenon.

The central concept of the model, that of high-risk situations, is based mainly on retrospective accounts of relapses of patients, and these may underreport the physical and craving elements. Instead, a retrospective explanatory account of the process that would inevitably be more psychological should have been given. On the other hand, a greater emphasis on the effects of conditioned craving could be accommodated within the model. Because the model has not been revised, clinicians must decide how strong an emphasis to place on craving in relapse prevention programmes. It is also left to researchers to study these processes in vitro or by such methods as diary keeping rather than relying on retrospective accounts.

The identification of relapse as a process and not just an event has been important. Paradoxically, the attention to relapse has also provided an important stimulus to research into recovery processes. Indeed, some of the research that was designed to address questions of relapse has subsequently developed into research into recovery processes. The identification and explication of high-risk situations, relapse precipitants, and coping strategies had an important but relatively nonspecific impact upon the delivery of treatment interventions in the national services of many European countries. This is reflected not so much in the provision of formal relapse prevention programmes (Wanigaratne et al., 1992) but in a rather more general manner, with the concepts being used as guidelines for the planning and delivery of treatment. To some extent, this is not surprising because relapse prevention methods are often seen not so much as alternatives to existing treatment methods but rather as applications of conventional techniques that are widely used in European clinical psychology practice.

In the United States the dominant model of addiction treatment is the twelve-step model, but it is less so in Europe. Marlatt coined the term *relapse prevention* with the expectation that a comprehensive alternative approach will be more acceptable to the addiction treatment establishment in the United States if it has disease connotations. The appropriateness of the term in the wider arena of addictions has been subject to much controversy; this will be discussed later. The response in the United States to relapse prevention is relevant here. Despite initial hostility to relapse prevention and fundamental conceptual differences between the two approaches, it can be said that in practice the approach has been absorbed and integrated into much of the twelve-step treatment programmes.

CURRENT EMPIRICAL STATUS

GENERAL METHODOLOGICAL REMARKS

Relapse rates from different studies are difficult to compare because of variations in concepts, definitions, methods, and situational conditions. Selection of patients, duration of treatment and follow-up period, type and measurement of success criteria, and the method to calculate success rates all make direct comparisons extremely difficult. Further problems arise when studies from different countries in Europe or from North America and Europe are compared. Süß (1995), for example, stated that short-term, outpatient, controlled treatment studies with small sample size dominate in the United States, whereas field studies on inpatient treatment with large sample sizes are preferred in Germany.

Conclusions about the long-term efficacy of different treatment modalities can only be derived from follow-up studies, although comparing of these follow-up studies is difficult due to different methodological problems (Fichter et al., 1992; Rist, 1996; Süß, 1995). Most of the treatment programmes contain several treatment components that are difficult to compare (Rist, 1996). Thus, Wetterling and Veltrup (1997) set forth several aspects to consider when comparing outcome studies:

1 Differences in local care,
2 Comparability of studies of different countries,
3 Preconditions for treatment admissions (selection),
4 Indications for special treatment strategies,

5 Differential utilization of care,

6 Economic aspects (comparison of cost-effectiveness and efficiency testing).

Meta-analyses are one way to enhance comparisons between studies, but often relevant data are lacking or nonexperimental studies have to be included. Another approach to enable treatment comparisons is if researchers follow common standards for treatment. The German Society for Addiction Research and Therapy (Deutsche Gesellschaft für Suchtforschung und Suchttherapie, 1987, 2d ed., 1992; English version, 1994) has published such a set of standards. Their publication includes data collection standards for major patient characteristics, treatment and outcome characteristics, and for the calculation of outcome figures (Platt, Bühringer, Widmann, Künzel & Lidz, 1996). For example, success rates for abstinence-oriented treatment were calculated in four different ways: success rates of planned discharges (F1) and of all discharged patients (F3) based on those for whom follow-up information was collected. Success rates for planned discharges (F2) and for all patients including also those for whom no follow-up information was available were also calculated (F4). The calculations for F2 and F4 were more conservative, counting all patients for whom follow-up information was unavailable as "relapsed." Thus, the true scores of outcomes for planned discharges lie between F1 and F3, and for all discharges between F2 and F4. The lower the response rate, the higher the differences between F1 and F3, and between F2 and F4. This underscores the need for adequate response rates and methods for better estimating relapse among nonrespondents.

RELAPSE RATES

ALCOHOL

This section provides an overview of average relapse rates of pharmacological and psychosocial treatment for alcohol-dependent patients. Keep in mind that the type and duration of treatment for alcohol dependents, as well as the length of the follow-up period, differ widely among European states, and even more between the United States and Europe. In general, the treatment duration is much longer in Europe (especially in Germany; standard duration until recently: 2–6 months) than in the United States, and to a much higher degree the treatment takes place in residential settings.

Correspondingly, relapse is defined differently in Europe and the United States. Although many European clinicians would consider any alcohol intake as a relapse, clinicians in the United States use the terms *lapse* or *slip* for minor or brief periods of alcohol intake and the term *relapse* as an intensive and continuing alcohol intake. This American perspective is slowly influencing the European definition. Therefore, the meaning of relapse is becoming blurred in Europe, so reported relapse rates can not be compared easily. In addition, a middle category ("improved," "abstinence after short relapse") with very different definitions makes comparison of relapse rates even more difficult. Many studies do not report these relevant data for comparison.

Relapse rates after pharmacological treatment

In a time when research on the neurobiological and neuropharmacological patterns of dependence is becoming more dominant, the role of pharmacological treatment of alcohol dependents is gaining more prominence among practitioners with the introduction of new drugs. According to Besson (1997), useful pharmacological agents for the treatment of alcohol dependents can be classified into four groups:

- Agents to treat withdrawal,
- Aversive agents,
- Therapeutic agents for comorbidity,
- New agents to reduce craving for alcohol or to prevent relapse.

These new agents derive from research in four areas, based on neurobiological hypotheses:

- The glutamatergic hypothesis with acamprosate,
- The opioid hypothesis with naltrexone,
- The serotonergic hypothesis with the new antidepressants,
- Other hypotheses, like the dopaminergic, peptidic, etc.

Many drugs have been tested in clinical trials over the past ten years, including all the above noted groups of drugs. Not all of these agents have been tested in large clinical studies, and according to Soyka (1997) only a few have been introduced into practice.

Meta-analyses of randomised controlled studies of different forms of pharmacotherapy in alcohol treatment (e.g., Batel, 1995) indicate that several agents have demonstrated safety and efficacy during different periods of follow-up, including acamprosate (long term), naltrexone (intermediate term), fluoxetine, and citalopram (short term). Studies of zimeldine, nialamide, L-dopa, viloxazine, and tetrabamate failed to demonstrate efficacy for these agents in treatment of alcoholism.

In a review of outcome studies following disulfiram, Hughes and Cook (1997) give a critical judgment of the methodological quality of these studies.

The findings support the general use of oral disulfiram, as it has been shown to lead to a reduced quantity of alcohol consumed and a reduced number of drinking days. However, evidence for an effect in increasing the number of abstainers is lacking. Hughes and Cook conclude that disulfiram should be employed as part of a comprehensive treatment programme.

Of the major new agents, however, acamprosate has undergone several studies in controlled clinical trials around Europe. This anticraving compound has been registered for relapse prophylaxes in weaned alcoholics in various European countries. Acamprosate, the $Ca(2+)$-salt of N-acetyl-homotaurinate, interacts with NMDA receptor-mediated glutamatergic neurotransmission in various brain regions and reduces $Ca(2+)$ fluxes through voltage-operated channels. Its efficacy has been demonstrated statistically, it is well tolerated, and it interacts with alcohol. Acamprosate can also be associated with disulfiram therapy. Acamprosate, as a specific modulator of the glutamatergic system, appears to be one of the most promising new pharmacological agents in relapse prevention when the patient benefits from psychosocial support (Pelc, 1997). The initial three-month treatment studies on the efficacy of acamprosate in relapse prevention were conducted in France by Lhuintre et al. (1985, 1990). In the initial study of 85 patients, a significant reduction in the rate of relapses within three months after cessation of alcohol use was showed. In the following study, these findings were replicated. In recent years, the efficacy of the drug has been examined in a number of phase II, III, and IV studies, including several large placebo-controlled double-blind studies of six and twelve months' duration, in various European countries (Soyka, 1996). These studies with acamprosate analyzed the relapse prevention effect when given in addition to a traditional psychosocial treatment programme. The outcome of these studies is referred to in the section on relapse prevention below.

A possible alternative to acamprosate is, according to some researchers, the nonselective long-acting opioid antagonist naltrexone (Feuerlein, Küfner, & Soyka, 1998). In Europe, however, there have been no major placebo-controlled, double-blind studies of the drug as a treatment to reduce relapses in alcohol-dependent patients as there have been in the United States (O'Malley et al., 1992; Volpicelli et al., 1992).

Relapse rates after psychosocial treatment

Studies on short-, medium-, and long-term treatment outcome of alcohol abuse and relapse rates vary between single case studies (Brewer, 1993) and more controlled studies with hundreds of patients. Table 4.2 contains selected

Table 4.1: Treatment Outcomes of Acamprosate Interventions for Alcohol Dependents

STUDY	COUNTRY	N	INTERVENTION MODALITIES	FOLLOW-UP	DROP-OUT RATE	COM-PLETERS RATE	DAYS OF CONTINU-OUS ABSTI-NENCE	RELAPSE RATE (PERCENT-AGE)	ABSTINENCE RATE (PER-CENTAGE)
Paille et al. (1995)	France	538	prospective randomized-controlled, double-blind study; acamprosate as a supplement to outpatient psychosocial intervention 1.3g vs. 2.0g vs. placebo	90 d 180 d 360 d 540 d	56	44	223 vs. 198 vs. 173	24 vs. 19 vs. 22	39 vs. 41 vs. 33 27 vs. 32 vs. 19 18 vs. 19 vs. 11 11 vs. 15 vs. 9
Saß et al. (1996)	Germany	272	multisite, randomized-controlled, double-blind study; acamprosate as a supplement to outpatient psychosocial intervention for 48 weeks	48 w	41 (a) vs. 60	59 (a) vs. 40	224 (a) vs. 163	61 (a) vs. 73	39 (a) vs. 17

Whitworth et al. 1996	Austria	455	multisite, randomized-controlled, double-blind study; acamprosate as a supplement to outpatient psychosocial intervention for 360 days	1 y	60	40	230 (a) vs. 183	39 (a) vs. 38	12 (a) vs. 5
Geerlings et al. (1997)	The Netherlands Belgium Luxembourg	262	multisite, randomized-controlled, double-blind study; acamprosate as a supplement to outpatient psychosocial intervention	6 m	59 (a) vs. 69	41 (a) vs. 31	61 (a) vs. 43	23 (a) vs. 28	11 (a) vs. 5
Poldrugo (1997)	Italy	246	multisite, randomized-controlled, double-blind study; acamprosate, six months	6 m	47 (a) vs. 62	53 (a) vs. 38	168 (a) vs. 121	6 (a) vs. 4	43 (a) vs. 30

Table 4.2: Treatment Outcomes of Psychosocial Interventions for Alcohol Dependents

STUDY	COUNTRY	N	INTERVENTION MODALITIES	FOLLOW-UP	DROPOUT RATE (PERCENT-AGE)	RELAPSE RATE/POOR (PERCENT-AGE)	ABSTINENCE RATE (PER-CENTAGE)
Jung et al. (1987)	Germany	491	inpatient behavior therapy	12 m 48 m	28	58 71	42 29
Doyle et al. (1994)	GB	44	inpatient alcohol unit	median 4 y (<10 y)		61.4	38.6
Garcia et al. (1995)	Spain	36	Relapse prevention vs. conventional care	3 y		40 vs. 78.6	64.3 vs. 13
Callejo et al. (1995)	Spain	978	community programme	6 m 1 y 2 y	40 37 49	56 68 72	44 32 28
Klijnsma et al. (1995)	GB	28	outpatient detoxification	2 m		40	29*

Study	Country	N	Intervention	Follow-up				
Veltrup (1995)	Germany	211	short inpatient treatment	12 m			81	19
Veltrup (1995)	Germany	65	detoxification	12				9
Saß (1996)	Germany	136	detoxification + placebo	12				21
Shaw et al. (1997)	GB	112	1 month intensive residential programme	6 m 1 y 9 y				43 33 15
Favre & Gillet (1997)	France	1043	residential programme	5 y	38	46.8		28.5
Patterson et al. (1997)	GB	127	1 year community psychiatric nurse aftercare vs. standard aftercare	5 y				36 vs. 5
Wetterling & Veltrup (1997)	Germany	201	detoxification	12				17

* Rate for good outcome: abstinence rate (25%) plus controlled drinking with 4 units per day (4%).

Table 4.3: Multisite Treatment Outcome Studies on Psychosocial Interventions for Alcohol Dependents

STUDY	TYPE OF INTERVENTION	N CENTERS	N PATIENTS	FOLLOW-UP RESULTS (F3)[1]		
				6 month	18 month	48 month
Küfner & Feuerlein, 1989;	2–6 month inpatient treatment (MEAT Study)	21 (Germany)	1,410			
Feuerlein & Küfner, 1992	All			67% + (11%)	53% + (9%)	46% + (3%)
	Male			69% + (10%)	55% + (9%)	49% + (3%)
	Female			61% + (14%)	47% + (8%)	41% + (2%)
Maffli, 1996	2–12 month inpatient treatment (Switzerland)	8	915		83 month (F3)[1,2,3]	
	All				12% + (25%)	
	Male				14% + (24%)	
	Female				7% + (27%)	

1 % of patients with abstinence in the total follow-up period (% of improved cases in brackets)
2 Outcome figures based on all clients with follow-up information (see 4.1)
3 Calculation from a representative subsample (N=135)

single-site and multisite studies on different kinds of detoxification, psychosocial outpatient, or residential treatment. The term *psychosocial* is used for all types of comprehensive interventions based on a varying combination of psychological (e.g., individual or group therapy) and social (e.g., job training) measures. The results of these studies indicate that alcohol patients are relatively difficult to treat. Depending on the treatment setting or follow-up period the abstinence rates vary between 9 and 44%.

But engagement following detoxification with voluntary agencies can also result in a better outcome. Klijnsma et al. (1995) found that outpatient detoxification is cost-effective in the treatment of alcohol-dependent patients because it is six times cheaper than inpatient detoxification. In addition to the 33% of subjects with good outcome, 32% showed improvement.

More interesting are some multisite studies and a meta-analysis of European and North American studies. The MEAT study in Germany included about 1,400 patients from 21 inpatient treatment centers, with the usual residential treatment duration at that time (1985–90) of two to six months (Küfner & Feuerlein, 1989; Feuerlein & Küfner, 1992). Follow-ups were carried out at six, eighteen, and forty-eight months after discharge. The average rate of planned discharge was 82.9%; the response rate in the follow-ups varied between 85% (6 m.) and 81% (48 m.). Success rates were calculated by formula F3, which was introduced above, taking the number of patients with total abstinence during the full follow-up period (table 4.3). Compared to North American studies the results show higher success rates. Relapse rates (without "improved" cases) were around 22% (6 months), 38% (12 months), and 51% (48 months). But keep in mind that the average treatment was four times longer in the European studies than in the North American ones. Maffli (1996) conducted a study with similar type and length of inpatient treatment in Switzerland. Eight treatment centers with 915 patients were included, but only one follow-up was done, with an average of 83 months (between 70 and 101 months). The average length of treatment was 5.5 months (1 to 567 days), and 70% had a regular discharge. Only 36% of the total population could be reached in the follow-up study, but in a representative sample of 15% of the patients the rate of successful interviews was 85%, so the results from this subgroup were taken for the total population (formula F3). Table 4.3 shows that the Swiss results (63% relapses) are similar to the German forty-eight-month follow-up data, even though the Swiss follow-up period was longer.

Süß (1995) found 320 publications for his meta-analysis, from both North America and Europe. The number included 183 publications from the review of Miller & Hester (1986). He excluded 62 because of formal criteria (grey

Table 4.4: Meta-analysis of Treatment Outcome Studies for Alcohol Dependents

	DURATION OF TREATMENT	FOLLOW-UP PERIOD	ABSTINENCE				ABSTINENCE 1 AND IMPROVED STATUS			
			F1	F2	F3	F4	F1 [2]	F2	F3	F4
All studies	1–4 m	14 m	47.9%	45.6%	42.9%	34%	61.8%	59.3%	56%	40.7%
Minimal / no interventions	—	9.9 m	[85.7%]			21.2%	62.3%			25.1%
Disulfiram	6.5 m	14.4 m	39.6%			23.2%	62.1%			28.6%
Eclectic therapies	1.7 m	13.2 m	45.9%			33.0%	61.4%			44.5%
Germany	4 m	15.6 m	67.4%			42.1%	75.9%			47.8%
Others	1.1 m	12.3 m	35.9%			29.7%	54.6%			43.3%
Behavioral therapies	1.6 m	14.4 m	58.0%			44.5%	62.8%			54.2%
Germany	2.8 m	13.9 m	76.2%			52.8%	81.6%			60.4%
Other	1.0 m	16.6 m	50.7%			40.4%	57.4%			51.5%

Source: Süß, 1995; 23 experimental and 21 nonexperimental field studies.

literature, dissertations that could not be found), 123 because of contextual criteria (studies with anticraving substances, programmes with controlled drinking), and 81 because of methodological reasons (small sample sizes, no clear data on abstinence). Finally, he included 54 publications on 23 experimental and 21 nonexperimental studies. Results were analysed (1) for abstinence in the total follow-up period and (2) for clear improvement, at least six months before the follow-up period. Effect sizes were additionally calculated for experimental studies. All results were reanalysed for formulas F1, F2, F3, and F4.

There is an interesting difference in the origin of the studies. Sixteen of the 23 experimental studies were carried out in North America, and only 7 in Europe (Great Britain and Finland). The nonexperimental studies predominantly came from Europe (14 from Germany, 1 from Scotland), and only 6 from North America. The average length of treatment was between 1 and 4 months, the length of follow-up period about 14 months (table 4.4). Differences could be found between the studies carried out in Germany and in other European countries (plus one exception from North America). Follow-up figures on relapse rates from German treatment centers seem to be somewhat lower, depending on the different calculations F1–F4 (independent of the type of treatment), but the treatment duration again is 2 to 4 times longer. One can also see that behavior therapy programmes are slightly shorter and have slightly higher success rates. Further analyses were made for the length of treatment, for the severity of the patient problems, and for the effect sizes in the experimental studies.

ILLEGAL DRUGS

The literature on relapse and relapse prevention for drug dependence in Europe in general and in the individual European states reflects the different treatment philosophies. Whereas methadone maintenance was relatively earlier implemented in some countries like Great Britain or the Netherlands, others like France or Germany did this rather recently, around 1990. Therefore, relapse issues were studied in the latter countries in the context of drug-free treatment programmes (predominantly residential), whereas studies in other countries were carried out mainly in methadone maintenance programmes. The comparison of these two treatment modalities is even more difficult than comparisons between programmes for alcohol dependents. Usually the treatment duration of methadone maintenance is much longer than in abstinence programmes, so comparing follow-up figures between patients still *in* methadone maintenance and patients *after* abstinence pro-

Table 4.5: Treatment Outcome of Methadone Maintenance for Drug Dependents

STUDY	COUNTRY	N	INTERVENTION MODALITIES	FOLLOW-UP	DROPOUT RATES (PERCENTAGE)	RETENTION RATE (PERCENTAGE)	ABSTINENCE RATE (PERCENTAGE)
Wilson, Watson, & Ralston (1994)	Scotland	46	methadone maintenance in general practice, 18 months			83	78
Rosenbach & Hunot (1995)	England	80	pre- and post-methadone treatment			83 vs. 13	57 vs. 39
Del Rio, Mino, & Perneger (1997)	Switzerland	111	methadone maintenance 1 year	1.5 y	15.2	84	
Raschke (1994)	Germany	795	outpatient methadone maintenance, average duration 15 months	1–4 y		91.3	3 after substitution 61 after follow-up
Ministerium f. Arbeit, Gesundheit u. Soziales NRW (1997)	Germany	244	outpatient methadone maintenance, average duration 5 years	1 y 3 y 5 y 7 y		87 66 53 48	51 101 121
Küfner et al. (1999)	Germany	123	outpatient methadone maintenance, average duration 18 months			53.3	111

grammes is like comparing apples and pears. In the following section, results of single studies are presented first and some multicentre studies are presented in more detail. Because of the complex pattern of physiological, psychological, and social disorders of drug dependents, there is no "pure" pharmacological treatment for them. Different kinds of psychosocial interventions are always delivered in maintenance programs, and therefore we differentiate in this chapter between maintenance- and abstinence-oriented interventions.

Relapse rates after methadone maintenance

Selected results of treatment outcome from methadone maintenance studies are summarized in table 4.5. Most studies report retention and not relapse rates, and because methadone maintenance is not per se abstinence-oriented but its goal is harm reduction, we differentiate between retention and abstinence rates in methadone treatment. In general, table 4.5 indicates that retention rates are between 83 and 91% with average treatment duration of one and a half years. Depending on the study, the follow-up time, and the definition of abstinence, the rate varies around 5–10% (total abstinence, including abstinence from methadone) and 50–80% (still in maintenance, but no other drugs).

An interesting study in England investigated the implications of a drug policy change by introducing an oral methadone treatment programme for problem opiate users in 1990 (Rosenbach & Hunot, 1995). Their study compared one client group before (39) and one client group after (41) methadone prescribing had commenced. Findings indicated that 83% of the postmethadone group compared to 13 percent of the premethadone group remained in treatment for longer than six months. Furthermore, the results revealed that clients in the postmethadone group were more likely to stop drug injection and continue illicit drug use. Also, the rate of detected crime was reduced and subjects improved their personal relationships. Strang et al. (1997) present encouraging data that underlines the benefits in the immediate postrecruitment phase (1 month) of outpatient treatment of opiate addicts with oral methadone: rates of drug use had reduced to one-fifth (heroin) and to one-quarter (cocaine). Also, the number of injectors decreased and the measures of physical and psychological health improved.

The differential effect of methadone and other substitutes is also relevant in Europe, particularly England. Two randomised double-blind studies conducted in England compared the differential effect of lofexidine and methadone as well as lofexidine and clonidine, respectively, in inpatient treatment

Table 4.6: Multisite Treatment Outcome Study on Drug Dependents

AUTHOR	COUNTRY	NO. OF PROGRAMMES	N	INTERVENTION MODALITIES	FOLLOW-UP	RESPONSE RATE (PERCENTAGE)	ABSTINENCE RATE (PERCENTAGE)
Gossop et al. (1998)	GB	54	1075	residential vs. community treatment services	1 year	72	44
							21

of opiate withdrawal and in the detoxification of opiate addicts in hospital (Bearn, Gossop, & Strang, 1996; Kahn et al., 1997). Both studies indicate that lofexidine resulted in significantly less hypotension and adverse effects.

Some other studies deal with detoxification efficacy in drug addicts. Detoxification procedures are necessary to get the addict off drugs as one of the first steps in the abstinence-oriented treatment of drug addicts. This process of detoxification is not in itself a sufficient treatment, but it is very important that it is carried out as effectively as possible and with the least discomfort for the patients. Recent interest in ultra-rapid detoxification procedures using opiate antagonists during benzodiazepine-induced general anaesthesia has sought to reduce the duration of it as well as the discomfort for the patients. Gossop and Strang (1997) questioned the benefits of the procedure, however, because there is not yet convincing evidence of its effectiveness or about the extent of adverse reactions. On the other hand, other authors like Brewer (1997) favour this procedure because it appears to help patients avoid withdrawal or shorten its discomforts.

Merrill & Marshall (1997) reported on another brief inpatient opioid detoxification procedure using naloxone. An accompanying supply of clonidine and diazepam was used to treat withdrawal symptoms. After six days, 75% of patients successfully completed detoxification; thus patients could participate in a relapse prevention programme. There is now but one multisite study that compares methadone maintenance and abstinence programme approaches in terms of patient selection, amount of intervention (also in terms of costs), and situation of the patient at different times after the beginning of interventions (including cost-effectiveness analysis). This is the study currently in progress in Great Britain: the National Treatment Outcome Research Study (NTORS), which is the largest study of treatment outcomes for drug misusers ever conducted in the United Kingdom. This study monitors the progress of 1,075 clients, who were recruited into either residential or community treatment services. The residential services were specialist inpatient and rehabilitation programmes. The community-based services were methadone maintenance and methadone reduction programmes. These four treatment modalities are said to be representative of the main types of treatment provided within the United Kingdom. A sum of 54 programmes participated in NTORS. After one year, 76% of the cohort (818 clients) were contacted, and from 769 (72%) outcome data were obtained (table 4.6). After one year there was an overall decline in drug taking and other problem behaviours, significant in view of the severity and chronicity of the problems presented at intake. Abstinence rates for illicit opiate use (heroin and non-prescribed methadone) were more than doubled (Gossop, 1998).

Relapse after psychosocial (abstinence-oriented) treatment

Examples of selected European studies are described in table 4.7. Dropout rates are high and relapse rates differ between 30 and 90% at one- to two-year follow-ups for all clients in treatment (form F3 or F4).

A similar large multisite study with 300 patients from 13 residential drug-free therapeutic communities in Germany was carried out between 1985 and 1990. Follow-up interviews including urine analysis were scheduled 3, 12, and 24 months after regular discharge or dropout. The response rate over all three follow-ups was 72% (Hanel, 1992; Haderstorfer & Künzel-Böhmer, 1992; Herbst, 1992). The relapse rate of the regular discharged patients was 49%, whereas that of the dropouts was at 79% (table 4.6). After a four-year follow-up the relapse rate was 77% for dropouts and 65% for treatment completers.

A further multisite study was carried out in Germany between 1987 and 1993, with 9,000 patients from 41 residential treatment facilities (Küfner et al., 1994). The purpose was to study (1) the rates of different types of dropout and planned discharge, (2) the rates for relapse during and at the end of treatment, (3) factors that influence these characteristics, and (4) the impact of different treatment improvements to reduce the high rate of dropout in residential treatment facilities. Follow-up surveys were not carried out, but the study gives a good overview of relapse during and at the end of treatment in Germany around 1990. The regular discharges of 29% seemed higher compared to corresponding rates in therapeutic communities of the American study Client-Oriented Data Acquisition Process (CODAP), a national data system used in the USA by NIDA until 1981 (about 20%). Furthermore, 53% of the clients in the study group terminated their treatment prematurely by their own decision, and 15% were discharged involuntarily by the treatment center.

The project also studied the relapse pattern during residential treatment and the relation between relapse and dropout. Planned discharges had relapses during treatment of 6 to 8% (cannabis, heroin) to about 13% (alcohol and analgetics, multiple responses possible), altogether 23% of the regular discharges. Depending on a drug, between 12 and 34% of the relapses were unknown to the therapists during the whole treatment process. According to the therapists, about 30% of the dropouts (dropouts are 68% of all clients in treatment) were due to relapses.

RISK AND PROTECTIVE FACTORS

EXTERNAL FACTORS

In an interesting article by Uitenbroek (1996), data were collected between 1988 and 1994 by a telephone survey of 30,000 persons living in Glasgow and Edinburgh. The author found that annually, alcohol use is the highest in the summer and in December. From this, one could derive that alcohol-dependent patients need special attention during these times of the year.

COMORBIDITY

The comorbidity of personality disorders and alcohol dependence is a risk factor for progressing more rapidly from moderate drinking to alcohol-related problems. Patients with these risk factors were more likely to discontinue treatment prematurely, indicating that patients with alcohol dependence and personality disorders are more likely to relapse after treatment if the personality disorder is not treated as well. Such patients need a different approach to treatment than those who have only alcohol dependence (Powell & Peveler, 1996). Ravndal & Vaglum (1995) investigated the influence of personality disorders on treatment completion in a hierarchical therapeutic community for drug abusers. They identified different personality disorders among dropouts and "completers." Completers were more likely to have histrionic traits, whereas dropouts were more likely to have schizotypal traits.

According to another study (Doyle, Delaney, & Tobin, 1994), patients who had a history of childhood personality difficulties and unsatisfactory schooling experiences were more likely to relapse. Such patients also had considerable concurrent illicit drug use and ongoing legal problems associated with continuing problem drinking. The poor outcome group furthermore continued to make heavy demands on medical services over the follow-up period.

Baving and Olbrich (1996) studied the role of coexisting depression in alcohol patients. Alcohol patients with coexisting depression exhibit heavier alcohol abuse, more severe physical damage, and greater liability to both psychotropic drug abuse and overdose behavior than nondepressive alcoholics. Depressed alcoholics also experience more frequent and more severe relapses and are at greater risk for suicide. According to the authors, the greater risk of suicide among depressed alcoholics may be due to three possible non-mutually exclusive types of association:

Table 4.7: Treatment Outcome of Abstinence-Oriented Interventions for Drug Dependents

STUDY	COUNTRY	N	INTERVENTION MODALITIES	FOLLOW-UP	DROPOUT RATES (PERCENTAGE)	RETENTION RATE (PERCENTAGE)	RELAPSE RATE (PERCENTAGE)	ABSTINENCE RATE (PERCENTAGE)
Dawe et al. (1993)	England	186	cue-exposure (CE), drug dependence unit (DDU), and general ward (GW) vs. control (C) DDU, C GW	6 weeks 6 months				CE DDU:67 C DDU: 64 CE GW: 50 C DDU: 11
De Los et al. (1997)	Spain	275	inpatient detoxification programme		17.8	82.2		
Gomez et al. (1995)	Spain	17	prison detoxification with naltrexone-guanfacine (5 days)		11.8	88.2		
Herbst (1992)	Germany	297	inpatient treatment	4 y	40	60	77/95 65/85	
Keaney, Wanigaratne, & Pullin (1995)	England	61	outpatient relapse prevention vs. control		21 vs. 68			

Küfner et al. (1994)	Germany	5678 (34 sites) vs. 3123	inpatient crisis intervention vs. control		71 vs. 73	29 vs. 27	29	37
Landabaso et al. (1996)	Spain	90	outpatient naltrexone treatment			75.5		
Marina et al. (1996)	Spain	334	drug-free clinics	3.3 y				
Moreno & Rosado (1996)	Spain	47	outpatient naltrexone treatment for 2 years	12 months				
Oppenheimer, Sheehan, & Taylor (1990)	England	150	inpatient treatment	3.6 y	23	77		37
Ravndal & Vaglum (1994)	Norway	13	hierarchical community-based treatment	(1.5 y) + 2 m			46	54
Ravndal & Vaglum (1995)	Norway	144	hierarchical community-based treatment	(1.5 y) + 2 months	80	20		
Sheehan, Oppenheimer, & Taylor (1993)	England	150	inpatient treatment	3.6 y			76	24

1 The ingestion of alcohol may be an attempt at self-medication of depressive symptoms;
2 Depression and alcohol abuse may, independently of each other, both be attributable to an underlying, possibly genetic, factor; and
3 Depression may be a result of alcoholism: either induced by heavy alcohol consumption as a consequence of alcohol withdrawal or as a psychoreactive phenomenon.

Independent from the type of association between alcohol and depressive disorder, for patients suffering from both disorders special treatment modalities have to be offered. The role of depression as a risk factor for the development of alcohol dependence could also be demonstrated in a study in which according to patients with alcohol dependence the presence of depressive mood is one reason for relapse (Veltrup, 1994).

COGNITION AND EMOTION

According to social learning theory, positive alcohol expectancies would increase the probability of drinking, and negative expectancies would decrease the risk. It is also recognized that the subjective evaluation of expectancies ought to moderate the impact, although the evidence for this in social drinkers is problematic. Jones and McMahon (1994) studied the negative and positive alcohol expectancies as predictors of abstinence in alcohol-dependent men (n = 53). The patients were treated and then were successfully followed up at one and three months after discharge to assess their compliance with the treatment goal of total abstinence. The results show that at one month, neither demographic variables nor alcohol expectancies were associated with outcome consumption. At three months, however, the demographic variable, age, total negative expectancy (but not total positive), and the two subscales — global positive expectancy and continued-drinking negative expectancy (representing longer term expected negative consequences) — were, leading to the conclusion that the role of negative alcohol expectancies and drinking decisions are important for relapse.

Jones and McMahon (1996a) addressed the speculation that the moderating effect of alcohol expectancies would be more evident in clinical populations than in social drinkers. They show that both expectancy and value, independently and equally, predict patients' abstinence survivorship following discharge from a treatment programme. When expectancy evaluations are processed against expectancy through multiplicative composites (i.e., expectancy × value), their predictive power is equivalent only to either expectancy or value on its own. Jones & McMahon (1996b) also demonstrated the role of negative outcome expectancies assessed at admission to treatment in predicting the number of days until first drink. Implications for planning treatment in terms of changing the negative outcome expectancy to a positive one are derived in order to prevent relapses.

The role of motivation as a prognostic factor for successful treatment of alcohol disorders has been shown in several reviews and studies (Arend, 1994; Fleischmann et al., 1995; John et al., 1995; Petry, 1993, 1996; Pfeiffer et al., 1988; Schwoon, 1992; Veltrup et al., 1993, 1994, 1996). The alcohol patients' experience of satisfaction with the initial assessment interview seems to enhance engagement in treatment. A study in England showed a similar result (Hyams et al., 1996). Thus, the first contact with a patient is prognostic for engagement in therapy and, therefore, probably for abstinence or relapse.

Also, patients' acceptance and appraisal of therapeutic components is important for the success of therapy and progress in further treatments. In a prospective study, Zähres, Stetter, & Mann (1993) asked 72 alcohol patients at the beginning of treatment and before discharge to evaluate different treatment components. Medical care and the protective nature of the inpatient detoxification treatment were assessed as valuable by detoxification patients who were not long-term patients. Moreover, patients wanted to keep a distance from their familiar environment and at the same time improve relationships with other patients. Therefore, patients liked group therapy though they expected more help from individual treatment. Consequently, abstinence-oriented and relapse prevention programmes respectively have to fulfill patients' interests in stabilization and support.

Certain attribution styles can lead more often to relapse than others. In one study, for example, the attributional styles of abstainers and relapsers were examined in a sample of 31 illicit drug users in a study by Birke et al. (1990). No significant differences were found in attributional styles, although relative to the relapse group there was a tendency for abstainers to score higher on internality and stability of attribution for negative events, but lower on globality. Both negative affect and interpersonal conflict, but not social pressure, were found to be important precipitants for relapse.

Given the high relapse rate of opiate addicts following detoxification, Powell et al. (1993) tried to identify any subjective variables that mediate outcome so they could be used as targets of treatment. They tested personality, cue-elicited craving, outcome expectancy for drug use, and self-efficacy for resisting drug use in 43 opiate addicts receiving inpatient detoxification in either a specialized addiction unit or a general psychiatric ward. These 43 patients were randomly allocated either to an inpatient detoxification unit or to a control group. Subjects were then followed up at between one and three months and again at six months after discharge. At the first follow-up the frequency of drug use was not predicted by any of the subjective variables. At six months, however, subjects with lower self-efficacy and higher positive outcome expectancies were found to be using less often, although latency to first lapse was greater among subjects with higher anxiety and neuroticism scores. The authors suggest that greater awareness of personal vulnerability may promote effective coping strategies.

Drug dreams are related to craving and to relapses, as reported by Christo & Franey (1996). They interviewed 101 drug users at baseline when six weeks abstinent. Some of the subjects reported having drug-related dreams, and they reported having more drug dreams when abstinent than when using drugs. Ninety percent of subjects were followed up with after six months. A higher dream frequency at baseline (after six weeks of abstinence) was prospectively related to greater drug use at follow-up. Drug dream frequency at follow-up was found to be related to craving and lack of sleep.

COPING STRATEGIES

The results of Kaufmann et al. (1993) show clearly that the quality of health concept, coping resources, and coping patterns are significant as prognostic factors in heroin addicts for their rehabilitation seven years later. A study by Bish et al. (1996) demonstrated the role of coping strategies in protecting individuals against long-term tranquilizer use. A sample of long-term benzodiazepine users were followed up over a period of six months. By the time of follow-up slightly more than half of the participants had withdrawn completely or had reduced their daily dose. Analyses showed that reduction was unrelated to factors associated with the drugs themselves. Significant associations, however, were found between participants' coping responses and long-term benzodiazepine use and the individuals' reduction or cessation of benzodiazepine use in the six-month study period. The findings suggest that interventions that encourage cognitive behavioural and affective aspects of coping appear to be more likely to succeed and prevent relapse.

Maintaining abstinence is not easy for most patients. Besançon (1993) in France was interested in time to reestablish dependence, and he investigated 31 subjects who had been dependent on alcohol, had subsequently been abstinent for at least two months, and had a relapse into dependence. He found that the median time to dependence when relapsing was seven days, which is 700-fold more accelerated than median time to first dependence. Time to subsequent dependence was not related to abstinence. Subjects had felt as if they were healed, so that this inadequate self-concept was a risk factor for relapse. These findings suggest the importance of cognitive treatment for relapse prevention.

SOCIAL INTERACTIONS

The importance of relationships to parents, partners, and peers seems to be important particularly for treatment, but especially for female addicts. For female addicts poor outcome was strongly related to destructive relationships with male coresidents in the outpatient period (Ravndal & Vaglum, 1994).

A study carried out in the Netherlands showed that an increase in alcohol intake is found more often if there are chronic social impairments (Cornell et al., 1996). This study indicates that chronic social impairments can also lead to more relapses after treatment.

TREATMENT-RELATED FACTORS

Relatively few European studies examined treatment factors in relation to outcome. They show that different treatment aspects, such as using former addicts as staff members, or the type of activity offered to drug users, such as family network, occupational information, vocational and pedagogical counselling, rehabilitative measures and sensation-seeking activity influence largely the treatment outcome (Berg, Andersen, & Alveberg, 1997). But these activities are also correlated with the length of stay for male clients, and the authors suggest that these clients tend to stay longer in facilities that provide activities to directly enhance functioning in a drug-free life. Strang et al. (1997) compared the outcome of general versus specialist psychiatric inpatient care with a randomized study design across 186 opiate addicts. The patient outcomes differed across the two settings. In a "specialist" setting more patients completed treatment (45 versus 18 percent) and during seven months' follow-up, of those patients who reached the end of treatment, significantly more ex-"specialist" than ex-"general" inpatient subjects were opiate-free. The use of a structured assessment interview as an intervention to reduce dropout rates due to anxiety and lack of clarity among "problem" drinkers in outpatient relapse prevention groups was illustrated by Keaney, Wanigaratne, & Pullin (1995).

Compared to studies in the United States relatively few European studies compared the differential efficacy of methadone dosages. In a study by Del Rio, Mino, and Perneger (1997), the patient retention rate in methadone maintenance was 84% after twelve months. Dropouts were less frequent in the highest and lowest doses and more likely among patients who enrolled in the first and second years of the programme. Dropping out was highly associated with using opioids for 7 years and with unstable income at baseline. Another study investigated the patterns of craving and pharmacokinetics in long-term opiate addicts in methadone maintenance therapy in the Netherlands: a significant relation was found between higher methadone dose and higher craving levels, a finding that counters much of the accepted knowledge on methadone maintenance treatment. The authors identified three specific craving patterns that related to daily fluctuations: high peak of the craving score just before the patients receive methadone around 9 a.m., around noon, and between 2 p.m. and 10 p.m. The results suggest that factors of pharmacokinetics like anticipatory conditional responses and/or circadian influences might also affect craving. These findings should be considered for relapse prevention (De Vos et al., 1996).

Results of a multicentre study on different treatment aspects and their impact on premature discharge in drug addicts (Küfner et al., 1994) indicate that experience-oriented approaches like long cottage stays, sailing, or similar activities are positively correlated to retention rates. The SWEDATE study and the study by Garcia, Cuesta, and Cuadrado (1995) prove also the relevance of educative treatment approaches. In trained subjects, relapse rates were lower and abstinence rates were higher.

The role of treatment duration for treatment outcome in drug addicts is a common finding in the European and some American literature (e.g., McLellan et al., 1994; Herbst, 1992; for an overview for Germany see Küfner, 1998) but not in some other American publications (e.g., Hester & Miller, 1995). Herbst (1992) showed that, four years after a regularly terminated treatment of at least eight months, drug-free inpatient treatment programmes for opiate or cocaine addicts are more successful than often assumed. After four years, one-third of the clients were still free from opiates, cocaine, or substitutes. The probability of success was significantly lower for clients with shorter treatment periods and for dropouts.

A study conducted in the Netherlands showed successful behaviour changes of drug-using inmates who attended a drug-free detention programme (Breteler et al., 1996). Two groups of detainees in separate prisons were examined at the beginning of detention, at release or transfer, and at two years after the end of detention. The authors investigated post-programme contact of subjects with treatment agencies, their changes in criminal recidivism, and their substance abuse, by use of regression analysis. Their results indicate that detainees who started drug use early, had not previously been in a drug-free detention programme, frequently expressed self-esteem, and had many family problems attended meetings with drug treatment agencies more often. The results also show that a legal source of income was associated with decreases in addiction severity and in the number of dates on which hard drugs were used. From these overall results one can conclude that a drug-free detention program assists inmates in stopping drug use, and normal social integration and functioning are necessary to ensure a successful treatment outcome.

Klijnsma et al. (1995) found that outpatient detoxification is cost-effective for the treatment of alcohol-dependent patients, because it is six times cheaper than inpatient detoxification. Aside from one-third of subjects with good outcome, 32% showed improvement. Almost 40% of patients were not improved, however. Thus engagement following detoxification with voluntary agencies was associated with a better outcome.

OTHER ASPECTS

In various studies familial aggregation of alcohol disorders (Klein, 1983), low social integration (John, 1984; Pfeiffer et al., 1988), and age lower than forty (Veltrup, 1995) could be demonstrated as risk factors for relapse.

The predictive multicentre study of the French Society of Alcohology (Favre & Gillet, 1997) pointed out that the following factors are associated with favorable course after treatment: advanced age, marriage, children, a stable family life, the absence of any painful event before the hospitalisation, admission in a department specialised in alcohol, a longer stay in hospital, more frequent use of institutional and directive groups, and family contact with the nursing team.

In a one-year follow-up after treatment, Sheehan et al. (1993) found a reduction in opiate use, as well as in injecting and sharing equipment. Sustained abstinence from opiates was associated with increased employment, enhanced social stability, and better mental health. Injectors of multiple drugs at intake were less likely to be long-term abstainers. In another follow-up study of 334 patients it was found that those who were abstainers had been mentally healthier and committed fewer crimes before treatment (Marina et al., 1996). There were no significant differences in excessive alcohol abuse, however, or between the number of HIV cases of heroin users and nonusers.

RELAPSE PREVENTION

The following is not limited to studies based on the narrow concept of behavioural-oriented, specific relapse prevention programmes. In a wider context, studies are included that compare two or more different treatment interventions to detect effective relapse prevention components that decrease relapse rates. Programmes that compare treatment effects with an untreated control group are therefore not included here. As relapse prevention components differ widely between alcohol and drug dependents, those substances are discussed separately. In general, intervention studies of effective relapse prevention programmes, compared to standard outcome rates, are rather rare in Europe.

ALCOHOL

Major approaches for relapse prevention are the combination of pharmacological agents with traditional psychosocial programmes and cue exposure as an adjunct to the usual psychosocial programmes.

Relapse prevention by combined pharmacological and psychosocial treatment

Table 4.1 shows particular results of some major European multisite, double-blind, randomized controlled studies (Paille et al., 1995; Poldrugo, 1997; Saß et al., 1996; Whitworth et al., 1996; Geerlings et al., 1997; see also Holter et al., 1997; Roussaux et al., 1996; Saß, Mann & Soyka, 1996; Ladewig et al., 1993; Nalpass et al., 1990; Lhuintre et al., 1990; for an overview see Soyka, 1996, 1997b; Wilde & Wagstaff, 1997). Outcome figures differ widely among the studies, indicating average relapse rates from 55 to 75% (6 months' follow-up after treatment), 55 to 85% (1 year), and 80 to 90% (2 years). However, the success of the combined pharmacological and psychosocial treatment can not be sufficiently assessed.

Also, the efficacy of different dosages of acamprosate was the scope of two studies (Paille et al., 1995; Pelc et al., 1994). Paille and his colleagues (1995) investigated in a prospective placebo-controlled, randomized double-blind study the effect of acamprosate at two dose levels in alcohol-dependent patients, followed up for twelve months. After detoxification, each of the 538 patients included was randomly assigned to one of three groups: 177 patients received the placebo, 188 received 1.3 g/day of acamprosate (low-dose group), and 173 received 2.0 g/day (high-dose group) for twelve months. That was followed by a single-blind six-month period on placebo. Abstinence rates were the highest for the high-dose group, middle for the low-dose group, and lowest for the placebo group. The difference was significant at a six-month follow-up, but not at twelve months. The mean number of days of continued abstinence after detoxification was 153 and 197 for the high-dose group (6 and 12 months) and 102 and 165 for the placebo group, with the low-dose group reporting 135 and 189 days. Clinic attendance was significantly better in the acamprosate groups than in the placebo group at six months and twelve months. During the six-month posttreatment period, no increased relapse rate or residual drug effect was observed. The side effect profile for acamprosate was good compared with controls, with only diarrhea being reported more frequently. This study confirms the pharmacological efficacy of acamprosate and its acceptability.

Despite the fact that many studies proved the reduction effect of acamprosate in both animal models (Boismare et al, 1984; Gewiß et al., 1991; Spanagel et al., 1996a, b, c; see also Littleton, 1995; Soyka, 1997a and b) and clinical conditions, there are opposing views on these studies. In a review by Moncrieff & Drummond (1997), the authors critically state that the evidence from randomized controlled trials for the efficacy of some of the main candidates like acamprosate, naltrexone, bromocriptine, selective serotonin reuptake inhibitors, and buspirone are based on studies that have significant methodological problems. The authors cite such examples as failure to test the integrity of the double blind, the exclusion or estimation of outcome in early withdrawals, and the comparison of groups on multiple outcome measures with selective reporting of results. In addition, the generalizability of some studies was limited by the procedures used for sample selection. In view of the potential adverse effects of pharmacological treatment, the evidence is not strong enough to support the introduction of any of these substances into routine clinical practice at present. The results of all appropriate medical treatment trials must also be interpreted in light of side effects, and there must be assurance that the overall improvement in functioning observed with the drug is significant and outweighs other liability. In addition, medications are almost always used in combination with education, counselling, and behavioral therapies, so the impact of these additional treatments must also be considered.

Relapse prevention by psychosocial treatment

Approaches directed at improving social and marital relationships, self-control, and stress management have been proven to reduce relapse rates. A paper by Hodgson (1994) gives an overview of the variety of approaches that have been used in the treatment of alcohol problems.

A controlled trial of cue exposure was conducted with dependent drinkers engaged in an insight-orientated therapy programme (McCusker & Brown, 1995). The authors investigated responses to an alcohol-associated stimulus compared with a neutral stimulus at the beginning and at the end of treatment. Compared with a control group, which did not receive intervening cue-exposure sessions, subjects who received such interventions manifested reductions in heart rate, salivation, and arousal responses to the alcohol-associated, compared with the neutral stimulus. They did not, however, show corresponding reductions in subjective estimates of craving and anxiety.

The clinical effectiveness of cue-exposure (CE) treatment in alcohol dependence was also evaluated in a controlled trial by Drummond and Glautier (1994). Thirty-five men who were detoxified and severely alcohol dependent received either CE or relaxation control (RC) treatment. CE subjects had 400 minutes' exposure to the sight and smell of preferred drinks over ten days in a laboratory setting. RC subjects spent identical amounts of time in the laboratory but had relaxation therapy and only 20 minutes' exposure to alcohol cues. During six-months' follow-up, personal interview was achieved with 91% of subjects. CE subjects had a more favourable outcome than the RC subjects in terms of latency (length of time to relapse of heavy drinking) (p < .01) and total alcohol consumption (p < .05). Significant predictors of latency to heavy drinking and dependence included skin conductance level and experimental condition. Results point to the potential importance of cue exposure as a treatment for addictive behavior.

The effects of brief group psychotherapy in relapse prevention were tested by Sandahl & Ronnberg (1990). The group focused on the patients' capacity to formulate their own treatment goals including controlled drinking, programmed relapse, and total abstinence. Twelve months after completion of the eight-week outpatient group treatment, 35 patients were followed up. The follow-up results were significantly better than before treatment and also than for a comparison group of alcohol-dependent patients. The positive treatment effects were found to be associated with the course leader's encouragement of personal decision making, increased awareness of risk situations, and improved coping skills. That brief interventions can be very effective in the treatment of alcohol disorders was also derived by John et al. (1996). According to Drummond (1997), however, the importance of brief interventions is often exaggerated in the context of alcohol treatment because of lack of generalizability of the research in this area.

ILLEGAL DRUGS

Pharmacological interventions

In contrast to the treatment of alcohol dependents, pharmacological interventions with opioid addicts usually are not implemented to stabilize abstinence but as an alternative approach to abstinence-oriented treatment, e.g. with methadone, LAAM, or buprenorphine. An exception is naltrexone, which sometimes is studied as an adjunct to an abstinence-oriented programme. Again there is no "pure" pharmacological treatment, but it is always in combination with psychosocial interventions.

Relapse prevention by combined pharmacological and psychosocial treatment

In two Spanish follow-up studies the outcomes of outpatient naltrexone programmes are reported. In the first study from Moreno & Rosado (1996), 47 heroine addicts with a mean age of 25 years (range 18–37) were followed-up at twelve months after treatment. The authors got information from 93.6% of the initial sample and demonstrated a significant decrease in opiate use by the subject after three months in a naltrexone programme. In another Spanish follow-up study of opiate addicts in a naltrexone programme (Landabaso et al., 1996) the opiate addicts were followed-up at six months after treatment. The results show that nearly 75% of the patients stayed in a treatment programme at the end of the study. Patients undergoing pharmacological treatment for more than six months remain abstinent longer with very few relapses. The use of naltrexone in long-term programmes did not increase the side effects.

A further Spanish study (Gomez et al., 1995) dealt with the treatment of 17 heroin addicts, to whom a combination of naltrexone-guanfacine was given over five days. Fifteen out of the 17 patients (88.2%) ended successfully their treatment and continued in a rehabilitation programme with naltrexone. They remained in treatment one month after they had completed the detoxification phase. The results confirm the clinical use of naltrexone-guanfacine and rapid detoxification, allowing a rapid detoxification with good tolerance by the patients.

Relapse prevention by psychological treatment

A controlled trial (Dawe et al., 1993) studied whether cue exposure can reduce relapse in opiate addiction. One hundred eighty-six subjects were randomly allocated to one of two in-patient treatment settings: a special ten-week drug dependence programme and four weeks in a behavioral-general treatment unit without such a programme. In each setting, following drug withdrawal, subjects had either cue exposure for at least six sessions over three weeks or a control condition. Six weeks later and six months posttreatment, patients were followed-up. The results indicate that cue exposure and control subjects did not differ in cue reactivity. Also, all groups showed a significant decrement in cue-elicited craving, withdrawal responsive, and negative mood.

DISCUSSION

There are many similarities between the United States and the European countries, but there are also many differences. In particular, there are differences between some of the priorities and concerns of Europe and the United States. The heat of the arguments surrounding treatment goals other than abstinence has been much less evident in Europe. As a consequence, it has been very easy to work with many of the concepts of the relapse model, in particular the notion that addicted individuals might subsequently use drugs or drink. That this should be used as a central part of the clinical process in helping patients to cope with the processes involved in avoiding the drift from a lapse to a relapse has not been so politically charged nor so diversified within the treatment community. In this respect, the distinction between a lapse and a relapse has been widely incorporated into many of the treatment programmes provided in Europe. Nor has this distinction been regarded as a radical departure from standard practice. In several European countries, harm reduction practices have been widely introduced and implemented in ways that have proved to be much more problematic in the United States. An obvious example is that way in which needle and syringe exchange schemes were introduced in Britain (Stimson, 1995).

The notion of high-risk situations has also had a broad but extremely important impact on European clinical practice. Many treatment programmes have used this as one of the key targets within their assessment procedures and subsequently as an important part of the clinical work that is done with clients to increase recovery chances. Because many of the high-risk situations that have been identified have been social and environmental, the incorporation of the concept into European clinical practice has also tended to focus the attention of both therapists and patients more acutely on the ways in which treatment outcomes can be affected by these "real-life" social factors. This has contributed to many clinical treatment practices becoming less reliant upon intrapsychic styles of thinking and more reliant upon social models. However, the very importance of the concept of high-risk situations in Europe has also led to some dissatisfaction with the imprecision that is inherent in some applications of the term (Sutton, 1993).

One of the few specifically intrapsychic factors that has been influential in European thinking has been the notion of "craving." A good deal of interest has been shown in the formulation and understanding of what is meant by craving (Heather & Stallard, 1989) and in ways in which treatment programmes can be organised to reduce relapses associated with craving (De Vos et al., 1996; Di Bello et al., 1995; Veltrup, 1994). In Europe, as in the United States, the interest in craving and in psychological concepts and theories of dependence has drawn from and has also stimulated an interest in biological research into neural networks and neurochemistry. Considerable interest has been shown in the neurobiology of craving.

It is always difficult to provide any single summary regarding developments within Europe. Europe is an extremely diverse collection of countries with different histories, cultures, and languages. The linguistic diversity should not be underestimated. The language of science is English. In some of the European countries, the research and clinical communities in the addictions are familiar with and at ease with the English language. In other countries, English is unfamiliar and infrequently used. It is as a direct consequence of this that the impact of work that is published in English-language journals is felt more in some countries than others. Conversely, the work that is done in some European countries is written and published almost entirely in languages other than English and is, therefore, inaccessible to most North American readers.

Despite this not inconsiderable problem of communication, and bearing in mind that the vast majority of the work published on relapse has been from North America or written in English, it is interesting to note how much impact the work on relapse has had upon Europe. For many European countries, the primary significance of the work surrounding the issue of relapse has not been due to the impact of any specific model (or models) nor due to any specific intervention. Instead, the influence has been broader, but certainly not less important for that reason. The concepts of the relapse models and the types of treatment approaches used in relapse work have both fitted into current styles of thinking in many European countries and have had an important influence in their effect on developments in those countries.

References

Arend, H. (1994). *Alkoholismus—Ambulante Therapie und Rückfallprophylaxe.* Beltz Psychologische Verlags Union: Weinheim.

Batel, P. (1995). The treatment of alcoholism in France. *Drug and Alcohol Dependence* 39 (supplement 1): 15–21.

Baving, L., & Olbrich, H. (1996). *Alcoholism and Depression.* European Addiction Research 2(1): 29–35.

Bearn, J., Gossop, M., & Strang, J. (1996). Randomised double-blind comparison of lofexidine and methadone in the in-patient treatment of opiate withdrawal. *Drug and Alcohol Dependence* 43(1–2): 87–91.

Berg, J. E., Andersen, S., & Alveberg, P. Ø. (1997). Former addicts as members of staff, and type of activity offered to drug misusers: Do these factors influence rate of completion? *Addiction Research* 5(1): 39–48.

Berglund, G. W., Bergmark, A., Björling, B., Grönbladh, L., Lindberg, S., Oscarsson, L., Olsson, B., Segraeus, V., & Stensmo, C. (1991). The SWEDATE project: Interaction between treatment, client background, and outcome in a one-year follow-up. *Journal of Substance Abuse Treatment* 8, 161–169.

Besançon, F. (1993). Time to alcohol dependence after abstinence and first drink. *Addiction* 88(12): 1647–1650.

Besson, J. (1997). [New drugs in the treatment of alcoholism.] [Article in French.] *Schweizer Medizinische Wochenschrift* 127: 1574–1578.

Birke, S. A., Edelmann, R. J., & Davis, P. E. (1990). An analysis of the abstinence violation effect in a sample of illicit drug users. *British Journal of Addiction* 85: 1299–1307.

Bish, A., Golombok, S., Hallstrom, C., & Fawcett, S. (1996). The role of coping strategies in protecting individuals against long-term tranquilizer use. *British Journal of Medical Psychology* 69: 101–15.

Boismare, F., Daoust, M., Moore, N., et al. (1984). A homotaurine derivate reduces the voluntary intake by rats: Are cerebral GABA receptors involved? *Pharmacology, Biochemistry and Behavior,* 21: 787–89.

Borg, S. (1996). Treatment of alcohol dependence: Experiences of using biological markers in monitoring and prevention of relapse. *Alcohol & Alcoholism* 31(6): 621–24.

Breteler, M. H. M., van den Hurk, A. A., Schippers, G. M., & Meerkerk, G.-J. (1996). Enrollment in a drug-free detention programme: The prediction of successful behavior change of drug-using inmates. *Addictive Behaviors* 21: 665–69.

Brewer, C. (1993). Recent developments in disulfiram treatment. *Alcohol & Alcoholism* 4, 383–95.

Brewer, C. (1997). Ultra-rapid, antagonist-precipitated opiate detoxification under general anaesthesia or sedation. *Addiction Biology* 2: 291–302.

Brownell, K. D., Marlatt, G. A., Lichtenstein, E., & Wilson, G. T. (1986). Understanding and preventing relapse. *American Psychologist* 41, 765–82.

Brünger, M., Löschmann, C., & Koch, U. (1997). In-patient-treatment of alcohol addicts between 1983 and 1993. *Sucht* 43(1): 37–55.

Callejo, P. C., Gonzalez, R. G., Guitian, M. D. P., & Martinez, M. J. N. (1995). Treatment for alcoholics in a community programme: Outcome after six months, one year and two years. *Adicciones* 7(2): 169–77.

Christo, G., & Franey, C. (1996). Addicts' drug-related dreams: Their frequency and relationship to six-month outcomes. *Substance Use & Misuse* 31: 1–15.

Connors, G. J., Carroll, K. M., Di Clemente, C. C., Longabaugh, R., & Donovan, D. M. (1997). The therapeutic alliance and its relationship to alcoholism treatment participation and outcome. *Journal of Consulting and Clinical Psychology* 65(4): 588–98.

Cornell, M., Knibbe, R. A., Knottnerus, J. A., Volovics, A., & Drop, M. J. (1996). Predictors for hidden problem drinkers in general practice. *Alcohol Alcohol* 30: 287–96.

Dawe, S., Powell, J., Richards, D., Gossop, M., Marks, I., Strang, J., & Gray, J. A. (1993). Does post-withdrawal cue exposure improve outcome in opiate addiction? A controlled trial. *Addiction* 88: 1233–45.

Del Rio, M., Mino, A., & Perneger, T. V. (1997). Predictors of patient retention in a newly established methadone maintenance treatment programme. *Addiction* 92(10): 1353–60.

Deutsche Gesellschaft für Suchtforschung und Suchttherapie e.V. (Hrsg.) (1992). *Dokumentationsstandards 2 für die Behandlung von Abhängigen*. Freiburg: Lambertus.

Deutsche Gesellschaft für Suchtforschung und Suchttherapie e.V. (Hrsg.) (1992). *Documentation Standards 2 for the Treatment of Substance Abuse*. Freiburg: Lambertus.

De Vos, J. W., van Wilgenburg, H., van den Brink, W., Kaplan, C. D., & De Vries, M. W. (1996). Patterns of craving and pharmacokinetics in long-term opiate addicts in methadone maintenance therapy. *Addiction Research* 3:285–95.

Di Bello, M. G., Gambassi, F., Mugnal, L., Masini, E., & Mannaioni, P. F. (1995). Gamma-hydroxybutyric acid induced suppression and prevention of alcohol withdrawal syndrome and relief of craving in alcohol dependent patients. *Alcologia* 7(2): 111–18.

Donovan, D. M., & Marlatt, G. A. (1993). Recent developments in alcoholism: Behavioral treatment. *Recent developments in Alcoholism* 11: 397–411.

Doyle, H., Delaney, W., & Tobin, J. (1994). Follow-up study of young attenders at an alcohol unit. *Addiction* 89(2): 183–89.

Drummond, D. C. (1997). Alcohol interventions: Do the best things come in small packages? *Addiction* 92(4): 375–79.

Drummond, D. C., & Glautier, S. (1994). A controlled trial of exposure treatment in alcohol dependence. *Journal of Consulting and Clinical Psychology* 62: 809–17.

Favre, J.-D., & Gillet, C. (1997). Follow-up of patients with alcohol dependence: results after five years and predictive factors. *Alcoologie* 19(3): 313–30.

Feuerlein, W., & Küfner, H. (1992). Results of inpatient treatment of alcoholics: Follow-ups after 18 and 48 months [Munich Evaluation of Alcoholism Treatment, MEAT]. In H. M. Emrich & M. Wiegand (eds.), *Integrative biological psychiatry*. Berlin, Heidelberg: Springer.

Feuerlein, W., Küfner, H., & Soyka, M. (1998). *Alkoholismus- Mißbrauch und Abhängigkeit. Entstehung—Folgen—Therapie.* Stuttgart: Thieme.

Fichter, M. M., & Frick, U. (1992). *Therapie und Verlauf von Alkoholabhängigkeit.* Berlin: Springer.

Fleischmann, H., & Klein, H. E. (eds.) (1995). *Behandlungsmotivation, Motivationsbehandlung. Suchtkranke im psychiatrischen Krankenhaus.* Freiburg: Lambertus.

Garcia, R., Cuesta, P., & Cuadrado, P. (1995). Assessment of two intervention modalities on alcoholics: A three-year follow-up. *Adicciones* 7(2): 131–48.

Geerlings, P. J., Ansoms, C., & Van den Brink, W. (1997). Acamprosate and prevention of relapse in alcoholics. *European Addiction Research* 3(3): 129–37.

Gewiss, M., Heidbreder, C. H., Opsomer, L., et al. (1991). Acamprosate and diazepam differentially modulate alcohol-induced behavioral and cortical alterations in rats following chronic inhalation of ethanol vapour. *Alcohol Alcohol* 26: 129–37.

Gomez, G., Cabañas, L., & Onate, P. (1995). Rapid detoxification with out-patients in Carabanchel Prison. *Adicciones* 7: 441–51.

Gossop, M. (1987). *Living with Drugs,* Aldershot: Winwood House/Gower.

Gossop, M. (1989). *Relapse and addictive behavior.* London: Tavistock/Routledge.

Gossop, M. (1998). The national treatment outcome study. Changes in substance use, health and criminal behaviours one year after intake. 3rd Bulletin of Department of Health, National Addiction Centre, London.

Gossop, M., Green L., Phillips, G., & Bradley, B. (1990). Factors predicting outcome among opiate addicts after treatment. *British Journal of Clinical Psychology* 29 (2): 209–16.

Gossop, M., & Strang, J. (1997). Rapid anaesthetic-antagonist detoxofication of heroin addicts: what origins, evidence base and clinical justification? *British Journal of Intensive Care* 7(2): 66–69.

Grabowski, J. (1986). Acquisition, maintenance, cessation, and reacquisition: An overview and behavioral perspective on relapse to tobacco use. In Tims, F. M., & Leukefeld, C. G., *Relapse and recovery in drug abuse,* NIDA Research Monograph no. 72, Washington, D.C.: US Govt. Printing Office, pp. 36–48.

Haderstorfer, B., & Künzel-Böhmer, J. (1992). The Munich multicenter treatment evaluation study: Results of the first follow-up. In G. Bühringer & J. J. Platt (eds.),

Drug addiction treatment research: German and American perspectives. Malabar, Fla.: Krieger, pp. 353–66.

Hanel, E. (1992). Client characteristics and the therapeutic process in residential treatment centers for drug addicts. In G. Bühringer & J. J. Platt (Hrsg.), *Drug addiction treatment research: German and American perspectives.* Malabar, Fla.: Krieger, pp. 187–96.

Heather, N., and Stallard, A. (1989). Does the Marlatt model underestimate the importance of conditioned craving in the relapse process? In M. Gossop (ed.), *Relapse and Addictive Behaviour,* London: Tavistock/Routledge.

Herbst, K. (1992). Verlaufsanalyse bei Drogenabhängigen nach stationärer Behandlung. *Sucht* 38, 147–54.

Hester, R. K., & Miller, W. R. (eds.). (1995). *Handbook of alcoholism treatment approaches: effective alternatives.* 2d ed. Boston: Allyn and Bacon.

Hiltunen, A. J., Koechling, U. M., Voltaire-Carlsson, A., & Borg, S. (1996). Subpopulations of alcohol-dependent patients: Differences in psychological functioning between high- and low-frequency alcohol consumers. *Alcohol & Alcoholism* 31: 429–38.

Hodgson, R. (1994). Treatment of alcohol problems. *Addiction* 89: 1529–34.

Holter, S. M., Landgraf, R., Zieglgänsberger, W., & Spanagel, R. (1997). Time course of acamprosate action operatn ethanol self-administration after ethanol deprivation. *Alcoholism, Clinical and Experimental Research* 21: 862–68.

Hubbard, R. L., Rachal, J. V., Craddock, S. G., & Cavanaugh, E. R. (1984). Treatment outcome prospective study (TOPS): Client characteristics and behaviors before, during and after treatment. In F. M. Times & J. P. Ludford (eds.), *Drug abuse treatment evaluation: strategies, progress, and prospects,* (NIDA Research Monograph 51) Tockville, Md.: NIDA, pp. 42–68.

Hughes, J. C., & Cook, C. C. H. (1997). The efficacy of disulfiram: A review of outcome studies. *Addiction* 92(4): 381–95.

Hyams, G., Cartwright, A., & Spratley, T. (1996). Engagement in alcohol treatment: the client's experience of, and satisfaction with, the assessment interview. *Addiction Research* 4: 105–23.

John, U. (1984). Erfolgskriterien bei Alkoholabhängigen nach einer Therapie: Aspekte sozialer Integration und Abstinenz. *Suchtgefahren* 30: 168–77.

John, U., Hapke, U., Rumpf, H.-J., Hill, A., & Dilling, H. (1996). *Prävalenz und Sekundärprävention von Alkoholmißbrauch und -abhängigkeit in der medizinischen Versorgung.* Baden-Baden: Nomos.

John, U., Veltrup, C., & Driessen, M. (1995). Motivationsarbeit mit Alkoholabhängigen. *Psychiat. Praxis* 24: 184–88.

Jones, B. T., & McMahon, J. (1994). Negative and positive alcohol expectancies as predictors of abstinence after discharge from a residential treatment programme: a one-month and three-month follow-up study in men. *Journal of Studies on Alcohol* 55: 543–48.

Jones, B. T., & McMahon, J. (1996a). A comparison of positive and negative alcohol expectancy and value and their multiplicative composite as predictors of post-treatment abstinence survivorship. *Addiction* 91: 89–99.

Jones, B. T., & McMahon, J. (1996b). Changes in alcohol expectancies during treatment relate to subsequent abstinence survivorship. *British Journal of Clinical Psychology* 35 (2): 221–34.

Kahn, A., Mumford, J. P., Rogers, G. A., & Beckford, H. (1997). Double-blind study of lofexidine and clonidine in the detoxification of opiate addicts in hospital. *Drug and Alcohol Dependence* 44(1): 57–61.

Kaufmann, B., Dobler-Mikola, A., & Zimmer-Hofler, D. (1993). The significance of self-concept and coping for long-term rehabilitation of heroin addicts. *Sucht* 39: 244–54.

Keaney, F., Wanigaratne, S., & Pullin, J. (1995). The use of a structured assessment interview as an intervention to reduce dropout rates in outpatient relapse prevention groups for "problem" drinkers. *International Journal of the Addictions* 30(10): 1355–62.

Klein, M. (1983). Katamnestische Untersuchungen in einer Fachklinik für Alkoholabhängige. *Suchtgefahren* 29: 181–86.

Klijnsma, M. P., Cameron, M. L., Burns, T. P., & McGuigan, S. M. (1995). Out-patient alcohol detoxification — outcome after 2 months. *Alcohol & Alcoholism* 30(5): 669–73.

Körkel, Joachim (Hrsg.) (1988). *Der Rückfall des Suchkranken.* Berlin: Springer.

Körkel, J., Lauer, G., & Scheller, R. (1995). *Sucht und Rückfall. Brennpunkte deutscher Rückfallforschung.* Stuttgart: Enke.

Küfner, H. (1998). Ergebnisse der Suchtbehandlung. *Sucht Aktuell* 1 and 2, 29–34.

Küfner, H., Denis, A., Roch, I., Arzt, J., & Rug, U. (1994). *Stationäre Krisenintervention bei Drogenabhängigen. Ergebnisse der wissenschaftlichen Begleitung des Modellprogramms. Schriftenreihe des Bundesministeriums für Gesundheit Band 37.* Baden-Baden: Nomos.

Küfner, H., & Feuerlein, W. (1989). *In-patient treatment for alcoholism.* Berlin: Springer.

Küfner, H., Feuerlein, W., & Huber, M. (1988). Die stationäre Behandlung von Alkoholabhängigen: Ergebnisse der 4-Jahres-Katamnesen, mögliche Konsequenzen für Indikationsstellung und Behandlung. *Suchtgefahren* 34, 157–272.

Küfner, H., Feuerlein, W., & Huber, M. (1988). Ergebnisse zur Abstinenz in der MEAT-Studie. *Suchtgefahren* 34: 157.

Küfner, H., Vogt, M., & Weiler, D. (1999). *Modellprojekt für die Substitution mit Metha-*

don zur Vorbereitung und Einleitung einer medizinischen Rehabilitation von Drogenabhängigen. Baltmannsweiler: Schneider.

Ladewig, D., Kmecht, T. H., Leher, P. H., et al. (1993). Acamprosat—Ein Stabilisierungsfaktor in der Langzeitentwöhnung von Alkoholabhängigen. *Ther Umshau* 1993: 50: 180–188.

Landabaso, M. A., de Corres, B. F., Sanz, J., de Apodaca, J. R., Perez, B., & Gutierrez, M. (1996). A follow-up study of opiate addicts in an antagonist treatment. *Adicciones* 8: 67–74.

Lhuintre, J. P., Daoust M., Moore, N., et al. (1985). Ability of calcium bisacetyl homotaurine: A GABA agonist to prevent relapse in weaned alcoholics. *Lancet* 1: 1014–16.

Lhuintre, J. P., Moore, N., Tran, G., et al. (1990). Acamprosate appears to decrease alcohol intake in weaned alcoholics. *Alcohol Alcohol* 25: 613–22.

Litman, G. K., Eiser, J. R., Rawson, N. S. B., and Oppenheim, A. N. (1977). Towards a typology of relapse: a preliminary report. *Drug and Alcohol Dependence* 2, 157–62.

Litman, G. K., Eiser, J. R., Rawson, N. S. B., and Oppenheim, A. N. (1979). Differences in relapse presipitants and coping behaviours between alcohol relapsers and survivors. *Behaviour Research and Therapy* 17, 89–94.

Litman, G. K., Stapleton, J., Oppenheim, A. N., and Peleg, M., (1983). An instrument for measuring coping behaviours in hospitalised alcoholics: implications for relapse prevention treatment. *British Journal of Addiction* 78, 269–76.

Littleton, J. (1995). Acamprosate—how does it work? Addiction 90: 1179–88.

Maffli, E. (ed.). (1996). *Alkoholismusbehandlung in der Schweiz. Neue Forschungsergebnisse—neue Orientierungen für die Praxis.* Lausanne: ISPA.

Marina, P. A., Vazquez-Barquero, J. L., Jimenez, J. M., & Erkoreka, I. (1996). The benefits of achieving abstinence: a follow-up study of Spanish heroin addicts. (In Spanish.) *Adicciones* 8(3): 295–309.

Marlatt, G. A. (1982). Relapse prevention: A self-control program for the treatment of addictive behaviors. In R. B.Stuart (ed.), *Adherence, Compliance and Generalisation in Behavioral Medicine.* New York: Brunner/Mazel.

Marlatt, G. A. (1995). *Harm reduction approach to alcohol abuse in young adults.* Paper presented at the World Congress of Behavioural and Cognitive Therapies, Copenhagen, Denmark.

Marlatt, G. A., and George, W. (1984) Relapse prevention: Introduction and overview of the model. *British Journal of Addiction* 79: 261–73.

Marlatt, G. A., and Gordon, J. R. (1980). Determinants of relapse: Implications for the maintenance of behavior change. In P. Davidson and S. Davidson (eds.), *Behavioral Medicine.* New York, Brunner/Mazel, pp. 410–57.

Marlatt, G. A., & Gordon, J. R. (1985). *Relapse prevention: Maintenance strategies in the treatment of addictive behaviors.* New York: Guilford.

McCusker, C. G., & Brown, K. (1995). Cue-exposure to alcohol-associated stimuli reduces autonomic reactivity but not craving and anxiety, in dependent drinkers. *Alcohol & Alcoholism* 30: 319–27.

McLellan, A. T., Alterman, A. I., Metzger, D. S., Grissom, G. R., Woody, G. E., Luborsky, L., & O'Brien, C. P. (1994). Similarity of outcome predictors across opiate, cocaine, and alcohol treatments: Role of treatment services. *Journal of Consulting and Clinical Psychology* 6: 1141–58.

McMahon, J., & Jones, B. T. (1996). Post-treatment abstinence survivorship and motivation for recovery: the precictive validity of the Readiness to Change (RCQ) and Negative Alcohol Expectancy (NAEQ) Questionnaires. *Addiction Research* 4: 161–76.

Merrill, J., & Marshall, R. (1997). Opioid detoxification using naloxone. *Drug and Alcohol Review* 16(1): 3–6.

Miller, W. R., & Hester, R. K. (1986). Matching problem drinkers with optimal treatments. In W. E. Miller & N. Heather (eds.), *Treating addictive behaviors: Processes of change* (pp. 175–203). New York: Plenum.

Ministerium für Arbeit, Gesundheit und Soziales des Landes Nordrhein-Westfalen (Hg.) (1997). *Medikamentengestützte Rehabilitation i.v.-Opiatabhängiger.* Katamnese.

Moncrieff, J., & Drummond, D. C. (1997). New drug treatments for alcohol problems: a critical appraisal. *Addiction* 92: 939–47.

Moreno, R. M., & Rosado, T. G. (1996). Follow-up of a 12-month naltrexone maintenance programme. *Adicciones* 8: 5–18.

Nalpass, B., Dabadie, H., Parot, P., & Paccalin, J. (1990). L'amprosate. De la pharmacologie a la clinique, *Encephale* 16: 175–79.

O'Malley, S. S., Jaffe, A. J., Chang Schottenfeld, R. S., Meyer, R. E., & Rounsaville, B. J. (1992). Naltrexone and coping skills therapy for alcohol dependence: a controlled study. *Archives of General Psychiatry* 49: 881–87.

Oppenheimer, E., Sheehan, M., & Taylor, C. (1990). What happens to drug misusers? A medium-term follow-up of addicts new to treatment. *British Journal of Addiction* 85: 1255–60.

Paille, F. M., Guelfi, J. D., Perkins, A. C., Royer, R. J., Steru, L., & Parot, P. (1995). Double-blind randomized multicentre trial of Acamprosate in maintaining abstinence from alcohol. *Alcohol & Alcoholism* 30: 239–47.

Patterson, D. G., Macpherson, J., & Brady, N. M. (1997). Community psychiatric nurse aftercare for alcoholics: A five-year follow-up study. *Addiction* 92(4): 459–68.

Peele, S. (1985). *The Meaning of Addiction.* Lexington, Mass.: Lexington Books.

Pelc, I. (1997). [Alcoholism: relapse prevention.] [Article in French] *Revue Medicale de Bruxelles* 18: 272–276.

Pelc, I., LeBon, O., & Verbanck, P. (1994). Acamprosate in the treatment of alcohol dependence: A six month post-detoxification study. *Alcoholism, Clinical and Experimental Research* 18: 38A.

Pelc, I., Verbanck, P., LeBon, O., Gavrilovic, M., Lion, K., & Lehert, P. (1997). Efficacy and safety of acomprosate in the treatment of detoxified alcohol-dependent patients. *British Journal of Psychiatry* 17(7): 73–77.

Petry, J. (1993). *Behandlungsmotivation*. Beltz Psychologische Verlags Union, Weinheim.

Petry, J. (1996). Suchtentwicklung und Motivationsdynamik. *Psychotherapeut* 41: 225–35.

Pfeiffer, W. E., Fahrner, E. M., Feuerlein, W. (1988). Soziale Anpassung und Rückfallanalyse bei ambulant behandelten Alkoholabhängigen. *Suchtgefahren* 34: 357–68.

Platt, J. J., Bühringer, G., Widman, M., Künzel, J., & Lidz, V. (1996). Uniform standards for substance user treatment research: An example from Germany for the United States and other contries. *Substance Use and Misuse* 31(4), 479–92.

Poldrugo, F. (1997). Acamprosate treatment in long-term community-based alcohol rehabilitation programme. *Addiction* 92: 1537–46.

Polich, J. M., Armor, D. J., & Braiker, H. B. (1980). Patterns of alcoholism over four years. *Journal of Studies on Alcohol* 5: 397–416.

Powell, G., & Peveler, R. (1996). Nature and prevalence of personality disorders amongst patients receiving treatment for alcohol dependence. *Journal of Mental Health* 5: 305–14.

Powell, J., Dawe, S., Richards, D., Gossop, M., Marks, I., Strang, J., & Gray, J. (1993). Can opiate addicts tell us about their relapse risk? Subjective predictors of clinical prognosis. *Addictive Behaviors* 18: 473–90.

Raschke, P. (1994). *Substitutionstherapie. Ergebnisse langfristiger Behandlung von Opiatabhängigen*. Freiburg: Lambertus.

Ravndal, E., & Vaglum, P. (1995). The influence of personality disorders on treatment completion in a hierarchical therapeutic community for drug abusers: A prospective study. *European Addiction Research* 1(4): 178–86.

Riegas, V. (1997). Die Erhöhung der Behandlungsmotivation Alkoholabhängiger in der Anfangsphase einer Langzeitrehabilitationsmaßnahme. (Motivating alcoholics to undergo treatment in the initial stages of a long-term rehabilitation programme.) (In German.) *Sucht* 43(5): 349–66.

Rist, F. (1996). Therapiestudien mit Alkoholabhängigen. In Mann, K., & Buchkremer, G. (eds.). *Suchtgrundlagen, Diagnostik, Therapie*. Stuttgart: G. Fischer, Stuttgart, pp. 243–54.

Rosenbach, A., and Hunot, V. (1995). The introduction of a methadone programme to a drug-free treatment service: implications for harm reduction. *Addiction* 90(6): 815–21.

Roussaux, J. P., Hers, D., & Ferauge, M. (1996). [Does acamprosate deminish the appetite for alcohol in weaned alcoholics?] [Article in French.] *Journal de Pharmacie de Belgique* 51: 65–68.

Sandahl, C., & Ronnberg, S. (1990). Brief group psychotherapy in relapse prevention for alcohol dependent patients. *International Journal of Group Psychotherapy* 40: 453–76.

Saß, H., Mann, K., & Soyka, M. (1996). Medikamentöse Unterstützung der Rückfallprophylaxe bei alkoholkranken Patienten mit Acamprosat — Ergebnisse einer doppelblinden, randomisierten, placebokontrollierten Studie. *Sucht* 5: 316–22.

Saß, H., Soyka, M., Mann, K., & Zieglgänsberger, W. (1996). Relapse prevention by acamprosate. Results from a placebo-controlled study on alcohol dependence. *Archives of General Psychiatry* 53: 673–80.

Saunders, W., and Allsop, S. (1989). Relapse: A critique. In M. Gossop (ed.), *Relapse and Addictive Behaviour*, London: Tavistock/Routledge.

Schwoon, D. R. (1992). Motivation — ein kritischer Begriff in der Behandlung Suchtkranker. In G. Wienberg (ed.). *Die vergessene Mehrheit — Zur Realität der Versorgung alkohol- und medikamentenabhängiger Menschen*, Bonn: Psychiatrie, pp. 170–82.

Shaw, G. K., Waller, S., Latham, C. J., Dunn, G., & Thomson, A. D. (1997). Alcoholism: A long-term follow-up study of participants in an alcohol treatment programme. *Alcohol & Alcoholism* 32(4): 527–35.

Sheehan, M., Oppenheimer, E., & Taylor, C. (1993). Opiate users and the first years after treatment: Outcome analysis of the proportion of follow-up time spent in abstinence. *Addiction* 88(12): 1679–89.

Soyka, M. (1996). Clinical efficacy of acamprosate in the treatment of alcoholism. In M. Soyka (ed.). *Acamprosate in relapse prevention of alcoholism* (pp. 155–71). Berlin: Springer.

Soyka, M. (1997a). Wirksamkeit von Acamprosat in der Rückfallprophylaxe der Alkoholabhängigkeit. *Nervenheilkunde* 14: 83–86.

Soyka, M. (1997b). Relapse prevention in alcoholism: Recent advances and future possibilities. *Drug Therapy* 7(4): 313–27.

Spanagel, R., Holter, S. M., Allingham, K., Landgraf, R., & Zieglgänsberger, W. (1996a). Acamprosate and alcohol: I. Effects on alcohol intake following alcohol deprivation in the rat. *European Journal of Pharmacology* 305: 39–44.

Spanagel, R., Putzke, J., Stefferl, A., Schobitz, B., & Zieglgänsberger, W. (1996b). Acamprosate and alcohol: II. Effects on alcohol withdrawal in the rat. *European Journal of Pharmacology* 305: 45–50.

Spanagel, R., Zieglgänsberger, W., & Hundt, W. (1996c). Acamprosate and alcohol: III. Effects on alcohol discrimination in the rat. *European Journal of Pharmacology* 305: 51–56.

Stimson, G. (1995). AIDS and injecting drug use in the UK, 1987–1993: The policy response and the prevention of the epidemic. *Social Science and Medicine* 41(5), 699–716.

Strang, J., Finch, E., Hankinson, L., Farrell, M., Taylor, C., & Gossop, M. (1997). Methadone treatment for opiate addiction: Benefits in the first month. *Addiction Research* 5(1): 71–76.

Strang, J., Marks, I., Dawe, S., Powell, J., Gossop, M., Richards, D., & Gray, J. (1997). Type of hospital setting and treatment outcome with heroin addicts: Results from a randomised trial. *British Journal of Psychiatry* 171(10): 335–39.

Süß, H.-M. (1995): Zur Wirksamkeit der Therapie bei Alkoholabhängigen: Ergebnisse einer Meta-Analyse. *Psychologische Rundschau* 46: 248–66.

Sutton, S. (1993). Is wearing clothes a high risk situation for relapse? The base rate problem in relapse research. *Addiction* 88: 725–27.

Tata, P. R., Rollings, J., Collins, M., Pickering, A., & Jacobson, R. R. (1994). Lack of cognitive recovery following withdrawal from long-term benzodiazepine use. *Psychological Medicine* 24(1): 203–13.

Uitenbroek, D. G. (1996). Seasonal variation in alcohol use. *Journal of Studies on Alcohol* 57: 47–52.

Unnithan, S., Gossop, M., & Strang, J. (1992). Factors associated with relapse among opiate addicts in an out-patient detoxification programme. *British Journal of Psychiatry* 161: 654–67.

Vaillant, G. E. (1983). *The natural history of alcoholism.* Cambridge, Mass.: Harvard University Press.

Veltrup, C. (1994): Erfassung des "Craving" bei Alkoholabhängigen mit Hilfe eines neuen Fragebogens (Lübecker-Risiko-Rückfall-Fragebogen). *Wiener Klinische Wochenschrift* 106: 75–79.

Veltrup, C. (1995). *Abstinenzgefährdung und Abstinenzbeendigung bei Alkoholabhängigen nach einer umfassenden stationären Entzugsbehandlung.* Münster: Waxmann.

Veltrup, C., & Driessen, M. (1993). Erweiterte Entzugsbehandlung für alkoholabhängige Patienten in einer psychiatrischen Klinik. *Sucht* 39: 168–72.

Veltrup, C., Junghanns, K., Weber, J., Urbinat, C., Driessen, M., Wetterling, T., John, U., & Dilling, H. (1996). Stationäre Motivationstherapie (Entzug II) für alkoholabhängige Patienten. *Schleswig-Holsteinisches Ärzteblatt* 48: 364–67.

Veltrup, C., Schnofl, A., Weber, J., Driessen, M., & John, U. (1994). Verhaltenstherapeutische Überlegungen zur Motivationsarbeit bei Alkoholabhängigen (pp. 40–51). In W. Scheiblich (ed.), *Sucht aus der Sicht psychotherapeutischer Schulen.* Freiburg: Lambertus.

Volpicelli, J. R., Alterman, A. L., Hayashida, M., & O'Brien, C. P. (1992). Naltrexone in the treatment of alcohol dependence. *Archives of Neurology* 19: 603–17.

Wanigaratne, S. D., Wallace, W., Pullin, J., Keaney, F., & Farmer, R. (1990). *Relapse Prevention for Addictive Behaviours: A Manual for Therapists.* Oxford: Blackwell.

Watzl, H., & Cohen, R. (1989). *Rückfall und Rückfallprophylaxe.* Berlin: Springer.

Wetterling, T., & Veltrup, C. (1997). *Diagnostik und Therapie von Alkoholproblemen. Ein Leitfaden.* Berlin: Springer.

Whitworth, A. B., Fischer, F., Lesch, O. M., Nimmerrichter, A., Oberbauer, H., Platz, T., Potgieter, A., Walter, H., & Fleischhacker, W. W. (1996). Comparison of acamprosate and placebo in long-term treatment of alcohol dependence. *Lancet* 347: 1438–42.

Wilde, M. I., & Wagstaff, A. J. (1997). Acamprosate: A review of its pharmacology and clinical potential in the management of alcohol dependence after detoxification. *Drugs* 6: 1038–53.

Wilson, P., Watson, R., & Ralston, G. E. (1994). Methadone maintenance in general practice: Patients, workload, and outcomes. *British Medical Journal* 309(6955): 641–44.

Yates, F. (1996). Developing therapeutic computer programs with particular reference to a programme to teach coping strategies to problem drinkers. *Journal of Mental Health* 5(1): 57–63.

Zähres, S., Stetter, E., & Mann, K. (1993). Components of a combined detoxification and motivation treatment: Investigations into alcoholic patients' point of view. (In German.) *Sucht* 39(5): 332–42.

II

Research on Relapse and Recovery in the Addictions

FIVE

RELAPSE AFTER DRUG ABUSE TREATMENT

Robert L. Hubbard, Patrick M. Flynn, S. Gail Craddock,
& Bennett W. Fletcher

Previous research has consistently documented that treatment for drug abuse reduces use during and after treatment (Gerstein et al., 1994; Hubbard et al., 1989; Hubbard et al., 1997; Institute of Medicine, 1996; McLellan et al., 1997; National Opinion Research Center at the University of Chicago, 1997; Simpson, 1997; Simpson & Curry, 1997; Simpson & Sells, 1990). The major national multisite studies of treatment (e.g., DARP — Drug Abuse Reporting Program, TOPS — Treatment Outcome Prospective Study, DATOS — Drug Abuse Treatment Outcome Studies) all provide evidence of treatment effectiveness (Institute of Medicine, 1996). Notwithstanding the overall effectiveness of treatment, relapse can and does occur. In view of the threats of AIDS/HIV, the epidemic of cocaine use, and the reemergence of heroin use, it is important to improve treatment and the provision of continuing care in the community. Understanding the process and timing of relapse is critical to this effort. Recent research by Simpson and his colleagues (1999) has begun to examine these issues and has shown relapse to be related to problem severity levels at intake, type of treatment received, and most importantly length of stay in treatment. Cocaine-dependent treatment clients with low levels of problems at intake to treatment (i.e., 0–3 problems on the intake severity index)

This chapter is an extension and update of the chapter by Robert L. Hubbard and Mary Ellen Marsden "Relapse to Use of Heroin, Cocaine, and Other Drugs in the First Year After Treatment," in NIDA Research Monograph 72, *Relapse and Recovery in Drug Abuse*. Dr. Marsden also provided helpful comments on the initial drafts of this chapter.

had the lowest relapse rates regardless of treatment modality compared to the medium- and high-severity groups (Simpson et al., 1999). Longer lengths of stay produced better outcomes among medium- to high-problem severity groups. Among the high-problem severity group, long-term residential clients staying in treatment at least ninety days had the most favorable relapse rates (Simpson et al., 1999).

In this chapter, we focus on relapse to heroin and cocaine use by examining various definitions of relapse, time to relapse, and the changes in patterns of use. The change from pretreatment use to after-treatment use and the timing of relapse is presented. Comparisons of the nature of relapse in two treatment eras is examined using data from two national, multisite, longitudinal studies of drug abuse treatment effectiveness sponsored by the National Institute on Drug Abuse. The studies were conducted about ten years apart. The first era and data are represented by the Treatment Outcome Prospective Study (TOPS), which included treatment admissions between 1979 and 1981. The second era and data are represented by the adult participants in the Drug Abuse Treatment Outcome Studies (DATOS) admitted to treatment between 1991 and 1993.

MULTIDIMENSIONAL ASPECTS OF RELAPSE

Relapse to drug abuse often occurs following treatment and is a major concern to treatment providers. Goals of most treatment approaches include the prevention of relapse, the delay of relapse, and/or the reduction in severity of use at relapse. Relapse is often characterized in terms of the use of a single substance such as heroin, alcohol, or tobacco during or after treatment. This basic definition fails to capture the nature of drug abuse and may lead to misguided policy and practice guidelines. The understanding of relapse to drug abuse is complicated by drug-abuse patterns that involve multiple use of a wide range of licit and illicit drugs (Craddock et al., 1985). A common pattern among clients entering treatment in the 1970s and 1980s was the weekly or more frequent use of drugs including marijuana, cocaine, alcohol, and heroin (Hubbard et al., 1985). Heroin abusers also commonly substituted other drugs for heroin. Increasing popularity and use of cocaine occurred during the follow-up period for TOPS clients in the early 1980s. In the middle to late 1980s and 1990s, cocaine use became more prominent, and weekly or more frequent use was reported by more than half of the clients admitted to treatment (Craddock et al., 1997). Cocaine was commonly used with alcohol and marijuana but infrequently with other nonopioid drugs.

A number of definitions of relapse can be formulated, and data are presented herein to illustrate the definitions and the implications of the alternative definitions. Under these formulations, relapse may be defined as use after treatment of a specific pretreatment drug or nonmedical use of its substitutes, or it may refer to an overall use pattern. The first basic relapse definition involves posttreatment return to use of a specific drug (e.g., cocaine) that was used before treatment. It does not consider posttreatment or pretreatment use levels or the timing of use. The second type of relapse is the nonmedical substitution of another drug for a principal pretreatment drug (e.g., other narcotics as a substitute for heroin). The third, more comprehensive definition of relapse is the posttreatment resumption of the pretreatment pattern of drug use (e.g., multiple use of heroin, cocaine, marijuana, and alcohol) or the development of new patterns of use. For this chapter, the initial focus is on the specific drugs heroin and cocaine and then on the multidimensional definitions of drug use that best describe the patterns used within and across the two studies.

Within each type of relapse, quantitative measures, such as frequency and severity, indicate the extent of relapse and add an important dimension to the description of drug use patterns and use of specific drugs. The timing dimension considers the latency, duration, and episodic nature of relapse (Mann et al., 1984). Drug abuse treatment clients may continue drug use throughout treatment or may cease use during treatment, only to resume use before leaving treatment or at various times after treatment. The first posttreatment use may be brief and have little clinical significance, or use may continue for weeks, months, or years. The lengths of periods of use and abstinence after treatment are variable and the periods are cyclical (see Maddux and Desmond, 1974).

A brief episode of infrequent use may not indicate serious relapse. Brief episodes of heavy use, however, even those separated by long intervals of abstinence, may be predictive of serious relapse in the future. Relapse needs to be defined by level and severity and within the context of overall use patterns. Indices of multiple drug use patterns have been developed and used in major national studies (Bray et al., 1982; Savage and Simpson, 1976). To appropriately study relapse, the pretreatment pattern of drug use and the overall posttreatment pattern should be considered. Posttreatment marijuana use by a client who used heroin daily before treatment and by another who used only marijuana are not equivalent. Shifts to less serious drug use patterns can be viewed as indicators of improvement rather than relapse.

Given the complexity of relapse, a number of key questions need to be addressed. Does the multidimensional construct of relapse provide more useful information than simple measures of relapse and time to relapse? Is relapse similar for different drugs? Is the construct of relapse and its dimensions similar across different eras of drug use? Is relapse similar for different types of drug users? To begin to address some of these key questions, the analyses in this chapter focus on relapse to heroin and cocaine use for large samples of clients in two national studies of treatment effectiveness during two different eras, one decade apart.

METHODS

The Treatment Outcome Prospective Study (TOPS) and the adult phase of the Drug Abuse Treatment Outcome Studies (DATOS) used personal interviews to obtain detailed drug use histories. The TOPS sample used here included 9,989 clients who entered 41 detoxification, outpatient methadone, long-term residential, and outpatient drug-free treatment programs in 10 cities from 1979 to 1981 (Hubbard et al., 1984). Three different samples totaling 5,000 of these clients were reinterviewed at 3 months, 12 months, 2 years, and 3–5 years after treatment. The DATOS sample included 10,010 clients who entered 96 outpatient methadone, long-term residential, outpatient drug-free, and short-term inpatient programs in 11 cities from 1991–93 (Flynn et al., 1997). Most of the analyses reported in this paper are based on the pretreatment and posttreatment drug-use patterns of 2,280 clients from 1979 and 1980 TOPS admission cohorts, and 2,966 clients from 1991–93 DATOS admission cohorts who were interviewed at intake and approximately one year after they left treatment (except for long-term methadone clients still in treatment at follow-up (Flynn et al., 1997).

The drug-use measures developed for this chapter are based on the comprehensive assessments of nonmedical use of nine different drug types. These include heroin, other opiates, cocaine, sedatives or barbituates, amphetamines or stimulants, hallucinogens or psychedelics, inhalants, marijuana, and alcohol. These assessments were obtained in interviews covering the year before admission and the first year of follow-up approximately one year after termination. Quantity and frequency of alcohol use and frequency of use of all types of drugs for nonmedical purposes during the twelve-month periods before and after treatment were obtained. Clients were asked to report their frequency of use on a nine-point scale from nonuse to use four or more times per day. At the follow-up, clients were asked how much time elapsed before use of specific drugs was resumed after leaving treatment. For heroin and for the clients' primary drug of abuse at the time of follow-up, questions were asked about the time until daily use was resumed.

Four measures of relapse to heroin and cocaine were developed for this chapter to illustrate the multidimensional nature of relapse. The measures are:

Any Posttreatment Use Among All Clients	Percentage of all clients reporting any use in the year after treatment.
Any Posttreatment Use Among Pretreatment Weekly or Daily Users	Percentage of clients who used weekly or more frequently before treatment and reported any use in the year after treatment.
Percent of Daily Users Among Posttreatment Users	Among those who used a drug in the posttreatment year, the proportion who used daily.
Resumption of Pattern of Use	Percentage of clients with each drug use pattern in the year before treatment who used the same pattern in the posttreatment year

For all measures equivalent coding and questions were used to compare results for heroin and cocaine relapse in the two study eras.

NATURE AND EXTENT OF RELAPSE

Drug use in the first year of follow-up was common in both TOPS and DATOS. About one in three reported weekly or daily heroin use in TOPS and about one in six reported weekly or daily use of heroin in DATOS in the year after treatment. Cocaine use was reported by about half of TOPS clients and one-third of DATOS clients. Although such simple frequency data on posttreatment use are informative, relapse can be described more appropriately in the context of pretreatment use. The pretreatment use of cocaine was much higher among DATOS clients in 1991–93 than among TOPS clients in 1979–81. In TOPS, weekly or daily cocaine use ranged from 17 to 30 percent, compared to 42 to 67 percent in DATOS, in the three comparable treatment modalities (Craddock et al., 1997).

TYPES OF RELAPSE

The magnitude of the relapse rates for heroin and cocaine shown in table 5.1 differs by drug and definition of relapse. Although the overall relapse rates for all clients differed, the relapse rates among pretreatment weekly users were more similar across eras for both drugs. Posttreatment use rates for cocaine and heroin were 10–20 percent higher in 1979–81 than in 1991–93 admissions.

Table 5.1 Types of Relapse Rates in the Year After Treatment for Heroin and Cocaine

| | DRUG USED POSTTREATMENT (PERCENTAGES) | | | |
| | HEROIN | | COCAINE | |
TYPES OF RELAPSE	TOPS	DATOS	TOPS	DATOS
Any posttreatment use among all clients	31.9	16.2	44.0	35.7
Any posttreatment use among pre-treatment weekly or daily users	58.6	47.0	65.0	47.3
Posttreatment daily use among post-treatment users	28.3	33.1	13.2	20.7

Among those who relapsed, the percentage relapsing to posttreatment *daily use* was higher among heroin than cocaine users. Among DATOS clients, about one-third of posttreatment users relapsed to daily use within the first year after treatment while about one-fifth of posttreatment users of cocaine relapsed to daily use.

TIME UNTIL RELAPSE

The DATOS participants were asked when they first used heroin and cocaine after leaving treatment. In table 5.2, the distributions of the periods between termination from treatment and first use of heroin and cocaine are presented for all former clients who reported any use in the first year after treatment. About 43–44 percent of the clients who used heroin in the year after treatment in either study were using the drug within the week after treatment termination, and another 20 percent resumed use within the first month after discharge. About half the remaining clients relapsed one to three months after termination. Cocaine was used within a week of termination by 29–32 percent of clients in both studies. After one month, half had relapsed. Somewhat higher percentages (20–30) did not relapse to cocaine use until three months after treatment termination. This accounted for a mean of about three weeks longer to relapse to cocaine use when compared to heroin use.

It is also important to investigate whether the timing of relapse was different for those who relapsed to daily use. Table 5.3 shows the time until first re-

Table 5.2 Time Until First Use in the First Year After Treatment Among Clients Who Reported Posttreatment Use of Heroin and Cocaine

| WEEKS AFTER TERMINATION | DRUG USED POSTTREATMENT (PERCENTAGES) | | | |
| | HEROIN | | COCAINE | |
	TOPS	DATOS	TOPS	DATOS
Within 1 week	44.2	42.9	32.3	29.2
2–4 weeks	21.4	18.2	24.6	20.4
5–13 weeks	15.8	19.3	17.6	19.9
14 or more weeks	18.6	19.7	25.5	30.4
No. of posttreatment users	720	457	984	993
Mean weeks to relapse among POTStreatment users	7.9	8.5	10.3	11.7

lapse for daily users of heroin and cocaine. Almost one-half of posttreatment daily heroin and cocaine users were using daily at treatment termination. On the other extreme, about one in five had been out of treatment at least three months before beginning daily use. A higher proportion of clients in DATOS were using heroin and cocaine within the first week after discharge and fewer were abstinent for more than three months. Extending the period between treatment termination and daily use seems to be important to establishing reductions and long-lasting abstinence. The variations in the timing of the relapse for daily users suggest that the course of relapse to daily use may differ by drug and be affected by the environment in which the drugs were used.

The timing of relapse for daily users appears to be different from the timing of relapse to first use. Those who were to become daily users were most likely to relapse immediately following termination. First daily use for those who did not immediately start using heroin daily after treatment was more evenly spread over the three-month time span than was first use of the same drug.

CHANGE IN PATTERNS

Describing posttreatment use of a specific type of drug does not provide a complete picture of relapse. Here the concept of relapse to drug use is broad-

Table 5.3 Time Until First Use in the First Year After Treatment Among Clients Who Reported Posttreatment Daily Use of Heroin and Cocaine

| | DRUG USED POSTTREATMENT (PERCENTAGES) | | | |
| | HEROIN | | COCAINE | |
WEEKS AFTER TERMINATION	TOPS	DATOS	TOPS	DATOS
Within 1 week	45.6	57.3	42.0	50.2
2–4 weeks	20.7	12.0	19.1	19.0
5–13 weeks	15.5	18.0	19.8	14.1
14 or more weeks	18.1	12.7	19.1	16.6
No. of posttreatment users	386	150	126	205

ened to consider differences between pretreatment and posttreatment patterns. Multiple drug use by both TOPS and DATOS respondents before treatment was common. Comparisons of the use patterns of clients in the TOPS and Drug Abuse Reporting Program (DARP) research provided evidence of the increasing prevalence of multiple drug use between the DARP and TOPS eras (Hubbard et al., 1985). The focus on daily use of heroin and other narcotics in the studies on treatment clients in the 1970s (DARP) was no longer fully descriptive of the extent of drug use or relapse during the 1980s. In the 1980s, cocaine became the principal drug of interest and led to the focus on cocaine in the 1990s (DATOS).

Several approaches were used in TOPS analyses (Bray et al., 1982; Hubbard et al., 1985) to examine patterns of multiple drug use including a set of drug use patterns adapted from the DARP classification framework (Simpson, 1974). The extensive variety of combinations of weekly use of eight drug types used by TOPS clients suggested that broad rather than specific categories were required to describe clinically useful patterns. Patterns were defined by hierarchical rules that required weekly or more frequent use of key drugs or drug types. In TOPS, two types of heroin users were defined: those who used other narcotics and those who did not use other narcotics. Next, among the remaining clients, users of narcotics other than heroin and users of non-narcotics (excluding marijuana and alcohol) were classified. Finally, alcohol/marijuana users and minimal users (clients who did not report weekly

Table 5.4. Relapse to Weekly or Daily Use of Heroin and Cocaine by
Pretreatment Drug Use Pattern

	POSTTREATMENT USE (PERCENTAGES)			
	HEROIN		COCAINE	
PRETREATMENT DRUG USE PATTERN	TOPS	DATOS	TOPS	DATOS
Heroin-other narcotics/no cocaine	33.4	21.6	13.9	11.6
Heroin-other narcotics and cocaine	45.5	27.0	42.0	30.1
Cocaine only	11.8	0.9	41.2	22.6
Cocaine and alcohol	16.7	1.8	25.0	25.1
Cocaine with other drugs	8.9	1.5	29.1	30.1
Marijuana and/or alcohol	5.4	0.7	7.6	6.7
Less than weekly use/no use	9.8	3.1	10.1	10.3

use of any drug or alcohol) were the residual group. The resulting five categories are hierarchical: clients were included in the less serious patterns only
if they did not meet the criteria for the more serious patterns. The defining
characteristics of the patterns did not identify all drugs used by the clients.
Rather, they indicated key drugs and the levels used. For DATOS, the development of a pattern was based on cocaine use and the combinations of
drugs used with cocaine. Each pattern variable was contextual in that it was
useful in describing the types and combinations of use present during either
the TOPS or the DATOS eras.

To demonstrate the hierarchical pattern approach and compare TOPS and
DATOS clients, a pattern based on heroin, other narcotics, cocaine, and other
nonnarcotic drugs (including marijuana) is shown in table 5.4. The first pattern considers weekly or daily heroin (or other narcotic) use in combination
with weekly or daily cocaine use. The second pattern is defined by weekly or
daily heroin or other narcotic use, and the third pattern, by weekly or daily
cocaine use. The fourth pattern contains clients who report weekly or daily
use of one or more nonnarcotic drugs (marijuana, sedatives, barbiturates,
amphetamines, hallucinogens, and inhalants), while the final pattern reflects
no use or less than weekly use of any illegal drug. Although the defining characteristics of the patterns are exactly the same for both studies, actual use

is manifested differently within each treatment era. For example, marijuana use within each of the patterns was much higher in TOPS than DATOS.

With the exception of the cocaine pattern and the less than weekly use/no use pattern, former TOPS clients were more likely than former DATOS clients to resume the same drug use pattern following drug treatment (refer to percentage in boxes in table 5.4). TOPS clients in the pretreatment cocaine pattern, however, were much more likely than DATOS clients to be using one or more non-narcotic drugs (especially marijuana), and a much higher proportion are categorized into the posttreatment other non-narcotic pattern (33%) than DATOS clients (4%). Table 5.4 clearly indicates that former DATOS clients are more likely than former TOPS clients to fall into the fifth drug treatment pattern in the year following treatment.

SUMMARY

This chapter briefly assessed the multidimensional nature of relapse to drug use, the length of posttreatment abstinence periods for heroin and cocaine, resumption of drug use patterns, and the differences in relapse across two decades of treatment admissions.

Rates of relapse defined in various ways showed important differences among heroin users. Relapse to daily heroin use, for example, was higher than relapse to daily cocaine use. The timing of relapse was similar for heroin and cocaine. Approximately 80 percent of clients who relapsed did so within the first three months after leaving treatment. Between 10 and 15 percent were using at follow-up. More emphasis on aftercare and postdischarge counseling that focuses on prevention or relapse might help reduce relapse rates and increase periods of remission for relapsing clients and may have been responsible for the decreases in all types of relapse among DATOS clients.

Considerations of the complementary concept of reduction in overall use patterns (in addition to reductions in use of individual drugs) could help researchers and clinicians better understand posttreatment use. Because of the complexity of drug abuse, different conceptualizations of relapse and reduction in drug use need to be examined. The drug abuse pattern measure used here is one way to describe the shift among patterns. It was clear that relapse differed among types of pretreatment heroin users. In particular, clients using cocaine (in the absence of heroin or other narcotics) in two admission cohorts had very different patterns of relapse in the two decades.

The analyses presented in this chapter indicate the complex nature of relapse among former drug abuse treatment program clients. Other types of analyses like survival analysis or failure rate analysis could also be used to examine the timing or relapse in more detail. To learn how treatment can minimize the risk of relapse and lengthen abstention periods, studies are needed to:

- Describe the multidimensional nature of relapse (type, extent, timing, and the overall drug use pattern) and the relapse to use of specific drugs within the context of multiple and changing drug use patterns;
- Identify the correlates of relapse, particularly behavior, during treatment and in the first three months after leaving treatment; and
- Assess the effects of relapse prevention efforts like discharge planning, continuing care services, and self-help participation in the first months following termination.

Relapse is a complex and dynamic process that must be examined more carefully by researchers and clinicians. The extensive treatment histories of many clients entering and re-entering programs suggest that recovery from drug use is a long-term challenge, and relapse may occur all too frequently. Such relapse can be addressed through interventions guided by an understanding of the recovery process. The process of recovery can be conceptualized and investigated as a long-term maturation or development in much the same way that addiction and treatment careers have been examined (Anglin et al., 1997). A better understanding of this process should lead to improved treatment and continuing care services in the community that will reduce overall relapse rates, extend remission periods, and reduce both the frequency and duration of relapse episodes.

References

Anglin, M. D., Hser, Y. I., & Grella, C. E. (1997). Drug Addiction and Treatment Careers Among Clients in Drug Abuse Treatment Outcome Study (DATOS). *Psychology of Addictive Behaviors,* 11(4), 308–323.

Bray, R. M., Schlenger, W. E., Craddock, S. G., Hubbard, R. L., & Rachal, J. V. (1982). *Approaches to the Assessment of Drug Use in the Treatment Outcome Prospective Study.* Prepared for the National Institute on Drug Abuse. Research Triangle Institute Report No. RTI/1901/01-5S.

Craddock, S. G., Bray, R. M., & Hubbard, R. L. (1985). *Drug Use Before and During Drug Abuse Treatment: 1979–1981 TOPS Admission Cohorts.* DHHS Publication No. (ADM) 85-1387. Rockville, Md.: National Institute on Drug Abuse.

Craddock, S. G., Rounds-Bryant, J. L., Flynn, P. M., & Hubbard, R. L. (1997). Characteristics and Pretreatment Behaviors of Clients Entering Drug Abuse Treatment: 1969 to 1993. *American Journal of Drug and Alcohol Abuse* 23, 43–59.

Flynn, P. M., Craddock, S. G., Hubbard, R. L., Anderson, J., & Etheridge, R. M. (1997). Methodological Overview and Research Design for the Drug Abuse Treatment Outcome Study (DATOS). *Psychology of Addictive Behaviors* 11(4), 230–243.

Gerstein, D. R., Harwood, H. J., Fountain, D., Suter, N., & Malloy, K. (1994). *Evaluating Recovery Services: The California Drug and Alcohol Treatment Assessment (CALDATA)* (California Department of Alcohol & Drug Programs Report No. ADP 94-629). Sacramento, Calif.

Hubbard, R. L., Bray, R. M., & Craddock, S. G. (1985). Issues in the Assessment of Multiple Drug Use Among Drug Treatment Clients. In M. Braude & H. M. Ginzburg, eds., *Strategies for Research on the Interactions of Drugs of Abuse*. National Institute on Drug Abuse Research Monograph 68. DHHS Pub. No. (ADM) 86-1453. Washington, D.C.: Supt. of Docs.

Hubbard, R. L., Craddock, S. G., Flynn, P. M., Anderson, J., & Etheridge, R. M. (1997). Overview of 1-Year Follow-Up Outcomes in the Drug Abuse Treatment Outcome Study (DATOS). *Psychology of Addictive Behaviors,* 11, 261–278.

Hubbard, R. L., Marsden, M. E., Rachal, J. V., Harwood, H. J., Cavanaugh, E. R., and Ginzburg, H. M. (1989). *Drug Abuse Treatment: A National Study of Effectiveness.* Chapel Hill, N.C.: University of North Carolina Press, 1989.

Hubbard, R. L., Rachal, J. V., Craddock, S. G., & Cavanaugh, E. R. (1984). Treatment Outcome Prospective Study (TOPS): Client Characteristics and Behaviors Before, During, and After Treatment. In F. M. Tims & J. P. Ludford, eds., *Drug Abuse Treatment Evaluation: Strategies, Progress, and Prospects*. National Institute on Drug Abuse Research Monograph 51. DHHS Publication No. (ADM) 84-1329. Washington, D.C.: Supt. of Docs.

Institute of Medicine (1996). *Pathways of Addiction: Opportunities in Drug Abuse Research.* Washington, D.C.: National Academy Press.

Leshner, A. I. (1997). Introduction to the Special Issue: The National Institute on Drug Abuse's (NIDA's) Drug Abuse Treatment Outcome Study (DATOS). *Psychology of Addictive Behaviors,* 11(4), 211–215.

Maddux, J. F., & Desmond, D. P. (1974). Obtaining Life History Information About Opioid Users. *American Journal of Drug and Alcohol Abuse,* 1, 181–191.

Mann, N. R., Charuvastra, V. C., & Murphy, V. K. (1984). A Diagnostic Tool with Important Implications for Treatment of Addiction: Identification of Factors Underlying Relapse and Remission Time Distributions. *International Journal of Addictions,* 19(1), 25–44.

McLellan, A. T., Woody, G. E., Metzger, D., McKay, J., Durell, J., Alterman, A. I., & O'Brien, C. P. (1997). Evaluating the Effectiveness of Addiction Treatments: Reasonable Expectations, Appropriate Comparisons. In J.A. Egertrson, D.M. Fox, and A.I. Leshner, eds., *Treating Drug Abusers Effectively* (pp. 7–40). Malden, Mass.: Blackwell.

National Opinion Research Center at the University of Chicago (1997). *The National Treatment Improvement Evaluation Study: Final Report.* (DHHS, SAMHSA, CSAT Report). Rockville, Md.

Savage, L. J., & Simpson, D. D. (1976). *Measures of Illicit Drug Use: National Followup Study of Admissions to Drug Abuse Treatment in the DARP During 1969–1971.* Institute of Behavioral Research Report, 76–14. Fort Worth: Texas Christian University.

Simpson, D. D. (1974). Patterns of Multiple Drug Abuse. In Sells, S. B., ed., *The Effectiveness of Drug Abuse Treatment,* vol. 1. Cambridge, Mass.: Ballinger.

Simpson, D. D. (1997). Effectiveness of Drug Abuse Treatment: A Review of Research from Field Settings. In J. A. Egertrson, D. M. Fox, and A.I. Leshner (eds.), *Treating Drug Abusers Effectively* (pp. 41–73). Malden, Mass.: Blackwell.

Simpson, D. D., & Curry, S. J., eds. (1997). Drug Abuse Treatment Outcome Study (DATOS) [special issue]. *Psychology of Addictive Behaviors,* 11.

Simpson, D. D., Joe, G. W., Fletcher, B. W., Hubbard, R. L., & Anglin, M. D. (1999). A National Evaluation of Treatment Outcomes for Cocaine Dependence. *Archives of General Psychiatry,* 56, 507–514.

Simpson, D. D., and Sells, S. B. (1990). *Opioid Addiction and Treatment: A 12-Year Follow-Up.* Malabar, Fl.: Robert E. Krieger.

SIX

RELAPSE: CONTRIBUTING FACTORS, CAUSATIVE MODELS, AND EMPIRICAL CONSIDERATIONS

David S. Festinger, David F. Rubenstein,
Douglas B. Marlowe, & Jerome J. Platt

Increasing attention on relapse prevention and its utility as a drug-free intervention has inspired interest in the multitude of possible correlates that might prevent, reduce, or predict the return to drug or alcohol use once abstinence has been achieved.

Prior to the 1970s and 1980s, very little was known about the determinants of relapse among addicted individuals. Although researchers noted the high relapse rates found in their studies (e.g., Emrick, 1974; Hill & Blane, 1967; Hunt & Matarazzo, 1973; Hunt, Barnett, & Branch, 1971), scant information existed regarding the characterization, determinants, or consequences of relapse. Following the then-current zeitgeist, most research on alcoholism and drug dependence flowed from the widely accepted disease model of addiction.

The disease model (Jellinek, 1960) regarded substance dependence as a sickness. The medical or disease model should likely have incorporated theories of genetics, endocrinology, neurology, and biochemistry; however, because of its often nonscientific interpretation, the disease model has frequently been oversimplified with the notion that drug dependence is a primary, progressive, chronic, and relapsing disease. This interpretation, focusing solely on the internal concepts of craving and loss of power, may in part explain the lack of attention given environmental, situational, or psychological factors involved in relapse.

Beginning in the 1970s, a number of studies focusing on determinants of relapse among treated alcoholics shifted the focal point of relapse from endogenous factors to environmental factors and life events. These early investigations led to an abundance of theories and models of the relapse process, each with its unique combination of internal and/or external determinants. In this chapter, we describe a number of factors that have been posited as possible determinants of relapse, review several major theories of relapse, and discuss possible shortcomings of these theories, with an emphasis on methodology and assessment.

DETERMINANTS OF RELAPSE

The lasting popularity of the disease model of addictions exemplifies how specific content areas can be hindered by unidimensional characterizations. The science of psychology, itself shifting from decades of introspection and black-box theorizing to decades of pure behaviorism, has only recently begun to explore multidimensional paradigms like the biopsychosocial model in an attempt to explain more of the variance and better to account for clinical phenomena. Multivariate theories have become a significant facet of our current zeitgeist, which is clearly evident in recent models of addiction and relapse, many of which have incorporated factors related to the individual's environment, the personal characteristics of the individual at risk for relapse, and the pharmacology of the psychoactive substance.

These variables can be broken down into personological factors, environmental factors, and pharmacological factors. These factors will be defined followed by a review of several theories of relapse that contain and explicate more fully the role of these factors in relapse and relapse prevention.

PERSONOLOGICAL FACTORS

Personological factors refer to an individual's characteristics and/or internal states. These factors influence an individual's likelihood of either maintaining abstinence or relapsing. For example, anxiety, depression, and anger (Shiffman, 1982) as well as "negative emotional states" and "positive emotional states in a social context" (Connors, Longabaugh, and Miller, 1996) may precipitate relapse. There has been some attempt to demarcate the severity of a return to substance use by differentiating a "lapse" from a "relapse" (Marlatt, 1985). The term *lapse,* according to Marlatt, should be reserved to describe a "slip" or initial transgression following a period of abstinence, as opposed to a *relapse,* which refers to a full return to regular use patterns. Using this differentiation, it has been noted that relapses are more commonly due to "negative emotional states or stress events," whereas lapses are more frequently related to situational factors. This finding has important implications for the development and implementation of relapse prevention strategies. It may be critical to focus on the development of coping strategies to manage stressful situations to prevent deterioration from lapse to relapse and to focus on the management of corrosive affective states to prevent the worsening of a relapse already in progress.

Motivation to remain abstinent from using substances, to avoid behaviors that increase vulnerability to relapse, and to implement coping strategies that sustain sobriety is another personological factor to consider. Miller and Rollnick (1991), for example, have developed a therapeutic intervention (motivational interviewing) to increase patients' readiness for change. Incorporating Prochaska and DiClemente's (1982) five-stage model of change (precontemplation, contemplation, determination, action, maintenance), Miller and Rollnick's (1991) approach provides specific interventions related to the patient's current level of motivation. According to Miller and Rollnick, the potential for relapse may be most likely in individuals in the precontemplation stage of this stages-of-change model. For example, a study by Stotts et al. (1996) indicated that women smokers were most likely to relapse when they were in this early stage of change.

One's belief in his or her ability to master a situation using his or her own resources (self-efficacy) is another factor associated with relapse prevention (Marlatt, 1985). According to Marlatt, a relapse to substance use may occur when an individual is faced with a high-risk situation, feels he or she has insufficient skills to cope with the situation, believes old behaviors are likely to return, and feels little control over the situation. Marlatt and Gordon also note that whether a full relapse occurs depends on how the individual perceives the cause of the initial use and how he or she responds to it. Subsequently, the extent to which an individual employs coping strategies, coupled with the effectiveness of these strategies, determines his or her likelihood of preventing relapse (Bliss et al., 1989; Connors, Longabaugh, & Miller, 1996).

An individual's perception of his or her experiences is another personological factor that may influence a person's vulnerability to relapse. Several models, including the person-situation interaction model (Litman, 1980) and the cognitive appraisals model (Sanchez-Craig, 1976), have posited that peoples' perceptions and distortions of high-risk situations, the utility of their drug use, and their own coping skills are associated with sensitivity and likelihood of relapse (Donovan & Chaney, 1985).

Internal mood states, level of motivation, and self/environment perception are theorized to be important personological determinants of relapse.

Empirically, however, little is known about these factors and their ultimate function in relapse.

PHARMACOLOGICAL/PHYSIOLOGICAL FACTORS

Pharmacological/physiological factors also play a role in relapse. Exposure to situational cues may trigger physiological changes that may make an individual more susceptible to craving and relapse (Ludwig, Wikler, & Stark, 1974). Wise (1988) further discusses neurobiology of craving and the role of positive and negative reinforcement in the development of drug addiction, in the initiation of relapse, and in sustaining drug use.

Chronic urges may have a powerful impact on relapse (Brandon, Tiffany, & Baker, 1987). A study done by Heather, Stallard, and Tebbutt (1991) showed that heroin addicts reported that substance-related temptations and urges were most powerful in predicting relapse. Connors et al. (1996) reviewed a number of models related to the psychobiology of relapse including the opponent-process and acquired motivation model (Solomon, 1980), which involve positive and negative reinforcement as motivation for substance use and/or relapse; the craving and loss of control model (Ludwig, Wikler, & Stark, 1974), in which exposure to interoceptive or exteroceptive cues and cognitive labeling may cause craving, which can trigger lapse/relapse; and the urges and craving model (Tiffany, 1990), in which an individual weaves intentional nonautomatic cognitive processes (which guide behavioral relapse prevention strategies) into automatic cognitive processes to slow and impede substance use behaviors sustained by these nonautomatic cognitive processes.

Relapse and its relation to withdrawal symptoms were also noted in a number of models reviewed by Connors, Maisto, and Donovan (1996), including the alcohol withdrawal symptoms model (Mossberg, Liljeberg, & Borg, 1985; Roelofs & Dikkenberg, 1987), the post-acute withdrawal syndrome model (Gorski & Miller, 1979), and the withdrawal/kindling model (Adinoff, O'Neill, & Ballenger, 1995).

ENVIRONMENTAL FACTORS

A number of studies have found that environmental factors are associated with relapse. Brownell et al. (1986) report that interpersonal conflict and stressful interpersonal relationships, peer pressure, and exposure to cues related to addictive behaviors leave individuals prone to relapse.

It is often difficult to differentiate personological from situational or environmental factors. Although Miller, Westenberg, Harris, and Tonigan (1996), found that cognitive appraisal variables, client coping resources, craving experiences, and affective/mood states (all personological) were predictive of relapse, O'Farrell and Cutter (1996) found that relapse in individuals using alcohol was more likely in those who had spouses that behaved (communicated and expressed themselves) negatively toward the patient (situational/environmental).

Environmental experiences/stressors and perception of these stressors and coping strategies to manage such stressors in combination with perception of social support may influence the potential for relapse. Individuals attempt to cope with these stressors through their identified and preferred coping strategies; when they fail, patients rely on previously used, albeit problematic strategies, and for individuals with addiction histories, this often means a return to substance abuse.

MODELS OF RELAPSE PREVENTION

As described, a wide array of variables have been examined as possible correlates or determinants of relapse. Many of these variables have been shown to explain significant portions of variance in relapse. Most clinical phenomena are influenced by a combination of factors, however, each factor individually or in combination predicting pieces of variance in the ultimate outcome. As theory and empirical research have continued to identify individual predictor variables, scientists have begun to build multivariate models to, as accurately as possible, predict an addict's likelihood of relapsing following a period of abstinence. In the past two decades a variety of such models have been developed to account for these variables and their potential interaction.

COGNITIVE-BEHAVIORAL MODEL

The cognitive-behavioral model of relapse (Marlatt, 1985b; Marlatt, 1996) focuses on the self-efficacy that drug-dependent individuals develop over time with continued abstinence. The longer one is able to remain drug or alcohol free, the stronger his or her sense of self-control becomes. Eventually, however, the individual will face a high-risk situation, another key component of this model. These situations may vary but are usually determined by both cognitive and environmental factors.

When an individual finds him or herself in a high-risk situation, he or she has but two main options, to use or to abstain. If the individual has the skills necessary to abstain, then these skills along with his or her sense of self-control are reinforced and strengthened. Alternatively, if the individual

is unable or lacks the skills or capacity to abstain, and transgresses, an abstinence violation effect (AVE) is hypothesized to occur. This is best described
as a period of cognitive dissonance resulting from contradiction between the
individual's cognitions or beliefs, and their actual behaviors. This is best illustrated through a case example:

> Joe, who has remained abstinent from cocaine for several weeks follow-
> ing years of chronic dependence, decides to attend a party. He convinces
> himself that he has no intention to use and that he is strong enough to
> resist the greatest temptation. Throughout the evening many people offer
> him the drug, but he resists. Later that evening he is offered cocaine by a
> female whom he finds attractive, and he finds it impossible to resist. Later,
> conflicted by his transgression, he begins to see himself as a failure.

In the above example, Marlatt and his colleagues would define Joe's transgression as a slip. It is not considered a complete relapse because Joe did not
yet return to his full baseline behavior in quantity, rate, or chronicity. He used
only one time. What happens next will determine whether or not he will actually relapse. According to the model, if this slip is not managed correctly and
redefined as a learning experience, it could have detrimental consequences.
In this case the individual, unable to employ adequate coping strategies, experiences an AVE. This effect can be overwhelming, as it produces significant
dissonance ("I shouldn't be using, it's destroying my life, but I used"), depression, anxiety, confusion, guilt, embarrassment, shame, and profoundly
diminished self-esteem. These powerful negative mood states often lead the
individual to believe he has no control and to the assumption that the only
way to cope with such negative emotions is through continued drug use. This
is particularly likely if the individual maintains positive outcome expectancies regarding the drug's effects. These beliefs in turn occasion continued use
and full relapse.

SELF-EFFICACY AND OUTCOME EXPECTATIONS MODEL

This model of relapse, posited by Wilson (1978), grew out of Bandura's (1977)
social learning theory. The self-efficacy and outcome expectations model
proposes that relapse is a function of an individual's expected outcome for
using or not using, and belief in his or her ability to enact the behaviors required to produce a specific outcome. According to the model, the stronger
the level of negative expectancies the individual experiences, and the less
control he or she perceives, the greater the likelihood of relapse.

The term *outcome expectancy,* coined by Bandura (1984, 1986), should not be confused with the term *expectancy* as used by Roehling and Goldman (1987); they are quite different concepts (Solomon & Annis, 1989). Roehling and Goldman use the term only to describe the anticipated consequences of *continued use* of a substance, whereas Bandura uses the term to describe the expected consequences of either *modifying or completely abstaining from substance use.*

Thus, the model posits that both positive and negative outcome and self-efficacy expectancies interact to either occasion or prevent relapse following an achieved period of abstinence. In other words, according to Bandura (1984), "The type of outcomes people anticipate depends on their judgments of how well they will be able to perform in certain situations: It is because expected outcomes are highly dependent on self-efficacy judgments that expected outcomes may not add much on their own to the prediction of behavior."

In the case illustration described above, Joe's expectancy for outcome of maintained abstinence may very well have been positive (e.g., "If I remain drug-free I'll be happy, healthier, and I'll have more money"). Even when such a positive outcome is expected, however, when coupled with a negative judgment of self-efficacy (e.g., "I'll never be able to stay clean. If I snort even one line I'm going to end up using every day") it is likely to occasion relapse. This brings to mind the concept of learned helplessness (Seligman, 1975), where Joe anticipates little if any efficacy in his ability to alter an expected outcome.

COGNITIVE APPRAISALS MODEL

According to this model of relapse (Sanchez-Craig, 1976), an individual's perception and appraisal of an aversive situation are more influential in determining relapse than is the situation itself (Donovan & Chaney, 1985). Thus, a person may appraise a situation as positive, negative, or neutral and respond accordingly. This model incorporates both the individual and the situation but focuses mainly on the person's interpretation of the situation. Such interpretations may vary and be modified as a function of additional information. They may also be affected by an individual's knowledge of available coping strategies and his or her ability to apply them. When coping skills are not available, the individual may experience stress and other negative emotional states that may exacerbate with continued exposure to stressful situations.

Sanchez-Craig (1976) theorized that interpretations of aversive situations play a significant role in alcoholism. For example, an alcoholic may see continued drinking as an efficient way of coping with negative conditions, or simply as a fun activity—a positive appraisal that may have developed through experiences in which alcohol use relieved, masked, or delayed aversive situations. Frequent use of alcohol as a coping mechanism may in addition prevent other, more appropriate coping strategies from developing, ultimately leaving the individual relying on alcohol as his or her way of coping with stress. According to this model, an individual who attempts to abstain from or reduce consumption is prone to relapse when he or she encounters any stressful situation, particularly one previously connected with alcohol or drug use. Additionally, inaccurate appraisals may further complicate the situation and contribute to more drinking.

Utilizing the cognitive appraisals model to understand Joe's dependence and risk of relapse, we could say that Joe may believe cocaine helps him deal with aversive situations. In the past Joe sought treatment and initiated abstinence in response to new stressors, including the threat of homelessness and losing his job. These stressors compelled him to realize the negative consequences of continued cocaine use. At the party he was able to refuse offers of cocaine and other drugs several times until he was offered the drug in a certain situation. This situation, being approached by an attractive female, may have made him nervous or simply amorous. In either case, he may have disregarded the negative long-term consequences and focused only on the immediate perceived benefits (e.g., "cocaine will make me feel more confident about myself," or "cocaine will increase my sexual stamina"). These inaccurate or inappropriate appraisals thus led Joe to relapse. Afterward he may have further misappraised the situation (e.g., "I totally blew it, I might as well give up"), regressing further toward his baseline dependence. Unless Joe's appraisal of cocaine use as a negative mechanism is reinforced over time, the stronger learned desire will continue to determine his behavior.

PERSON-SITUATION INTERACTION MODEL

Littman, Eiser, Rawson, and Oppenheim (1979) hypothesized a formulation of relapse described as an interactional perspective (Litman, 1980). According to the person-situation interaction model (Litman, Eiser, Rawson, & Oppenheim, 1979), the likelihood of relapse is determined by an interaction among: (1) situations that are dangerous for the individual in terms of bringing about relapse, (2) the availability of coping skills or strategies necessary to deal with these high-risk situations, (3) the effectiveness of these skills or strategies, and (4) the individual's self-perception, self-esteem, and degree of learned helplessness. Littman et al. (1979) suggest that if an individual sees him or herself as a helpless victim of feelings and situations, he or she will be less likely to engage in appropriate coping responses necessary to prevent relapse. Alternatively, if an individual develops effective coping skills and strategies, that person will experience positive changes in self-esteem and perception.

Thus, according to the model, individuals who encounter more high-risk situations (e.g., negative moods, offerings of drugs or alcohol, interpersonal anxiety, or diminished cognitive vigilance) and have fewer coping skills will be more likely to relapse. Recall that Joe was doing rather well in most situations, as when he was able to say no to offers of cocaine several times during the evening. What made him finally transgress? According to Litman's model it may have been the combination of a high-risk situation and a limited coping repertoire, the match between Joe's coping skills and the person-situation interaction, or his perceived capability of handling the situation and remaining abstinent. Joe knew how to, as the once popular war on drugs slogan suggested, "just say no." When presented with a more complex situation, however, that of being offered the drug repeatedly throughout the evening, and then by an attractive female or a more persistent individual, this coping strategy itself was not sufficient in preventing relapse.

There is obviously some overlap in construct between the person-situation interaction model and both the cognitive-behavioral model (Marlatt, 1985; Marlatt, 1996) and the self-efficacy and outcome expectations model (Wilson, 1978). However, there are several significant differences (Donovan & Chaney, 1985). First, although self-perception is clearly a major component of the model, the concept of self-efficacy is not fully integrated into the model. Second, the person-situation interaction model clearly does not address an individual's positive expectancies of substance use.

OPPONENT-PROCESS AND ACQUIRED MOTIVATION MODEL

First introduced by Solomon (1980), the opponent-process model incorporates reinforcement theory in its explanation of the process of addiction and relapse. According to the model the hedonic characteristics of reinforcers usually arouse affective opponent processes. The action of these is (a) mitigation of the hedonic potency of the reinforcer, (b) the occurrence of an opponent hedonic aftereffect, and (c) the development of a new acquired motivation, which may over time predominate in its control over drug or alcohol use. Solomon (1980) presented a variety of examples and data to support this hypothesis (for a complete review of these data see Solomon, 1980).

According to Solomon (1980), when a body experiences a positive reinforcer, it will act to reduce or normalize its effects. The reinforcer first engages a process that leads to an emotional or hedonic state (a). A secondary process (b) then engages an opposing emotional state. Solomon suggests that the two processes differ in several ways. First, although the "a" process appears to track the stimulus intensity properties over time, the opposing "b" processes do not. Instead, these opposing processes usually have a long latency, a high inertia, and a slow decay following termination of the stimulus. Second, while the "a" processes initiated by the onset of the reinforcer remain unmodified over repeated presentations of the reinforcer, the "b," or secondary, opposing processes are often strengthened by use and weakened by disuse. Strengthening of the opponent processes occurs only when they are aroused at inter-reinforcer intervals less than the time necessary for the opponent process to decay to near baseline. This time interval is known as the critical decay duration of the opponent process.

In terms of addiction, use of a specific psychoactive substance can be seen as a stimulus. The ensuing "a" state could be a euphoric, excited mood, while the opposing "b" state might be a depressed, guilty, or irritable mood. Over time these mood states may become conditioned to stimuli associated with the drug-using situation, such as passing a former copping site, smelling burned matches, or seeing a liquor bottle, and ensuing feelings of depression, hopelessness, or guilt. Relapse potential is thus likely to increase when an individual is confronted with stimuli that evoke either positive "a" processes, in which he or she may desire to attain the positive feelings, or the "b" processes, where the individual may use in order to attain relief from the associated negative emotional state (Connors, Maisto, & Donovan, 1996).

In our case example, cocaine was Joe's initial stimulus. The "a" state was a feeling of euphoria, disinhibition, and stimulation. The opposing "b" state, however, involved feelings of depression, anhedonia, and fatigue. As Joe's dependence increased he gradually habituated to the "a" state and it became less novel. Subsequently the opposing state predominated, and Joe found himself increasingly using drugs to stave off this state rather than to evoke the former. Thus, according to this model this newly acquired motivation was likely responsible for his relapsing. Each time he was approached with an offer of the drug he found himself less able to cope with the ensuing negative emotions until he finally transgressed.

CRAVING AND LOSS OF CONTROL MODEL

According to Ludwig, Wikler, and Stark (1974), craving for alcohol involves a cognitive, subclinical, conditioned withdrawal syndrome. They hypothesized that cravings are initiated by both interoceptive and exteroceptive stimuli. Through classical conditioning, a variety of stimuli evoke sensations similar to those experienced during initial abstinence and psychophysiological withdrawal.

Interoceptive stimuli refer to the effects of psychoactive substances on visceral and cerebral neuronal receptors. Their physiological and neurophysiological effects are hypothesized to closely match those elicited during past withdrawals, including effects to both the central and autonomic nervous systems. These effects may in turn promote craving.

Exteroceptive stimuli refer to all situational and environmental circumstances that were previously paired or associated with drug use. These might include situations like handling money, passing a bar, or going to a party. They might also include situations that affect an individual in a manner similar to that experienced during withdrawal. For example, an interpersonal conflict may elicit dysphoria similar to that experienced during initial abstinence. In this case the argument might precipitate craving.

According to the craving and loss of control model, it is how the individual interprets the interoceptive or exteroceptive stimuli that determines whether or not a craving will occur. The sense of craving (Connors, Maisto, & Donovan, 1996) may be seen as a "cognitive label" used to refer to feelings associated with these stimuli. Through classical conditioning, individuals who experience more frequent or more intense withdrawal symptoms will likely acquire more conditioned stimuli with the ability to elicit cravings.

In applying this model to our case example, we see that while attending the party, Joe may have been confronted with a number of interoceptive and exteroceptive stimuli. These in turn may have evoked strong craving sensations (similar to those experienced during past withdrawal experiences) and ultimately led to his relapsing in an effort to alleviate these feelings.

CONDITIONED COMPENSATORY RESPONSE MODEL

Borrowing from research on the development of drug tolerance (Poulos, Hinton, & Siegel, 1981; Siegel, 1983) and the works of Ludwig and Wikler (Wikler, 1980; Ludwig, Wikler, & Stark, 1974), the conditioned compensatory response model asserts that the administration of a drug constitutes a conditioning trial where the conditioned stimuli (CS) include all cues experienced during drug administration. Formerly neutral stimuli like holding money, walking by a buying site, or talking to a former drug-using associate, when repeatedly paired with drug ingestion [the unconditioned stimulus (US)], come to evoke conditioned responses (CRs) similar to the unconditioned responses (URs) evoked by drug ingestion. Thus, the previously neutral stimuli, after repeated pairings with the US (Unconditioned stimuli), may begin to evoke physical reactions similar in nature to the URs.

Siegel (1983) further hypothesized that the CRs may occur in a direction opposite the original URs to preserve homeostasis by compensating for the impending pharmacological effects of the drug. These anticipatory compensatory responses may account for the development of acquired tolerance (Niaura et al., 1988).

According to this hypothesis, the same process that accounts for the development of tolerance contributes to the development of withdrawal symptoms (Hinson & Siegel, 1980). Thus, if an individual encounters CS in the absence of the actual drug (e.g., during abstinence) the resulting CRs may be compensatory. When not attenuated by drug ingestion, this will likely lead to a state of homeostatic imbalance (Niaura et al., 1988). According to this model the drug-dependent individual learns to avoid these withdrawal symptom–like CRs by using regularly (Hinson & Siegel, 1980).

Regarding our case example, this model would suggest that Joe's relapse may have been motivated by a need to preserve homeostasis. When confronted by stimuli previously associated with drug use (e.g., the party, loud music, excitement), Joe may have begun to experience withdrawal-like symptoms. To escape these Joe decided to use.

CONDITIONED APPETITIVE MOTIVATION MODEL

Moving away from models that assert that relapse is motivated by a desire to relieve withdrawal, Stewart, deWit, and Eikelboom (1984) hypothesized that drug use is motivated by appetitive processes. The conditioned appetitive motivation model stems from observations that relapse often occurs in situations involving no significant withdrawal, or related distress. According to the model, neutral stimuli, through classical conditioning, come to evoke positive motivational states similar to those elicited by drug ingestion itself. These conditioned incentive stimuli (Niaura et al., 1988) prime reinitiation of drug use by enacting neural states similar to the original effects of the drug. Subsequently, drug ingestion or stimuli that have been paired with the drug may bring about a desire for the drug and precipitate a relapse.

According to this model, Joe may have been responding to classically conditioned stimuli when he relapsed. Cues at the party (e.g., music, celebration, the smell of alcohol and/or cigarette smoke, etc.) that in the past had been repeatedly paired with the positive affective effects of cocaine use began to elicit a strong motivational desire to use. Accordingly, Joe's desire for cocaine was precipitated by a variety of conditioned stimuli.

URGES AND CRAVING MODEL

The last model we will present (Wise, 1988; Tiffany, 1990) deals with the operation of nonautomatic cognitive processes used to allow or disallow automatic drug-using behaviors. According to the urges and craving model, automatic processes are fleeting, autonomous, and effortless. They happen below the level of ordinary awareness. On the other hand, nonautomatic processes are generally slower and more arduous, and they require choice, generation, implementation, and maintenance of specific strategies, as well as the modification or termination of these strategies in response to environmental changes.

A drug-dependent individual must exert significant effort and control in order to initiate and maintain abstinence. These efforts are mediated primarily through intentional, nonautomatic cognitive processes. However, drug use is controlled by automatic schemata, which are triggered by a variety of internal and external stimuli. The schemata, which are referred to as "drug-use action plans" (Tiffany, 1990), may thus lead to relapse in the absence of any conscious intention. According to Tiffany (1990), addicts are particularly prone to this form of relapse if their nonautomatic processing is focused on some other task and if the current environmental conditions are conducive to the drug-use action plan.

This model proposes that negative mood states may precipitate relapse. Several of the models discussed interpret the relation between negative mood states and relapse by viewing mood states as conditioned stimuli that occasion drug use (Ludwig et al., 1974; Solomon, 1980). Others (Marlatt, 1985) proposed that negative mood states evoke a desire for drug use based on the expectation that the drugs will relieve the emotional pain. Tiffany (1990) believed that negative affect may precipitate relapse in another manner. He theorized that negative mood states may evoke nonautomatic processing, which may compete with the nonautomatic processes focused on maintaining abstinence. Additionally, negative mood states may inhibit the appropriation of nonautomatic cognitive processes used to maintain abstinence. For example, an extremely depressed individual may simply lack the motivation or interest necessary to engage relapse prevention strategies (Shiffman, 1982).

This model would suggest that Joe's nonautomatic cognitive processes had been effectively engaged at the beginning of the party. However, at some point in the night Joe may have become distracted (i.e., depressed, anxious, sexually preoccupied), at the expense of his focus on abstinence. This distraction, coupled with conducive conditions and availability of the drug, subsequently precipitated a relapse.

ASSESSMENT AND METHODOLOGICAL ISSUES

The determinants and models of relapse presented here provide information and theoretical frameworks of use in describing, understanding, and possibly predicting relapse among psychoactive substance users who are able to initiate abstinence. Each of the models has demonstrated some degree of construct and predictive validity. Still, future research is necessary, along with improved methodology, to improve current models (Connors, Maisto, & Donovan, 1996) to where they will be of applied use in reducing substance abuse relapse. A number of possible limitations exist regarding current and past research on relapse. Donovan (1996) delineates a variety of possible shortcomings. These include (1) definition of relapse, (2) retrospective versus prospective studies, and (3) single versus multiple determinants. These limitations are pervasive throughout the relapse literature.

DEFINITION

The ninth edition of *Webster's English Dictionary* defines the term *relapse* as follows: (1) the act or an instance of backsliding, worsening, or subsiding; (2) a recurrence of symptoms of a disease after a period of improvement; (3) to slip or fall backward into a former worse state. According to these definitions, the term *relapse* connotes simply a step backwards. The definitions do not clarify (1) how much of a backslide is necessary, (2) how many symptoms are required, or (3) what exactly characterizes a "worse state."

This lack of definitional clarity is equally evident in the variety of meanings given the term in the available literature (Chiauzzi, 1991; Litman, 1986; Marlatt, 1985; Shiffman, 1982; and Wilson, 1978). Examples of these include: (1) a process that leads to substance use; (2) a discrete event marked by the first use in a particular amount of time; (3) returning to the same intensity of use; (4) daily use for a number of consecutive days; (5) a consequence of substance use requiring treatment; (6) substance use that results in a loss of control (Donovan, 1996). As discussed earlier, Marlatt (1985) has offered a definitional distinction between the terms *lapse* and relapse, with the former referring to the first use after a period of abstinence, and the latter to a full return to chronic use.

This lack of agreement on a definition of relapse is a significant obstacle in evaluating the literature on relapse models. According to Miller, Westerberg, Harris, and Tonigan (1996), different individual determinants may be predictive depending on the differing outcomes associated with the divergent connotations of relapse (e.g., complete abstinence, asymptomatic use, reduced but problematic drinking, or unremitted impairment).

Donovan (1996) points out that the definition of relapse has implications regarding (1) determination of base rates of relapse and (2) conceptualization and methodology involved in assessment and prediction models. With regard to assessment models, a relatively static assessment model might be sufficient to examine relapse when it is conceptualized as a discrete event. One could merely collect a number of measures at baseline and from these attempt to predict outcome (relapse). This would, according to Donovan (1996), similarly be true if the information collected were of immediate precipitants to relapse rather than historical information. Alternatively, if relapse is conceptualized as the end point in a process (Marlatt, 1985, Litman, 1986), then such static assessments would not be sufficient. Instead, such processes would require more dynamic assessment models, which could measure specific components of the process at different points in time.

Miller (1996) asserts that the term *relapse* "serves no useful diagnostic purpose." He suggests that conceptualizing relapse as a binary or dichotomous event is both arbitrary and misleading. Although he accepts that it is useful in developing binary outcome taxonomies, Miller posits that "dichotomy, be it diagnostic or descriptive, belies the longitudinal complexity of addictive behaviors." Indeed, it is well accepted that dichotomizing outcomes often leads to significant loss of information. Miller further showed that the binary conceptualization of relapse may actually be harmful. Believing that there are only two states of substance use (abstinence or out-of-control use) may lead individuals to interpret a slip as a complete failure. According to Marlatt's abstinence violation effect (1985), this may result in a true relapse or a return to baseline substance use.

PROSPECTIVE VERSUS RETROSPECTIVE DESIGNS

A second critical issue and limitation for research on relapse is the overreliance on retrospective assessment. Indeed, most relapse models rely on a client's retrospective self-report of the antecedents to their relapse. The resulting data are thus vulnerable to a number of biases, including memory errors and self-presentation distortions (Brandon et al., 1987). Relapses, according to Marlatt (1978), tend to be traumatic events associated with significant feelings of failure and guilt. Individuals who relapse may try to make retrospective sense of their transgressions, and thus they may be prone to remembering negative precipitants of the relapse (O'Doherty & Davies, 1987).

Although relapse has consistently been found to be associated with negative mood states like depression, loneliness, anger, frustration, and guilt, the retrospective nature of most of the supporting studies makes these findings difficult to interpret (Litman et al., 1979; Marlatt & Gordon, 1985). Without benefit of prospective data, all that is known is that negative mood states covary with relapse (Hodgins, el-Guebaly, & Armstrong, 1995). A variety of stressors may be caused or increased by a relapse to substance abuse, and any of these may, over time, be falsely interpreted as causes of relapse. Additionally, large amounts of alcohol or other psychoactive substances may elicit negative mood states. Correlation is not causation, however, and an effect should not be misconstrued as a determinant.

Evidence also exists for a mood-congruent memory bias (Blaney, 1986). According to this research, depressed individuals are more likely or show a bias to recall recent negative events (Hodgins, el-Guebaly, & Armstrong, 1995). In other words, inducing negative mood states can cause individuals to recall more negative life events and depressive symptomatology rather than induce positive mood states. Similarly, individuals who are suffering the depressogenic effects of considerable substance use are likely to overendorse negative recent events/precipitants, particularly on self-report measures.

In his review of assessment issues and domains in the prediction of relapse, Donovan (1996) delineates five specific factors that may contribute to inaccurate classification of true relapse precipitants. These are as follows: (1) In accordance with attribution theory, individuals may externalize failures and internalize successes. This may lead to an overidentification of external, nonpersonal precipitants to relapse. (2) Alcohol and other psychoactive substances are known to diminish information processing and short- and long-term memory, reducing the overall verity of self-reported precipitants. (3) Intoxication may cause individuals to catastrophize, which may cause individuals to attribute their relapse to negative mood states. (4) Recalled precipitants may be skewed by the depression, guilt, and overall dissonance theorized to accompany the abstinence violation effect. (5) Finally, in accordance with the AVE, patients tend to blame themselves and their lack of self-efficacy for the relapse.

SINGLE VERSUS MULTIPLE AND INTERACTIVE DETERMINANTS

The last major limitation of many of the models and research efforts embodied in the relapse literature is the overreliance on unidimensional and univariate assessment processes. For example, Marlatt's relapse taxonomy system is mutually exclusive. This permits only one precipitant to relapse to be identified. This precipitant is the one closest in time to the actual relapse occurrence. Although Marlatt's theory of the relapse process has more breadth and incorporates emotional states; social and interpersonal context; the availability, adequacy, and volition to employ coping skills; and the individual's sense of self-efficacy, the more reductionistic taxonomy is the model used for assessment in much of his research. According to Donovan (1996), relying solely on immediate precipitants because of their temporal proximity may lead to the false assumptions that they are the "real" or "primary" causes of outcome, and that more distal factors are less or not significant determinants.

Shiffman (1989) recommends a multilayer assessment to reliably predict relapse, asserting that models cannot rely on only one level, disregarding others. According to Donovan (1988), Marlatt's relapse taxonomy requires expansion to permit the incorporation of multiple variables exerting different degrees of influence across a range of time, varying in overall proximity to the relapse. Shiffman's (1989) three-tier approach to the assessment of precipitants to relapse. Precipitants include (1) identification of distal personological characteristics, (2) intermediate or background factors that may change over time, and (3) immediately proximal precipitants, which occur immediately prior to the relapse.

CONCLUSION

Clearly, a combination of factors contributes to the process of relapse. We have organized these factors into personological, pharmacological/physiological, and environmental categories in delineating their relation to relapse. We have also reviewed various models of relapse, each rooted in specific theories of human behavior. Given the large number of models that propose to explain the relapse process, it is likely that many of these models contain elements that may serve specific functions in the relapse process. We believe it is necessary to integrate various models in developing a comprehensive and potentially empirically supported explanation of the relapse process. Most models have generated some degree of empirical support, yet they fail to account for large percentages of variance in outcome. Each model must now integrate and incorporate features of other approaches in order to extend their overall value in understanding, describing, and predicting relapse-related behaviors. Integration of multiple factors, including psychological, environmental, and physiological ones, would be consistent with the biopsychosocial zeitgeist. Finally, studies are needed to address limitations regarding the lack of clarity around an operational definition of relapse, the need to replace retrospective with prospective studies, and the need to expand a vision that includes multiple determinants of relapse.

References

Adinoff, B., O'Neill, H. K., & Ballenger, J. C. (1995). Alcohol withdrawal and limbic kindling: A hypothesis of relapse. *American Journal on Addictions, 4*, 5–17.

Bandura, A. (1977). Self-efficacy: Toward a unifying theory of behavioral change. *Psychological Review, 84*, 191–215.

Bandura, A. (1984). Recycling misconceptions of perceived self-efficacy. *Cognitive Therapy and Research, 8*, 231–255.

Bandura, A. (1986). *Social foundations of thought and action.* Englewood Cliffs, N.J.: Prentice-Hall.

Blaney, P. H. (1986). Affect and memory: A review. *Psychological Bulletin, 99*, 229–246.

Bliss, R. A., Garvey, A. J., Heinold, J. W., & Hitchock, J. L. (1989). The influence of situation and coping on relapse crisis outcomes after smoking cessation. *Journal of Consulting and Clinical Psychology, 57*, 3, 443–449.

Brandon, T. H., Tiffany, S. T., & Baker, T. B. (1987). Characterization of the process of smoking relapse. In F. Tims & C. Leukefeld (eds.), *Relapse recovery in drug abuse* (National Institute on Drug Abuse Research Monograph, *72*, 104–117.

Brownell, K. D., Marlatt, G. A., Lichtenstein, E., & Wilson, G. T. (1986). Understanding and preventing relapse. *American Psychologist, 41* (7), 765–782.

Chiauzzi, E. J. (1991). *Preventing Relapse in Addictions: A Biopychosocial Approach,* New York: Pergamon Press.

Connors, G. J., Longabaugh, R., & Miller, W. R. (1996). Looking forward and back to relapse: implications for research and practice. *Addiction, 91*, S191–S196.

Connors, G. J., Maisto, S. A., & Donovan, D. M. (1996). Conceptualizations of relapse: A summary of psychological and psychobiological models. *Addiction, 91*, S5–S13.

Connors, G. J., Maisto, S. A., & Zywiak, W. H. (1996). Understanding relapse in the broader context of post-treatment functioning. *Addiction, 91*, S173–S189.

Cronkite, R. C., & Moos, R. H. (1980). Determinants of the posttreatment functioning of alcoholic patients: A conceptual framework. *Journal of Consulting and Clinical Psychology, 45*, 305–316.

Donovan, D. M. (1988). Assessment of addictive behaviors: implications of an emerging biopsychosocial model, in: Donovan, D. M., & Marlatt, G. A. (eds.) *Assessment of Addictive Behaviours,* New York, Guilford, pp. 3–48.

Donovan, D. M. (1996). Marlatt's classification of relapse precipitants: Is the emperor still wearing clothes? *Addiction, 91*, S131–137.

Donovan, D. M., & Chaney, E. (1985). Alcoholic relapse prevention and intervention: Models and methods. In Marlatt, G. A., & Gordon, J. R. (eds.), *Relapse prevention: Maintenance strategies in the treatment of addictive behaviors.* New York: Guilford.

Emrick, C. D. (1974). A review of psychologically oriented treatment of alcoholism. *Quarterly Journal of Studies on Alcohol, 35,* 523–549.

Gorski, T. T. & Miller, M. (1979). *Counseling for Relapse Prevention* (Hazel Creste, IL, Alcoholism Systems Associates).

Heather, N., Stallard, A., & Tebbutt, J. (1991). Importance of substance cues in relapse among heroin users: Comparison of two methods of investigation. *Addictive Behaviors, 16,* 41–49.

Hill, M. J., & Blane, H. T. (1967). Evaluation of psychotherapy with alcoholics: A critical review. *Quarterly Journal of Studies on Alcohol, 28,* 76–104.

Hinson, R. E., & Siegel, S. (1980). The contribution of Pavlovian conditioning to ethanol tolerance and dependence. In H. Rigter & J. Crabbe, Jr. (eds.), *Alcohol tolerance and dependence.* Amsterdam: Elsevier.

Hodgins, D. C., el-Guebaly, N., & Armstrong, S. (1995). Prospective and retrospective reports of mood states before relapse to substance use. *Journal of Consulting and Clinical Psychology, 63*(3), 400–407.

Hunt, W. A., Barnett, L. W., & Branch, L. G. (1971). Relapse rates in addiction programs. *Journal of Clinical Psychology, 27,* 455–456.

Hunt, W. A., & Matarazzo, J. D. (1973). Three years later: Recent developments in the experimental modification of smoking behavior, *Journal of Abnormal Psychology, 81,* 107–114.

Jellinek, E. M. (1960). *The disease concept of alcholism.* New Haven: Hillhouse.

Litman, G. K. (1980). Relapse in alcoholism: Traditional and current approaches. In G. Edwards & M. Grant (eds.). *Alcoholism treatment in transition.* London: Croom Helm.

Litman, G. K. (1986). Alcoholism survival: The prevention of relapse. In W. K. Miller & N. Heather (eds.), *Treating addictive behaviors,* 391–405.

Litman, G. K., Eiser, J. R., Rawson, N. S. B., & Oppenheim, A. N. (1979). Differences in relapse precipitants and coping behavior between alcohol relapsers and survivors. *Behavior Research and Therapy, 17,* 89–94.

Ludwig, A. M., & Stark, L. M. (1974). Alcohol craving: Subjective and situational aspects. *Quarterly Journal of Studies on Alcohol, 35,* 899–905.

Ludwig, A. M., Wikler, A., & Stark, L. M. (1974). The first drink: Psychobiological aspects of craving. *Archives of General Psychiatry, 30,* 539–547.

Marlatt, G. A. (1978). Craving for alcohol, loss of control and relapse: A cognitive-behavioral analysis. In P. E. Nathan, G. A. Marlatt, & T. Loberg (eds.), *Alcohol-*

ism: New directions in behavioral research and treatment (pp. 227–314). New York: Plenum.

Marlatt, G. A. (1985). Relapse prevention: Theoretical rationale and overview of the model. In G. A. Marlatt & J. R. Gordon, (eds.), *Relapse prevention: Maintenance strategies in the treatment of addictive behaviors.* New York: Guilford.

Marlatt, G. A. (1985) Cognitive factors in the relapse process. In G. A. Marlatt & J. R. Gordon (Eds.) *Relapse prevention: Maintenance Strategies in the treatment of addictive behaviors.* New York: Guilford.

Marlatt, G. A. (1996). Taxonomy of high-risk situations for alcohol relapse, *Addiction, 91.* S37–S50.

Marlatt, G. A., & Gordon, J. R. (1980). Determinants of relapse: Implications for the maintenance of behavior change. In P. Davidson & S. M. Davidson (eds.), *Behavioral medicine: Changing health lifestyles.* (pp. 1410–1452) New York: Brunner/Mazel.

Marlatt, G. A., & Gordon, J. R. (1985). *Relapse Prevention: Maintenance Strategies in the Treatment of Addictive Behaviors.* (New York: Guilford).

Miller, W. R. (1996). What is relapse? Fifty ways to leave the wagon, *Addiction, 91:* S15–S28.

Miller, W. R., & Rollnick, S. (1991). *Motivational Interviewing: Preparing people for change in addictive behavior.* New York: Guilford.

Miller, W. R., Westenberg, V. S., Harris, R. J., & Tonigan, J. S. (1996). What predicts relapse? Prospective testing of antecedent models. *Addiction, 91,* S155–S171.

Mossberg, D., Liljeberg, P., & Borg, S. (1985). Clinical conditions in alcoholics during long-term abstinence: A descriptive, longitudinal treatment study. *Alcohol, 2,* 551–553.

Niaura, R. S., Rosenhow, D. J., Binkoff, J. A., Monti, P. M., Pedraza, M., & Abrams, D. B. (1988). Relevance of cue reactivity to understanding alcohol and smoking relapse. *Journal of Abnormal Psychology, 97,* 123–152.

O'Doherty, F., & Davies, J. B. (1987). Life events and addiction: A critical review. *British Journal of Addiction, 82,* 127–137.

O'Farrell, T. J., & Cutter, H. S. G. (1996). Expressed emotion and relapse in alcoholic patients. Poster presented at the 30th annual meeting of the Association for the Advancement of Behavior Therapy. New York, N.Y., November 21–24.

Pomerleau, O. F., Adkins, D. E., & Pertschuk, M. (1978). Predictors of outcome and recidivism in smoking cessation treatment. *Addictive Behaviors, 3,* 65–70.

Poulos, C. X., Hinton, R. E., & Siegel, S. (1981). The role of Pavlovian processes in drug tolerance and dependence: Implications for treatment. *Addictive Behaviors, 6,* 205–212.

Prochaska, J. O., & DiClemente, C. C. (1982). Transtheoretical therapy: Toward a more integrated model of change. *Psychotherapy: Theory, Research, and Practice, 19,* 276–288.

Roehling, P. V., & Goldman, M. S. (1987). Alcohol expectancies and their relationship to actual drinking experiences. *Psychology of Addictive Behaviors, 1,* 108–113.

Roelofs, S. M. & Dikkenberg, G. M. (1987). Hyperventilation and anxiety: alcohol withdrawal symptoms decreasing with prolonged abstinence, *Alcohol, 4,* 215–220.

Sanchez-Craig, M. (1976). Cognitive and behavioral coping strategies in the reappraisal of stressful social situations. *Journal of Counseling Psychology, 23*(1), 7–12.

Seligman, M. E. P. (1975). *Helplessness: On depression, development, and death.* San Francisco: Freeman.

Shiffman, S. M. (1982). Relapse following smoking cessation: A situational analysis. *Journal of Consulting and Clinical Psychology, 50,* 71–86.

Siegel, S. (1983). Classical conditioning, drug tolerance, and drug dependence. In R.G. Smart, F. B. Glaser, Y. Isreal, et al. (eds.), *Research advances in alcohol and drug problems,* vol. 7, New York: Plenum.

Solomon, K. E., & Annis, H. M. (1989). Development of a scale to measure outcome expectancy in alcoholics. *Cognitive Therapy and Research, 13,* 409–420.

Solomon, R. L. (1980). The opponent-process theory of acquired motivation. *American Psychologist, 35*(8), 691–712.

Stewart, J., de Wit, H., & E. Kolboom, R. (1984). The role of conditioned and unconditioned drug effects in the self-administration of opiates and stimulants, *Psychological Review, 91,* 251–268.

Stotts, A. L., DiClemente, C. C., Carbonari, J. P., & Dolan-Mullen, P. (1996). Stages of change and pregnancy smoking cessation: The prediction of postpartum relapse. Poster presented at the 30th annual meeting of the Association for the Advancement of Behavior Therapy. New York, N.Y., November 21–24.

Tiffany, S. (1990). A cognitive model of drug urges and drug-use behavior: Role of automatic and nonautomatic processes. *Psychological Review, 97*(2), 147–168.

Wikler, A. (1980). *Opioid dependence: Mechanisms and treatment.* New York: Plenum.

Wilson, G. T. (1978). Booze, beliefs, and behavior: Cognitive processes in alcohol use and abuse. In P. E. Nathan, G. A. Marlatt, & T. Loberg (eds.). *Alcoholism: New directions in behavioral research and treatment.* New York: Plenum.

Wise, R. A. (1988). The neurobiology of craving: Implications for the understanding and treatment of addiction. *Journal of Abnormal Psychology, 97,* 118–132.

SEVEN

THE ROLE OF MOTIVATION AND READINESS IN TREATMENT AND RECOVERY

George De Leon, Gerald Melnick, & Frank M. Tims

Substance abuse is a complex problem involving numerous subpopulations and comorbidities. Researchers have attempted to provide a general recovery-stage model that formulates a common process. Motivation for change is an underlying dynamic variable believed to dominate the early stages of such recovery-stage models. Clinicians have long recognized the importance of motivational and readiness factors in recovery from chemical dependency, and within the past decade or so several lines of inquiry have empirically established the relevance of these factors for both treatment and recovery. Stages of Change formulations have generated studies related to motivation and readiness, particularly in the areas of smoking cessation and control of alcoholism. Clinical research on motivational enhancement strategies has demonstrated efficacy in engaging resistant clients in the treatment process.

Recent research on treatments for abusers of illicit substances has clarified the importance of motivation in retention and outcomes in the treatment process. This line of inquiry reflects the systematic accrual of empirically based knowledge from mulitmodality and program-based treatment evaluation studies (see Anglin & Hser, 1990; Platt, 1995; Simpson, 1993; Simpson, Joe, & Brown, 1997; De Leon, 1993). These studies have documented the effectiveness of drug treatment in terms of reductions in drug use, crime, improved employment, and psychological status, and it has demonstrated the relation between retention and posttreatment outcomes. The motivational studies logically derived from the need to improve retention, matching the client to treatment setting, and our understanding of the treatment process.

In this chapter we illuminate the current status of motivational and readiness factors in treatment and recovery by reviewing theoretical formulations and developing research. The extensive clinical and research literature on the general topic of motivation among substance users is much beyond our focus here. We make limited reference to the writings on the concept, sources, or types of motivation. Miller (1983) provides a comprehensive review of early literature surveying perspectives on motivation, trait theory, therapist perceptions, and determinants of motivation, noting that these areas have been separated from treatment.

The research on expectancy and self-efficacy research is also not discussed in this chapter. Although there may be relationships between expectancy and motivation, the two concepts remain distinct as do their measures. Beliefs about such outcomes as self-change (expectancy) differ from the components of such motivations as problem recognition, desire for change, and readiness to engage in the actions that produce change.

The initial section clarifies the motivational construct in the context of current recovery-stage formulations. The second section reviews empirical findings on motivation and readiness, drawn primarily from the aforementioned three lines of inquiry, stage formulations, motivational enhancement, and studies in the major federally funded drug treatment modalities. The final section discusses clinical and research issues to further illuminate the role of motivation in recovery.

TREATMENT AND RECOVERY

Some clarification of terms is needed to interpret the theoretical and empirical material discussed in relation to motivation and readiness. These involve conceptual distinctions between treatment and recovery, rehabilitation, and within the motivational construct itself.

Treatments consist of the various strategies or interventions employed to assist individuals in reducing or eliminating their substance-use problems. Treatments are formal in that they are typically medical, mental health, and social services implemented in particular settings and in prescribed ways. The *treatment process* refers to how individuals change in relation to the various intervention or assistance strategies.

Recovery refers to a continuing process of individual change from active use or addiction to maintained abstinence. The recovery process may or may not include formal treatment. A further distinction is needed between recovery, rehabilitation, and habilitation. Recovery is a medically derived term that refers to overcoming a disease or disorder like chemical dependency; it is usually measured in terms of relapse or maintained abstinence.

Rehabilitation and habilitation imply broader changes. Rehabilitation refers to repair of, or return to, a functional lifestyle unimpeded by drug use; habilitation involves learning a functional lifestyle for the first time. The three terms are related in that sustained recovery may require the changes associated with rehabilitation and/or habilitation, and achieving the latter requires continued abstinence. The role of motivation/readiness in treatment, recovery, rehabilitation, and habilitation needs to be theoretically and empirically clarified.

THE MOTIVATIONAL CONSTRUCT

Two basic types of motivation, external and internal, have an impact on recovery from substance abuse. External motivation is generally defined as perceived outside pressures or coercion to change, or to enter and/or remain in treatment. The sources of coercion are usually legal, family, or employment pressures, although health concerns may also qualify. Internal motivation refers to pressures to change that arise from within the individual. These pressures are typically negative self-perceptions concerning drug use, and the desire for a more fulfilling lifestyle.

The research on extrinsic motivation has been largely confined to studies of legal pressure (see reviews in Leukefeld & Tims, 1988; Platt, 1995). Generally, these studies bear out the importance of external motivation as a predictor of treatment retention and outcomes. Consistent findings support relations between legal pressure and retention in therapeutic communities (TCs) (Condelli, 1986; De Leon, 1988; Hubbard, Collins, Rachal, & Cavanaugh, 1988; Pompi & Resnick, 1987; Sansome, 1980; Sheffet et al., 1980; Siddall & Conway, 1988; Siddiqui, 1989; Vickers-Lahti et al., 1995). Studies in other modalities report similar findings (e.g., Anglin, Brecht, & Maddahian, 1989; Hubbard, Collins, Rachal, and Cavanaugh, 1988; Collins & Allison, 1983; Gerstein & Harwood, 1990; Platt et al., 1988; Desmond & Maddux, 1996).

The research on family and employment pressures is less conclusive with respect to motivation. Though limited, these studies do support the clinical conclusion that family and job pressures can be effective in influencing treatment seeking and program retention (e.g., Condelli, 1986; Deitch & Zweben, 1996; Biase, Sullivan, & Wheeler, 1986).

Studies of internal motivation have utilized various ways of assessing motivation, including unstructured interviews, questionnaires, and scales.

Nevertheless, they reveal consistent findings with respect to the reasons for self-quitting drug use or seeking drug treatment. These reasons are broadly classified into the perceived negative consequences of drug use and the fatigue with the drug-abuse lifestyle (Cunningham, Sobell, Sobell, & Gaskin, 1994; Joe, Chastain, & Simpson, 1990). Typical examples include the realization of being addicted, health fears, the need to reduce a chaotic lifestyle, "hitting bottom or wearing out," or simply the sum of negative experiences (e.g., Crawford, Washington, & Senay, 1983; Mann, Charavustra, & Murphy, 1984; Murphy, Bentall, & Owens, 1989; Varney et al., 1995).

The positive internal motivators for quitting drugs, like the desire for better relationships or other positive consequences, have not been similarly addressed. One positive motivator, however, the extent of commitment to abstinence, has been shown to predict abstinence among alcoholics, opiate abusers, and cigarette smokers (Hall, Havassy, & Wasserman, 1990). In a large-scale European study, a measure of "future orientation" was viewed as a positive element correlated with readiness to renounce drug use (Zimmer-Hoefler & Meyer-Fehr, 1986).

Research has mainly addressed the separate effects of external and internal motivation, although a few studies have examined their relative contributions to both treatment and recovery. These studies reveal that internal motivation is more important than external pressures in smoking cessation (Curry, Wagner, & Grothaus, 1990), response to alcohol treatment (Ryan, Plant, & O'Malley, 1995), commitment to renounce drugs (Zimmer-Hoefler & Meyer-Fehr, 1986), retention in a TC (Siddiqui, 1989), and seeking referral services (Melnick, De Leon, & Zingaro, 1996).

Regardless of the initial source of motivation, external or internal, stable recovery appears to depend on the continuing influences of intrinsic motivational factors (e.g., Cunningham, Sobell, Sobell, and Gaskin, 1994; Curry, Wagner, & Grothaus, 1990; Deci & Ryan, 1985, De Leon, 1988; Zimmer-Hoefler & Meyer-Fehr, 1986). Although external pressure may influence internal motivation, it cannot substitute for it in the recovery process. Overall, the research on external and internal motivation clarifies the motivational construct with respect to treatment and recovery. External motivation is more adequately characterized as external *pressure* to further distinguish it from the internal motivational variables underlying recovery. These variables refer to certain cognitions and perceptions expressed in self-statements concerning changing drug-use behaviors. Thus the cognitive/perceptual elements of motivation (e.g., "tired of the drug life") are separate from the behavioral elements of motivation (seeking treatment). This distinction underlies the components of the motivational construct that have been identified in the stage formulations and related research discussed below.

MOTIVATION AND RECOVERY STAGE FORMULATIONS

Much of the recent research on motivation has been generated by theoretical formulations of the role of motivation in the recovery process. There is no single or unified theory of recovery for substance abuse, although there are various recovery perspectives that derive from clinical experience and some research in several areas. Some examples of these are twelve-step approaches (e.g., Alcoholics Anonymous), the therapeutic community view of recovery (e.g., De Leon, 1993; De Leon, 1995; De Leon & Ziegenfuss, 1986; De Leon & Rosenthal, 1989), neurobehavioral programming (e.g., Rawson, Shoptaw, Obert, & McCann, 1995), recovery training (Zackon, McAuliffe, & Chien, 1985), relapse prevention (Marlatt & Gordon, 1985), and Stages of Change (e.g., Gorski, 1989; Prochaska, DiClemente, & Norcross, 1992).

These different perspectives converge on a developmental view of change or recovery that depicts the abuser/addict as moving from a status of active use and problem denial to one of stabilized abstinence and longer-term maintenance of a drug-free status. Progress is directional but erratic, marked by backward and forward steps. Various substages of recovery are characterized in behavioral and cognitive terms. Specific treatment interventions or assistance may be employed to move the client to the next stage of treatment or recovery, although the change process can occur without these interventions. Although each of these theories differs in important respects, a consistent developmental theme emerges that stresses the importance of motivation as a precursor to taking steps toward abstinence in the early stages of recovery.

Empirical support for the recovery perspective is developing in research from different areas of addiction, like treatments for smoking and obesity (e.g., Prochaska, DiClemente, & Norcross, 1992); alcohol treatment (e.g., Miller & Hester, 1986); relapse prevention for alcohol problems (e.g., Marlatt & Gordon, 1985); outpatient treatment for cocaine and opiate abuse (e.g., Rawson, Shoptaw, Obert, and McCann, 1995); and the treatment process in residential therapeutic communities for opiate, cocaine, and other drug abusers (e.g., De Leon & Rosenthal, 1989; De Leon, 1993).

Tables 7.1 and 7.2 summarize the elements of two different stage perspectives that have guided recent research on motivation. The Stages of Change model (Prochaska, DiClemente, & Norcross, 1992) is a transtheoretical model of the change process that represents both dynamic and motivational aspects of the change process. The model has been applied to smokers (e.g., Glynn,

Table 7.1: The Stages of Change

---

1. *Precontemplation:* Ignorant of problem or unwilling to change.

2. *Contemplation:* Thinking seriously about change and engaged in making a decision based on an evaluation of the pros and cons of problem behavior and the change.

3. *Preparation:* Resolution of the decision-making process and commitment to a plan of action to be implemented in the near future.

4. *Action:* The change plan is implemented and the behavior is changed.

5. *Maintenance:* This stage is achieved when the action plan has been sustained successfully for three to six months. Stages terminate when change is integrated into lifestyle.

Based on DiClemente & Prochaska, in press.

Boyd, & Gruman, 1990); weight control (e.g., Prochaska et al., 1992); and alcoholism (Institute of Medicine, 1989) but has yet to be adequately studied for other substance abusers, particularly opioid and cocaine abusers.

The Integrated Recovery model (De Leon, 1996) is a ten-stage paradigm describing the recovery process of serious substance abusers treated in long-term TCs. The motivational and readiness stages of this model have been the subject of developing research in the areas of treatment entry, retention, and outcomes as well as treatment process in residential TCs and in other modalities.

MOTIVATION AND THE STAGES OF CHANGE

Although the Stages of Change are described in terms of their discrete characteristics, recent research in alcoholism has begun to focus on the importance of a continuous underlying motivational variable. The central instrument for the Stages of Change consists of a basic algorithm that has proven sufficient for discriminating the various stages over a wide range of individuals. However, when more homogeneous groups, such as admissions to treatment programs, are examined, the algorithm fails to recognize those who are likely to show greater compliance with treatment or better treatment outcomes (DiClemente & Prochaska, in press). In addition to the algorithm, several objective instruments have been developed to place individuals within a specific stage. Factor analytic studies, however, have consistently failed to confirm the existence of the separate stages.

Table 7.2. The TC Stages of Integrative Recovery

Pretreatment Stages

1. *Denial:* Active abuse and/or associated problems, with no problem recognition or problem acceptance.

2. *Ambivalence:* Some problem recognition, but inconsistent acceptance of the consequences of continued use on self and others

3. *Motivation (Extrinsic):* Some recognition and acceptance of drug use and associated problems, but it is attributed to external influences and not seen as reason for seeking change.

4. *Motivation (Intrinsic):* Acceptance of drug use as a central problem, and recognition of associated problems.

5. *Readiness for Change:* Willingness to seek change options that are not treatment related. In this stage individuals are intrinsically motivated but have not actually accepted the necessity for treatment.

6. *Readiness for Treatment:* Rejection of all other options for change except treatment.

Treatment-Related Stages

7. *Deaddiction:* Detachment from active drug use, pharmacological and behavioral detoxification.

8. *Abstinence:* Stabilized drug freedom for a continuous period, usually beyond the individual's longest historical period of drug freedom.

9. *Continuance:* Sobriety plus personal resolve to acquire or maintain the behavior, attitudes, and values, associated with drug-free lifestyle.

10. *Integration and Identity Change:* The interrelation of treatment influences, recovery stage experiences, and broader life experiences resulting in self-perceived change in social and personal identity.

Based on De Leon, 1996.

The Readiness to Change Questionnaire (RTCQ) was developed for use with alcohol abusers in general medical settings. The instrument consists of three factored subscales that can be used to place individuals at the precontemplation, contemplation, and action stages (Rollnick, Heather, Gold, & Hall, 1992) and successfully predicts reduced drinking among alcoholic abusers in the action stage (Heather, Rollnick, & Bell, 1993). Like the basic Stages of Change algorithm, however, the RTCQ does not reliably differentiate among admissions to alcohol treatment programs, nor does it retain the same factor structure corresponding to the three identified stages of change (Gavin, Sobel, & Sobel, 1994).

Two other instruments have been developed to differentiate stages of change among admissions to treatment programs. The Stages of Change Readiness and Treatment Eagerness (SOCRATES) was developed specifically for alcohol abuse (Miller & Tonigan, 1996). Although the items were developed in reference to the Stages of Change model, factor analysis yielded three rather than the expected five dimensions. Instead of measuring the stage constructs, these new scales appear to measure continuously distributed motivation processes. Isenhart (1994) similarly found three subgroups using the SOCRATES.

The University of Rhode Island Change Assessment scale (URICA) was developed to further operationally define the stages of change. A factor analysis failed to confirm the five stages, however, and cluster analyses yielded as many as seven to nine different clusters (McConnaughy, Prochaska, & Velicer, 1983; McConnaughy, DiClemente, Prochaska, & Velicer, 1989). A cluster analysis has yielded a typology based on alcohol abusers entering treatment consisting of five profiles: precontemplation, ambivalent, participation, uninvolved, and contemplation. Four of these clusters were later confirmed by Carney and Kivlahan (1996).

Thus, the relation between the clusters and the stages is complex. The clusters do not yield groups in concordance with the stages, and they cannot be used to reliably place individuals within stages (DiClemente & Prochaska, in press). Furthermore, in tests with polydrug users the URICA failed to demonstrate the same factor structure as in earlier studies (Belding, Iguchi, & Lamb, 1996). This study found that the Stages of Change algorithm and URICA may measure different phenomena. Recently published findings from Project MATCH (1997) utilized an aggregate score from the URICA to determine an overall measure of motivation. This measure demonstrated a consistently linear relation between motivation and treatment outcome among outpatients. Although motivation was not a predictor among clients entering aftercare following residential treatment, the authors note that low-motivated clients would likely not have completed the inpatient program, so the sample of completers most likely represents a truncated group of highly motivated clients. Thus, much of the research designed to assess the stages reflects the role of continuously distributed motivational variables.

MOTIVATION/READINESS STUDIES IN METHADONE MAINTENANCE AND THERAPEUTIC COMMUNITIES

The research on motivational factors among abusers of illicit substances in the federally funded treatment programs emerged from studies of client predictors of retention and outcomes and subsequently from investigations of treatment process. This section reviews two ongoing research programs in methadone maintenance and therapeutic communities that are systematically investigating the role of motivation and readiness factors in drug treatment.

The studies at Texas Christian University (TCU) by Simpson and associates and at the Center for Therapeutic Community Research (CTCR) by De Leon and colleagues have utilized similar constructs, operational definitions, and measurement and analytical strategies. The focus of the work has been to clarify the contribution of the motivational factor to retention, outcomes, and the treatment process.

THE CTCR STUDIES

Studies at the Center for Therapeutic Community Research (CTCR) have provided a theoretical framework and an instrument (the Circumstances, Motivation, and Readiness, or CMR) for assessing three components of the motivational construct: circumstances, motivation, and readiness. The psychometric properties of these scales are sound, and their predictive validity is now well established. CMR data have been obtained on several thousand admissions to residential therapeutic communities, outpatient settings, and special populations including adolescents, mentally ill chemical abusers, and criminal justice clients (Melnick, 1999).

The CMR Intake Version is an 18-item factored version of the original 42-item CMRS (e.g., De Leon & Jainchill, 1986; De Leon, Melnick, Kressel, & Jainchill, 1994). The CMR is derived from confirmatory factor analysis with studies of drug abusers in long-term residential TCs, drug-free outpatients, and patients in methadone maintenance treatment. The instrument is self-administered and employs Likert-type items rated on a five-point scale from *strongly disagree* (1) to *strongly agree* (5). The reading level is approximately third grade.

Briefly, confirmatory factor analysis shows four CMR scales: *Circumstances 1 (pressure to enter treatment)* refers to extrinsic reasons to engage in treatment, such as fear of jail or family pressure. *Circumstances 2 (pressure to leave treatment)* refers to external pressure to leave treatment, such as financial problems or family pressure. *Motivation (internal pressures)* refers to intrinsic factors relating to the sense of things getting worse, the fear of hurting others, and the desire for a better life. *Readiness (perceived need for treatment)* refers to the perceived necessity for treatment in order to change. The total CMR score assesses the individual's overall potential, or his or her willingness to enter and stay in treatment.

Studies with nontreatment samples have found lower motivation among drug abusers not entering treatment. Lipton (1991) found lower motivation and readiness scores among non-treatment seekers compared to clients on a TC waiting list. Studies involving homeless women demonstrated that CMRS scores predicted entry into a women's TC (Erickson, Stevens, McKnight, & Figuerodo, 1995).

Prediction studies of retention in TCs have demonstrated consistent linear relations between CMRS scores and remaining in treatment, with high-scoring clients twice as likely to remain in treatment for thirty days or more (De Leon, Melnick, Kressel, & Jainchill, 1994). Separate analyses confirmed these findings for inner-city minority drug abusers (De Leon, Melnick, Shocket, & Jainchill, 1993) and for a range of illicit drugs including cocaine, heroin, and marijuana (De Leon, Melnick, & Kressel, 1997).

Another study of adults and adolescents entering TC residential treatment demonstrated a linear relation between age and motivation, and between motivation and retention at each age level (see fig. 7.1). The findings of this study firmly support the long-held clinical impression that younger substance users are less internally motivated to change than older addicts. Regardless of age, however, higher motivated clients are more likely to stay in treatment (Melnick, De Leon, Hawke, Jainchill, & Kressel, 1997).

More recently, a theoretical formulation has been outlined for interpreting the motivational contribution to the treatment process in TCs (De Leon, 1995; De Leon, 1997). Briefly, all of the activities of the TC, both formal and informal, are viewed as interrelated interventions that address the multidimensional disorder of the "whole person." Meeting community expectations for complete participation in all of the roles and activities of the community facilitates social and psychological changes in the individual.

Within this general theoretical framework, a process formulation has been outlined that consists of a dynamic interaction between the individual and the TC community, its context and expectations. Thus, treatment process can be indirectly investigated in relationships involving client motivation, changes in participation during treatment, and eventual outcomes.

Figure 7.2 illustrates recent findings supporting this formulation obtained

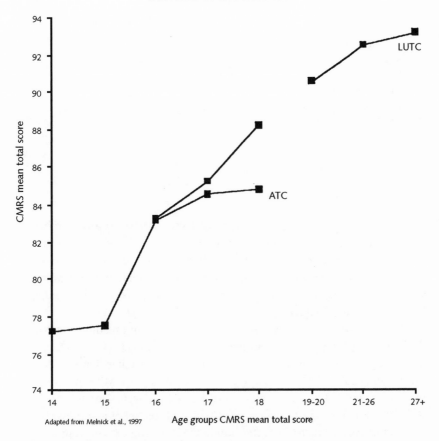

Fig. 7.1. CMRS by age in TC admissions. (LUTC: N = 1,899; ATC: N = 656)

from progress and outcome studies on inmates in prison therapeutic community settings. Motivation showed a direct effect on treatment status (entering postprison aftercare), which in turn demonstrated a direct effect on outcome variables of reincarceration and relapse. There were no direct effects of motivation on the outcome variables. Thus, motivation influenced treatment, which affected outcomes (De Leon, 1997).

THE TCU STUDIES

The TCU research conducted by Dwayne Simpson and associates has focused upon the role of motivation in treatment retention and more recently in the treatment process, particularly in methadone maintenance and other treat-

Chi-square= 0.664; df=1; prob. level=0.415

*   # of days from prison relapse to first incarceration
*   Any drug use within 1 year of prison release

From Melnick & De Leon, 1996.

Fig. 7.2. TC prison program path analyses (N = 279). Relapse to drug use at one year.

ment settings. This research utilizes three factor scales: drug use problems, desire for help, and treatment readiness, which reflect the multidimensional concept of motivation in the CMR and in the Stages of Change. Studies in methadone maintenance have found a relation between high motivation and retention as well as engagement in treatment (Simpson & Joe, 1993; Simpson, Joe, Rowan-Szal, & Greener, 1995).

The TCU studies have also assessed motivational and readiness factors in the large-scale Drug Abuse Treatment Outcome Study (DATOS) of abusers of illicit drugs entering several treatment modalities (Fletcher, Tims, & Brown, 1997; Flynn et al., 1997). Based upon twenty items of the CMRS that were administered in DATOS, three factors were derived that were similar to the TCU scales (problem recognition, desire for help, and treatment readiness). These were significant predictors of retention in DATOS programs in all modalities (Joe, Simpson, & Broome, 1998).

The TCU studies have identified relations between motivation and a number of treatment process variables. Client motivation at intake is associated with therapeutic relationships (Simpson, Joe, Rowan-Szal, & Greener, 1997), more favorable perceptions of counselor competence and support from peers (Broome et al., 1997), and increased session attendance (Simpson, Joe, Rowan-Szal, & Greener, 1997).

Simpson and associates have proposed a general model for treatment process and have focused on measures of client engagement, including attendance, cooperation, dependability, and motivation (Simpson, Joe, & Rowan-Szal, 1997; Joe, Simpson, & Broome, in press). Cognitive strategies, such as node-link mapping (Dansereau, Joe, & Simpson, 1993; Simpson, Joe, & Rowan-Szal, in press)—a system for visually displaying a problem by the relationship between its components on paper—have been found to strengthen the therapeutic relationship between counselor and patient, which led to attendance of a greater number of sessions. Further research identified the influences of motivation and the node-link cognitive mapping procedure on the therapeutic alliance, and the subsequent effect of the alliance on total number of sessions and outcome variables. The investigators conclude that node-link cognitive strategies function as a motivational enhancement in the treatment process.

The models and results in the TCU and CTCR studies converge in illustrating the role of motivational/readiness factors in both retention in treatment and in the treatment process. Although significant, these factors alone explain relatively little variance of outcomes, such as retention or posttreatment status. As the research indicates, motivation interacts with treatment-related interventions, which eventually lead to positive outcomes.

MOTIVATIONAL ENHANCEMENT

The role of motivation in substance users has been considerably illuminated by clinical efforts to enhance motivation for change in general and for treatment in particular. Research focuses on various approaches that directly or indirectly attempt to increase the likelihood that individuals will enter and/or remain in treatment. Prominent among these is the work of Miller and associates, who have developed a collection of counseling strategies termed Motivational Interviewing that have been extensively evaluated (Miller, 1983; Miller & Rollnick, 1991; Miller & Hester, 1986; Rollnick & Morgan, 1995).

Motivational Interviewing emerged in part from a body of research demonstrating the effectiveness of various brief interventions (e.g., psychotherapy, skills training, conditioning) in reducing problem drinking (see review by Miller & Rollnick, 1991, pp. 31–32). These interventions were presumed to be motivational in that they altered decisions and commitments to change. The active elements of these interventions were identified (e.g., feedback, advice, empathy, etc.) and organized into strategies to help people address their ambivalence about change.

The Stages of Change formulation has been utilized to focus the goals and strategies of specific Motivational Interviewing sessions. For example, a cost-benefit analysis of drug abuse is implemented in the precontemplation and contemplation stages, where enhancing motivation is seen as the critical issue. Goals and strategies are stressed for people in the preparation stage, where motivation is perceived as already sufficient and the type of action to be taken becomes the critical issue (Rollnick & Morgan, 1995).

Motivational Interviewing has produced positive effects in the form of increased retention in treating alcoholism (Galbraith, 1989; Miller & Roll-nick, 1991; Bien, Miller, & Boroughs, 1993) and in methadone treatment for opioid abuse (Van Bilsen & Van Emst, 1986). However, some investigators have found it necessary to modify the techniques to incorporate more di-rect approaches when treating more difficult clients (Saunders, Wilkinson & Allsop, 1991).

Clinical applications of Motivational Interviewing are described in Miller and Rollnick (1991). Several of these are particularly relevant to relapse pre-vention (e.g., Allsop & Saunders, 1991) and maintaining client changes (Kent, 1991). Motivational Interviewing is also relevant to recovery theories, such as the Stages of Change (DiClemente, 1991).

Various other approaches are presumed to enhance motivation indirectly. For example, behavioral conditioning techniques such as contingency man-agement are successful in increasing retention in both outpatient (Higgins et al., 1993; Rowan-Szal et al., 1994) and residential settings (Kadden & Mau-riello, 1991). Although not targeted specifically toward altering motivational factors, the effects of these approaches may be mediated by these factors.

The above hypothesis gains support from efforts to enhance retention in a therapeutic community program. These efforts have utilized techniques based on role modeling ("senior professor" group seminars) and focused counseling (e.g., individual and group sessions addressing treatment suit-ability). Research indicates that these interventions can significantly reduce early dropout (De Leon, 1991). Furthermore, the motivational intervention increases retention among the least motivated clients (De Leon, Hawke, Jain-chill, & Melnick, in press). As noted in the TCU studies, the node-link cogni-tive strategies may have functioned indirectly as a motivational enhancement in the treatment process.

MOTIVATION IN RECOVERY: STATUS AND IMPLICATIONS

Motivation and readiness appear to be the most significant *client-related* fac-tors in the recovery process thus far identified by the prediction research. Highly motivated clients are more likely to enter and remain in treatment, which results in better outcomes. Further advances in understanding the role of motivation in treatment and recovery require clarification of several issues. This final section briefly discusses several of these issues that have theoretical and practical, as well as research, implications.

CLARIFYING THE CONTRIBUTION OF MOTIVATION
IN TREATMENT AND RECOVERY

Current research indicates differences in the extent to which motivation contributes directly or indirectly to outcomes. In the TCU and CTCR studies, motivation contributes to outcomes indirectly as a critical variable in the treatment process. Motivation alone explains relatively little of the variance of retention or outcomes but interacts with treatment interventions that lead to positive outcomes.

In various studies grounded in the Stages of Change formulation, however, there appears to be a relatively large direct contribution of motivation to outcomes. For example, the action stage (which implies high readiness for change) predicts cessation of smoking (e.g., Prochaska, DiClemente, & Norcross, 1992). More recently, in Project Match, motivational scores at admission (a single score based on all items of the URICA) predicted improvements incrementally across the months of the posttreatment follow-up period (Project Match, 1997). Project Match did not report on interactions between initial motivation and treatment in the separate 12-Step, Cognitive-Behavioral Therapy, and Motivation Enhancement Therapy conditions, however, which obscures the possible indirect contributions of motivation to outcomes.

Studies are needed to resolve the direct and indirect contribution of motivation to recovery. Research thus far suggests that the role of motivation in recovery reflects a complex interaction between subgroups of substance abusers and treatment intensity. For some substance abusers, high motivation alone will result in positive outcome regardless of treatment intensity; for others high motivation plus some minimal treatment will sustain recovery; and for still others, high motivation plus intense treatment is needed to sustain recovery. For example, the patients in methadone maintenance treatment programs and TCs are chronic abusers of illicit substances, many of whom are socially deviant and psychologically troubled. For these patients, high initial motivation facilitates their engagement in a long and intense treatment that is needed to produce a positive impact. Thus, the TCU and CTCR research underscore the indirect effects of motivation and direct effects of the treatment on outcomes.

In Project Match, the study sample consisted of primary alcoholics without serious psychiatric disorder, illicit drug use, or serious social deviancy. Brief, similar verbal treatments of relatively low intensity (maximum of 12 sessions) were implemented for these highly motivated clients, who volunteered to be research subjects. Not unexpectedly, the results showed uniform reductions in alcohol use across the three comparative treatment conditions. For these clients, initial motivational levels alone, or some (unmeasured) interaction with treatment, remained important in directly predicting outcomes.

COMPONENTS OF THE MOTIVATIONAL CONSTRUCT

Although the utility and validity of the motivational construct has been demonstrated, further clarity is needed with respect to the construct itself. Recovery stage formulations are similar in defining the components of the motivational construct with current measures and instruments showing surprising agreement in yielding two or three factors. In general, these factors relate broadly to the constructs of motivation and readiness in which motivation represents internal motivation to change, and readiness represents a decision to take action.

Motivation and readiness

Generally, recovery theory consistently accounts for two types of influences — motivation to change, and a readiness to take action based on that motivation. In current formulations there is some consensus as to the meaning and measurement of readiness in the recovery process. The concept describes individuals who have problem recognition, want to change, and actively initiate actions needed to change. In the Stages of Change algorithm, the individual advances through the stages from precontemplation to contemplation and then to preparation, moving from being unmotivated to being motivated and finally to formulating a plan of action. The SOCRATES, an instrument based on the Stages of Change model (Miller & Tonigan, 1996), yielded three factors, two of which, ambivalence (contemplation) and recognition (a combination of low precontemplation and high determination/preparation) appear to be related to motivation and readiness for change, respectively. A third factor, taking steps, included action and maintenance items. Isenhart (1994) also identified three subgroups based on the SOCRATES, characterized as uninvolved, ambivalent, and active, of which ambivalent and active appear to refer to motivation and readiness.

In terms of differential effects, Stages of Change research does report distinct outcomes in smoking cessation between those in the action stage and those in earlier stages. The terms motivation and readiness are frequently used interchangeably (e.g., Project Match), however, and few studies have addressed the issue of readiness for treatment as distinct from motivation for change.

It may be possible to detect meaningful differences between these concepts, however. For example, in the report of the DATOS motivational instrument based on the CMRS, readiness was the strongest predictor of retention among admissions to long-term residential and outpatient methadone treatment, while motivation was the best predictor among admissions to drug-free outpatient treatment (Joe, Simpson, & Broome, in press).

Readiness for change and readiness for treatment

In addition to identifying an overall concept of readiness, theory and research in the TCs and methadone maintenance treatment programs have underscored the distinction between readiness for change and readiness for treatment (e.g., De Leon, 1995). The former describes individuals who may elect a number of change strategies other than treatment, and the latter describes individuals who elect treatment as the main change strategy. Much of the research literature has failed to draw a sharp distinction between readiness for change and readiness for treatment.

The distinction between readiness for change and readiness for treatment is underscored in the ten-stage Integrative Recovery model (De Leon, 1996). Although frequently subsumed under motivation, two types of readiness are distinguished. Motivation is defined as internal pressure to change, and two forms of readiness are proposed: readiness to change involving a willingness to take action, and readiness for treatment referring specifically to the perception that treatment is necessary in order to achieve self-change (e.g., De Leon & Jainchill, 1986).

Although framed in terms of the Stages of Change, the three-factor model proposed by Simpson and associates (Simpson & Joe, 1993; Joe, Simpson, & Broome, in 1998) is more similar to the motivation, readiness for change, and readiness for treatment concepts of the Integrative Recovery model. Thus, drug use problems defined as movement from precontemplation to contemplation relate to motivation for change, desire for help defined as cognitive movement toward action relates to readiness for change, and treatment readiness defined as commitment to formal treatment appears to mirror readiness for treatment.

Implications of motivation and readiness distinctions

To date, research has not reported on these theoretical differences in readiness. Indeed, motivational and readiness differences in general may depend upon the populations studied. Among the treatment seekers, scale scores tend to be high, with relatively low variance. The most consistent scale differences with respect to retention or outcomes are obtained on the readiness-for-treatment scale or more usually on the total score. These findings are not unexpected. Treatment seekers are relatively homogeneous in their motivation, compared to their readiness for treatment; and in current stage perspective, readiness assumes motivation. The collinearity among the scales, therefore, renders the total score a sensitive measure. These points further underscore the importance of refinement of measures to uncover motivational/readiness differences among treatment-seeking individuals.

Non-treatment seekers, however, are more heterogeneous in motivation as well as readiness. For example, substance users in hospitals, prisons, shelters, drug treatment referral centers, and in some detoxification clinics reveal consistently lower scores than treatment seekers and greater variability in motivational and readiness levels (Lipton, Morales, & Goldsmith, 1991; Sacks et al., 1997; De Leon et al., 2000; Melnick, De Leon, & Zingaro, 1996).

Motivation and readiness as dynamic variables

The research thus far indicates the importance of initial motivation/readiness in facilitating client engagement in treatment activities. Subsequent research must clarify the changing contribution of motivation throughout the course of treatment (or in the various stages of recovery). In this regard, one hypothesis based on the TC process is that initial motivation leads to treatment participation, which results in positive changes that in turn sustain motivation to continue to participate in treatment. And conversely, lack of progress (outcomes during treatment) may weaken motivation to continue and lead to premature dropout (De Leon, 1995; De Leon, 1998).

Thus the research to date emphasizes the utility and importance of motivation as a multidimensional construct separately from stage formulations. However, refinement of the construct will better capture individual differences, explain more variance in outcomes, and guide clinical assessment and enhancement strategies.

MOTIVATION AND RECOVERY WITHOUT TREATMENT

A distinct group of substance abusers are those who recover without formal treatment. These cases may be labeled as recovery, which is spontaneous in the natural history of the disorder (Waldorf & Biernacki, 1981) or in the developmental maturation of the addict (Winick, 1962). Motivational and readiness factors are implied in each of these recovery examples without significant formal treatment.

There are no firm statistics as to the rates of such recoveries from illicit drugs of abuse. Early studies of samples of narcotic addicts followed longitudinally offer rough estimates of 15–20% of spontaneous recovery. Among smokers, self-quitting rates are alleged to be considerably higher, as inferred from the Stages of Change literature (Prochaska, DiClemente, & Norcross, 1992).

A relation between motivation and self- or spontaneous recovery is illuminated in the ethnographic and natural history studies of narcotic addicts (e.g., Anglin, 1988; Biernacki, 1986; Winick, 1962). Some older addicts "mature out" of their addiction. These heroin abusers appear to surrender their addiction without formal treatment interventions, making use of their ties to the community, family, and religion. Self-quitters among smokers seem to decide to stop their use of tobacco by utilizing a wide variety of strategies and methods.

Research is needed to clarify how individuals recover without treatment. One interpretation of the phenomenon emphasizes a covert interaction between motivation and readiness to change and unmeasured change influences (see De Leon, 1998). In different functional ways, various influences/interventions, not necessarily delivered in treatment settings, interact with motivational factors to incrementally result in recoveries. For example, treatment completers followed five to ten years after residency in TCs continue to utilize social relationships, family, work, and leisure activities to sustain their recoveries. Thus, recovery without treatment is not simply self-cure, but a special interaction between motivational/readiness factors and change-producing influences that are mediated outside of formal treatment. Understanding how these individuals change can provide valuable insights into the recovery process but does not invalidate the need for treatment. As a special group they do not represent the majority of substance abusers for whom formal treatment options are necessary.

MOTIVATIONAL ENHANCEMENT AND THE DISAFFILIATED

The past five years have witnessed increased efforts to treat such special populations of substance abusers as the homeless (Erickson et al., 1995), the homeless mentally ill (Sacks et al., 1997; Rahave & Link, 1995), and prison inmates (Wexler et al., in press). Many of these serious substance abusers are socially disaffiliated, unhabilitated, and/or antisocial. These subgroups often do not have a personal or social stake in changing themselves, with or without treatment. They view their drug use as embedded in their lifestyle. For some, the drug life is the only life in which they experience self-efficacy or social potency, for example as dealers, hustlers, or criminals. For others, drug use is a psychoactive relief from the persistent dysphoria associated with chronic personal frustration and their perceived social impotency. They may express a wish to change but they are not convinced of the possibility of change nor of their energy to effect change.

In terms of a recovery paradigm, many of these individuals are not motivated to change at all or are apparently incapable of moving to readiness. To engage them in the change process often depends on their perceptions of the opportunity for developing self-efficacy and social potency before they seriously consider surrendering drug use and associated behaviors and attitudes. Enhancing motivation among these subgroups of substance users presents a formidable challenge for clinicians as well as researchers.

CONCLUSIONS

Clinical observation and theoretical formulations are grounded in the assumption that motivational/readiness factors are essential in the recovery process. This assumption receives critical empirical support from several lines of inquiry, Stages of Change research, and motivational enhancement, as well as treatment retention and treatment process studies. Several broad conclusions can be drawn from this developing research.

First, motivation as a broad multidimensional construct referring to cognitions and perceptions of the individual's need for and readiness to change has now been empirically demonstrated. The research to date has clarified the distinctions between intrinsic and extrinsic motivation, readiness for change, and readiness for treatment.

Second, motivation and readiness are prominent constructs and measurable factors in stage formulations of recovery and of the treatment process. However, the research to date emphasizes the utility and importance of motivation as a multidimensional, continuously distributed process separate from stage formulations. The refinement of the construct will better capture individual differences, explain more variance in outcomes, and guide clinical assessment and enhancement strategies.

Third, motivational factors alone (or any other client variable) do not directly result in recovery. Functionally, these factors move the individual to engage in the activities or interventions, treatment or otherwise, that lead to recovery. Thus, motivational factors are essential to recovery, but their contribution is inherently limited by the complexity of the recovery process itself.

Finally, motivation itself can be enhanced through various intervention strategies. Studies on motivational enhancement indicate that addressing components of motivation can result in positive outcomes through increasing treatment acceptance or retention. However, the distinctions between recovery, rehabilitation, and habilitation evident across various subgroups of substance abusers imply a different understanding of the role of motivation in treatment and recovery.

References

Allsop, S., & Saunders, B. (1991). Reinforcing robust resolutions: Motivation in relapse prevention with severely dependent problem drinkers. In W. R. Miller & S. Rollnick (eds.), *Motivational Interviewing: Preparing People to Change Addictive Behavior.* New York: Guilford.

Anglin, M. D. (1988). The efficacy of civil commitment in treating narcotics addiction. Special issue: A social policy analysis of compulsory treatment for opiate dependence. *Journal of Drug Issues, 18*(4), 527–545.

Anglin, M. D., Brecht, M., & Maddahian, E. (1989). Pretreatment characteristics and treatment performance of legally coerced versus voluntary methadone maintenance admissions. *Criminology, 27*(3), 537–557.

Anglin, M. D., & Hser, Y.I. (1990). Treatment of drug abuse. *Drugs and Crime: Crime and Justice: A Review of Research,* vol. 13 (M. Tonry and J. Q. Wilson, eds.). Chicago: University of Chicago Press, pp. 393–460.

Belding, M. A., Iguchi, M. Y., & Lamb, R. J. (1996). Stages of change in methadone maintenance: Assessing the convergent validity of two measures. *Psychology of Addictive Behaviors, 10* (1), 157–166.

Biase, D. V., Sullivan, A. P., & Wheeler, B. (1996). Daytop iminversity-phase 2-college training in a therapeutic community: Development of self concept among drug free addict/abusers, in therapeutic communities for addictions. In G. De Leon & J. T. Ziegenfuss (eds.), *Therapeutic communities for addictions: Readings in theory, research, and practice.* Springfield, Ill.: Charles C. Thomas.

Bien, T. H., Miller, W. R., & Boroughs, J. M. (1993). Motivational interviewing with alcohol outpatients. *Behavioral & Cognitive Psychotherapy, 21,* 347–356.

Biernacki, P. (1986). *Pathways from heroin addiction: Recovery without treatment.* Philadelphia: Temple University Press.

Broome, K. M., Knight, D. K., Knight, K., Hiller, M. L., & Simpson, D. D. (1997). Peer, family, and motivational influences on drug treatment process and recidivism for probationers. *Journal of Clinical Psychology, 53*(4), 387–397.

Carey, K. B. (1996). Substance use reduction in the context of outpatient psychiatric treatment: a collaborative, motivational, harm reduction approach. *Community Mental Health Journal, 32,* 291–310.

Carney, N. M., & Kivlahan, D. R. (1995). Motivational subtypes among veterans seeking substance abuse treatment: Profiles based on stages of change. *Psychology of Addictive Behaviors, 9*(2), 135–142.

Collins, J. J., & Allison, M. (1983). Legal coercion and retention in drug abuse treatment. *Hospital and Community Psychiatry, 34,* 1145–1149.

Condelli, W. S. (1986). Client evaluations of therapeutic communities and retention. In G. De Leon and J. T. Ziegenfuss (eds.), *Therapeutic communities for addictions: Readings in theory, research, and practice.* Springfield, Ill.: Charles C. Thomas, pp. 131–140.

Condelli, W. S., & De Leon, G. (1993). Fixed and dynamic predictors of retention in therapeutic communities. *Journal of Substance Abuse Treatment, 10,* 11–16.

Cox, W. M., & Klinger, E. (1987). Research on the personality correlates of alcohol use: Its impact on personality and motivational theory. *Drugs & Society, 1,* 61–83.

Crawford, G. A., Washington, M. C., & Senay, E. C. (1983). Careers with heroin. *International Journal of the Addictions, 18*(5), 701–715.

Cunningham, J. A., Gavin, D. R., Sobell, L. C., Sobell, M. B., & Breslin, F. C. (1997). Assessing motivation for change: Preliminary development and evaluation of a scale measuring the costs and benefits of changing alcohol or drug use. *Psychology of Addictive Behaviors, 11,* 107–114.

Cunningham, J. A., Sobell, L. C., Sobell, M. B., & Gaskin, J. (1994). Alcohol and drug abusers' reasons for seeking treatment. *Addictive Behaviors, 19,* 691–696.

Curry, S. J., Wagner, E. H., & Grothaus, L. C. (1990). Intrinsic and extrinsic motivation for smoking cessation. *Journal of Consulting and Clinical Psychology, 58*(3), 310–316.

Dansereau, D. F., Joe, G. W., & Simpson, D. D. (1993). Node-link mapping: A visual representation strategy for enhancing drug abuse counseling, *Journal of Counseling Psychology, 40*(4), 385–395.

Deci, E. L., & Ryan, R. M. (1985). *Intrinsic motivation and self-determination in human behavior.* New York: Plenum.

Deitch, D., & Zweben, J. E. (1996). The impact of social change on treating adolescents in therapeutic communities. *Journal of Psychedelic Drugs, 8*(3).

De Leon, G. (1988). Legal Pressure in Therapeutic Communities. In: *Compulsory Treatment of Drug Abuse: Research and Clinical Practice,* NIDA Research Monograph 86, DHHS Publication No. (ADM) 88-1578, Leukefeld, C. G., and Tims, F. M. (eds.), pp. 160–177. Rockville, Md.: National Institute on Drug Abuse.

De Leon, G. (1991). Retention in drug-free therapeutic communities National Institute on Drug Abuse (NIDA) Research Monograph 106, *Improving Drug Abuse Treatment,* pp. 218–244, DHHS Pub. No. ADM 91-1754. Superintendent of Documents, U.S. Government Printing Office, Washington, D.C.

De Leon, G. (1993). What psychologists can learn from addiction treatment research. *Journal of Addictive Behaviors, 7,* 103–109.

De Leon, G. (1995). Therapeutic communities for addictions: A theoretical framework. *International Journal of the Addictions, 30*(12), 1603–1645.

De Leon, G. (1996). Integrative recovery: A stage paradigm. *Substance Abuse, 17*(1), 51–63.

De Leon, G. (1997). Therapeutic communities: Motivation in the treatment process. Symposium presentation, American Psychological Association Convention, Chicago, Ill., August.

De Leon, G. (1998). Reconsidering the self selection factor in addiction treatment research. Commentary in *Psychology of Addictive Behaviors, 12*(1), 3–13.

De Leon, G., Hawke, J., Jainchill, N. & Melnick, G. (in press). Therapeutic communities: enhancing retention in treatment using "senior professor" staff. *American Journal of Drug & Alcohol Abuse.*

De Leon, G., & Jainchill, N. (1986). Circumstance, motivation, readiness and suitability as correlates of treatment tenure. *Journal of Psychoactive Drugs, 18,* 203–208.

De Leon, G., Jainchill, N., & Hawke, J.M. (1996) Enhancing short-term retention in therapeutic communities. Presented at the American Sociological Association, New York City, August.

De Leon, G., & Rosenthal, M. S. (1989). Treatment in residential communities. In T.B Karasu (ed.) *Treatments of psychiatric issues, 2.* (1379–1396). Washington, D.C.: American Psychological Association Press.

De Leon, G., Melnick, G., Schoket, D., & Jainchill, N. (1993). Is the therapeutic community culturally relevant? Findings on race/ethnic differences in retention in treatment. *Journal of Psychoactive Drugs, 25*(1), 77–86.

De Leon, G., Melnick, G., Kressel, D., & Jainchill, N. (1994). Circumstances, motivation, readiness, and suitability (the CMRS scales): Predicting retention in therapeutic community treatment. *American Journal of Drug and Alcohol Abuse, 20,* (4), 495–515.

De Leon, G., Melnick, G., & Kressel, D. (1997). Motivation and readiness for therapeutic community treatment among cocaine and other drug abusers. *American Journal of Drug and Alcohol Abuse, 23*(2), 169–189.

De Leon, G., Melnick, G., Thomas, G., Kressel, D., & Wexler, H. K. (2000) Motivation for treatment in a prison-based therapeutic community. Manuscript submitted to *American Journal of Drug and Alcohol Abuse, 26*(1), 294–307.

De Leon, G., & Ziegenfuss, J. (eds.) (1986). *Therapeutic communities for addictions: Readings in theory, research, and practice.* Springfield, Ill.: Charles C. Thomas.

Desmond D. P., & Maddux J. F. (1996). Compulsory supervision and methadone maintenance. *Journal of Substance Abuse Treatment, 13*(1), 79–83.

DiClemente, C. C. (1991). Motivational interviewing and the stages of change. In W. R. Miller & S. Rollnick (eds.), *Motivational interviewing: Preparing people to change addictive behavior,* New York: Guilford.

DiClemente, C. C., & Hughes, S. O. (1990). Stages of change profiles in outpatient alcoholism treatment. *Journal of Substance Abuse Treatment, 2,* 217–235.

DiClemente, C. C., & Prochaska, J. O. (1998). Toward a comprehensive, transtheoretical model of change: Stages of change and addictive behaviors. In Miller, W. R., & Heather, N. (eds). *Treating addictive behaviors.* New York: Plenum.

Erickson, J. R., Stevens, S., McKnight, P., & Figuerodo, A. J. (1995). Willingness for treatment as a predictor of retention and outcomes. *Journal of Addictive Diseases, 14,* 135–150.

Fletcher, B. W., Tims, F. M., & Brown, B. S. (1997). Drug Abuse Treatment Outcome Study (DATOS): Treatment evaluation research in the United States. *Psychology of Addictive Behaviors, 11*(4), 216–229.

Flynn, P. M., Craddock, S. G., Hubbard, R. L., Anderson, J., & Etheridge, R. M. (1997). Methodological overview and research design for the Drug Abuse Treatment Outcome Study (DATOS). *Psychology of Addictive Behaviors, 11*(4), 230–243.

Galbraith, I. G. (1989). Minimal interventions with problem drinkers: A pilot study of the effect of two interview styles on perceived self-efficacy. *Health Bulletin, 47,* 311–314.

Gavin, D. R., Sobel, L. C., & Sobel, M. B. (1994). Evaluation of the Readiness to Change Questionnaire with problem drinkers in treatment. Unpublished manuscript, Addiction Research Foundation, Toronto.

Gerstein, D. R., & Harwood, H. J. (eds.). (1990). *Treating drug problems: Volume One: A study of the evolution, effectiveness, and financing of public and private drug treatment systems.* Washington, D.C.: National Academy Press.

Glynn, T. J., Boyd, G. M., & Gruman, J. C. (1990). Essential elements of self-help/minimal intervention strategies for smoking cessation. *Health Education Quarterly, 17*(3), 329–345.

Gorski, T. T. (1989). *Passages through recovery: An action plan for preventing relapse.* San Francisco: Harper and Row.

Hall, S. M., Havassy, B. E., & Wasserman, D. A. (1990). Commitment to abstinence and acute stress in relapse to alcohol, opiates, and nicotine. *Journal of Consulting and Clinical Psychology, 58*(2):175–181.

Heather, N., Rollnick, S., & Bell, A. (1993). Predictive validity of the Readiness to Change Questionnaire. *Addiction, 88,* 1667–1677.

Hendricks, V. M. (1991). *Addiction and psychopathology: A multidimensional approach to clinical practice.* Rotterdam: European Addiction Research Institute.

Higgins, S. T., Budney, S. J., Bickel, W. K., Foerg, F. E., Donham, R., & Badger, G. J. (1993). Incentives improve outcome in outpatient behavioral treatment of cocaine dependence. *Archives of General Psychiatry, 51,* 568–576.

Horvath, A. T. (1993). Enhancing motivation for treatment of addictive behavior. *Psychotherapy, 30,* 473–480.

Hubbard, R. L., Collins, J. J., Rachal, J. V., & Cavanaugh, E. R. (1988). The criminal justice client in drug abuse treatment. In C. G. Leukefeld and F. M. Tims (eds.), *Compulsory Treatment of Drug Abuse.* National Institute on Drug Abuse Research Monograph 86, DHHS publication ADM 88-1578. Rockville, Md.: National Institute on Drug Abuse.

Institute of Medicine (1989). *Prevention and treatment of alcohol problems: Research opportunities.* Washington, D.C.: National Academy Press.

Isenhart, C. E. (1994). Motivational subtypes in an inpatient sample of substance abusers. *Addictive Behavior, 29,* 463–475.

Joe, G. W., Chastain, R. L., & Simpson, D. D. (1990). Reasons for addiction stages. In Simpson, D. D., & Sells, S. B. (eds.) *Opioid addiction and treatment: A 12-year follow-up.* Malabar, Fla.: Krieger, 73–102.

Joe, G. W., Simpson, D. D., & Broome, K. M. (1998). Effects of readiness for drug abuse treatment on client retention and assessment of process. *Addiction, 93,* 1177–1190.

Kadden, R. M., & Mauriello, I. J. (1991). Enhancing participation in substance abuse treatment using an incentive system. *Journal of Substance Abuse Treatment, 8,* 113–124.

Kent, R. (1991). Motivational interviewing and the maintenance of change. In W. R. Miller & S. Rollnick (eds.), *Motivational interviewing: Preparing people to change addictive behavior,* New York: Guilford.

Lawental E., McLellan, A. T. Grissom, G. R., Brill, P., & O'Brien, C. (1996). Coerced treatment for substance abuse problems detected through workplace urine surveillance: Is it effective? *Journal of Substance Abuse, 8*(1), 115–128.

Leukefeld, C. G., & Tims, F. M. (1988). Compulsory treatment: A review of findings. In C. G. Leukefeld & F. M. Tims (eds.), *Compulsory treatment of drug abuse: Research and clinical practice.* NIDA Research Monograph 86, DHHS Publication No. ADM 89-1578, Washington, D.C.: U.S. Government Press, pp. 236–249.

Lipton, D. S., Morales, E., & Goldsmith, D. S. (1991). Pathways into Treatment: A study of the drug treatment entry process. *Final Project Report.* National Institute on Drug Abuse, Rockville, Md.

Mann, Nancy R., Charuvastra, V. C., & Murphy, V. K. (1984). A diagnostic tool with important implications for treatment of addiction: Identification of factors underlying relapse and remission time distributions. *International Journal of the Addictions, 19*(1) 25–44.

Marlatt, G. A., & Gordon, J. R. (eds.) (1985). *Relapse prevention: Maintenance strategies in the treatment of addictive behaviors.* New York: Guilford, pp. 201–279.

McBride, C. M., Cury, S. J., Stephens, R. S., Wells, E. A., Hoffman, R. A., & Hawkins, D. J. (1994) Intrinsic and extrinsic motivation for change in cigarette smokers, marijuana smokers, and cocaine users. *Psychology of Addictive Behaviors, 8*(4), 243–250.

McConnaughy, E. A., DiClemente, C. C., Prochaska, J. O., & Velicer, W. F. (1989). Stages of change in psychotherapy: A follow-up report. *Psychotherapy: Theory Research and Practice, 4,* 494–503.

McConnaughy, E. A., Prochaska, J. O., & Velicer, W. F. (1983). Stages of change in psychotherapy: Measurement and sample profiles. *Psychotherapy: Theory, Research and Practice, 20,* 368–375.

Melnick, G. (1999). Assessing Treatment Readiness in Special Populations: Final Report of Project Activities, NIDA Grant No. 2 R01 DA07377-03. National Institute on Drug Abuse, Rockville, Md.

Melnick, G., De Leon, G., Hawke, J., Jainchill, N., & Kressel, D. (1997). Motivation and readiness for therapeutic community treatment among adolescents and adult substance abusers. *American Journal of Drug and Alcohol Abuse, 23*(4), 485–507.

Melnick, G., De Leon, G., & Zingaro, M. (1996, August). The multimodal CMRS: Report on concurrent validity. Poster presented at the American Psychological Association Meeting, Division 50, Substance Abuse. Toronto, Canada.

Michalec E. M., Rohsenow DJ. Monti PM. Varney SM. Martin RA. Dey AN. Myers MG. Sirota AD. (1996). A Cocaine Negative Consequences Checklist: development and validation. *Journal of Substance Abuse.* 8(2):181–93, 1996.

Miller, W. R. (1983). Motivational interviewing with problem drinkers. *Behavioral Psychotherapy, 11,* 147–172.

Miller, W. R. (1985). Motivation for treatment: A review with special emphasis on alcoholism. *Psychological Bulletin, 98* (1), 84–107.

Miller, W. R., & Hester, R. R. (1986). *Treating addictive behaviors: Processes of change.* New York: Plenum.

Miller, W. R., & Rollnick, S. (eds.) (1991). *Motivational interviewing: Preparing people to change addictive behavior.* New York: Guilford.

Miller, W. R., & Tonigan, J. S. (1996). Assessing drinkers' motivations for change: The Stages of Change Readiness and Treatment Eagerness Scale (SOCRATES). *Psychology of Addictive Behaviors, 10*(2) 81–89.

Murphy, P. N., Bentall, R. P., & Owens, R. G. (1989). The experience of opioid abstinence: The relevance of motivation and history. *British Journal of Addiction, 84,* 673–679.

Platt, J. J. (1995). *Heroin addiction: Theory, research, and treatment.* Vol. 2: *The addict, the treatment process, and social control.* Malabar, Fl.: Krieger.

Platt, J. J., Buhringer, G., Kaplan, C. D., Brown, B. S., & Taube, D. O. (1988). The prospects and limitations of compulsory treatment for drug addiction. Special issue: A social policy analysis of compulsory treatment for opiate dependence. *Journal of Drug Issues, 18*(4), 505–525.

Pompi, K. F., & Resnick, J. (1987). Retention of court-referred adolescents and young adults in the therapeutic community. *American Journal of Drug and Alcohol Abuse, 13,* 309–325.

Prochaska, J. O., & DiClemente, C. C. (1992). Stages of change in the modification of problem behaviors. *Progress in Behavior Modification, 28,* 183–218.

Prochaska, J. O., DiClemente, C. C., & Norcross, J. C. (1992). In search of how people change: Applications to addictive behaviors. *American Psychologist, 47,* 1102–1114.

Prochaska, J. O., Norcross, J. C., Fowler, J. L., Follick, M. J., & Abrams, D. B. (1992). Attendance and outcome in a work-site weight control program: Processes and stages of change as process and predictor variables. *Addictive Behaviors, 17,* 35–45.

Prochaska, J.O., Velicier, W.F., Rossi, J.S., Goldstein, M.G., Marcus, B.H., Rakowski, W., Fiore, C., Harlow, L.L., Redding, C.A., Rosenbloom, D., Rossi, S.R. (1994). Stages of change and decisional balance for 12 problem behaviors. *Health Psychology, 13,* 39–46.

Project MATCH Research Group (1997). Matching alcoholism treatment to client heterogeneity: Project MATCH post-treatment drinking outcomes. *Journal of Studies on Alcohol, 58*(1), 7–29.

Rahav, M., & Link, B. G. (1995). When social problems converge: Homeless, mentally ill, chemical abusing men in New York City. *International Journal of the Addictions, 30,* 1019–1042.

Rawson, R. A., Shoptaw, S. J., Obert, J. L., & McCann, M. J. (1995). An intensive outpatient approach for cocaine abuse treatment: The Matrix model. *Journal of Substance Abuse Treatment, 12,* 117–127.

Rollnick, S., Heather, N., Gold, R., & Hall, W. (1992). Development of a short "Readiness to Change" Questionnaire for use in brief opportunistic interventions. *British Journal of Addictions, 87,* 743–754.

Rollnick, S., & Morgan, M. (1995). Motivational interviewing: Increasing readiness for change. In A. M. Washton (ed.), *Psychotherapy and substance abuse: A practitioner's handbook.* New York: Guilford Press, pp. 179–191.

Rowan-Szal, G., Joe, G. W., Chatham, L. R., & Simpson, D. D. (1994). A simple reinforcement system for methadone clients in a community-based treatment program. *Journal of Substance Abuse Treatment, 11:* 217–223.

Ryan, Richard M., Plant, Robert W., O'Malley, S. (1995). Initial motivations for alcohol treatment: Relations with patient characteristics, treatment involvement, and dropout. *Addictive Behaviors, 20*(3) 279–297.

Sacks, S., Sacks, J., De Leon, G., Bernhardt, A. I., & Graham, S. (1997). Modified therapeutic community for mentally ill chemical "abusers": Background; influences; program description; preliminary findings. *Substance Use & Misuse, 32*(9), 1217–1259.

Sansome, J. (1980). Retention patterns in a therapeutic community for the treatment of drug abuse. *International Journal of the Addictions, 15,* 711–736.

Saunders, B., Wilkinson, C., & Allsop, S. (1991). Motivational intervention with heroin users attending a methadone clinic. In W. R. Miller & S. Rollnick (eds.), *Motivational interviewing: Preparing people for change.* New York: Guilford Press, pp. 191–202.

Saunders, B., Wilkinson, C., & Phillips, M. (1995). The impact of a brief motivational intervention with opiate users attending a methadone program. *Addiction, 90* (3), 415–424.

Sheffet, A. M., Quinones, M. A., Doyle, K. M., Lavenhar, M. A., El Nakah, A., & Louria, D. B. (1980). Assessment of treatment outcomes in a drug abuse rehabilitation network: Newark, New Jersey. *American Journal of Drug and Alcohol Abuse, 7,* 141–174.

Siddall, J. W., & Conway, G. L. (1988). Interactional variables associated with retention and success in residential drug treatment, *International Journal on the Addictions, 23,* 1241–1254.

Siddiqui, Q. (1989). *The relative effects of extrinsic and intrinsic pressure on retention in treatment.* Ph.D. dissertation, City University of New York.

Simpson, D. D. (1993). Drug treatment evaluation research in the United States. *Psychology of Addictive Behaviors, 7*(2), 120–128.

Simpson, D.D., & Joe, G.W. 1993. Motivation as a predictor of early dropout from drug abuse treatment. *Psychotherapy, 30,* 357–368.

Simpson, D.D., Joe, G.W. & Brown, B.S. (1997). Treatment retention and follow-up outcomes in the Drug Abuse Treatment Outcome Study (DATOS). *Psychology of Addictive Behaviors, 11*(4), 294–307.

Simpson, D. D., Joe, G. W., & Rowan-Szal, G. A. (1997). Drug abuse treatment retention and process effects on follow-up outcomes. *Drug and Alcohol Dependence, 47,* 227–235.

Simpson, D. D., Joe, G. W., Rowan-Szal, G., & Greener, J. (1995). Client engagement and change during drug abuse treatment. *Journal of Substance Abuse, 7,* 117–134.

Simpson, D. D., Joe, G. W., Rowan-Szal, G. A., & Greener, J. M. (1997). Drug abuse treatment process components that improve retention. *Journal of Substance Abuse Treatment, 14*(6), 565–572.

Tims, F. M., Ludford, J. P. (eds.) (1984). *Drug abuse treatment evaluation: Strategies, progress and prospects.* Institute on Drug Abuse Research Monograph 51. Rockville, Md.: National Institute on Drug Abuse.

Van Bilsen, H. P., & Van Emst, A. J. (1986). Heroin addiction and motivational milieu therapy. *International Journal of the Addictions, 21,* 707–713.

Varney S. M., Rohsenow, D. J., Dey, A. N. Myers, M. G., Zwick, W. R., & Monti, P. M. (1995). Factors associated with help seeking and perceived dependence among cocaine users. *American Journal of Drug & Alcohol Abuse, 21*(1):81–91.

Vickers-Lahti, M., Garfield, F., McCusker, J., Hindin, R., Bigelow, C., Love, C., & Lewis, B. (1995). The relationship between legal factors and attrition from a residential drug abuse treatment program. *Journal of Psychoactive Drugs, 27*(1):17–25.

Waldorf, D., & Biernacki, P. (1981). The natural recovery from opiate addiction: Some preliminary findings. *Journal of Drug Issues,* 11, 343–365.

Waisberg, J. L. (1990). Patient characteristics and outcome of inpatient treatment for alcoholism. *Advances in Alcohol and Substance Abuse, 8*(3–4):9–32.

Wexler, H. K., De Leon, G., Thomas, G., Kressel, D., & Peters, J. (1999). The Amity Prison TC evaluation. *Criminal Justice and Behavior,* 26(2):147–167.

Winick, C. (1962). Maturing out of narcotic addiction. *Bulletin on Narcotics, 14,* 1–7.

Zackon, F., McAuliffe, E. E., & Chien, J. (1985). Addict aftercare: Recovery training and self-help treatment. NIDA Research Monograph Series, DHHS Publication (ADM) 85-134. Rockville, Md.: National Institute on Drug Abuse.

Zimmer-Hoefler, D., & Meyer-Fehr, P. (1986). Motivational aspects of heroin addicts in therapeutic communities compared with those in other instituttions. In G. De Leon and J. T. Ziegenfuss (eds.), *Therapeutic communities for addictions: Readings in theory, research and practice.* Springfield, Ill.: Charles C. Thomas.

EIGHT

THE ROLE OF COMORBIDITY IN RELAPSE AND RECOVERY

Rajita Sinha & Richard Schottenfeld

Substance use disorders often exist in conjunction with psychiatric disorders, and their co-occurrence has profound implications for assessment, classification, etiology, and treatment of both disorders (Clarkin & Kendall, 1992). Altered mood and mental status and psychiatric symptoms may co-occur independently of the substance use disorder as part of a psychiatric disorder, or secondary to substance intoxication and acute and protracted withdrawal states, thus making assessment and diagnosis of comorbidity challenging for the clinician. Further, patients with concurrent psychiatric and substance use disorders generally have a worse prognosis than those with either disorder alone. Patients with comorbid substance use disorders and psychiatric symptoms, for example, tend to seek professional treatment more frequently, have a poorer prognosis, show higher relapse and treatment dropout rates, and require additional treatment approaches, including medications and modifications in standard recovery approaches, as compared to substance abusers without psychiatric symptomatology (McLellan, 1986). It is increasingly evident that the traditional separation between substance abuse and mental health treatment has been inadequate in addressing comorbidity, and there is a great need for integrated approaches in the treatment of comorbid disorders. In this chapter, we first review current findings on the classification, prevalence, and prognosis of co-occurring substance use and psychiatric disorders, and then present an integrated treatment approach to address relapse and recovery issues among patients with comorbid substance abuse and psychiatric symptomatology. In the interest of providing an integrated clinical approach, we broadly categorize the comorbid disorders into two groups, (1) the psychotic dually diagnosed population, i.e., those who have an identified history of schizophrenia, schizoaffective disorder, other psychotic disorders and organic brain syndromes, and (2) the nonpsychotic dually diagnosed population, which includes individuals with co-occurring substance abuse and anxiety, affective and/or personality disorders. The integrated clinical approach will focus broadly on these two categories of individuals.

CLASSIFICATION ISSUES

For the purposes of this chapter, comorbidity is defined as the coexistence of substance use and psychiatric disorders in a person at a given period of time, regardless of the order of their appearance (Wittchen et al., 1996; Hirschfield et al., 1990). Individuals with co-occurring substance use and psychiatric illnesses have also been labeled as *dually diagnosed* (Weiss et al., 1992). Although dual diagnosis can refer to any combination of DSM-IV (APA, 1994) psychiatric disorders, the term is most commonly used to describe an individual with a substance use disorder who also exhibits a coexisting psychiatric disorder. This is different from the term *dually addicted,* which refers to addiction to more than one substance. Despite such distinctions, dual diagnosis is a broad term, in which the comorbidity may range from the abuse or dependence on any number of substances, such as alcohol, cocaine, opiates, marijuana, and/or sedatives/benzodiazepines, in association with co-occurring chronic and serious mental illnesses such as schizophrenia and other psychotic disorders, or other nonpsychotic Axis I psychiatric disorders such as affective anxiety disorders and Axis II personality disorders.

Clearly, different combinations of disorders that may be labeled as dual diagnosis lead to heterogeneity with regard to clinical presentations and prognostic implications. Patients with dual diagnosis may include: (1) a homeless person with schizophrenia, who is addicted to cocaine, (2) an alcoholic woman with panic and borderline personality disorder who just lost her job, and (3) a depressed, high-functioning executive who quietly abuses alcohol at night. Thus, patients with comorbid disorders or dual diagnoses vary with respect to type and severity of substance use and psychiatric disorder, level of functioning, social support, and capacity for independent living. These variations in severity of disorder and level of functioning add unique complexity to dual diagnosis and make assessment and treatment planning especially challenging. The prognostic implications of these varied clinical presentations are discussed in the sections on prognosis and treatment.

EPIDEMIOLOGY OF CO-OCCURRING DISORDERS

Estimates of prevalence of psychiatric and substance use disorders have come both from population studies, based on individuals selected from the general population, and from clinical studies that assessed individuals entering various substance abuse and mental health specialty treatment services.

POPULATION STUDIES

Two major epidemiologic studies supported by the National Institute of Mental Health examining the rates of prevalence of psychiatric disorders provide the most recent data regarding comorbidity. The first was the Epidemiologic Catchment Area (ECA) study, which interviewed more than 20,000 respondents in a series of five community epidemiologic surveys (Regier et al., 1990). The second study, the National Comorbidity Survey (NCS), interviewed 8,098 individuals in the 15–54 age range and examined both the prevalence of psychiatric diagnoses and risk factors associated with psychiatric disorders (Kessler et al., 1994; 1996). Although the lifetime prevalence rates of substance use disorder (including alcohol and drugs) averaged 23% in the general population, substance use disorders were twice as likely to co-occur among individuals diagnosed with psychiatric disorders, when compared to individuals with no psychiatric disorders. Conversely, psychiatric disorders were three times more likely to co-occur in individuals with a lifetime substance use disorder as compared to those without a substance use disorder (Regier et al., 1990; Kessler et al., 1994). In addition, co-occurrence of psychiatric disorders was more strongly associated with greater severity of the substance use disorder (Kessler et al., 1996). Finally, among individuals with co-occurring disorders, the psychiatric disorder was generally more likely to occur first, although, among men, alcohol use disorders generally preceded onset of affective disorders (Kessler et al., 1996). Thus the above findings indicate that co-occurrence of substance use and psychiatric diagnoses is highly prevalent in the general population, with psychiatric diagnoses often occurring first in an individual's life prior to substance abuse.

CLINICAL STUDIES

High rates of comorbid substance use and psychiatric disorders have been reported in clinical samples of individuals entering treatment for either psychiatric disorders or substance use problems. In general, lifetime rates of substance use disorders among individuals treated at mental health facilities for such psychiatric disorders as schizophrenia, bipolar disorder, affective and anxiety disorders, and Axis II personality disorders range from 25–75% (Ries & Ellingson, 1990; Caton et al., 1989; Pepper et al., 1981; Galanter et al., 1988; Greenfield et al., 1995), with prevalence rates varying due to differences in samples studied, psychiatric diagnoses, and assessment methodology. For example, in urban settings the rates of comorbidity averaged 60% as compared to 25–30% in suburban settings (Lehman et al., 1994; Mowbray et al., 1995; Hien et al., 1997). Similarly, rates of dual diagnosis among inpatient psychiatric facilities range from 35–65%, while outpatient settings report 25–50% rates of comorbidity (McElvey et al., 1987; Crowley, 1974; Grilo et al., 1997). Prevalence of substance use disorders varies by psychiatric diagnosis as well. For example, approximately 65% of bipolar disorder patients have an addiction, most commonly alcoholism (Dunner et al., 1979; Hasin et al., 1985), while 25–35% of patients treated for depression and anxiety disorders experience co-occurring substance use disorders (Hasin et al., 1985; Tsuang et al., 1995). Comorbid substance abuse occurs in the range of 45–75% among schizophrenics in treatment, with alcohol use being more common than use of cocaine, marijuana, and opiates (Safer, 1987; Zeidonis & Fisher, 1996). Finally, substance use disorders are common among individuals with Axis II personality disorders, especially among those with antisocial personality disorders (range of 20–30%) and those with borderline personality disorder (60–65%) (Dulit et al., 1990; Vaglum & Vaglum, 1985; Grilo et al., 1997).

Studies of individuals seeking treatment for alcohol and drug problems have reported co-occurrence of lifetime psychiatric disorders in the range of 65–75%, with antisocial personality (ASP) disorder, anxiety disorders, affective disorders, borderline personality disorder, and psychosexual disorders being most common (McLellan et al., 1979; Ross et al., 1988; Nace et al., 1983). In addition, similar to the population studies, clinical studies of substance use patients also show that those who abuse both alcohol and drugs are more likely to have a psychiatric disorder and, further, their alcohol and drug abuse has been found to be more severe than that of patients without psychiatric disorders (Ross et al., 1988).

Prevalence patterns of comorbid psychiatric disorders also vary according to the specific substance of abuse. For example, among alcoholics, ASP, other substance use disorders, and major depression were found to be most common, with lifetime rates ranging from 41–45% (Hesselbrock et al., 1985). These were followed by diagnoses of phobias occurring in 27%, obsessive compulsive disorder in 12%, and panic disorder in 10%. In women, the onset of most psychopathologies preceded alcohol abuse. In men, with the exception of ASP and panic disorder, the onset of psychiatric disorders was more often secondary to alcohol abuse/dependence. Among cocaine abusers, co-occurrence of affective disorders, anxiety disorder, and alcoholism was most common, with lifetime rates ranging from 60–65% (Rounsaville et al., 1991). These were followed by ASP, occurring in 23%, and attention deficit disorder, occurring in 34%. Alcoholism and affective disorders usually followed the onset of cocaine abuse, whereas anxiety disorders, ASP, and attention deficit disorder preceded drug abuse.

In early studies with clinical samples of opiate addicts, major depression was found to be the most common comorbid psychiatric diagnosis, with life-time rates ranging from 53–60%. The other most common Axis I disorders included alcoholism (29%), ASP (22%), and anxiety disorders (15%), while Axis II personality disorders were reported in 65% of the sample (Rounsaville et al., 1982a; Khantzian & Treece, 1985; Kosten et al., 1982). A more recent study, however, reported lower lifetime estimates, with rates of major depression at 20%, anxiety disorders at 8%, other substance use disorders at 65%, and Axis II personality disorders at 35% (Brooner et al., 1997). The differences in findings between these studies have been attributed to differences in diagnostic methods and assessment tools, and to variability in populations being studied. In summary, consistent with epidemiologic studies, the data from clinical studies indicate higher rates of comorbidity in clinical populations than found in the general population, and underscore the need to address coexisting psychiatric symptoms in initiating recovery and preventing relapse among substance abusers.

IMPACT ON PROGNOSIS

Clinical experience suggests that comorbidity has a profound impact on the clinical course and outcome of both substance use and psychiatric disorders. In general, psychological symptoms such as irritability, anxiety, depression, and anger are common reasons for relapse to substance use (Marlatt & Gordon, 1985; Wallace, 1989). Further, active substance use among psychiatric patients is associated with a generally less favorable treatment response for psychiatric symptoms. Research examining the effects of alcoholism on the long-term course of major depression has consistently reported that remission in alcoholism strongly and significantly increased the chances of remission with major depression and also reduced chances of depression relapse (Mueller et al., 1994; Hasin et al., 1996). Coexistent alcohol dependence in individuals with bipolar disorders has also been found to be a predictor of recurrence of psychiatric symptoms (Tohen et al., 1990). Dually diagnosed individuals with psychotic disorders are more likely to relapse to psychiatric illness and have higher rates of rehospitalization and more episodes of violent and suicidal behavior when compared to psychotic individuals without substance use disorders (Craig et al., 1985; Drake et al., 1989; Ridgeley et al., 1990; Haywood et al., 1995; Strakowski et al., 1993). Finally, among individuals treated for Axis II personality disorders, those with comorbid substance use tend to have worse long-term outcomes than those without substance use disorders (Links et al., 1995). These findings support clinical observations suggesting that presence of comorbid substance use disorders is associated with less favorable psychiatric outcomes among individuals treated for psychiatric disorders.

Several studies have examined the impact of co-occurring psychiatric symptoms on substance abuse treatment outcomes. An early study by McLellan et al. (1983) found that patients with low psychiatric problem severity improved the most while those with high psychiatric problem severity showed least improvement overall, and those with mid-range psychiatric problem severity showed differential improvement based on type of treatment provided. Among opiate-dependent patients, Rounsaville et al. (1982b) found that although improvement of depressive symptoms was related to better treatment retention, those who met criteria for major or minor depression at intake had poorer drug use outcomes, i.e., they had either relapsed or continued drug use when assessed at the six-month follow-up period. In cocaine abusers, Carroll et al. (1993) found that severity of drug use, severity of psychiatric symptomatology, and presence and severity of alcoholism at baseline was significantly associated with poorer long-term substance abuse outcomes when assessed one year later.

The effects of Axis II personality disorders on substance abuse outcomes, specifically the more commonly occurring antisocial personality and borderline personality disorders, have also been examined. In general, these two Axis II disorders are associated with an earlier onset of substance use, more polydrug use, and worse outcomes in drug abuse treatment (Nace et al., 1983; Woody et al., 1985; Rounsaville et al., 1986). In methadone-maintained patients, Cacciola et al. (1996) recently reported that patients with personality disorders, specifically cluster B disorders (borderline, histrionic, and antisocial), showed the poorest overall outcomes, including retention rates, as compared to those without personality disorders. In contrast, when these researchers examined the effects of antisocial personality disorder on treatment response among alcohol- and cocaine-dependent men, they found that although the ASP group had more severe problems at admission and follow-up, both the ASP and non-ASP groups showed comparable improvement in substance use outcomes when assessed at seven-month follow-up (Cacciola et al., 1995). Although these findings suggest that the ASP group is as responsive to treatment as the non-ASP group, it is important to note that two subgroups of antisocial substance abusers have been identified, and that there may be differences in outcome depending on the diagnostic subtype, those with high emotional distress and additional psychiatric diagnoses and those with high psychopathy and low emotional distress (Liskow et al., 1990; Rousar et al., 1994). There is some evidence to suggest that those in the ASP group with greater emotional distress are more treatment-responsive than those with high psychopathy and low levels of emotional distress (Rutherford et al., 1993).

Presence of such psychiatric disorders as major depression, ASP, and drug abuse among alcoholics has also been associated with worse treatment outcomes, as compared to alcoholics without other psychiatric disorders (Rounsaville et al., 1987); however, gender differences in the above findings have been observed. Alcoholic men with major depression, ASP, and drug abuse had poorer outcomes than men without additional psychopathology. Alcoholic women with major depression, however, had better outcome in drinking-related measures, while ASP and drug abuse in women were associated with poorer outcome. In two prospective follow-up studies, Hasin and colleagues showed that individuals with alcoholism and comorbid affective disorders were less likely to achieve abstinence when assessed at a two-year follow-up (Hasin et al., 1989), and that those with unipolar depression were more likely to meet current alcoholism diagnoses five years after initial assessment than their counterparts with bipolar disorder (Hasin et al., 1991).

In treating comorbid disorders, the hypothesis that matching individuals to specific treatments to address their dual problems may improve treatment outcome has gained recent attention (McLellan et al., 1997). Several previous studies have shown that specific types of counseling and psychotherapies are associated with better outcomes among individuals with comorbid disorders. For example, patients with comorbid depression and cocaine abuse showed greater improvement with relapse prevention and coping skills treatment than with clinical management (Carroll et al., 1993; 1995). Among methadone-maintained opiate-dependent individuals, those with psychiatric problems showed greater improvements when receiving cognitive-behavioral psychotherapy or short-term dynamic psychotherapy as compared to drug counseling (Woody et al., 1984). Kadden et al. (1989) and Litt et al. (1992) have documented that sociopathic alcoholic individuals have improved treatment outcomes when treated in structured group settings providing coping skills training, while interactional group therapy was more effective for less sociopathic alcoholics. However, in a large multisite psychotherapy trial with alcohol-dependent individuals (Project MATCH), very few of the matching hypotheses were borne out. Individuals with low psychiatric problem severity had more days of abstinence with twelve-step facilitation treatment, while all treatments were comparable in effectiveness for the high psychiatric severity subgroup (Project MATCH Research Group, 1997). In summary, the above findings indicate that Axis I and Axis II psychiatric symptomatology is often associated with poor substance abuse treatment outcomes and suggest that there is a need to develop specialized, integrated treatment approaches for individuals with comorbid psychiatric and substance use disorders.

INTEGRATED TREATMENT APPROACH

At the beginning of this chapter we identified two broad groups of comorbid disorders, those in which, in addition to substance use disorders, psychotic disorders such as schizophrenia and schizoaffective disorders occur comorbidly, and those in which a nonpsychotic psychiatric condition such as depression, anxiety, bipolar disorder, and/or Axis II personality disorder coexists with a substance use disorder. Such a categorization of the dual-diagnosis population has been made because of the clinical implications for assessment, classification, and treatment. In this section, we first discuss the assessment and treatment planning issues, including pharmacological treatment issues for comorbid disorders. This is followed by a description of the integrated therapy approach for patients with comorbid psychotic disorders and those with nonpsychotic Axis I and Axis II disorders.

DIAGNOSTIC ASSESSMENT AND TREATMENT PLANNING

A common diagnostic dilemma in assessing comorbid disorders stems from the fact that psychiatric symptoms may occur independently of the substance use disorder or secondary to the substance use. For example, panic, anxiety, sleep disturbances, or depression may be concomitants of persistent heavy drinking or alcohol withdrawal, and they may resolve spontaneously during the first two to four weeks following initiation of abstinence. They may also occur independently of the drinking and require specific treatment. Table 8.1 outlines the specific psychiatric symptoms that may be induced by substance

Table 8.1: Psychiatric symptoms commonly associated with the following substance-induced states

SPECIFIC SUBSTANCE	SUBSTANCE INTOXICATION	ACUTE WITHDRAWAL	PROTRACTED WITHDRAWAL
Alcohol	Mood lability—sadness, irritability, impaired judgment; impaired social/occupational functioning; inappropriate sexual/aggressive behavior; attention and memory impairment; incoordination	Insomnia; psychomotor agitation, anxiety, perceptual disturbances (hallucinations, illusions); dysphoria, autonomic dysfunction (sweating, pulse rate)	Anxiety, insomnia, autonomic dysfunction; dysphoric mood
Cannabis	Euphoria, with inappropriate laughter and grandiosity; sedation, lethargy; impaired judgment; distorted sensory perceptions; impaired motor performance	Irritability; anxious or depressed mood, nervous, tense, sleep disturbances, appetite change, tired, trouble concentrating, distorted sensory perceptions	Not well established
Cocaine	Euphoria or blunted affect; hypervigilance; anxiety; tension or anger; change in sociability; interpersonal sensitivity; paranoid ideation	Fatigue; insomnia/hypersomnia; increased appetite; psychomotor agitation or retardation; anhedonia; drug craving	Fatigue; anxiety; dysphoric mood; drug craving; insomnia

Nicotine	Not well established	Dysphoric or depressed mood; insomnia; irritability, frustration or anger; anxiety, difficulty concentrating; restlessness/impatience; increased appetite	Not well established
Opiates	Initial euphoria followed by apathy, dysphoria, psychomotor agitation or retardation, impaired judgment, impaired attention and memory	Anxiety, restlessness, irritability, increased sensitivity to pain; dysphoric mood; insomnia, increased achiness, drug-seeking behavior, craving	Anxiety; insomnia, dysphoria; anhedonia; drug craving
Sedatives/Hypnotics or Anxiolytics	Mood lability; inappropriate sexual or aggressive behavior; impaired judgment, memory and attention difficulties; incoordination	Insomnia, anxiety, autonomic hyperactivity; psychomotor agitation	Anxiety; insomnia; dysphoric mood

Information adapted from the *Diagnostic and Statistical Manual of Mental Disorders* (DSM-IV), APA, 1994, and other empirical findings.

intoxication, acute withdrawal, and/or protracted withdrawal states for the most commonly used substances of abuse. In addition to the psychological symptoms, it is important to note that there are physical signs of intoxication and withdrawal as well (APA, DSM-IV, 1994). Although the psychiatric symptoms outlined in table 8.1 and other physical symptoms may be substance-induced, their existence does not rule out a preexistent psychiatric or medical condition, and careful assessment of the substance use disorders should be considered a routine part of all psychiatric or medical evaluations.

A comprehensive assessment of the patient must include a detailed history of his or her symptoms, an assessment of physical and mental status, information from screening instruments and diagnostic interviews, urine toxicology testing, breathalyzer and various biochemical tests, and, finally, any information provided by family members or significant others. In addition to the diagnostic assessment, it is important to assess the patient's motivation for changing substance use behaviors, as his or her readiness to change has a profound impact on implementing an appropriate treatment plan. The reader is referred to Schottenfeld and Pantalon (1999), which describes in depth the assessment strategies that should be used in a comprehensive evaluation of substance use disorders.

The level of clinical care with regard to the immediate treatment needs of the patient should be determined based on the assessment of the patient's history and current clinical presentation. A need for immediate hospitalization may be indicated from the assessment of suicidal and homicidal ideation, intent, or plan; positive symptoms of psychosis, such as auditory or visual hallucinations, or delusions; intensity, duration, and recency of substance use; level of depressed affect; and mental status with regard to thought content and process. If immediate hospitalization is not required, then an assessment of whether the patient may need partial hospitalization or intensive outpatient services prior to regular outpatient care needs to be determined. The American Society for Addiction Medicine (ASAM) has developed patient placement criteria that provide guidelines for matching type and severity of the patient's symptoms to various levels of care (ASAM Patient Placement Criteria, 1991a,b). The criteria are specified along the six dimensions of (1) intoxification and/or potential withdrawal; (2) biomedical condition and complications; (3) emotional/behavioral conditions and complications; (4) treatment acceptance/resistance; (5) relapse/continued use potential; and (6) recovery environment. Such criteria can be useful in training clinicians in assessment and determining the appropriate treatment plan for a patient.

PHARMACOLOGICAL CONSIDERATIONS IN TREATING COMORBIDITY

In addition to a diagnostic assessment and an evaluation of motivation and level of care needed for the patient, the initial assessment should also include an evaluation of the need for pharmacological treatments to address psychiatric symptoms. Although psychotic symptoms and mania may be substance-induced, acute management of psychotic and manic symptoms is critical and may require hospitalization and/or immediate pharmacological treatment. The American Psychiatric Association (1995) has established practice guidelines for the treatment of substance use disorders that review the medical management of acute psychiatric symptoms associated with substance intoxication and withdrawal states.

In addition to the more severe psychiatric symptoms of psychosis and mania, depression, anxiety, irritability, sleep disturbances, and other psychiatric symptoms commonly exist secondary to substance intoxication, acute withdrawal, and protracted withdrawal states, and a thorough assessment of the history of psychiatric symptomatology and substance use history needs to be conducted in evaluating the need for pharmacological treatment. It is important to establish the chronology of symptom development (i.e., whether the signs and symptoms predate or follow the onset of repetitive substance use), whether symptoms were present during extended drug-free periods, and the impact of each disorder on the presentation, clinical course, and outcome of the other. The probability that the patient has a comorbid psychiatric disorder that will persist independently of attainment of abstinence is increased if there is a history of psychiatric symptoms predating the onset of substance use disorder or during previous drug-free periods or if there is a family history of at least one first-degree biological relative having a documented history of similar illness (APA, 1995).

The appropriate timing of pharmacological treatment of anxiety and depressive disorders and the use of benzodiazepines in patients with comorbid substance use disorders are somewhat controversial. Because severe anxiety and depressive disorders are quite common and typically self-limited in duration in newly abstinent alcohol-dependent individuals, many authorities recommend delay in institution of pharmacological treatment for at least 2–4 weeks following initiation of abstinence (Anthenelli & Schuckit, 1993). During a four-week period of abstinence, depression and anxiety symptoms generally remit among alcohol- and cocaine-dependent individuals. Other authorities, however, note that anxiety and depressive symptoms may contribute to the likelihood of relapse or treatment attrition, and they suggest that earlier initiation of pharmacological treatment for these psychiatric disorders may be warranted in some patients, especially those with indications that the disorder will persist without pharmacologic treatment (Rounsaville & Kranzler, 1989).

The use of benzodiazepines for substance-dependent individuals with anxiety symptoms is controversial because benzodiazepines and other CNS depressants have high abuse potential in patients with substance abuse disorders. For individuals requiring anti-anxiety medications, such agents as buspirone or even beta-blockers such as propranolol are generally preferable to benzodiazepines. Additionally, a key task in the treatment of patients with addictive disorders is to teach them ways of coping with feelings of anxiety or other affective states without necessarily turning to medications for immediate relief. Thus it is critical to help patients learn to differentiate between normal, transient emotional states requiring self-management strategies and persistent anxiety disorders that may benefit from pharmacologic intervention. Nonpharmacologic relaxation techniques and other behavioral approaches may be beneficial for patients with transient anxiety or persistent anxiety disorders.

Recent studies in alcoholism support the early initiation of pharmacotherapy for nonpsychotic, affective, and anxiety disorders. Antidepressant agents such as the serotonin reuptake inhibitors and such anxiolytics as buspirone have been shown to reduce alcohol consumption among depressed and anxious alcoholics. In trials of depressed alcoholics, fluoxetine treatment initiated seven days after a patient's last drink was shown to decrease alcohol consumption and reduce depressive symptoms (Cornelius et al., 1993; 1995). In alcoholics with anxiety disorders, Kranzler et al. (1989; 1994) showed that buspirone treatment (once again initiated one week after last drink) decreased anxiety symptoms as well as craving for alcohol, and further delayed relapse to heavy drinking, while also increasing treatment retention when compared to placebo. These findings indicate that there may be a role for treating concurrent anxiety and depressive symptomatology in alcohol-dependent patients, with at least short-term goals of reduction of psychiatric symptoms, better engagement in treatment, and decreased risk of relapse in the early recovery phase (Litten & Allen, 1995).

One area that is not controversial is the treatment of persistent depression despite prolonged abstinence or stable agonist replacement treatment such as methadone among opiate-dependent individuals. In such cases, patients respond to treatment with antidepressant medication with reduction of depressive symptoms and increased engagement in substance abuse treatment, and withholding pharmacological treatment is not warranted. In addition, several other treatments have shown modest effectiveness in addressing comorbid symptomatology. For example, among cocaine abusers with comorbid psychiatric conditions, lithium for comorbid bipolar disorder, desipramine for comorbid depression, and methylphenidate for comorbid ADHD have been used effectively (APA Practice Guidelines, 1995). In addition, Ziedonis and Kosten (1991) have shown that desipramine or amantadine treatment for depressed, cocaine-abusing methadone maintenance patients may reduce cocaine use.

INTEGRATED TREATMENT FOR COMORBID PSYCHOTIC DISORDERS AND SUBSTANCE ABUSE

Recent attention on the treatment of dual-diagnosis patients has primarily focused on the need for integrated assessment of and treatment for patients with substance use disorders and chronic psychotic illness, identified here as the first group of dually diagnosed patients. For this group of patients, clear guidelines for integrated treatment in inpatient, partial hospital and outpatient settings have been outlined (Minkoff, 1989; Minkoff & Drake, 1991; Carey, 1989; Ziedonis & Fisher, 1996). These integrated approaches focus on the simultaneous stabilization of both the psychiatric illness as well as substance use. The primary goals of stabilization include initiation of and compliance with psychotropic medications and motivating patients to reduce substance use. Abstinence from substance use is viewed as a more realistic long-term goal rather than a short-term requirement, as these patients have more frequent relapses and may be difficult to engage initially (Carey, 1989; Rosenthal et al., 1992b; Ziedonis & Fisher, 1996). Following the simultaneous initiation into psychiatric and substance abuse treatment, integrated treatment includes continuation of medication, supportive psychotherapy, peer group support for sobriety, psychoeducation, self-help groups, relapse prevention skills training, case management, family support, and occupational therapy (Rosenthal et al., 1992a; Weiss et al., 1995).

One of the main challenges in treating dually diagnosed patients has been treatment engagement. Ziedonis and Fisher (1996) outline a motivationally based treatment (MBT) that includes careful screening and assessment of the psychotic, dually diagnosed patient and integrates the above-mentioned interventions with a motivational enhancement model of treatment (Miller & Rollnick, 1991). In the MBT model of treatment, patients who have low motivation to change substance use behaviors may be most appropriate for harm-reduction goals, while abstinence goals may be appropriate for those with higher motivation. This model of treatment underscores the need for specific interventions to engage the patient based on his or her motivational level so as to prevent relapse to both the psychotic disorder as well as substance abuse. Engagement is critical in maintaining patients with these disorders in treatment, increasing compliance with psychotropic medications, and working toward the goal of abstinence from substance use.

INTEGRATED TREATMENT FOR COMORBID NONPSYCHOTIC DISORDERS AND SUBSTANCE ABUSE

Because psychiatric symptoms occur secondary to substance use, primary substance abuse treatment facilities may delay addressing psychiatric symptomatology. Conversely, in a mental health program, the extent of current substance use may not be assessed thoroughly while psychiatric symptoms gain primary attention and treatment. Failure to directly address concurrent substance use, however, contributes to early attrition and relapse. Thus, initial and ongoing assessment needs to focus on both psychiatric and substance use issues, and outcomes from both domains of functioning need to be used to address recovery issues comprehensively (Litten & Allen, 1995). Table 8.2 outlines the integrated treatment approach suggested for this group of patients.

PHASE 1: ASSESSMENT, ORIENTATION, AND ENGAGEMENT

Although most experts believe that initiating abstinence and detoxification is an important initial step in recovery from substance abuse and comorbid disorders (Khantzian, 1989; Rounsaville & Kranzler, 1989; Anthenelli & Schuckit, 1993), there are very few guidelines on how to intervene and initiate abstinence for this group of patients. Thus, in the first phase of treatment, the treatment goal is to engage the patient and elicit commitment to abstinence from substance use behaviors. This phase is brief and time-limited (up to 4–6 weeks), and it focuses primarily on the above-mentioned treatment target. Simultaneous pharmacotherapy for psychiatric symptoms is important and may be initiated during this phase of treatment, if necessary. This phase includes diagnostic and motivational assessment and the use of motivational enhancement techniques to better engage the patient in treatment (Miller & Rollnick, 1991; Miller et al., 1992). In conjunction with motivational enhancement therapy (MET) techniques, we outline additional interventions that address motivation and commitment to change substance use behaviors.

Table 8.2: Integrated treatment approach for comorbid disorders

---

Phase I: Assessment, orientation, and engagement in treatment

Assessment
  * Mental state
  * Psychiatric and substance use history
  * Assessment of motivation to change substance use and treat
    psychotic symptoms

Orientation to treatment and agreement on goals
  * Provide information on substances
  * Present theory of comorbid disorders
  * Provide treatment framework and it's promise
  * Collaborate on development of treatment targets and rules of
    treatment

Engagement to treatment: initiating abstinence and detoxification
  * Motivational enhancement strategies
  * Special additional strategies
  * Pharmacotherapy evaluation and medication initiation

Phase II: Abstinence, connection, and stability
  * Achieving abstinence
  * Decrease in psychiatric symptoms
  * Initiating adaptive skills training

Phase III: Recovery and preventing relapse
  * Breaking the link between dysregulated affect, craving, and
    substance use
  * Affect regulation and stress tolerance skills
  * Relapse prevention skills
  * Enhancing social support and new community relationships

Assessment of motivation to change substance abuse

The patient's willingness to change substance use behaviors is critical in initiating treatment of substance abuse in the nonpsychotic dually diagnosed population. The level of willingness varies widely. Some patients may not see their substance use as a problem at all; others may see the psychiatric symptoms as the main problem and not the substance use; and for others, substance use may be viewed as positive, associated with pleasure, enjoyment, and symptom reduction. Even patients who feel they could benefit from some reduction in use may feel so much shame and guilt that they may not easily tolerate revealing their use. Many patients who recognize their use as causing problems may not know how to address their substance use problem or feel that they may not succeed in remaining abstinent. Assessment of motivation or willingness to change therefore is an important aspect of assessment and treatment planning, because the specific approach used should depend on the patient's motivational level. Self-report assessment tools like the University of Rhode Island Change Assessment Questionnaire (URICA; Prochaska, DiClemente, & Norcross, 1992) or shorter versions of the Stages of Change Readiness and Treatment Evaluation Screening (SOCRATES) (Miller & Tonigan, 1996) or the Contemplation Ladder (Biener & Abrams, 1991) may be used to assess readiness to change substance use. Alternatively, questions regarding willingness to change can be addressed during a clinical interview as well.

Patients can generally be divided into three groups: (1) those who recognize their substance use problem and are ready to take steps to change their behavior or have already begun to make changes in their substance use (action stage), (2) those who are ambivalent about making changes (ambivalence or contemplation stage), and (3) those who do not see any need to change their behavior (precontemplation stage). Once the motivational level is determined, the first target of treatment is to address the patient's willingness to change substance use behaviors and initiate abstinence. Although harm-reduction models that view abstinence as a long-term goal may be useful for the psychotic dually diagnosed population, findings that abstinence-oriented short-term goals for the nonpsychotic dually diagnosed population lead to better retention in treatment and increased chances for long-term recovery (Rounsaville et al., 1982b, 1987; Hasin et al., 1991) suggest that the most appropriate short-term goal of phase 1 for this group of dually diagnosed individuals is initiating abstinence. This goal may be extremely difficult to achieve, however, especially for patients who do not believe they need to change their behavior. In such cases the treatment focus should be engagement and initiating abstinence by using MET and the strategies outlined below to initiate change in substance use behaviors.

Providing information   Providing feedback about the patient's drug use, information on risk factors for substance abuse problems, and the negative consequences of their substance use is an integral part of MET. The power of providing information about the disorder in a nonjudgmental and matter-of-fact psychoeducational format in helping individuals understand their disorders and motivate change has been documented in studies of brief interventions (see Bien et al., 1993, for review). We have developed a program that utilizes both treatment entry groups and individual counseling to increase the determination to initiate abstinence. In the treatment entry groups, patients receive brief handouts on the physiological and psychosocial effects of the various substances of abuse, and they also view engaging videos that focus on the personal experiences of individuals in recovery. The videos help to overcome stigma and provide hope for the person contemplating change. Group modalities are especially powerful as they are likely to lead to a discussion among patients about the effects of substance use, which in turn can be a powerful vehicle for change. In addition to the time-limited entry group, patients meet with an individual therapist who, using MET techniques, reviews each patient's responses to the information and integrates them with the individual feedback on the patient's substance use patterns.

Providing a framework for understanding comorbid disorders   In treating patients with comorbid disorders, we use a collaborative style and attempt to provide the patient with a working framework of how comorbid disorders develop and are maintained. Substance-dependent individuals frequently report that they use substances to cope with their anxiety, negative affect, and day-to-day stresses. In a large survey study, Cooper et al. (1992) demonstrated that drinking to cope with psychological distress was strongly predictive of tolerance, withdrawal, loss of control, and functional impairment symptoms of problem drinking. However, drinking to enhance positive affect was associated with quantity and frequency of drinking but not with symptoms of alcohol abuse/dependence, and drinking to celebrate or socialize with peers was related to neither quantity of alcohol consumption nor symptoms of abuse/dependence. Consistent with these findings, numerous studies have shown that individuals with alcohol or drug use disorders cite psychological distress as the most common reason for their relapse (Marlatt & Gordon, 1985; Wallace, 1989). Our recent laboratory studies have shown that alcoholics and cocaine abusers show increases in craving following psychological stress induction in the laboratory (Sinha et al., 1997a; Sinha et al., 1999). These findings are consistent with the "self-medication" hypothesis, which states that alcohol and drugs are used as a way of finding relief from psychological distress in dually diagnosed populations (Khantzian, 1989).

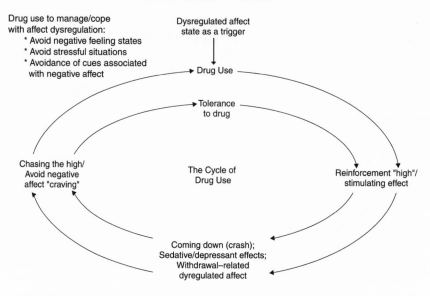

Fig. 8.1. The psychobiological model of co-morbid disorders.

Figure 8.1 provides an illustration of the psychobiological model for co-morbid disorders that is shared with patients in helping them understand the interface between psychiatric symptoms and the cycle of substance abuse/dependence. In this model, affect dysregulation associated with anxiety, depression, and personality disorders is shown as a trigger to drug use and relapse, and continued use of substances perpetuates the cycle by leading to affect dysregulation, anxiety, and depressive symptoms. The association between psychiatric symptoms and persistent substance use, withdrawal, and subclinical withdrawal states is clearly explained to patients. In our experience, providing information on the etiology and theory of comorbidity validates the patient's experience of his or her own problems and helps to motivate the patient to address the problems. In explaining the model to the patient, it is important to point out that unless the cycle is broken, psychiatric symptoms that are secondary to substance use will continue. Further, presenting the model provides hope, as it promises that by engaging in treatment, patients will learn alternate, adaptive ways of coping with negative affect, anxiety, depression, and stress, and the need to use substances to cope with psychological distress will be eliminated. The presentation style for describing the model is empathic and nonconfrontational, and the goal is to provide information, understanding, and hope. Eliciting the patient's response to this model, along with obtaining concrete examples of his or her recent relapses and drug use episodes to determine whether the model is consistent with the patient's understanding of his or her own problems, further helps in motivating patients to address change in substance use behaviors.

Assessment of pros and cons of substance use   An analysis of the "decisional balance," specifically examining the benefits of substance use and the negative consequences of drug use, can be a useful exercise in motivating the patient to quit. The motivational enhancement therapy (MET) manual (Miller et al., 1992) outlines clearly the use of such strategies in preparing individuals to change alcohol use behaviors. For patients who are unable to identify any negative consequences of their drug use, this strategy highlights that the treatment in this initial phase must focus on exploring the positive reasons as well as the adverse consequences of drug use. The parallel interventions of examining the pros and cons of use and the potential benefits of recovery work well in the initial engagement of patients.

Daily log of feelings, urges, and actions   Use of daily logs for thoughts, feelings, actions and triggers is a common intervention that is used in a variety of ways in most cognitive behavioral therapies. Table 8.3 provides the daily log that we use with this population to track their psychiatric symptoms, patterns of substance use, and urges to use drugs or engage in other maladaptive behaviors. We institute the log early in treatment even for individuals who are in the precontemplation stage. The log provides a tool for tracking substance use and the association between psychiatric symptoms and other maladaptive behaviors, including substance use. The log serves multiple purposes, including (1) obtaining information about the symptoms and their association over the previous week; (2) informing the direction and focus of the therapy session, and (3) helping the patient develop a sense of control over substance use and affective states. Each treatment session is started with a review of the log. When patients have difficulty complying with completing the log, it is completed in session prior to addressing any other issues.

Commitment strategies   Because nonpsychotic dually diagnosed patients generally have poor retention rates in treatment and difficulty in committing to and complying with treatment, we have adapted the commitment- and compliance-enhancing strategies developed for treating borderline personality disorder by Linehan (1993a) with these patients. *Pros and cons of committing to treatment* is a proactive treatment strategy that highlights the good points of the treatment, develops an action plan, and then identifies counter-

Table 8.3: Daily Log of Feelings, Urges and Actions.

Today I felt: {0–9}   (0 = not at all; 9 = highest)

Date	—/— Monday	—/— Tuesday	—/— Wednesday	—/— Thursday	—/— Friday	—/— Saturday	—/— Sunday
Good, happy							
Anxious, tense							
Miserable							
Angry							
Depressed							
Hopeful							
Empty, alone							
Unreal/disconnected							
Physically bad							

Today I felt an urge to: {0–9}   (0 = not at all; 9 = highest)

Date	—/—/— Monday	—/—/— Tuesday	—/—/— Wednesday	—/—/— Thursday	—/—/— Friday	—/—/— Saturday	—/—/— Sunday
Kill myself	( )	( )	( )	( )	( )	( )	( )
Binge or purge	( )	( )	( )	( )	( )	( )	( )
Drink or take drugs	( )	( )	( )	( )	( )	( )	( )
Injure myself	( )	( )	( )	( )	( )	( )	( )
Overdose	( )	( )	( )	( )	( )	( )	( )
Other	( )	( )	( )	( )	( )	( )	( )

Place * next to those days you acted on the urge.

Table 8.3: Continued

Describe what was important to you today—be specific

Monday _____

Tuesday _____

Wednesday _____

Thursday _____

Friday _____

Saturday _____

Sunday _____

This log was developed in collaboration with Christine Foerstch, Ph.D., at the Cornell-Westchester Personality Disorders Program.

arguments or reservations that may come up later when the patient is alone and without help in managing self-doubts. Once a commitment is made, Linehan recommends playing devil's advocate, if possible. In this intervention, the therapist poses arguments against making a commitment but makes sure that the counterarguments to commitment are slightly weaker than the patient's arguments for commitment. This strategy also helps in enhancing the patient's sense of choice and control.

In addition, Linehan recommends several marketing techniques, such as *foot-in-the-door* and *door-in-the-face* techniques, to enhance compliance and increase commitment. The foot-in-the-door technique increases commitment by making an easier first request followed by a more difficult request — for example, first getting an agreement to reduce substance abuse as a goal, then asking for a commitment to abstain from drugs for the coming week. In the door-in-the-face technique, the procedure is reversed. The therapist first requests something much larger than is actually wanted, and then requests something easier — for example, request abstinence from drug use for the coming week, then make a request to call the therapist or a sponsor before using any substances. Reminding patients of previous commitments, especially when they may be in a crisis or on the verge of dropping out, and then renegotiating their commitment to treatment goals also helps to sustain commitment and compliance.

Collaborative treatment planning   Matching patient's goals to therapist's goals and obtaining an explicit and collaborative treatment plan are critical in addressing the needs of the dually diagnosed population. Reviewing the patient's complaints, expectations from treatment, and previous treatment episodes along with the current assessment of their needs may identify some common priorities as well as differences. For example, a patient may want to address panic and anxiety symptoms with medication and insist that substance use is secondary to these symptoms or irrelevant. Negotiating a treatment plan and reaching agreement on treatment goals then become the first goal of treatment. Although the need to address anxiety symptoms may be met by evaluating possible pharmacologic interventions, it is also important to begin interventions outlined earlier to enhance commitment to reduce/abstain from substance use. An explicit time frame for obtaining a collaborative treatment plan and a consistent and constant focus on the plan is more effective than a vague agreement on obtaining a common set of goals for treatment. Equally important is working collaboratively with the treatment team, especially the pharmacotherapist, who may be involved in prescribing medications.

PHASE II: ABSTINENCE, CONNECTION, AND STABILITY

Once a patient makes a commitment to abstinence, acting on the commitment and initiating abstinence are critical. Some patients may require medically supervised withdrawal (see APA Practice Guidelines, 1995). For patients who can abstain on their own, providing increased frequency of contact and support during abstinence initiation is recommended. During this period, the primary focus of the therapist must be on achieving abstinence. Although the focus is on initiating abstinence, the therapist also targets establishing a therapeutic alliance with the patient. The therapist functions as a coach, validating and cheerleading the patient's efforts, and teaching ways of coping with cravings and daily stresses to achieve initial abstinence. Patients who self-initiate abstinence should be warned of the difficulties of withdrawal and asked ahead of time for a commitment to participate in a formal detoxification if they are unable to sustain abstinence by themselves.

Protracted withdrawal symptoms, including increased anxiety, depression, craving, and sleep disturbances, are common following cessation of alcohol, cocaine, and opiates and may last up to 6–8 weeks. The patient must be prepared for these symptoms so that the focus of treatment can be the management of these symptoms without relapse. During this period, the likelihood of relapse is extremely high, and continued intensive services may be needed to provide sufficient support and structure in this early recovery phase. Important therapy tasks include emphasis on maintaining the daily log and the patient's commitment to recovery, with the therapist often cheerleading the patient's ability to abstain even for a day.

PHASE III: RECOVERY AND PREVENTING RELAPSE

The major goals of this phase are maintaining and extending the brief periods of abstinence and preventing relapse to substance use and recurrence of psychiatric symptomatology. Patients should continue to complete daily logs, which are used to target the development of self-management skills, including adaptive coping strategies to manage high-risk situations, cravings, negative affect, and psychological distress. Patients may also need to continue on psychiatric medications. During this phase, relapse prevention approaches such as coping with cravings and high-risk situations are combined with teaching skills for identifying and labeling emotions, identifying maladaptive thoughts, and observing urges and bodily sensations associated with trigger situations. Once identification and labeling of these components of the trigger situations are learned, specific behavioral skills on coping with craving, high-risk situations, negative affect and psychological distress, interpersonal conflict situations, and cognitive dysregulation states such as racing thoughts and paranoid ideation are taught for accepting and managing the urges. We use a skills-training approach adapted from traditional relapse prevention and coping skills treatment for substance use disorders (Carroll et al., 1994; 1995) and from the skills-training approach used in Linehan's Dialectical Behavior Therapy (DBT) Skills Training Manual (Linehan, 1993b). Although the former skills treatment has been shown to have specific efficacy in drug abusers with psychiatric symptoms, the latter set of skills-training techniques has been proven effective with more severe personality-disordered individuals (Linehan et al., 1991; Linehan, 1993a,b). This combined approach focuses on helping dually diagnosed patients to learn more adaptive ways of coping with their negative affect states, psychological distress, anxiety, and depressed mood, thus preventing relapse.

ADDRESSING THE LINK BETWEEN DYSREGULATED AFFECT, CRAVING, AND SUBSTANCE USE

A review of the daily record at the start of every session is used to assess level of urges, anxiety and depressed affect, sleep problems, emotional lability, and occurrence of relapse. If a relapse has occurred, therapy focuses on identifying the eliciting events and associated thoughts, feelings, urges, and bodily sensations that led to the relapse, and the consequences of the relapse. Specific attention is paid to developing alternate behavioral, cognitive, and affective coping strategies to manage high-risk situations. For example, if boredom led to relapse, fostering involvement in rewarding or interesting activities might be the suggested behavioral coping strategy, along with identifying and challenging any judgmental thoughts and negative belief systems, and identifying and labeling the negative emotions associated with such a state. Among dually diagnosed clients, developing alternate, adaptive, behavioral coping strategies is often not adequate in managing trigger situations, and teaching skills to manage the cognitive and affective components of the high-risk situation is important to ensure change in the behavioral coping process. If the patient is in a specific crisis between therapy sessions, the patient is offered phone consultations to help prevent a relapse. If a patient has not relapsed to drug use, but is increasingly more depressed, anxious, or has resorted to other impulsive behaviors such as binging or parasuicidal behaviors, however, such behaviors become the focus of treatment, with the similar goal of generating alternate, adaptive ways of coping with the distress. The alternate, adaptive solutions are generated from the specific skills that the patient learns either in individual therapy or by participating in a skills-training group. The modality determination is primarily based on the severity of the patient's substance use disorder and severity of comorbid psychiatric symptomatology. Some patients with severe Axis I or II psychiatric disorders may benefit from participation in a skills-training group along with concurrent individual therapy. The skills-training group focuses on teaching the patients new psychosocial skills, while the individual therapy focuses on specific treatment goals and generalization of newly acquired skills to the specific problems that the patient is facing currently in his or her life. For other patients, especially those whose symptoms are less severe or who are at a later stage of treatment, skills training may occur as part of the individual therapy.

AFFECT REGULATION SKILLS TRAINING

The psychobiological model proposed for understanding comorbid disorders is based on the notion that affect dysregulation is a central dynamic in the development or perpetuation of addiction. A key element in this model is teaching patients ways of coping with emotional distress so that they are able to prevent relapse. We have adapted Linehan's skills training manual (Linehan, 1993b) for this purpose, and we teach patients mindfulness, emotion regulation, interpersonal effectiveness, and distress tolerance skills, in the context of the integrated treatment outlined here. The mindfulness skills focus on making the patients aware of their mind states, identifying thoughts, feelings, and urges and teaching ways of redirecting their attention to specific objectives in each situation. For example, dually diagnosed clients may focus primarily on their racing thoughts, feelings of hopelessness, or sleep difficulties, and teaching them ways to notice and describe additional components of each experience (the components of each experience are broken down into thoughts, emotions, urges/actions, and bodily sensations) increases their overall awareness and decreases the focus on specific symptoms. Emotion regulation skills focus on identifying primary and secondary emotions; labeling emotions; integrating feelings with thoughts, urges, and bodily sensations; modulating negative feeling states; identifying and increasing positive daily activities as a way of altering recurrent negative mood; and experiencing positive emotions. Interpersonal effectiveness skills focus on ways of being effective in an interpersonal situation with a focus on one's priorities and objectives. Finally, distress tolerance skills focus on identifying a crisis and learning ways of tolerating painful affect instead of resorting to impulsive, maladaptive behaviors.

RELAPSE PREVENTION SKILLS

The major challenge of treating substance abuse is to help the patient avoid a relapse. A well-established and effective strategy of avoiding relapse is to identify the high-risk situations that increase the likelihood of resuming drug use and help the patient anticipate and practice strategies for coping with these situations. Relapse prevention and coping skills treatment approaches are based on this premise, and several excellent texts elaborate on the specific interventions to achieve this goal (Marlatt & Gordon, 1985; Monti et al., 1989). For this patient population, however, relapse prevention skills are modified to relate specifically to the affect regulation skills discussed earlier to prevent relapses associated with psychological distress.

ENHANCING SOCIAL SUPPORT

A consistent finding in the literature on depression, anxiety disorders, and drug abuse is the protective influence of an adequate network of social supports (Mazure, 1995; Marlatt & Gordon, 1985). Patients with serious psychiatric symptoms and active substance abuse typically have difficulties managing and maintaining interpersonal relationships. We address this in two ways. First, patients are specifically taught ways of being effective in interpersonal relationships, including assertiveness training and a focus on priority of self-goals in the skills groups. Second, participation in self-help groups or twelve-step programs is strongly recommended, and the individual therapist actively problem-solves with the patient regarding participation in Alcoholics Anonymous (or Narcotics Anonymous) groups. Twelve-step programs can provide opportunities for developing social supports and relationships with others. In most urban and suburban settings, self-help groups are held daily, a "sponsor" system is available to provide the patient with individual guidance and support, and "after-care meetings" and activities provide additional support.

FUTURE RESEARCH AND CONCLUSIONS

Although it is well established that high rates of comorbidity exist among substance abusers and that presence of psychiatric symptomatology leads to poorer compliance and retention rates along with increased risk for relapse, there is great need for research on the etiology of comorbid disorders, factors that increase the risk of comorbid psychiatric and substance abuse disorders, and the effectiveness of differing treatment approaches. In addition, there is a strong need for obtaining empirical support for integrated treatment approaches such as the one proposed here. Clinically, we have implemented this model at our substance abuse treatment unit and have seen benefits, both in terms of better retention in treatment and improved substance use outcomes, but systematic and rigorous evaluation of the efficacy of this model of treatment is an important future goal. Finally, additional research is needed to evaluate pharmacologic interventions to assess timing of initiation of psychiatric medication. Collection of information on both substance use and psychiatric outcomes in the same population is important, and studies examining the optimal length of maintenance on medications for patients with nonpsychotic comorbid disorders are also necessary.

References

American Psychiatric Association (1994). *Diagnostic and Statistical Manual of Mental Disorders,* 4th ed. Washington, D.C.: American Psychiatric Association.

American Psychiatric Association (1995). *Practice Guideline for Treatment of Patients with Substance Use Disorders.* American Psychiatric Association: Washington, D.C.

American Society of Addiction Medicine (1991a). *ASAM patient placement criteria for the treatment of psychoactive substance use disorders.* Chevy Chase, Md.: American Society of Addiction Medicine.

American Society of Addiction Medicine and National Association of Addiction Treatment Providers (1991b). *ASAM/NAATP patient placement criteria for the treatment of psychoactive substance use disorders.* Chevy Chase, Md.: American Society of Addiction Medicine.

Anthenelli, R. M., Schuckit, M.A. (1993). Affective and anxiety disorders and alcohol and drug dependence: diagnosis and treatment. *Journal of Addictive Diseases,* 12(3), 73–87.

Bien, T. H, Miller, W. R., Tonigan, J. S. (1993). Brief interventions for alcohol problems: A review. *Addiction,* 88, 315–336.

Biener, L., Abrams, D. B. (1991). The contemplation ladder: Validation of a measure of readiness to consider smoking cessation. *Health Psychology,* 10: 360–365.

Brooner, R. K., King, V. L., Kidorf, M., Schmidt, C. W., Bigelow, G. E. (1997). Psychiatric and substance use comorbidity among treatment-seeking opioid abusers. *Archives of General Psychiatry,* 54(1), 71–80.

Brown, S. A., Inaba, B. A., Gillin, J. C., Schuckit, M. A., Stewart, M. A., Irwin, M. R. (1995). Alcoholism and affective disorder: Clinical course of depressive symptoms. *American Journal of Psychiatry,* 152(1), 45–52.

Cacciola, J. S., Alterman, A. I., Rutherford, M. J., Snider, E. C. (1995). Treatment response of antisocial substance abusers. *Journal of Nervous and Mental Disease,* 183(3), 166–171.

Cacciola, J. S., Rutherford, M. J., Alterman, A. I., McKay, J. R., Snider, E. C. (1996). Personality disorders and treatment outcome in methadone maintenance patients. *Journal of Nervous and Mental Disease,* 184(4), 234–239.

Carey, K. B. (1989). Emerging treatment guidelines for the mentally ill chemical abusers. *Hospital and Community Psychiatry* 40, 1037–1040.

Carroll, K. M., Nich, C., Rounsaville, B. J. (1995). Differential symptom reduction in depressed cocaine abusers treated with psychotherapy and pharmacotherapy. *Journal of Nervous and Mental Disease,* 183(4), 184–259.

Carroll, K. M., Power, M. D., Bryant, K. J., Rounsaville, B. J. (1993). One-year follow-up status of treatment-seeking cocaine abusers: Psychopathology and dependence severity as predictors of outcome. *Journal of Nervous and Mental Disease,* 181(2):71–79.

Carroll, K. M., Rounsaville, B. J., Gordon, L. T., Nich, C., Jatlow, P., Bisighini, R. M., Gawin, F. H. (1994). Psychotherapy and pharmacotherapy for ambulatory cocaine abusers. *Archives of General Psychiatry,* 51, 177–187.

Caton, C. L., Gralnick, A., Bender, S., Simon, R. (1989): Young chronic patients and substance abuse. *Hospital and Community Psychiatry,* 40, 1037–1040.

Clarkin, J. F., and Kendall, P. C. (1992). Comorbidity and treatment planning summary and future directions, *Journal of Consulting and Clinical Psychology,* 60, 904–908.

Cooper, M. L., Russel, M., Skinner, J. B., Windle, M. (1992). Development and validation of a three-dimensional measure of drinking motives. *Psychological Assessment,* 4, 123–132.

Cornelius, J. R., Salloum, I. M., Cornelius, M. D., Perel, J. M., Ehler, J. G., Jarrett, P. J., Levin, R. L., Black, A., Mann, J. J (1995). Preliminary report: Double-blind, placebo-controlled study of fluoxetine in depressed alcoholics. *Psychopharm. Bulletin,* 31(2), 297–303.

Cornelius, J. R., Salloum, I. M., Cornelius, M. D., Perel, J. M., Thase, M. E., Ehler, J. G., Mann, J. J. (1993). Fluoxetine trial in suicidal depressed alcoholics. *Psychopharm. Bulletin,* 29, 195–199.

Craig, T. J., Linm, S. P., El-Defrawi, M. H., Goldman, A. B. (1985). Clinical correlates of readmission in a schizophrenic cohort. *Psychiatric Quarterly,* 57, 243–249.

Crowley, T. J., Chesluk, D., Dilts, S., et al. (1974): Drug and alcohol abuse among psychiatric admissions. *Archives of General Psychiatry,* 30, 13–20.

Drake, R. E., Osher, F. C., Wallach, M. A. (1989). Alcohol use and abuse in schizophenia: A prospective community study. *Journal of Nervous and Mental Disease,* 177, 408–414.

Dulit, R. A., Fyer, M. R., Haas, G. L., Sullivan, T., Frances, A. J. (1990). Substance use in borderline personality disorder. *American Journal of Psychiatry,* 147, 1002–1007.

Dunner, D., Hensel, B. M., Fieve, R. R. (1979): Bipolar illness: Factors in drinking behavior. *American Journal of Psychiatry*, 136, 583–585.

Galanter, M., Castaneda, R., Ferman, J. (1988): Substance abuse among general psychiatric patients: Place of presentation, diagnosis, and treatment. *American Journal of Alcohol and Drug Abuse*, 14, 211–235.

Greenfield, S. F., Weiss, R. D., Tohen, M. (1995): Substance abuse and the chronically mentally ill: A description of dual diagnosis treatment services in a psychiatric hospital. *Comm. Mental Health Journal*, 31(3), 265–277.

Grilo, C. M., Martino, S., Walker, M. L., Becker, D. F., Edell, W. S., McGlashan, T. H. (1997). Controlled study of psychiatric comorbidity in psychiatrically hospitalized young adults with substance use disorders. *American Journal of Psychiatry*, 154(9), 1305–1307.

Goodwin, D. W., Guze, S. B., *Psychiatric Diagnosis*. New York: Oxford University Press, 1980.

Hasin, D. S., Endicott, J., Keller, M. B. (1989). RDC alcoholism in patients with major affective syndromes: Two-year course. *American Journal of Psychiatry* 146:318–323.

Hasin, D. S., Endicott, J., Keller, M. B. (1991). Alcohol problems in psychiatric patients: 5-year course. *Comprehensive Psychiatry* 32:303–316.

Hasin, D. S., Endicott, J., Lewis, C. (1985): Alcohol and drug abuse in patients with affective syndromes. *Comprehensive Psychiatry*, 26, 283–295.

Hasin, D. S., Tsai, W. Y., Endicott, J., Mueller, T. I., Coryell, W., Keller, M. (1996). Five-year course of major depression: effects of comorbid alcoholism. *Journal of Affective Disorders*, 41(1), 63–70.

Haywood, T. W., Kravitz, H. M., Grossman, L. S., Cavanaugh, J. L., Davis, J. M., Lewis, D. A. (1995). Predicting the "revolving door" phenomenon among patients with schizophrenic, schizoaffective and affective disorders. *American Journal of Psychiatry*, 152(6), 856–861.

Hein, D., Zimberg, S., Weisman, S., First, M., Ackerman, S. (1997). Dual diagnosis subtypes in urban substance abuse and mental health clinics. *Psychiatric Services*, 18(8), 1058–1063.

Hesselbrock, M. N., Meyer, R. E., Keener, J. J. (1985). Psychopathology in hospitalized alcoholics. *Archives of General Psychiatry*, 42, 1050–1055.

Hirschfeld, R. M. A, Hasin, D., Keller, M. B., Endicott, J., Wunder, J. (1990). Depression and alcoholism: comorbidity in a longitudinal study. In J. D. Maser & C. R. Cloninger (eds.), *Comorbidity of mood and anxiety disorders*. Washington, D.C.: American Psychiatric Press, pp. 293–304.

Kadden, R. M., Cooney, N. L., Getter, H., et al. (1989). Matching alcoholics to coping skills or interactional therapies: Posttreatment results. *Journal of Consulting and Clinical Psychology*, 57, 698–704.

Kessler, R. C., McGonagle, K. A., Zhao, S., Nelson, C. B., Hughes, M., Eshleman, S., Wittchen, H., Kendler, K. S. (1994). Lifetime and 12-month prevalence of DSM-III-R psychiatric disorders in the United States. *Archives of General Psychiatry*, 51, 8–19.

Kessler, R. C., Nelson, C. B., McGonagle, K. A., Edlund, M. J., Frank, R. G., Leaf, P. J. (1996). The epidemiology of co-occurring addictive and mental disorders: Implications for prevention and service utilization. *American Journal of Orthopsychiatry*, 66:17–31.

Khantzian, E. J. (1989). The psychotherapy of dually diagnosed patients. *Journal of Substance Abuse Treatment*, 6, 9–18, 1989.

Khantzian, E. J., Treece, C. (1985). DSM-III psychiatric diagnosis of narcotic addicts: Recent findings. *Archives of General Psychiatry*, 42:1067–1071.

Kosten, T. R., Rousaville, B. J., Kleber, H. D. (1982). DSM-III personality disorders in opiate addicts. *Comprehensive Psychiatry*, 23, 572–581.

Kranzler, H. R., Meyer, R. E. (1989). An open trial of buspirone in alcoholics. *Journal of Clinical Psychopharmacology*, 9, 379–380.

Kranzler, H. R., Burleson, J. A., Delboca, F. K., Babor, T. F., Korner, P., Brown, J., Bohn, M. J. (1994). Buspirone treatment of anxious alcoholics: A placebo-controlled trial. *Archives of General Psychiatry*, 51, 720–731.

Kranzler, H. R., Meyer, R. E. (1989). An open trial of buspirone in alcoholics. *Journal of Clinical Psychopharmacology*, 9, 379–380.

Lehman, A. F., Myers, C., Corty, E., Thompson, J. W. (1994): Prevalence and patterns of "dual diagnosis" among psychiatric inpatients. *Comprehensive Psychiatry*, 35(2), 106–112.

Linehan, M. M. (1993a). *Cognitive behavioral therapy of borderline personality disorder.* New York: Guilford.

Linehan, M. M. (1993b). *The skills training manual for treating borderline personality disorder.* New York: Guilford.

Linehan, M. M., Armstrong, H. E., Suarez, A., Allmon, D., Heard, H. L. (1991). Cognitive-behavioral treatment of chronically parasuicidal borderline patients. *Archives of General Psychiatry*, 48, 1060–1064.

Links, P. S., Heslegrave, R. J., Mitton, J. E., van Reekum, R., Patrick, J. (1995). Borderline personality disorder and substance abuse: Consequences of comorbidity. *Canadian Journal of Psychiatry*, 40, 9–14.

Liskow, B., Powell, B., Nickel, E., Penick, E. (1990). Diagnostic subgroups of antisocial alcoholics: Outcome at 1 year. *Comprehensive Psychiatry*, 31(6), 549–556.

Litt, M. D., Babor, T. F., DelBoca, F. K., et al. (1992). Types of alcoholics, II: Application of an empirically derived typology to treatment matching. *Archives of General Psychiatry*, 49, 609–614.

Litten, R. Z., Allen, J. P. (1995). Pharmacology for alcoholics with collateral depression or anxiety: an update of research findings. *Experimental and Clinical Psychopharmacology*, 3:1, 87–93.

Ludwig, A. M., Wikler, A., Stark, L. H. (1974). The first drink: Psychobiological aspects of craving. *Archives of General Psychiatry*, 30: 539–547.

Marlatt, G. A., Gordon, J. R. (1985). *Relapse prevention: Maintenance strategies in the treatment of addictive behaviors*. New York: Guilford.

Mazure, C. M. (1995). *Does stress cause psychiatric Illness?* Washington, D.C.: American Psychiatric Press.

McElvey, M. J., Kane, J. S., Kellison, K. (1987): Substance abuse and mental illness: Double trouble. *Journal of Psychosocial Nursing*, 1, 20–25.

McLellan, A. T. (1986). Psychiatric Severity as a predictor of outcome from substance abuse treatments. In R.E. Meyer (ed.), *Psychopathology and Addictive Disorders*. New York: Guilford.

McLellan, A. T., Grissom, G. R., Zanis, D., Randall, M., Brill, P., O'Brien, P. (1997). Problem-service 'matching' in addiction treatment. *Archives of General Psychiatry*, 54, 730–735.

McLellan, A. T., Luborsky, L, Woody, G. E., O'Brien, C. P., Druley, K. A. (1983). Predicting response to drug and alcohol treatments: Role of psychiatric severity. *Archives of General Psychiatry*, 40:620–625.

McLellan, A. T., Woody, G. E., O'Brien, C. P. (1979): Development of psychiatric disorders in drug abusers. *New England Journal of Medicine*, 301, 1310–1314.

Merikangas, K. R., Leckman, J. F., Prusoff, B. A., et al. (1985). Familial transmission of depression and alcoholism. *Archives of General Psychiatry*, 42:367–372.

Meyer, R. E. (1986). How to understand the relationship between psychopathology and addictive disorders: Another example of the chicken and the egg. In: R. E. Meyer (ed.), *Psychopathology and Addictive Disorders*. New York: Guilford.

Miller, W. R., Rollnick, S. (1991). *Motivational interviewing: Preparing people to change addictive behavior*. New York, N.Y.: Guilford.

Miller, W. R., Tonigan, J. S. (1996). Assessing drinkers' motivation for change: The stages of change readiness and treatment eagerness scale (SOCRATES). *Psychology of Addictive Behaviors*, Vol. 10 (2), 81–89.

Miller, W. R., Zweben, A., DiClemente, C. C., Rychtarik, R. G. (1992). *Motivational enhancement therapy manual* Rockville, Md.: U.S. Department of Health and Human Services, Publication No. (ADM)92-1894.

Minkoff, K. (1989). An integrated treatment model for dual diagnosis of psychosis and addiction. *Hospital and Community Psychiatry*, 40:1031–1036.

Minkoff, K., Drake, R. E. (1991). *Dual diagnosis of major mental illness and substance disorder*. San Francisco: Jossey-Bass.

Monti, P. M., Abrams, D. B., Kadden, R. M., Cooney, N. L. (1989). *Treating alcohol dependence: A coping skills training guide.* New York: Guilford.

Mowbray, C. T., Solomon, M., Ribisl, K. M., et al. (1995): Treatment of mental illness and substance abuse in a public psychiatric hospital: Successful strategies and challenging problems. *Journal of Substance Abuse Treatment,* 12, 129–139.

Mueller, T. I., Lavori, P. W., Keller, M. B., Swartz, A., Warshaw, M., Hasin, D., Coryell, W., Endicott, J., Rice, J., Akiskal, H. (1994). Prognostic effect of the variable course of alcoholism on the 10-year course of depression. *American Journal of Psychiatry,* 151(5), 701–706.

Nace, E. P., Saxon, J. J., Shore, N. (1983). A comparison of borderline and nonborderline patients. *Archives of General Psychiatry,* 40, 54–56.

Pepper, B., Kirshner, M. C., Ryglewicz, M. (1981): The young adult chronic patient: overview of a population. *Hospital and Community Psychiatry,* 32, 463–469.

Prochaska, J. O., DiClemente, C. C., Norcross, J. C. (1992). In search of how people change: Applications to addictive disorders. *American Psychologist,* 47:1102–1114.

Project MATCH Research Group (1997). Matching alcoholism treatments to client heterogeneity: Project MATCH Posttreatment drinking outcomes. *Journal of Studies on Alcohol,* 58(1), 7–25.

Regier, D. A., Farmer, M. E., Rae, D. S., Locke, B. Z., Keith, S. J., Judd, L. L., Goodwin, F. K. (1990). Comorbidity of mental disorders with alcohol and other drug abuse: Results for the Epidemiological Catchment Area (ECA) study. *JAMA* 264, 2511–2518.

Ridgeley, M. S., Goldman, H. H., Willneberg, M. (1990). Barriers to the care of persons with dual diagnosis: Organizational and financing issues. *Schizophrenia Bulletin,* 16, 123–132.

Ries, R. K., Ellingson, T. (1990): A pilot assessment at one month of 17 dual diagnosis patients. *Hospital and Community Psychiatry,* 41, 1230–1233.

Rosenthal, R. N., Hellerstein, D. J., Miner, C. R. (1992a). Integrated services for treatment of schizophrenic substance abusers: Demographics, symptoms, and substance abuse patterns. *Psychiatry Quarterly,* 63, 3–26.

Rosenthal, R. N., Hellerstein, D. J., Miner, C. R. (1992b). A model of integrated services for outpatient treatment of patients with comorbid schizophrenia and addictive disorders. *American Journal of Addiction,* 1(4): 339–348.

Ross, H. E., Glaser, F. B., Germanson, T. (1988). The prevalence of psychiatric disorders in patients with alcohol and other drug problems. *Archives of General Psychiatry,* 45:1023–1032.

Rounsaville, B. J., Cacciola, B. A., Weissman, M. M., Kleber, H. D. (1981). Diagnostic concordance in a follow-up study of opiate addicts. *Psychiatric Research,* 16(3), 191–201.

Rounsaville, B. J., Dolinsky, Z. S., Babor, T. F., Meyer, R. (1987). Psychopathology as a predictor of treatment outcome in alcoholics. *Archives of General Psychiatry,* 44, 505–513.

Rounsaville, B. J., Foley, A., Anton, S., Carroll, K., Budde, D., Prusoff, B. A., and Gawin, F. (1991). Psychiatric diagnoses of treatment-seeking cocaine abusers. *Archives of General Psychiatry,* 48:43–51.

Rounsaville, B. J., Kosten, T. R., Weissman, M. M., Kleber, H. D. (1986). Prognostic significance of psychiatric disorders in treated opiate addicts. *Archives of General Psychiatry,* 43, 739–745.

Rounsaville, B. J., Kranzler, H. R. (1989). The DSM-III-R diagnosis of alcoholism. In A. Tasman, R. E. Hale, A. J. Frances (eds.), *Psychiatric update.* Washington, D.C.: American Psychiatric Press, 323–340.

Rounsaville, B. J., Weissman, M. M., Kleber, H., Wilber, C. (1982a). Heterogeneity of psychiatric diagnosis in treated opiate addicts. *Archives of General Psychiatry,* 39, 161–166.

Rounsaville, B. J., Weissman, M. M., Wilber, C. H., Crits-Christoph, K., Kleber, H. D. (1982b). Diagnosis and symptoms of depression in opiate addicts: Course and relationship to treatment outcome. *Archives of General Psychiatry,* 39, 151–156.

Rousar, E., Brooner, R. K., Regier, M. W., Bigelow, G. E. (1994). Psychiatric distress in antisocial drug abusers: relation to other personality disorders. *Drug and Alcohol Dependence,* 34, 149–154.

Rutherford, M. J., Cacciola, J. S., Alterman, A. I. (1993). Predictive validity of the psychopathy checklist — Revised in treated opiate addicts. In L. Harris (ed.), *Problems of drug dependence 1992* (NIDA Research Monographs 132). Rockville Md.: U.S. Department of Health and Human Services.

Safer, D. J. (1987). Substance abuse by adult chronic patients. *Hospital and Community Psychiatry,* 5, 511–514.

Schottenfeld, R. S., Pantalon, M. V. (1999). Assessment of the patient. In Galanter, M., & Kleber, H. D. (eds.), *Textbook of substance abuse treatment,* Washington, D.C.: American Psychiatric Press pp. 109–119.

Sinha, R., Catapano, D., O'Malley, S. (1999). Stress-induced craving and stress response in cocaine-dependent individuals. *Psychopharmacology,* 142, 343–351.

Sinha, R., Krishnan-Sarin, S., O'Malley, S. (1997). Stress responses and stress-induced craving in alcoholics. Poster presented at the Annual Meetings of the Research Society of Alcoholism, San Francisco, California, July 20–24.

Strakowski, S. M., Tohen, M., Stoll, A. L., Faedda, G. L., Mayer, P. V., Kolbrener, M. L., Goodwin, D. C. (1993). Comorbidity in psychosis at first hospitalization. *American Journal of Psychiatry,* 150(5), 752–757.

Tohen, M., Waterneaux, C. M., Tsuang, D. (1990). Outcome in mania: A 4-year prospective follow-up of 75 patients utilizing survival analysis. *Archives of General Psychiatry,* 47, 1106–1111.

Tsuang, D., Cowley, D., Ries, R., et al. (1995). The effects of substance use disorders on the clinical presentation of anxiety and depression in an outpatient psychiatric clinic. *Journal of Clinical Psychiatry,* 56, 549–555.

Vaglum, S., Vaglum, P. (1985). Borderline and other mental disorders in alcoholic female psychiatric patients: A case control study. *Psychopathology,* 18, 50–60.

Wallace, B. C. (1989). Psychological and environmental determinants of relapse in crack cocaine smokers. *Journal of Substance Abuse Treatment,* 6, 95–106.

Weiss, R. D., Greenfield, S. F., Najavits, L. M. (1995). Integrating psychological and pharmacological treatment of dually diagnosed patients. *NIDA Research Monographs,* 150:110–128.

Weiss, R. D., Mirin, S. M., Griffin, M. L. (1992). Methodological considerations in the diagnosis of coexisting psychiatric disorders in substance abusers. *British Journal of Addiction,* 87:179–187.

Wittchen, H.-U. (1996). Critical issues in the evaluation of comorbidity of psychiatric disorders, *British Journal of Psychiatry,* 168, 9–16.

Woody, G. E., McLellan, A. T., Luborsky, L., O'Brien, C. P. (1984). Severity of psychiatric symptoms as a predictor of benefits of psychotherapy: The VA-Penn study. *American Journal of Psychiatry,* 141, 1172–1177.

Woody, G. E., McLellan, A. T., Luborsky, L., O'Brien, C. P. (1985). Sociopathy and psychotherapy outcome. *Archives of General Psychiatry,* 42, 1081–1086.

Ziedonis, D. M., Fisher, W., (1996). Motivation-based assessment and treatment of substance abuse in patients with schizophrenia. *Directions in Psychiatry,* 16(11), 1–8.

Ziedonis, D. M., Kosten, T. R. (1991). Depression as a prognostic factor for pharmacological treatment of cocaine dependence. *Psychopharm. Bulletin,* 27, 337–343.

NINE

EFFICACY OF COERCION
IN SUBSTANCE ABUSE TREATMENT

Douglas B. Marlowe, David J. Glass,
Elizabeth P. Merikle, David S. Festinger,
David S. DeMatteo, Geoffrey R. Marczyk, & Jerome J. Platt

EFFICACY OF COERCION IN SUBSTANCE ABUSE TREATMENT

Coercion in substance abuse treatment is commonly viewed as being synonymous with a legal mandate to receive services. Clients who are involuntarily committed to treatment or referred to treatment by criminal justice authorities are typically defined as "coerced," while the remaining clients are defined as "voluntary." This has had several untoward consequences for measuring the effects of coercion on treatment outcome. First, statistical power is substantially reduced (by up to a third) when a continuous variable is dichotomized (e.g., Cohen, 1988). It is reasonable to assume that coercion is a continuous variable, with patients experiencing varying degrees and types of coercive pressures. Coercion should therefore lend itself to scalar measurement, which would permit the use of more sensitive statistical techniques.

Second, the content domain of coercion may have been inadequately sampled, which would further reduce its predictive utility for treatment outcome. Substance abusers are commonly subjected to a broad array of coercive treatment-entry pressures, not all of which emanate from legal sources (e.g.,

This research was supported by grant #R01-DA-10113 from the National Institute on Drug Abuse (awarded to Dr. Marlowe), a Bondi Fellowship from MCP Hahnemann University, and a dissertation grants-in-aid award from the American Psychology-Law Society (both awarded to Dr. Glass). Portions of these data were defended by Dr. Glass as part of a doctoral dissertation in clinical psychology and law at MCP Hahnemann University. The authors would like to thank Michael Dennis, Ph.D., for his valuable input on the statistical analyses.

Brown et al., 1987; Marlowe et al., 1996; Platt, 1995; Platt et al., 1988; Rotgers, 1992). In fact, many substance abusers view nonlegal pressures as being more influential to their decision to enter treatment than formal legal mandates. For instance, substance abusers commonly rate legal entanglements as being less influential to their decision to quit or reduce drug use than such other factors as emotional disturbances, health problems, interpersonal conflicts, and employment problems (e.g., Bardsley & Beckman, 1988; Blumberg et al., 1974; Brown et al., 1971; Simpson et al., 1986; Thom, 1987; Weisner, 1993). Assessment of the full range of these treatment-entry pressures might therefore improve prediction of tenure and outcome.

Finally, it is likely that clients have widely differing views about the impact of formal legal sanctions. Some substance abusers may habituate to threats from the criminal justice system due to a history of recurrent legal entanglements. Other clients may come from cultures in which legal problems are viewed as commonplace or even a "badge of honor" to be worn proudly. Thus, the mere presence of a legal mandate might not be nearly as influential as the client's *attitude* about the significance of legal troubles.

A number of review papers are available on the efficacy of formal legal mandates in substance abuse treatment (e.g., Brown et al., 1987; Leukefeld & Tims, 1988; Platt, 1995; Platt et al., 1988; Rachin, 1988; Rotgers, 1992; Stitzer & McCaul, 1987; Ward, 1979; Webster, 1986; Weissner, 1990); refer to those resources for more in-depth discussions of the topic. Generally speaking, civil commitment and diversion programs for substance abusers processed through the criminal justice system are expensive to implement effectively, and many of these programs fail to achieve the stated objectives. Platt (1995) concluded that such programs are typically effective only if the drug abuser is placed on long-term probation or parole (five to ten years), with close supervision, regular urine testing, and a realistic threat of reincarceration for serious instances of relapse.

This is commonly illustrated by a comparison of the California Civil Addict Program (CAP) to the New York Civil Commitment Program (CCP). In the CAP program, narcotic addicts were diverted from the criminal justice system to a seven-year civil commitment program, which included a period of incarceration at a minimum security facility followed by a community aftercare component with intensive parole supervision. Severe penalties, including reincarceration, were rapidly imposed for infractions of program or parole regulations. Subjects who entered the CAP condition significantly reduced daily narcotic use and criminal activities in comparison to individuals who were immediately discharged from the program due to procedural errors in the commitment process (McGlothlin et al., 1977). In contrast, the New York CCP program permitted narcotics addicts who were charged with relatively minor offenses to elect treatment participation for three to five years, during which time the criminal charges were held in abeyance. Most eligible addicts preferred the relatively shorter prison sentences to the longer commitment period. Further, because there was no provision for mandatory participation in aftercare, few clients completed the program (e.g., Inciardi, 1988). These data indicate that the impact of legal mandates is strongly affected by how those legal pressures are managed.

Reports are conflicting as to the efficacy of enhanced probation and parole programs. Clients in enhanced programs typically receive greater amounts and varieties of substance abuse services, including random urine monitoring and progressive sanctions for evidence of drug use. Some studies have reported significant improvements in outcomes for these programs over standard probationary interventions (Anglin, 1988; Chavaria, 1992; McGlothlin, 1979), while other studies have failed to detect significant differences in outcomes (McCabe, et al., 1975; Schottenfeld, 1989; Stitzer & McCaul, 1987). Regardless of whether subjects significantly reduce drug use while in enhanced probation or parole programs, rates of relapse are often substantial following termination of monitoring (e.g., Bailey, 1975; Brecht, et al., 1993).

Clients who receive mandatory referrals from criminal justice authorities to attend community residential treatment remain in those programs significantly longer than nonmandated subjects; however, there appear to be no significant differences between groups in substance use (Anglin, 1988; Collins & Allison, 1983; DeLeon, 1988; Inciardi, 1988; Simpson & Friend, 1988; but see Stark, 1992). In fact, some evidence suggests that nonmandated clients do somewhat better in some circumstances (Friedman et al., 1982). Similarly, studies of mandatory outpatient drug abuse treatment have yielded unimpressive results. Subjects who are legally mandated into methadone-maintenance treatment engage in equivalent levels of illegal narcotic use and criminal activities as nonmandated subjects during and immediately after treatment (Anglin, et al., 1989; Brecht, et al., 1993). One study of drug-free outpatient cocaine treatment reported that nonmandated subjects entered treatment with significantly more severe substance abuse problems than did subjects referred by legal authorities, and the nonmandated subjects benefited substantially more from treatment (Glass & Marlowe, 1994). As is found in residential settings, however, legally mandated outpatients remain in treatment significantly longer than nonmandated outpatients (Collins & Allison, 1983; Glass & Marlowe, 1994; Leukefeld, 1988).

Equivalent outcomes between legally mandated and nonmandated clients in community treatment settings have been proffered as evidence by some commentators that compulsory treatment "works," because mandated clients fare at least as well as "motivated" clients (e.g., Brecht et al., 1993; Collins & Allison, 1983; Leukefeld, 1988). Apart from merely affirming the null hypothesis, this rationale presumes that mandated and nonmandated patients are comparable at baseline. It is likely, however, that legally mandated subjects differ systematically from voluntary subjects at baseline on relevant variables such as drug use severity and antisocial propensities, which would be expected to confound comparisons of treatment effects. Because it is difficult or impossible to randomly assign clients to coercive or noncoercive treatment conditions, there is often no way to disentangle these confounds (cf. Platt, 1995; Rotgers, 1992).

As noted earlier, substance abusers are subjected to a wide range of treatment-entry pressures that should be amenable to dimensional assessment. Unfortunately, to date, there is no generally accepted behavioral formulation of coercion that encompasses this larger universe of pressures, nor has an adequate assessment technology been developed that would permit scalar measurement of this construct (e.g., Brown, et al., 1987; Lidz & Hoge, 1993; Marlowe, 1996; Platt, 1995; Platt et al., 1988; Rotgers, 1992).

Most available instruments measure global perceptions of coercive treatment-entry pressures and do not distinguish among different sources of these pressures. For example, the MacArthur Admission Experience Survey (MAES; Gardner et al., 1993) assesses general perceptions of having had control over the decision to enter psychiatric inpatient treatment, having made significant input into the decision to enter treatment, and having been forced, threatened, or cajoled to enter the hospital. The MAES does not distinguish between various sources of treatment-entry pressures (e.g., legal, familial), and its generalizability has not been established in nonpsychiatric inpatient samples. The Circumstances, Motivation, Readiness, and Suitability Scales (CMRS; DeLeon et al., 1994) assess events or conditions that influence clients to seek substance abuse treatment, including pressures stemming from legal, familial, and financial sources. However, the various sources of pressures are not scored separately and it is unclear whether the instrument samples the full range of perceived treatment-entry pressures.

Marlowe et al. (1996) sought to define the content domain of treatment-entry pressures. These investigators interviewed 260 clients at intake about their reasons for entering drug-free, outpatient cocaine abuse treatment. Most clients reported a predominance of treatment-entry pressures emanating from psychological, financial, social, familial, and legal domains, respectively. Within each of these domains, treatment entry was designed both to escape or avoid aversive consequences of drug use (e.g., imprisonment, eviction, divorce) as well as to obtain positive rewards or contingencies (e.g., respect of loved ones, improved health, improved self-esteem). These data confirm that legal mandates comprise only a portion of perceived treatment-entry pressures, and that clients enter treatment for a multitude of coercive and noncoercive reasons. Most importantly, clients generated *multidimensional profiles* of perceived treatment-entry pressures, which might prove useful for characterizing or classifying these individuals in terms of their reasons for entering treatment. Greater predictive utility should be attained by comparing clients on multiple dimensions rather than on single categorical indices such as legal status. For instance, clients who report significant legal pressures in combination with familial and social pressures might differ significantly in treatment response from clients who report only legal pressures or only financial pressures.

The present study further evaluated the content domain of perceived treatment-entry pressures among 100 clients in methadone maintenance treatment. Using cluster analytic techniques, subjects were classified according to their multidimensional profiles of reported treatment-entry pressures and the utility of these cluster typologies for predicting subsequent tenure and abstinence in treatment was examined. The clusters were also compared on the MAES and selected demographic variables.

METHODS

SUBJECTS

Participants were recruited from a methadone maintenance program in Trenton, New Jersey, during 1996 and 1997. Out of 330 consecutive admissions to the program, 100 clients (30%) agreed to participate in the study. All participants met DSM-IV criteria for primary heroin dependence. In addition to opiates, substantial proportions of participants reported abusing cocaine (35%), alcohol (26%), cannabis (14%), or benzodiazepines (3%). They averaged (±SD) 2.30 ± 2.33 prior substance abuse treatment episodes.

Subjects were predominantly male (62%), Caucasian (52%) or African American (35%), single (92%), unemployed (64%), and currently living with family members or friends (82%). Their mean age was 37.81 ± 7.33 years and their mean educational attainment was 11.79 ± 1.75 years. None of the participants was involuntarily committed for treatment; however, 22% of participants reported current legal involvement (11% on probation or parole, 9% facing criminal charges, 2% under investigation by child protective services). Clients who refused to participate in the study did not differ from the final cohort on demographic variables other than employment status. Clients who refused participation were more often employed (55%), $x^2(1, N = 330) = 15.80$, $p < .01$; and, indeed, the most common reason offered for refusing participation was a need to leave for work immediately after obtaining methadone. No data are available on the substance abuse patterns of clients who refused participation.

INSTRUMENTS

Survey of Treatment-Entry Pressures (STEP; Marlowe et al., 1996)

Participants were administered the STEP within ten days of admission. They were specifically asked: (1) "What made you decide to enter treatment at this time?" (2) "What problems was heroin causing you that made you seek help now?" (3) "What advantages do you envision as a result of entering treatment?" and (4) "Who or what influenced you to seek help now?" They were then asked to rate the importance of each pressure to their decision to enter treatment on a three-point Likert scale, from 1 ("a little important") to 2 ("moderately important") to 3 ("very important").

The procedures for tabulating subjects' responses are described elsewhere (Marlowe et al., 1996). First, responses were scored as containing either a positive or negative reinforcement schedule. In the case of negative reinforcement, treatment entry is intended to escape or avoid an aversive consequence of drug use; for example, "my wife said she would leave me if I didn't get help." In a positive reinforcement schedule, treatment entry is designed to obtain positive rewards; for example, "I wanted my children to respect me again." Second, responses were scored as being socially mediated or non-socially mediated. Social mediation indicates that the application of contingent reinforcement is perceived by the subject as being in the control of another person or entity. For example, a response that "my boss threatened to fire me if I didn't quit" would be scored as socially mediated because the boss has apparent control over the imposition of the contingent reinforcement (i.e., termination of employment). Finally, responses were scored according to the primary psychosocial domain from which they emanated (family, financial, social, medical, legal, psychiatric, or other).

Reinforcement schedule and social mediation were crossed in a two-by-two table to yield four general categories of treatment-entry pressures: co-

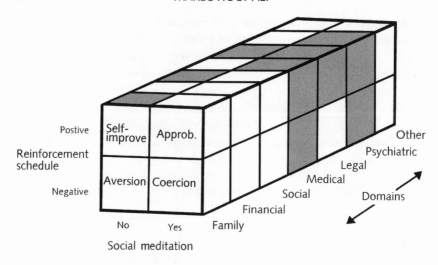

Fig. 9.1.

ercion (socially mediated negative reinforcement), aversion (non-socially mediated negative reinforcement), approbation (socially mediated positive reinforcement), and self-improvement (non-socially mediated positive reinforcement). These, in turn, were crossed with the seven psychosocial domains in the two-by-two-by-seven matrix depicted in figure 9.1. Fourteen of the possible 28 treatment-entry pressures were omitted from the analyses because they were rarely reported (reported by < 5% of subjects). The rarely reported pressures are shaded in figure 9.1. In addition, the "other" domain was excluded from further analyses because it was too heterogeneous to be useful or interpretable.

Table 9.1 provides sample items for the 14 prevalent treatment-entry pressures reported in the sample.

Inter-rater reliability of the STEP was calculated based on three raters who were advanced practicum students in a combined law and clinical psychology (J.D., Ph.D.) graduate program at MCP Hahnemann University and Villanova University School of Law. The raters independently scored interview responses in 3 rounds of 10 protocols, averaging 10 to 12 items per subject. Inter-rater agreement was computed for each round, and the raters were instructed to resolve all scoring discrepancies and to keep track of any agreed-upon decision rules. The resolved scores were used in all substantive analyses. A minimum criterion of 80% agreement was required on all scores (reinforcement schedule, social mediation, and psychosocial domain).

Table 9.1: Sample responses of prevalent* treatment-entry pressures

PRESSURE	SAMPLE RESPONSE
Financial aversion	"I was tired of being poor all the time."
Medical aversion	"The drugs were making me sick."
Psychiatric aversion	"I couldn't stand the depression any more."
Legal aversion	"I was afraid I'd wind up in jail."
Psychiatric self-improvement	"To improve my self-esteem."
Medical self-improvement	"I wanted to be healthy again."
Financial self-improvement	"So I could earn a living."
Family coercion	"My wife was going to leave me."
Social coercion	"I was afraid of losing all my friends."
Financial coercion	"The bill collectors keep harrassing us."
Legal coercion	"My probation officer was gonna violate me."
Family approbation	"I wanted my children's respect."
Social approbation	"So I could hang with my old cronies again."
Financial approbation	"I want to impress my boss and get ahead."

* Includes only those pressures that were reported by >5% of subjects in the current sample.

MacArthur Admission Experience Survey — Short Form (MAES; Gardner, et al., 1993).

Participants completed the MAES-SF at the same time as the STEP. The MAES-SF is a 14-item, true-false questionnaire that was designed to assess perceptions of coercion within the context of inpatient psychiatric admission. The word *hospital* was replaced with *program* to make it face-valid for outpatient treatment. The MAES-SF is made up of three subscales. The Perceived Coercion Scale (5 items) assesses clients' perceptions of having had control over the decision to enter treatment; the Negative Pressures Scale (6 items) assesses perceptions of having been forced, threatened, or cajoled to enter treatment; and the Voice Scale (3 items) assesses perceptions of having had significant input into the decision to enter treatment.

OUTCOME MEASURES

Clients submitted urine samples upon random notification on an average schedule of two times per month. The urine specimens were immediately tested on site for the presence of opiate and other drug metabolites. The total number of drug-free urines provided by the subject was used as an index of abstinence. Treatment attendance was measured by the total number of group and individual counseling sessions completed by the client, and treatment tenure was measured by the number of weeks that the client maintained enrollment in the program. Outcomes were tracked for 3 months from the date of intake; therefore, clients could provide up to 6 clean urine samples, maintain up to 12 weeks of enrollment in the program, and attend up to 14 counseling sessions.

DATA ANALYSES

Cluster typologies of clients were generated from the STEP using SPSS 7.5. Because this study was exploratory in nature, a hierarchical cluster analytic procedure was used that did not pre-specify the number or composition of the clusters (e.g., Rapkin & Luke, 1993). Ward's Method (Ward, 1963) was employed to minimize within-cluster variability and to maximize the distance between clusters. The final number of clusters was determined based upon their interpretability and their ability to discriminate between subjects on the outcome measures.

Between-cluster comparisons were performed on demographic variables, including gender, race, legal status, marital status, employment status, and living arrangements; the MAES Perceived Coercion Scale, Voice Scale, and Negative Pressures Scale; and the treatment outcome indices of tenure, attendance, and abstinence. These analyses were performed using ANOVA and Least Significant Difference (LSD) post hoc tests for continuous data and chi square for categorical data. The p-values were not Bonferroni-corrected because of the exploratory nature of this preliminary study.

RESULTS

Inter-rater reliability for the STEP was excellent over all three rating trials. Percentages of agreement were 97%, 87%, and 91%, respectively, for reinforcement schedule; 96%, 95%, and 95% for social mediation; and 98%, 81%, and 90% for psychosocial domain.

Table 9.2 presents descriptive statistics on the treatment-entry pressures reported by at least 5% of subjects in the total sample. Non-socially mediated medical, psychiatric, and financial pressures were reported most often, indicating that the majority of clients entered methadone maintenance predominantly to escape the aversive physical, psychological, and financial consequences of opiate use and to improve their conditions in these areas. Sub-

Table 9.2: Descriptive statistics on prevalent * treatment-entry pressures among 100 clients in methadone maintenance treatment

PRESSURE	% OF SUBJECTS**	MEAN (SD)	RANGE
Aversion	*97*	*9.24 (5.08)*	*0–14*
Financial aversion	70	3.12 (2.82)	0–12
Medical aversion	62	2.79 (2.94)	0–15
Psychiatric aversion	55	2.56 (2.30)	0–15
Legal aversion	16	0.78 (2.05)	0–12
Self-improvement	*85*	*5.71 (4.00)*	*0–21*
Psychiatric self-improvement	51	2.16 (2.58)	0–12
Medical self-improvement	50	1.95 (2.38)	0–12
Financial self-improvement	48	1.60 (1.98)	0–8
Coercion	*76*	*3.72 (3.37)*	*0–14*
Family coercion	54	1.76 (2.03)	0–9
Social coercion	28	1.02 (1.82)	0–8
Financial coercion	16	0.51 (1.22)	0–6
Legal coercion	10	0.43 (1.60)	0–12
Approbation	*61*	*3.19 (3.56)*	*0–15*
Family approbation	43	1.64 (2.18)	0–9
Social approbation	33	1.15 (1.91)	0–8
Financial approbation	11	0.40 (1.35)	0–9

* Includes only those pressures that were reported by >5% of subjects in the sample.
** Indicates the proportion of subjects who reported at least one treatment-entry pressure in that category. Means, standard deviations, and ranges are for weighted scores.

stantial numbers of clients also reported coercive and approbative pressures in the social and familial domains, indicating that they also entered treatment to avoid negative consequences from friends and loved ones and to improve these interpersonal relationships. A substantial minority of clients reported experiencing legal pressures to enter treatment.

There were no significant differences on these dimensional scores in terms of demographic variables. There were, however, non-significant trends concerning gender. Female clients tended to report more approbation, $F(1, 97)$ = 3.32, p <.10; more pressures in the social domain, $F(1, 97)$ = 2.99, p <.10; and more pressures in the family domain, $F(1, 97)$ = 3.20, p <.10.

A four-cluster solution accounted for 98% of the variance in perceived treatment-entry pressures, Wilks' lambda = .02, $F(42, 244) = 15.48$, $p < .0001$. The inclusion of more clusters did not add appreciably to the variance accounted for by a four-cluster solution, and it was difficult to interpret the additional clusters because they contained moderate elevations on multiple items. The mean profiles for the four clusters are presented in figure 9.2. Roughly half of the clients in the sample ($n = 46$, 46%) were classified into cluster 1 (medical/psychiatric), which has relative elevations on medical aversion, psychiatric aversion, medical self-improvement, financial aversion, and psychiatric self-improvement, respectively. Subjects in this cluster reported being predominantly influenced by non-socially mediated medical and psychological problems to enter methadone maintenance. Cluster 2 (financial) reveals fair resolution, with a single relative elevation on financial aversion. Clients in this cluster ($n = 41$, 41%) reported mostly financial problems leading them to seek treatment. Cluster 3 (diverse) has multiple elevations on a variety of scores, including psychiatric aversion, psychiatric self-improvement, family coercion, financial coercion, and financial approbation, respectively. Clients in this cluster ($n = 9$, 9%) reported a number of different pressures stemming from various psychosocial domains. Finally, cluster 4 (legal coercion) reveals very high resolution, with a single elevation on legal coercion. Clients in this cluster ($n = 3$, 3%) reported fearing legal repercussions if they did not enter treatment.

Cluster membership was significantly predictive of tenure and outcome during treatment (see table 9.3). Subjects in the various clusters differed significantly in their length of enrollment in the program, $F(3, 95) = 4.09$, $p < .01$. Post hoc pair-wise comparisons revealed that subjects in clusters 1 and 4 had a significantly longer tenure than did subjects in cluster 2. Similarly, the clusters differed significantly in the total number of drug-free urines provided by subjects, $F(3, 95) = 4.02$, $p < .01$. Again, subjects in clusters 1 and 4 fared significantly better than did subjects in cluster 2. Finally, the groups differed significantly in the number of counseling sessions attended, $F(3, 95) = 2.98$, $p < .05$. Subjects in cluster 1 attended significantly more counseling sessions than did subjects in cluster 2.

There were also significant differences between clusters on certain demographic variables. Clusters 2 and 4 contained significantly more males, x^2 (3, N = 99) = 9.39, $p < .05$, and there was a non-significant trend toward cluster 3 containing more clients with current legal involvement, x^2 (3, N = 99) = 6.78, $p < .10$.

There were no significant differences among clusters on the MAES scales. On average, however, subjects in cluster 4 did report experiencing relatively more coercion overall, as measured by the Perceived Coercion Scale, and relatively less input into the decision to enter treatment, as measured by the Voice Scale. Subjects in cluster 3 reported experiencing more negative pressures overall, as measured by the Negative Pressures Scale. The lack of statistical significance is likely attributable to insufficient power, given that there were only three subjects in the legal cluster.

DISCUSSION

The results of this preliminary study support our hypothesis that a multidimensional analysis of treatment-entry pressures would improve prediction of outcome over categorical comparisons of legally mandated versus nonmandated subjects. Cluster analyses of data derived from the STEP produced four interpretable profiles of perceived treatment-entry pressures among clients in methadone maintenance, and cluster membership was significantly predictive of tenure and outcome in treatment.

The majority of clients in this study reported entering methadone maintenance predominantly for non-socially mediated medical and psychological reasons (46% of subjects) or for financial reasons (41%). A substantial minority of clients entered treatment in response to diverse psychosocial pressures (9%), and a small, but noteworthy minority entered treatment in response to coercive legal pressures (3%). This confirms that legal pressures make up a small, but meaningful, segment of a broader content domain of treatment-entry pressures (cf. Brown et al., 1987; Marlowe et al., 1996; Platt, 1995; Platt et al., 1988).

Perceived legal pressures were apparently effective in maintaining this small subset of clients in treatment and contributing to their abstinence. Clients who were classified in the legal cluster had the longest tenure, attended the most counseling sessions, and provided the most clean urine samples (see table 9.3). It would be erroneous, however, to assume that legal pressures are prime or unique factors in drug abuse treatment entry. Rather, while they appear to be effective motivators for some clients in methadone maintenance, they may not be effective motivators for the majority of these clients.

It is noteworthy that clients in the legal cluster did not report any current legal involvement. They were not facing criminal charges, nor were they on probation or parole or under criminal investigation. Rather, they entered treatment because they feared the possibility or likelihood of legal problems in the future. This suggests that the existence of a formal legal sanction may not be the dispositive issue. As discussed earlier, clients' attitudes about legal

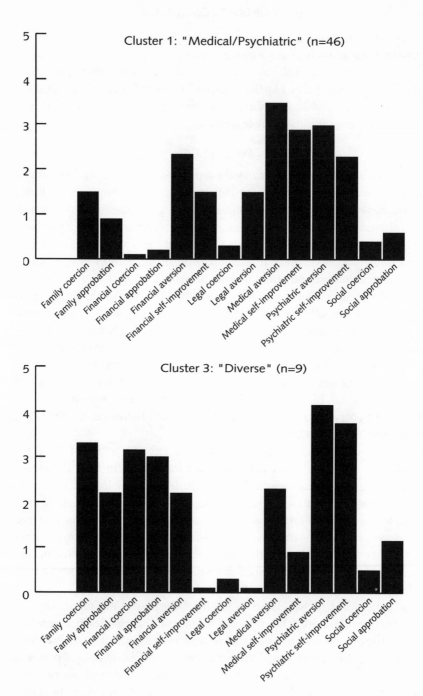

Fig. 9.2a.

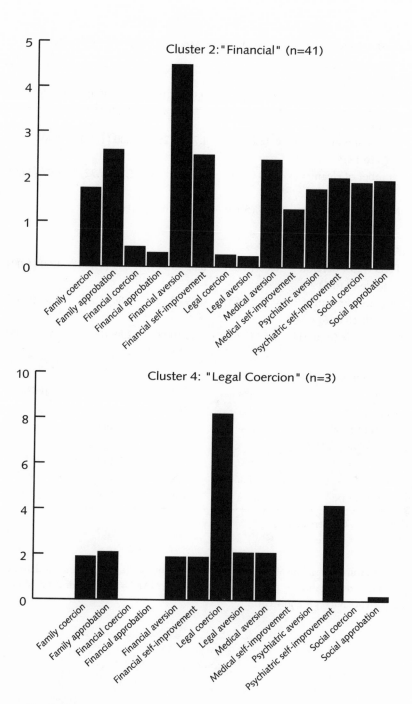

Fig. 9.2b.

Table 9.3: Between-cluster comparisons: Mean (SD) or % of subjects

DEPENDENT MEASURE	CLUSTER 1	CLUSTER 2	CLUSTER 3	CLUSTER 4
Outcome measures				
Weeks of tenure (0 to 12)[1]	6.48 (3.02)	4.71 (2.26)	6.00 (1.32)	8.00 (3.61)
Number of clean urines (0 to 6)[1]	2.80 (3.21)	1.12 (1.58)	1.78 (1.72)	4.67 (5.69)
Number of sessions (0 to 14)[2]	9.50 (5.10)	7.15 (4.04)	10.00 (3.00)	12.33 (5.03)
MAES scales				
Perceived Coercion Scale (0 to 5)	0.63 (0.88)	0.63 (0.97)	0.89 (1.17)	1.00 (1.00)
Negative Pressures Scale (0 to 6)	0.41 (0.83)	0.29 (0.72)	0.89 (1.27)	0.33 (0.58)
Voice Scale (0 to 3)	2.63 (0.64)	2.49 (0.84)	2.89 (0.33)	2.00 (1.00)
Demographic variables				
Male[3]	54%	76%	33%	100%
Caucasian	59%	46%	56%	33%
Current legal involvement[4]	28%	12%	44%	0%
Employed	36%	42%	11%	33%
Married	7%	7%	11%	33%
Living alone	22%	15%	11%	33%

1 Cluster 2 < Clusters 1 and 4.

2 Cluster 2 < Cluster 1.

3 $p < .05$.

4 $p < .10$. Current legal involvement = on probation or parole, facing criminal charges, or under investigation by child protective services. MAES = MacArthur Admission Experience Survey—Short Form.

problems may be more influential than the mere presence of a legal mandate. It might, therefore, be nonproductive or counterproductive to rely excessively on legal mandates to enforce drug treatment compliance without first ascertaining the client's belief system about the importance of legal repercussions.

Perceptions of treatment-entry pressures may bear some relation to clients' readiness or motivation for change. There might, in fact, be "good" and "bad" reasons for seeking drug abuse treatment. In the current sample, for instance, clients who reported entering methadone maintenance for medical and psychological reasons tended to succeed in treatment, while those who entered treatment to improve their financial conditions performed the poorest on all outcome measures. As several clients phrased it, being "sick and tired of being sick and tired" might be a very good reason to stop using heroin. In contrast, financial improvement is often an indirect or longer-term effect of abstinence, and thus might not be a sufficient motivator to maintain the client in treatment in the short term.

These data, therefore, have important implications for clinical practice. For the majority of clients in methadone maintenance treatment, it seems that motivation for change might be improved by focusing the client's attention on the medical and psychiatric sequelae of opiate dependence. In addition, the clinician might be advised to leverage or capitalize on informal familial and social pressures stemming from the client's natural social networks. For instance, if a client perceives operative familial pressures to enter treatment, then the clinician might be advised to include family members in conjoint interventions or to report attendance and related information to family members (with the informed consent of all parties). Such conjoint interventions might be particularly well suited to female opiate abusers, because females in this sample more often reported being influenced by approbative pressures in the family and social domains.

Because these analyses were exploratory in nature, however, it is necessary to replicate the clusters in other clinical samples and to confirm their predictive utility for treatment outcome in those settings. Additional clusters might emerge in other populations, and the relative proportions of clients that are classified into the various clusters might change as a function of sample characteristics. With a sufficiently large and heterogeneous sample, however, it should be possible to define the entire content domain of perceived treatment-entry pressures and to identify characteristic profiles for various patient groups. This would permit the development of a self-report instrument to assist clinicians with treatment planning in diverse clinical settings.

It is also important to relate perceptions of treatment-entry pressures to more definitive outcome measures. In the current study, urinalyses were performed only twice monthly, and outcomes were tracked only for three months postintake. Given the restricted range of these measures, it is particularly striking that statistical significance was reached on the outcome analyses. This suggests that there is probably a large effect size for the relation between treatment-entry pressures and clinical outcomes. With more rigorous outcome assessments and longer follow-up intervals, even larger effect sizes might be attained.

At present, however, it may be concluded that clients' perceptions of treatment-entry pressures at intake have substantial prognostic utility for tenure and outcome in substance abuse treatment. Properly conceptualized as a continuous and multidimensional construct, coercion therefore holds much promise for predicting, evaluating, and understanding treatment effects. Simply put, one of the best ways to anticipate compliance in substance abuse treatment might be to ask what brought the client into treatment in the first place.

References

Anglin, M. D. (1988). A social policy analysis of compulsory treatment for opiate dependence. *Journal of Drug Issues, 18,* 527–545.

Anglin, M. D., Brecht, M. L., & Maddahian, E. (1989). Pre-treatment characteristics and treatment performance of legally coerced versus voluntary methadone maintenance admissions. *Criminology, 27,* 537–557.

Bailey, W. C. (1975). Addicts on parole: Short term and long term prognosis. *International Journal of the Addictions, 10,* 423–437.

Bardsley, P. E., & Beckman, L. J. (1988). The health belief model and entry into alcoholism treatment. *International Journal of the Addictions, 23,* 19–28.

Blumberg, H. H., Cohen, S. D., Dronfield, B. F., Mordecai, E. A., Roberts, F. C., & Hawks, D. (1974). British opiate users: I. People approaching London treatment centers. *International Journal of the Addictions, 9,* 1–23.

Brecht, M., Anglin, M. D., & Wang, J. (1993). Treatment effectiveness for legally coerced versus voluntary methadone maintenance clients. *American Journal of Drug and Alcohol Abuse, 19,* 89–106.

Brown, B. S., Buhringer, G., Kaplan, C. D., & Platt, J. J. (1987). German/American report on the effective use of pressure in the treatment of drug addiction. *Psychology of Addictive Behaviors, 1,* 38–54.

Brown, B. S., Guavey, S. K., Meyers, M. B., & Stark, S. D. (1971). In their own words, addicts' reasons for initiating and withdrawing from heroin. *International Journal of the Addictions, 6,* 635–645.

Chavaria, F. R. (1992). Successful treatment in a criminal justice setting: A case study. *Federal Probation, 56,* 48–52.

Cohen, J. (1988). *Statistical power analysis for the behavioral sciences* (2d ed). Hillsdale, N.J.: Lawrence Erlbaum.

Collins, J. J., & Allison, M. (1983). Legal coercion and retention in drug abuse treatment. *Hospital and Community Psychiatry, 34,* 1145–1149.

DeLeon, G. (1988). Legal pressure in therapeutic communities. *Journal of Drug Issues, 18,* 625–640.

DeLeon, G., Melnick, G., Kressel, D., & Jainchill, N. (1994). Circumstances, motivation, readiness, and suitability (the CMRS scales): Predicting retention in therapeutic community treatment. *American Journal of Drug and Alcohol Abuse, 20,* 495–515.

Friedman, S. B., Horvat, G. L., & Levinson, R. B. (1982). The narcotic addict rehabilitation act: Its impact on federal prisons. *Contemporary Drug Problems, 82,* 101–111.

Gardner, W., Hoge, S. K., Bennett, N., Roth, L. H., Lidz, C. W., Monahan, J., & Mulvey, E. P. (1993). Two scales for measuring patients' perceptions of coercion during mental hospital admission. *Behavioral Sciences and the Law, 11,* 307–321.

Glass, D. J., & Marlowe, D. B. (1994, March). *Comparing state agency mandated and voluntary outpatients: treatment outcome and retention in a cocaine addiction program.* Paper presented at the 1994 Biennial Conference of the American Psychology-Law Society, Santa Fe, N.M.

Inciardi, J. A. (1988). Some considerations on the clinical efficacy of compulsory treatment: reviewing the New York experience. In C. G. Leukefeld & F. M. Tims (eds), *Compulsory treatment of drug abuse: Research and clinical practice,* pp. 126–138. NIDA Research Monograph No. 86. Rockville, Md.: National Institute on Drug Abuse, U.S. Government Printing Office.

Leukefeld, C. G. (1988). Opportunities for enhancing drug abuse treatment with criminal justice authority. In C. G. Leukefeld & F. M. Tims (eds), *Compulsory treatment of drug abuse: Research and clinical practice,* pp. 328–337. NIDA Research Monograph No. 86. Rockville, Md.: National Institute on Drug Abuse, U.S. Government Printing Office.

Leukefeld, C. G., & Tims, F. M. (Eds.) (1988). *Compulsory treatment of drug abuse: Research and clinical practice,* p. 17. NIDA Research Monograph No. 86. Rockville, Md.: National Institute on Drug Abuse, U.S. Government Printing Office.

Lidz, C. W., & Hoge, S. K. (eds.) (1993). Coercion: theoretical and empirical understanding. *Behavioral Sciences and the Law, 11,* 237–238.

Marlowe, D. B., Kirby, K. C., Bonieskie, L. M., Glass, D. J., Dodds, L. D., Husband, S. D.,

Platt, J. J., & Festinger, D. S. (1996). Assessment of coercive and noncoercive pressures to enter drug abuse treatment. *Drug and Alcohol Dependence, 42,* 77–84.

McCabe, O. L., Kurland, A. A., & Sullivan, D. (1975). Paroled narcotic addicts in a verified abstinence program: Results of a five-year study. *International Journal of the Addictions, 10,* 211–228.

McGlothlin, W. H. (1979). Criminal justice clients. In R. I. Dupont, A. Goldstein, & J. O'Donnell (eds.), *Handbook on drug abuse,* pp. 203–209. Rockville, Md.: National Institute on Drug Abuse, U.S. Dept. of Health and Human Services.

McGlothlin, W. H., Anglin, M. D., & Wilson, B. D. (1977). *An evaluation of the California Civil Addict Program.* Rockville, Md.: National Institute on Drug Abuse, U.S. Government Printing Office.

Platt, J. J. (1995). *Heroin addiction: Theory, research, and treatment.* Volume 2: *The addict, the treatment process, and social control.* Malabar, Fla.: Krieger.

Platt, J. J., Buhringer, G., Kaplan, C. D., Brown, B. S., & Taube, D. O. (1988). The prospects and limitations of compulsory treatment for drug addiction. *Journal of Drug Issues, 18,* 505–525.

Rachin, R. L. (ed.) (1988). A social policy analysis of compulsory treatment for opiate dependence. *Journal of Drug Issues, 18 (4).*

Rapkin, B. D., & Luke, D. A. (1993). Cluster analysis in community research: Epistemology and practice. *American Journal of Community Psychology, 21,* 247–277.

Rotgers, F. (1992). Coercion in addictions treatment. In J. W. Langebucher, B. S. McCrady, W. Frankenstein & P. E. Nathan (eds.), *Annual review of addiction research and treatment, 2,* 403–416.

Schottenfeld, R. S. (1989). Involuntary treatment of substance abuse disorders — Impediments to success. *Psychiatry, 52,* 164–176.

Simpson, D. D., & Friend, J. H. (1988). Legal status and long-term outcomes for addicts in the DARP follow-up project. In C. G. Leukefeld & F. M. Tims (eds.), *Compulsory Treatment of Drug Abuse: Research and clinical practice,* pp. 81–98. NIDA Research Monograph No. 86. Rockville, Md.: National Institute on Drug Abuse, U.S. Dept. of Health and Human Services.

Simpson, D. D., Joe, G. W., Lehman, W. E. K., & Sells, S. B. (1986). Addiction careers: Etiology, treatment, and 12-year follow-up outcomes. *Journal of Drug Issues, 16,* 107–121.

Stark, M. J. (1992). Dropping out of substance abuse treatment: A clinically oriented review. *Clinical Psychology Review, 12,* 93–116.

Stitzer, M. L., & McCaul, M. E. (1987). Criminal justice interventions with drug and alcohol abusers: The role of compulsory treatment. In E. K. Morris & C. J. Braukmann (eds.), *Behavioral approaches to crime and delinquency: A handbook of application, research, and concepts,* pp. 331–361. New York: Plenum.

Thom, B. (1987). Sex differences in help-seeking for alcohol problems — 2. Entry into treatment. *British Journal of Addiction, 82,* 989–997.

Ward, D. A. (1979). The use of legal coercion in the treatment of alcoholism: A methodological review. *Journal of Drug Issues, 9,* 387–393.

Ward, J. H. (1963). Hierarchical grouping to optimize an objective function. *Journal of the American Statistical Association, 58,* 236–244.

Webster, C. D. (1986). Compulsory treatment of narcotic addiction. *International Journal of Law and Psychiatry, 8,* 133–159.

Weisner, C. (1993). Toward an alcohol treatment entry model: A comparison of problem drinkers in the general population and in treatment. *Alcohol: Clinical and Experimental Research, 17,* 746–752.

Weisner, C. M. (1990). Coercion in alcohol treatment. In *Broadening the base of alcoholism treatment,* pp. 579–609. Institute of Medicine monograph. Washington, D.C.: National Academy Press.

TEN

ADOLESCENTS:
ISSUES IN RELAPSE AND RECOVERY

Sherilynn F. Spear, James R. Ciesla, Sharon Y. Skala, & Edyta D. Kania

Although the popular press gives a good deal of attention to adolescent substance abuse, articles in scholarly and professional journals are more likely to focus on adults. To the extent that it exists, scientifically sound literature on adolescents tends to concentrate on prevention and primary treatment. Only a relatively small body of literature deals with relapse and recovery among chemically dependent adolescents (Spear and Skala, 1995). Consequently, it is the adult literature that has largely directed the formulation of research issues on relapse and recovery among adolescents. Although the issues identified for adults certainly have implications for adolescents treated for chemical dependency, caution should be taken not to generalize indiscriminately from the adult to the adolescent population of substance abusers. Therefore, in this chapter we focus on relapse and recovery among adolescents. Specifically, we are concerned with: (1) reviewing the adolescent literature to identify what is known about the key issues related to relapse and recovery among adolescents treated for chemical dependency, (2) examining the implications of this literature for sustaining recovery begun by adolescents in primary treatment, and (3) suggesting a theoretical framework to guide future research on relapse and recovery among chemically dependent adolescents.

WHERE TO BEGIN

Although we do not want to generalize indiscriminately from adults to adolescents, there are areas of apparent similarity of relapse and recovery patterns for adolescents and adults. Thus, we can anticipate that for adolescents, as well for adults, relapse rates are high. The individual often fluctuates between use and nonuse. In addition, drug use is not a single behavior (DeJong, 1994)—it is part of a complex set of behaviors that link the individual to his or her social environment. In return, that social environment provides cues and opportunities for use as well as reinforces drug-using behavior. Consequently, the recovery process is complex and not clearly understood. Recovery is not likely to be a simple linear process of sustaining abstinence begun in primary treatment and then successfully continued as the person moves from the treatment to the community environment (Gerstein and Harwood, 1990; Marlatt and Gordon, 1980; Rounsaville, 1986). Continuing the process of extinguishing drug-using behavior while trying to recover or establish a nonusing lifestyle is particularly difficult if the individual returns to a community environment that is likely to reinforce drug-using behavior. In addition, drug use among adolescents as well as adults may be enmeshed with such other significant problems as histories of physical and sexual abuse, criminal behavior, and psychological disorders (Crowley, 1995; Dembo et al., 1990; Spear and Skala, 1995). Finally, from the clinical perspective, treatment for both adolescents and adults has been dominated by the "disease model." This model focuses on the onset of behavior and suggests that, once begun, the "disease" progresses with increasingly more serious consequences. Secondly, the disease model stresses the importance of professional (i.e., medical) intervention if the once-initiated process is to be brought under control. Thus, the disease model suggests a linear relapse pattern that, once begun, cannot be controlled by the individual. The theoretical underpinning of treatment with the disease model appears to be at odds with the complex and nonlinear relapse/recovery process suggested by research.

The similarities between chemically dependent adults and chemically dependent adolescents provide a framework from which to focus on the processes of relapse and recovery. In reviewing the literature that delineates the characteristics of the adolescents in the treatment population, the correlates of relapse and recovery, and the methodological and theoretical issues, we suggest a framework that is more adolescent-specific as well as discuss directions for further research.

CHARACTERISTICS OF ADOLESCENTS IN TREATMENT

Adolescents in treatment for chemical dependency range in age from 12 to 18 years. However, the majority are between 14 and 17 years old, with an average age of approximately 15.5 years (Spear and Skala, 1995; Cady, Winters, et al., 1996). The average age of onset of drug use in this population is about 12 years

(Spear, Ciesla, and Skala, 1999). More than 80% of the population is white and nearly two-thirds are male. Though families and the court system most frequently refer adolescents for treatment, other common referral sources include social agencies and schools (Spear and Skala, 1998; Cady, Winters, et al., 1996; Newcomb, 1995; Brown et al., 1989). The adolescents also report that the most common places in which they use drugs are at home and at school (Spear and Skala, 1995).

As indicated above, these adolescents often have other comorbidities. A significant proportion of the adolescents in treatment for chemical dependency have a history of physical and sexual abuse (Spear and Skala, 1998; Dembo, 1989; Harrison, Hoffmann, and Edwall, 1989; Hart, Mader, Griffith, and DeMendonca, 1989), and/or a history of delinquency (Dembo et al., 1989; Harrison and Hoffman, 1987). Females are more likely than males to report a history of physical and/or sexual abuse (Spear and Skala, 1998; Blood and Cornwall, 1996). In contrast, males are more likely to have a history of delinquency and to be referred for treatment by the court system.

In addition, research suggests that both males and females may have coexisting psychological disorders. Recent research indicates that many chemically dependent adolescents meet criteria for one or more additional psychiatric diagnoses, including conduct disorder, attention deficit/hyperactivity disorder, affective disorders, and mood disorders (McKay and Buka, 1994). McKay and Buka found that nearly 50% of their chemical dependency treatment sample met childhood and adult criteria for antisocial personality disorder.

Finally, it appears that chemically dependent adolescents are more likely to have substance-abusing parents and/or siblings and to perceive the functioning of their families as more chaotic (McKay and Buka, 1994; Spear and Skala, 1995). Greater adolescent drug use is observed within disrupted families (Newcomb, 1995). Spear, Ciesla, and Skala (1999) found that 88% of the adolescents in treatment for chemical dependency reported at least one other immediate family member having a problem with chemical dependency. Other researchers also suggest that inconsistent discipline, low and poor quality of parental interaction with their children, and low expectations for their children increase the chances of adolescent involvement with drugs (Hawkins, Catalano, and Miller, 1992).

IMPLICATION FOR RELAPSE AND RECOVERY

In general, researchers have found that the existence of one or more comorbidities appears to increase the risk of posttreatment drug use. Unfortunately, the studies that have examined the relation of comorbidities to relapse have tended to focus on one type of comorbidity: psychiatric problems, delinquency, histories of physical and/or sexual abuse, or dysfunctional families. Consequently, no overall picture emerges of the relative influence of these problems on the risk of relapse. Thus, we are left with the impression that the "more problems" the adolescent has, the greater the risk of relapse. Such comorbidities as correlates of relapse may help to identify adolescents at increased risk for relapse. They do not, however, clarify the process that leads to relapse or to recovery.

Although the risk of relapse among adolescents and adults appears to increase with the existence of comorbidities, there are other characteristics of adolescents in treatment for chemical dependency, which may uniquely influence treatment outcomes for them. These include age, continued dependence on dysfunctional families, and the pattern of drug use at home and at school. Adolescents are minors; the average age of those in treatment is about 15.5 years. Once they complete primary, residential treatment their options are quite limited. They can return home, go to jail, or run away. Most return to families in which there is at least one other member with a chemical dependency problem. They return to a home and school that were the primary places in which they used drugs in the past. Virtually all adolescents report being "offered something" within the first day of returning to school (Spear, Ciesla, and Skala, 1999). In addition, the adult literature suggests the efficacy of regaining a nonusing identity such as an employee, spouse, or parent as an important component of sustaining recovery. Because most of the adolescents began using by the age of 12, they have no such identity to recover. Indeed, adolescence is the time in which individual identities develop. Thus, age and minority status ensure that most adolescents will follow primary treatment by returning to an environment that both provides opportunities for drug use and reinforces it. Most adolescents do not have the power to choose a new environment nor the skill to function drug-free within the old one.

RELAPSE RATES AND PATTERNS

As indicated above, although relatively scarce, there are some studies that have focused on relapse rates and patterns among adolescents treated for chemical dependency. Two early, large-scale studies (Sells and Simpson, 1979; Hubbard et al., 1985) indicate that among adolescents relapse rates are high and that the greatest risk of relapse occurs during the first 6 to 12 months following treatment. More recent studies confirm these early findings and provide more detailed information on rates, patterns, and correlates of relapse among adolescents.

Brown et al. (1989) assessed relapse rates of 75 adolescents who had completed inpatient treatment and compared them with those of adults, suggesting that both relapse rates and timing of relapse for adolescents are similar to those for adults. Sixty-four percent of the adolescents had at least one instance of drug or alcohol use (isolated use incident) within 3 months of treatment. Following 6 months posttreatment, the isolated use incident rate was up to 70%. A somewhat lower percentage of the adolescents, 56%, returned to regular use within six months of completing primary treatment.

McKay and Buka (1994) found similar relapse rates among comorbid antisocial personality disorder–diagnosed adolescents who were interviewed approximately three months after inpatient treatment. Fifty-five percent of the 157 adolescents interviewed reported using at least once since leaving treatment. Although no information on the pattern of relapse was provided beyond three months, the study indicated that males had higher relapse rates than females (58% to 47%), and that younger subjects, as well as those who had shorter treatment stays, were also more likely to relapse.

Kennedy and Minami (1993) followed up on adolescents after completion of a specific treatment intervention, the Beech Hill Hospital/Outward Bound program. Adolescents and their parents were interviewed every three months during the year for which they were studied. Overall, Kennedy and Minami found a somewhat lower posttreatment drug use rate, 53%, than the Brown et al. (1989) study. As in the Brown et al. (1989) study, Kennedy and Minami found that the greatest risk of relapse occurred during the first three months following completion of primary treatment. The Kennedy and Minami study also indicates that "more severe (pretreatment) psychopathology and chemical use problems" as well as lack of attendance at AA/NA meetings were associated with posttreatment drug use.

In a 1994 article, Brown et al. report on a two-year follow-up study of 142 adolescents who completed an Alcoholics Anonymous twelve-step–based inpatient treatment program. Weekly aftercare meetings were also part of the treatment program. The adolescents were interviewed at 6, 12, and 24 months following inpatient treatment. Providing more detail in relapse patterns, this study found slightly lower regular use among the adolescents at two years following treatment than the 1989 Brown et al. study. The classification scheme placed the adolescents in one of five categories: abstainers (14%), non-problem users (13%), slow improvers (21%), worse with time (24%), and abusers (28%). According to Brown et al. (1994), 52% were major relapsers, i.e., returning to regular use, and 86% used at least once during the two-year study. In examining the demographic data in relation to relapse, Brown et al. (1994) found no consistent gender or ethnic differences across the outcome classifications. They did, however, find that a significant difference emerged for age, in that "the 'worse with time' group was significantly younger upon entering treatment compared to abstainers and abusers."

Studies by Spear and Skala (1995) and Spear, Ciesla, and Skala (1999) suggest similar results. One hundred thirteen adolescents and their parents were interviewed at 3, 6, 9, and 12 months following residential treatment. Drug use during the first year after completing primary treatment was measured as: (1) abstinence—no use, (2) isolated use incidents—at least once a year, but not as often as once a month, (3) monthly use—at least once a month, but not as often as once a week, and (4) weekly use—at least once a week or more. Only 7.9% of the adolescents remained abstinent at the end of the year. Slightly more, 10.6%, reported isolated-use incidents and 20.4% reported monthly use. More than 60% reported use on a weekly level. Essentially those adolescents in the weekly use category had returned to their pretreatment level of use.

The Spear et al. study reports slightly higher levels of use than Brown et al. One possible reason was that the Spear et al. study used multiple means of gathering relapse data. Random urine screens were administered during the first four months of aftercare. Both the adolescent and at least one parent were interviewed. If a parent was not available, other adults such as grandparents or parole officers were consulted. As a result, drug use data were confirmed by more than one source in 97% of the cases.

By examining patterns of relapse related first to gender and then to drug of dependence, Spear et al. went beyond previous studies. Distinct differences in pattern of drug use were found in relation to gender. A greater proportion of the females (26.8%) remained abstinent or had only isolated-use incidents compared to the males (13.9%). For those adolescents who returned to monthly use, the proportion of females who used monthly was 31.7% versus 13.9% for males. In contrast, 72.2% of the males returned to their pretreatment level of use versus 41.5% of the females. Finally, for males the time of greatest risk of returning to their pretreatment level of use was during the first three months after completing primary treatment. For females, the time of greatest risk of returning to their pretreatment level of use was during the first six months after completing primary treatment.

With respect to patterns of relapse in relation to drug of dependence, distinct differences were also found. Consistent with reports from other studies

(Ray and Ksir, 1996), alcohol and/or marijuana were the most common drugs of dependence. Not quite 11% (n=12) of the adolescents were dependent on marijuana only. For 31.9% (n=36) of the subjects, alcohol was the only drug of dependence. By far, the greatest percentage of adolescents were dependent on both alcohol and marijuana: 45.5% (n=51). An additional 12.4% (n=14) of the adolescents were dependent on drugs other than or in addition to alcohol and marijuana. Five of the 14 were cocaine-dependent and the remaining adolescents were dependent on amphetamines, inhalants, or barbiturates.

Because the number of adolescents dependent on "marijuana only" or on "other drugs" was so small, Spear et al. (1997) focused only on those adolescents dependent on alcohol (n=36) or on alcohol and marijuana (n=51). Of those dependent on alcohol, 36.2% either remained abstinent or had only isolated-use incidents throughout the year. A significantly lower proportion of those adolescents dependent on both alcohol and marijuana (13.8%) remained abstinent or had only isolated-use incidents during the same period. In addition, 44% of the alcohol-dependent adolescents returned to weekly or more frequent use in contrast to a larger proportion (63%) of those adolescents who were alcohol- and marijuana-dependent. If relapse is defined as using at least once per week, alcohol dependent adolescents are less likely to relapse than adolescents dependent on alcohol and marijuana. These results contrast with studies of adults that suggest similar or higher relapse rates for alcohol versus other drugs (Hunt et al., 1971; Catalano et al., 1990–91).

CORRELATES OF RECOVERY

Literature on factors associated with relapse and recovery provides no overall understanding of who is at elevated risk for relapse, the nature of the relapse/recovery process, or whether correlates influence the process or are merely associated with it. However, there is widespread agreement that recovery is a multidimensional phenomenon. As with drug-use behavior, recovery involves a complex set of social characteristics and behaviors that locate the individual within a social environment and link him or her to it. Researchers have looked at both pretreatment and posttreatment factors that appear to be correlated with relapse and/or recovery. These factors span a number of domains.

PRETREATMENT FACTORS

A number of studies suggest a relation between gender and treatment outcomes. Research indicates that males are more likely to relapse than females

(Catalano et al., 1989; Dembo et al., 1991; Shoemaker and Sherry, 1991; McKay and Buka, 1994; Spear, Ciesla, and Skala, 1999). Adolescents with higher levels of pretreatment drug use (Filstead and Anderson, 1983; McLellan et al., 1986; Shoemaker and Sherry, 1991; Catalano et al., 1990–91; Kennedy and Minami, 1993), greater family pathology, higher lifetime exposure to substance-abusing models (parents and other relatives), less parental involvement in treatment, and a diagnosis of psychological disorders and/or conduct disorder are also more likely to relapse (Filstead and Anderson, 1983; McLellan et al., 1986; Shoemaker and Sherry, 1991; McKay and Buka, 1994; Brown et al., 1994; Crowley and Riggs, 1995).

Some studies suggest that less time in primary treatment may be associated with increased likelihood of relapse (Booth, 1981; De Leon and Jainchill, 1986; Finney et al., 1980; Friedman and Glickman, 1987; Gerstein and Harwood, 1990; Sells and Simpson, 1979). Work by Jenson et al. (1993) indicates a relation between reported intentions to use drugs in the future and actual posttreatment drug use. Lower intentions to use are correlated with lower levels of actual posttreatment drug use.

It is important to note that there are many inconsistencies across studies that focus on the relation of pretreatment variables to posttreatment drug use (Catalano et al., 1990–91). For example, a series of studies reported in Brown et al. (1994) found no association between relapse and either level of pretreatment drug use or gender. It is not clear if different study findings reflect differences in the samples studied or differences in how relapse and/or the correlates are measured.

POSTTREATMENT FACTORS

A number of studies present data on posttreatment correlates of relapse (Brown et al., 1989; Brown et al., 1994; DeJong and Henrich, 1980; Shoemaker and Sherry, 1991). Despite using various posttreatment correlates and differing definitions of relapse, findings are similar to studies of posttreatment correlates of relapse for adults. Maintaining recovery seems to involve greater use of behavioral and cognitive coping skills, better overall functioning in school (Shoemaker and Sherry, 1991; Brown et al., 1994), and greater involvement in social and work-related activities (Brown et al., 1994). In contrast, the factors associated with relapse include lack of involvement in productive activities (work, school, leisure activities), return to the environment where the adolescent previously used drugs, and failure to establish social contact with nonusing friends (DeJong and Henrich, 1980). Finally, family factors appear to be important for recovery of adolescent drug abusers. Abstaining adolescents report consistently better family relationships than adolescents who used drugs in the posttreatment period (Brown et al., 1994).

IMPLICATIONS FOR RELAPSE AND RECOVERY

As with the characteristics of adolescents in treatment for chemical dependency, the results of studies that report correlates of relapse and/or recovery present no overall model of the relative influence of these factors. Nearly all of these adolescents can be characterized by one or more of these factors. What then can be gained from a review of such studies? Despite limitations, these correlational studies make a number of contributions to both research and clinical areas. First, the studies on pretreatment factors make clear the heterogeneous nature of the population of adolescents in treatment for chemical dependency. Second, they suggest the likelihood of a differential risk for posttreatment drug use. Third, they point to the need to develop risk models and begin to lay the groundwork for them. Fourth, risk models are an essential component of matching client to treatment not only by identifying clients at differential risk for relapse but also by suggesting how interventions should vary. Understanding what increases risk of relapse may provide a basis for a more sophisticated approach to intervention design that addresses intervention content not just varying the time in treatment or the intensity of the intervention.

Posttreatment correlates of relapse and/or recovery may also provide important guidance for future research and intervention design. However, they differ from pretreatment correlates in a number of important ways. Unlike pretreatment factors such as gender or a history of sexual and/or physical abuse, posttreatment factors may be influenced by the treatment process. In addition, posttreatment correlates may, in fact, be a component of treatment outcome. That is, they may be indicators of lifestyle variables that link the adolescent to a social environment. What is not clear is whether changes in friends, school, or work performance influence the probability of sustaining recovery or are an indicator of it. In other words, do such changes occur simultaneously with sustaining recovery or are they initiated at a different point in time? Are they precursors of sustaining recovery within the community environment or consequences of it?

Finally, the correlational studies, together with those focusing on adolescent relapse rates and patterns, direct attention to a number of methodological and theoretical weaknesses in the relapse and recovery literature for adolescents.

METHODOLOGICAL ISSUES
DEFINING RELAPSE

A precise and widely agreed upon definition of relapse is not present in the literature. Such a definition has eluded researchers for many years and has been the subject of a great deal of discussion. In its most general sense, relapse is a breakdown or setback in a person's attempt to change or modify any target behavior (Marlatt, 1985). In the context of substance abuse, relapse is generally characterized as the inability to abstain from drug or alcohol use after a commitment to do so. For some researchers, relapse is defined as any use incident following a period of nonuse. For others (Brown et al., 1989; Spear, Ciesla, and Skala, 1999) relapse is not defined as such. Rather, a wide range of levels and patterns of use is documented.

THEORETICAL DEFINITIONS

Some researchers have drawn upon theoretical models to operationalize relapse. The most prominent schools of thought are the disease model and the cognitive-social learning theory. Each is discussed in turn.

The disease model

The disease model emphasizes the biological aspects of addiction, focusing on a substance's pharmacological effects. Under this view, addicts are seen as largely incapable of exercising control over their behavior (Marlatt, 1985). Accordingly, relapse is viewed as the dichotomy, sick or well. One has relapsed if one has any use at all (Litman, Eiser, and Taylor, 1979). The problems with this all-or-nothing approach have been well documented. They include feelings of fatalism on the part of the recovering addict because they relate isolated use with complete relapse and treatment failure (Marlatt, 1985), which may lead to complete indulgence. The disease model view of relapse de-emphasizes psychological, social, and situational factors as determinants of relapse. Researchers applying the disease model operationalize relapse as use or no use de-emphasizing setting, frequency, intensity, and duration of use.

Social learning approach

Recent research has taken a more sophisticated approach to relapse, grounding relapse in cognitive-social learning theory. Marlatt (1978) and Marlatt and Gordon (1985) have all done a great deal of work with this model, including Marlatt and Gordon's detailed prevention model, which has garnered considerable attention. This approach allows for the inclusion of different rates and patterns of relapse as well as the measurement of psychological, social, and situational variables.

ATHEORETICAL DEFINITIONS

In addition to the theoretically grounded definitions of relapse discussed above, researchers and practitioners have characterized relapse in many ways that do not take into account underlying theory. In fact, most of the research on adolescent substance abuse that examines relapse bases its operational definitions of relapse on such circumstantial factors as the availability of information or the ease with which such information can be obtained. For this reason, definitions of relapse vary considerably. At one end of a continuum are the most conservative definitions, such as any use of an addictive substance; on the other end are more liberal definitions such as reported daily use or return to pretreatment levels of use. The lack of a widely agreed upon definition of relapse, theoretically based or not, has hampered research directed at understanding and, ultimately, preventing relapse.

IMPLICATIONS FOR RELAPSE AND RECOVERY

Using the disease model to guide the conceptualization of relapse appears to have a number of limitations. First, the view that any use incident will lead inevitably to a linear pattern of use, largely beyond the control of the individual, seems inconsistent with research findings that suggest that recovery is often a complex pattern of use and nonuse (Gerstein and Harwood, 1990; Marlatt and Gordon, 1980; Rounsaville, 1986). Second, the model does not take into account the role of the social context in the recovery process. Some of the clearest documentation of the role of social context comes from the experience of Vietnam veterans who became addicted to heroin but were relatively easy to treat successfully when they returned to the context of the United States (Leshner, 1997). High rates of successful treatment are attributed to change in the social environment and roles of the individuals. Third, the "any use" definition makes it difficult to assess the efficacy of new treatment approaches. As McAuliffe and Ashery (1993) note in an extensive review of treatment outcome studies, the impact of differential treatments is difficult to detect. A use versus nonuse definition of outcome is not likely to be sufficiently sensitive to detect differences. Lastly, at a clinical level, the disease model may suggest to the adolescent that a single use incident will inevitably lead to his or her return to the pretreatment level of use. Such a belief could in itself function as part of the dynamic of a self-fulfilling prophecy.

In contrast to the disease model conceptualization of relapse, atheoretically based approaches to measuring outcome examine different levels of posttreatment drug use as well as measure variables related to the social context of the recovery situation. As indicated in the discussion of the correlates of relapse and recovery, however, these studies provide no rationale for focusing on one set of social psychological variables versus another, nor is there an assessment of the relative influence of the range of correlates. In addition, the atheoretical approaches provide no explanation of the process by which recovery is sustained. Thus, they provide little direction to clinicians seeking to design more effective treatment approaches.

Finally, such sociobehavioral approaches as social learning theory can address the concerns raised in regard to the disease model and atheoretical approaches; however, there has been no consistent conceptualization of social learning theory as it applies to relapse and recovery processes, particularly among chemically dependent adolescents. One of the best-known social learning approaches in the field is the one proposed by Marlatt, but research using this model has focused primarily on adults. Secondly, with few exceptions (Marlatt and George, 1984; Annis, 1990; Spear and Akers, 1988), researchers who have used a social learning framework have not differentiated between initiating nonusing behavior and the variables involved in sustaining that behavior.

MEASURING RELAPSE

A second important methodological issue in studying posttreatment drug use among adolescents is how to measure use. Studies focusing on adults have stressed the importance of biochemical indicators of use. Thus, emphasis has been on such techniques as urine screens or hair sample assays. Indeed, studies failing to use such techniques are often perceived as flawed. Adolescents differ from many of the chemically dependent adults in that the drugs of choice and/or addiction in the adolescent population have predominantly been alcohol and marijuana. Using the "gold standard" techniques may be less reliable in measuring alcohol and marijuana than in measuring such substances as heroin or cocaine. Another common approach to measuring treatment outcomes for adolescents is use of self-reports and parental reports of the adolescents' posttreatment drug-use behavior. Although the issues of self-reports of various behaviors have been dealt with in the literature, there are few studies that compare drug-use self-reports and the outcomes of biochemical measures (Akers et al., 1985). Even more sparse are studies of the consistency of adolescent versus parent reports of posttreatment drug use.

In this section, we discuss the various ways researchers and practitioners measure relapse, the strengths and limitations of each technique, successful approaches that have been reported in the literature, and finally, future issues related to measuring relapse in adolescents. Measuring relapse is largely a function of conceptualizing relapse. Adherents of the disease model typically use less elaborate techniques because they gather less information. To disease modelists, simply determining if one has commenced using is usually considered sufficient. Those applying the cognitive-social learning theory or similar approaches tend to measure relapse at a finer grain of detail, often recording as much about the act of using and the circumstances of use as possible. The information collected often includes, but is not limited to, the exact quantities, duration, combinations of substances, time, place, company present, state of mind, and many other details regarding the circumstances of use. The approach to relapse must also take into account the reason for collecting relapse data—that is, whether the purpose is to conduct research, evaluate treatment, or track a particular client or group of clients as part of treatment.

For most practical purposes, there are two ways to measure relapse in adolescent populations. The first, self-report survey, is the most common way. The second and next most common method utilizes various bioassay techniques, mostly urinalysis. We will consider each in turn and then discuss a few less commonly used techniques.

Self-report surveys

Survey methods using self-report have been the mainstay for the past thirty years. The advantages of self-reports are well known to social scientists—they include safety, simplicity, reliability, and low cost. Validation studies widely cited before the mid-1980s indicate an acceptable concordance between self-report survey results and other more objective methods, including bioassays. Almost all of these studies were conducted on adults, so their generalizability to adolescents is the subject of some debate. More recent studies, again on adults, cast some doubt on the reliability of self-reports (Harrison, 1989). These newer studies with more accurate urinalysis and most recently with hair samples indicate that a larger than previously known amount of recent drug and alcohol use may go undetected in self report surveys; however, the self-report data in these studies were collected on adult arrestees who may have had legal reasons for underreporting their use.

An important adjunct to self-report surveys in adolescents is the use of proxies, particularly parental proxies, as a means of obtaining outcome or relapse information when adolescents are unwilling or otherwise unable to complete surveys or to corroborate adolescent responses. New research by Ciesla et al. (1999b) indicates that there is a high degree of concordance between adolescent and parental responses to questions relating to posttreatment use. Using proxy responses in adolescent populations enhances the accuracy of self-report survey information on relapse and can provide information on adolescents who are hard to contact. The Spear et al. research shows that adolescents' and parents' responses to questions about school and work performance, friends, and drug use are similar if the questions are not highly subjective, if they regard phenomena that are easily observable (e.g. "on time to work/school?" "runs away from home?" versus "takes responsibility for actions?" "accepts criticism well?"). In short, carefully designed self-report surveys using proxies to corroborate facts and, in some instances filling in for difficult-to-reach adolescents, can be a robust way to elucidate relapse and relapse behaviors (Spear et al., 1999).

Bioassay techniques

Clinical laboratory, or bioassay, techniques are considered by many to be the gold standard techniques to detect relapse. Bioassay techniques have several serious limitations however. The first is that the most commonly used urine tests, enzyme multiplied immunoassay (EMIT) and fluorescence polarization immunoassay (FPIA), have unacceptably short windows of detectability. Urine EMIT can detect cocaine for 2 to 3 days, opiates for 2 days, cannabis for up to 4 weeks, but these figures vary by route of ingestion, amount, frequency, and combinations of drugs used and by the physical characteristics of the individual including their state of hydration and fluid balance. Although both EMIT and FPIA can detect alcohol, most researchers agree that the window of detectability for alcohol is so short and unpredictable as to mitigate against using either test for detecting relapse of alcohol use in adolescents. What is more, these figures are from studies with adults. No validity or reliability studies of the EMIT or FPIA procedures have been conducted on adolescent treatment populations.

Second, bioassays can be prohibitively expensive both in terms of the direct costs of the tests themselves and follow-up tests for positives and also in terms of the indirect costs of the time and effort on the part of researchers or clinicians who must collect specimens and the adolescents who must take time to give them. Considering all of these factors, bioassay techniques have considerably more limitations as methods for detecting relapse in adolescents than many realize.

Perhaps the most important thing to bear in mind is that self-report surveys and bioassay techniques should not be considered mutually exclusive approaches to detecting relapse. The literature suggests that neither self-report surveys nor bioassays are completely accurate (Harrison & Hughes, 1997). Both have important strengths and limitations. What is likely to be the most effective metric of relapse in adolescents is the multipronged approach used by Spear et al., which used self-report surveys of the adolescents as the primary source of information, parental interviews for verification of adolescent responses and as proxies for unreachable adolescents, coupled with random clinical bioassays.

Other techniques

Other less common, less reliable, and less practical ways researchers have measured relapse in adolescents are drug arrests, drug sales, drug seizures, and treatment admissions or readmission. Most researchers agree that these approaches are not expeditious enough for widespread use. Drug arrests and treatment admissions or readmissions certainly signify relapse, but not all adolescents who have relapsed end up being arrested or admitted to treatment. Also, it is exceedingly difficult to use these indicators on defined populations. If one is tracking a specific group of posttreatment adolescents, the task of monitoring all of the possible places to which the adolescents might be admitted or readmitted can become overwhelming. Similarly, the task of monitoring arrests in multiple jurisdictions is not often found to be practical. Also, adolescent arrestees are increasingly being dealt with by juvenile justice interventions such as pretrial intervention or by drug courts, both of which have no standard method of or, indeed, may be enjoined by law from reporting details of the adolescents' cases.

IMPLICATIONS FOR RELAPSE AND RECOVERY

The issues raised concerning how to conceptualize and measure relapse among adolescents treated for chemical dependency have significant consequences for the results of treatment evaluation studies. Clearly, the definition of relapse changes the perceived level of treatment success. It may also alter the perception of what are the correlates of relapse and recovery. If relapse is "any use" versus relapse as "return to pretreatment levels of use," the identification of characteristics of the "at-risk adolescents" and correlates of relapse change. Secondly, because the predominant drugs of addiction are different for adolescents than for adults, various bioassay techniques that are considered the gold standard of measurement in adult studies may not be nearly as reliable in adolescent studies. Finally, the reliability of self-reports among adolescents and of proxy reports by parents or others are also unclear. Unquestionably, if such reports are reliable they would represent a cost-effective way for agencies to get a sense of the success of the interventions.

THEORETICAL ISSUES

Throughout this chapter we have raised the issue of the lack of a theoretical model that takes into account the complex nature of the relapse/recovery process. Although there are many worthwhile studies, existing research does not provide a general perspective that integrates previous findings and generates new research directions. Rather, what emerges from current research is a wide-ranging list of variables associated with relapse and/or recovery. On such a list, all variables are "equal." That is, there is no differentiation between types of variables such as those that locate the individual within a social context, for example, gender or age and processual variables that may be factors in initiating and/or sustaining a behavior. Secondly, because so much of the existing research focuses on a single type of correlate, for example, psychiatric disorders or delinquency, it is not possible to assess the relative influence of variables in the relapse/recovery processes. In addition, the use of an inadequately specified model of these processes is likely to artificially inflate the influence of the included variables on drug use behavior.

There are a few studies that have used a theoretical framework to depict the relapse/recovery process. Other than the disease model, the most commonly cited approach is social learning theory. Social learning theory is not a single conceptual framework, although many of the approaches subsumed under this title appear to be rooted in the social learning theory presented by Bandura (1977). Generally, social learning theory has come to refer to any number of social behavioral approaches that take into account behavioral modeling and reinforcement (Akers and Lee, 1996). As a theoretical framework, social learning theory includes the realization that there is likely to be a difference in the processes of initiating a behavior and sustaining that behavior. That is, the relative influence of the variables in the model change if the process is behavioral acquisition versus habituation. Key researchers in the field such as Marlatt, Annis, and Akers have noted the importance of distinguishing between these two processes. However, beyond the Bandura (1977) work as an overall frame of reference and the recognition of the importance of distinguishing between behavioral acquisition and habituation, there is little systematic overlap between such approaches as Marlatt's relapse prevention model (Marlatt and George, 1984), the Annis self-efficacy theory (1986), and the social learning theory developed by Akers and Cochran (1985).

As a general perspective, social behavioral theory includes a variety of exchange, social learning, and more radically behavioristic theories. Fundamental to all of these approaches is operant behavior or the idea of reinforcement, which posits that the consequences of behavior alter the probability of its performance in the future. The likelihood of successfully initiating a behavior increases with the consistency of positive reinforcement. Once a behavior is established, however, intermittent reinforcement is the more powerful pattern in sustaining the behavior. Social learning theory builds on the operant behavior principle by adding the concept of modeling—that is, people can learn from observing the behavior of others and the consequences of behavior for them. There is some evidence that modeling may have a greater influence on the process of initiating a behavior than on the process of continuing it (Akers and Lee, 1996; Spear and Akers, 1988).

The relapse and recovery processes among adolescents treated for chemical dependency involve both extinguishing existing behaviors associated with drug use and initiating and sustaining new behaviors associated with a drug-free lifestyle. Given that the adolescent is likely to return to the pretreatment home and school environment, both of which may provide opportunities for drug use and reinforce that behavior, extinguishing drug-using behavior will be difficult. In addition, this environment is less likely to provide the models and reinforcement for developing a nonusing lifestyle. A major challenge for researchers is to specify the variables that depict the behavior acquisition and continuation process and to work with clinicians to identify and assess continuing care interventions that take these variables into account.

Recognizing that the process of sustaining recovery is different from the process of initiating it, Marlatt and George (1984) developed a social learning model focused on sustaining recovery begun in primary treatment. In contrast to the disease model, which posits any use as the inevitable beginning of return to habitual drug use, the relapse prevention model of Marlatt and George views relapse as a transitional process that may or may not lead to continued drug use. Central to this model is the identification of high-risk situations and interventions that focus on the skill development necessary to help the individual cope with these situations. Research of Marlatt and colleagues has primarily targeted adults. In addition, the theoretical model itself is designed to deal specifically with relapse and recovery rather than general processes of behavior acquisition and maintenance.

Annis (1986) developed a social learning approach that is somewhat similar to that of Marlatt and George in that it focuses on the individual's learning to control his or her behavior in high-risk situations. This self-efficacy theory stresses increasing the individual's expectations of personal efficacy. In this theory, the clients' expectations of self-efficacy influence coping behavior. In other words, self-efficacy encourages the belief that the individual can successfully cope with high-risk situations. Successfully coping with those situations reinforces the individual's belief in his or her own self-efficacy. Self-efficacy is posited to influence not only the initiation of behavior but also continuation of it. As with the relapse prevention model, the self-efficacy model focuses on adults and is designed to deal with relapse by utilizing interventions that help the individual cope with the environment.

In contrast to the work of Marlatt and Annis, Akers developed a social learning theory that is not specific to relapse or recovery. Rather, it deals with the process by which behavior, any behavior, is initiated and sustained. In addition, Akers has applied the theory to drug use among adolescents (Akers and Lee, 1996; Spear and Akers, 1988). The advantage of the Akers social learning theory is that it applies the same set of variables to describe the general process of behavior acquisition and maintenance while recognizing the differential influence of the variables in the two processes. These variables include differential association, differential reinforcement, imitational learning (modeling), and cognitive definitions or attitudes that function as discriminative (cues) stimuli. Work with Spear and Akers (1988) focused specifically on the process that moves the individual from initiation to habituation. This test of the theory included the degree to which the individual could integrate the behavior into his or her lifestyle. In assessing the process of habituation, integration into lifestyle had the strongest influence of the variables in the model on the process.

IMPLICATIONS FOR RELAPSE AND RECOVERY

Researchers and clinicians have come to recognize the importance of focusing on issues associated with the process of sustaining recovery initiated in primary treatment once the individual returns to the community setting. Both Marlatt and Annis focus on the issue of designing interventions to sustain recovery. Both approach the issue of sustaining recovery guided by the principles of social learning theory. However, the emphasis is on designing effective interventions rather than testing a social learning approach to maximize understanding of the process by which the behavior is sustained. In addition, because the research has targeted adults, there are no findings on the applicability of the approach to adolescents.

In contrast to Marlatt and Annis, Akers' research is concerned with testing a more general social learning theory of behavior acquisition and maintenance applied to the specific situation of drug use. The same set of variables is tested regardless of the behavior of interest or the characteristics of the client. However, the theory recognizes that there may be an interactive effect between the characteristics of the individual and the variables in the model. In other words, the theory is able to take into account the heterogeneity of the treatment population. Quite often that heterogeneity is a function of those variables that locate individuals within the social context. For example, just as relapse rates may vary with gender, so too may the relative influence of the social learning variables.

Although this discussion may seem esoteric, it is, in fact, quite pragmatic. The idea of matching client to treatment suggests that there exists a heterogeneous treatment population and that interventions need to be adjusted to respond effectively to that heterogeneity. The Akers model has the potential to provide a means of directing research to identify the basis for making treatment adjustments.

FUTURE DIRECTIONS

As we finished the discussions for each of the issues raised in this chapter, we sought to synthesize the conclusions that could be drawn relative to the research and clinical implications that the issue has for relapse and recovery among adolescents treated for chemical dependency. Rather than repeat those discussions, we conclude with a few comments about future directions, particularly from a research perspective. A number of overall impressions emerge from the above discussion which suggest that future research needs to be directed toward issues related to sustaining recovery begun in primary treatment, specifically target adolescents, recognize the heterogeneity within the adolescent treatment population, measure posttreatment drug use in ways that take into account different levels and patterns of use, and, whenever possible, be conducted within a theoretical framework that can accommodate the complexity of the relapse/recovery processes and integrate past and future effort.

References

Akers, R. L., & Cochran, J. K. (1985). Adolescent marijuana use: A test of three theories of deviant behavior. *Deviant Behavior, 6,* 323–346.

Akers, R. L., & Lee, G. (1996). A longitudinal test of social learning theory: Adolescent smoking. *Journal of Drug Issues, 26,* 317–343.

Akers, R. L., Massey, J., Clarke, W., & Lauer, R. M. (1983). Are self-reports of adolescent deviance valid? Biochemical measures, randomized response, and the bogus popeline in smoking behavior. *Social Forces, 62,* 234–251.

Annis, H. M. (1986). A relapse prevention model for treatment of alcoholics. In W. R. Miller & N. Heather (Eds.), *Treating addictive behaviors: Processes of change* (pp. 407–433). New York: Plenum Press.

Annis, H. M. (1990). Relapse to substance abuse: Empirical findings within a cognitive-social learning approach. *Journal of Psychoactive Drugs, 22,* 117–124.

Bandura, A. (1977). *Social learning theory.* Englewood Cliffs, N.J.: Prentice-Hall.

Blood, L., & Cornwall, A. (1996). Childhood sexual victimization as a factor in the treatment of substance misusing adolescents. *Substance Use and Misuse, 31,* 1015–1039.

Booth, R. (1981). Alcohol halfway houses: Treatment, length and treatment outcome. *International Journal of the Addictions, 16,* 927–934.

Brown, S. A., Myers, M. G., Mott, M. A., & Vik, P. W. (1994). Correlates of success following treatment for adolescent substance abuse. *Applied and Preventive Psychology, 3,* 61–73.

Brown, S. A., Vik, P. W., & Creamer, V. A. (1989). Characteristics of relapse following adolescent substance abuse treatment. *Addictive Behaviors, 14,* 291–300.

Cady, M. E., Winters, K. C., Jordan, D. A., Solberg, K. B., & Stinchfield, R. D. (1996). Motivation to change as a predictor of treatment outcome for adolescent substance abusers. *Journal of Child & Adolescent Substance Abuse, 5,* 73–91.

Catalano, R. F., Hawkins, J. D., Wells, E. A., Miller, J., & Brewer, D. (1990–1991). Evaluation of the effectiveness of adolescent drug abuse treatment, assessment of risks for relapse and promising approaches for relapse prevention. *International Journal of the Addictions, 25(9A/10a),* 1085–1140.

Catalano, R. F., Wells, E. A., Jenson, J. M., & Hawkins, J. D. (1989). Aftercare services for drug-using institutionalized delinquents. *Social Service Review, 63,* 553–577.

Ciesla, J. R., S. F. Spear, S. Y. Skala (1999). Reliability over time of self-reports given by adolescents and their parents in substance abuse outcome research. *Journal of Child & Adolescent Substance Abuse. 9,* 57–73.

Crowley, T. J., & Riggs, P. D. (1995). Adolescent substance use disorder with conduct disorder and comorbid conditions. In E. Rahdert & D. Czechowicz (eds.), *Adolescent drug abuse: Clinical assessment and therapeutic interventions* (National Institute on

Drug Abuse Research Monograph No. 156, NIH Publication No. 95-3908, pp. 49–111). Rockville, Md.: U.S. Department of Health and Human Services, Public Health Service, National Institutes of Health.

DeJong, W. (1994). Relapse prevention: An emerging technology for promoting long-term drug abstinence. *The International Journal of the Addictions, 29,* 681–705.

DeJong, W., & Henrich, G. (1980). Follow-up results of a behavior modification program for juvenile drug addicts. *Addictive Behaviors, 5,* 49–57.

De Leon, G., & Jainchill, N. (1986). Circumstance, motivation, readiness, and suitability as correlates of treatment tenure. *Journal of Psychoactive Drugs, 18*(3), 203–208.

Dembo, R., Williams, L., LaVoie, L., Berry, E., Getreu, A., Wish, E. D., Schmeidler, J., & Washburn, M. (1989). Physical abuse, sexual victimization, and illicit drug use. *Violence and Victims, 4,* 121–138.

Dembo, R., Williams, L., LaVoie, L., Schmeidler, J., Kern, J., Getreu, A., Berry, E., Genung, L., & Wish, E. D. (1990). A longitudinal study of the relationships among alcohol use, marijuana/hashish use, cocaine use, and emotional/psychological functioning problems in a cohort of high-risk youths. *International Journal of the Addictions, 25,* 1341–1382.

Dembo, R., Williams, L., Schmeidler, J., Getreu, A., Berry, E., Genung, L., Wish, E. D., & Christensen, C. (1991). Recidivism among high risk youths: A 2-½ year follow up of a cohort of juvenile detainees. *International Journal of the Addictions, 26,* 1197–1221.

Finney, J. W., Moos, R. H., & Mewborn, C. R. (1980). Posttreatment experiences and treatment outcome of alcoholic patients six months and two years after hospitalization. *Journal of Consulting and Clinical Psychology, 48,* 17–29.

Filstead, W. J., & Anderson, C. L. (1983). Conceptual and clinical issues in the treatment of adolescent alcohol and substance misusers. *Child and Youth Services, 6*(1–2), 103–116.

Friedman, A. S., & Glickman, N. W. (1987). Residential program characteristics for completion of treatment by adolescent drug abusers. *Journal of Nervous and Mental Disease, 175,* 419–424.

Gerstein, D. R., & Harwood, H. J. (Eds.). (1990). *Treating drug problems* (vol. 1). Washington, D.C.: National Academy Press.

Harrison, L. D. (1989, November). *The validity of self-reported drug use among arrestees.* Paper presented at the 41st meeting of the American Society of Criminology, Reno.

Harrison, L., & Hughes, A. (1997). Introduction. The validity of self-reported drug use: Improving the accuracy of survey estimates. *National Institute on Drug Abuse Research Monograph, 167,* 1–16.

Harrison, P. A., & Hoffman, N. G. (1987). *CATOR 1987 Report: Adolescent Residential Treatment Intake and Follow-Up Findings.* St. Paul, Minn.: CATOR.

Harrison, P. A., Hoffmann, N. G., & Edwall, G. G. (1989). Sexual abuse correlates: Similarities between male and female adolescents in chemical dependency treatment. *Journal of Adolescent Research, 4*, 385–399.

Hart, L. E., Mader, L., Griffith, K., & DeMendonca, M. (1989). Effects of sexual and physical abuse: A comparison of adolescent inpatients. *Child Psychiatry and Human Development, 20*, 49–57.

Hawkins, J. D., Catalano, R. F., & Miller, J. Y. (1992). Risk and protective factors for alcohol and other drug problems in adolescence and early adulthood: Implications for substance abuse problems. *Psychological Bulletin, 112*, 64–105.

Hubbard, R. L., Cavenaugh, E. R., Craddock, S. G., & Rachal, J. V. (1985). Characteristics, behaviors, and outcomes for youth in the TOPS. In A. S. Friedman & G. M. Beschner (eds.), *Treatment services for adolescent substance abusers* (DHHS Publication No. ADM 85-1342, pp. 49–65). Washington, D.C.: U.S. Printing Office.

Hunt, W. A., Barnet, L. W., & Branch, L. G. (1971). Relapse rates in addiction programs. *Journal of Clinical Psychology, 27*, 455–456.

Jenson, J. M., Wells, E. A., Plotnick, R. D., Hawkins, J. D., & Catalano, R. F. (1993). The effects of skills and intentions to use drugs on posttreatment drug use of adolescents. *American Journal of Drug and Alcohol Abuse, 19*, 1–18.

Kennedy, B. P., & Minami, M. (1993). The Beech Hill Hospital: Outward bound adolescent chemical dependency treatment program. *Journal of Substance Abuse Treatment, 10*, 395–406.

Leshner, A. I. (1997). Addiction is a brain disease, and it matters. *Science, 278*, 45–47.

Litman, G. K., Eiser, J. R., & Taylor, C. (1979). Dependence, relapse, and extinction. A theoretical critique and a behavioral examination. *Journal of Clinical Psychology, 35*, 192–199.

Marlatt, G. A. (1978). Behavioral assessment of social drinking and alcoholism. In G. A. Marlatt & P. E. Nathan (Eds.), *Behavioral approaches to alcoholism,* (pp. 35–57). New Brunswick, N.J.: Rutgers Center of Alcohol Studies.

Marlatt, G. A., & George, W. H. (1984). Relapse prevention: Introduction and overview of the model. *British Journal of Addiction, 79*, 261–273.

Marlatt, G. A., & Gordon, J. R. (1980). Determinants of relapse: Implications for maintenance of behavior change. In P. O. Davidson & S. M. Davidson (eds.), *Behavioral medicine: Changing health lifestyles* (pp. 410–451). New York: Brunner/Mazel.

Marlatt, G. A., & Gordon, J. R. (eds.). (1985). *Relapse prevention: Maintenance strategies in the treatment of addictive behaviors.* New York: Guilford Press.

McAuliffe, W., & Ashery, R. S. (1993). Implementation issues and techniques in randomized trials of outpatient psychosocial treatments for drug abusers. II. Clinical and administrative issues. *American Journal of Drug and Alcohol Abuse, 19*, 35–50.

McKay, J. R., & Buka, S. L. (1994). Issues in the treatment of antisocial adolescent substance abusers. *Journal of Child and Adolescent Substance Abuse, 3,* 59–81.

McLellan, A. T., Luborsky, L., & O'Brien, C. P. (1986). Alcohol and drug abuse treatment in three different populations: Is there improvement and is it predictable? *American Journal of Drug and Alcohol Abuse, 12*(1&2), 101–120.

Newcomb, M. D. (1995). Identifying high-risk youth: Prevalence and patterns of adolescent drug abuse. In E. Rahdert & D. Czechowicz (eds.), *Adolescent drug abuse: Clinical assessment and therapeutic interventions.* (National Institute on Drug Abuse Research Monograph No. 156, NIH Publication No. 95-3908, pp. 7–37). Rockville, Md.: U.S. Department of Health and Human Services, Public Health Service.

Ray, O., & Ksir, C. (1996). *Drugs, society, and human behavior* (7th ed.). St. Louis, Mo.: Mosby.

Rounsaville, B. J. (1986). Clinical implications of relapse research. In F. M. Tims & C. G. Leukefeld (eds.), *Relapse and recovery in drug abuse* (National Institute on Drug Abuse Research Monograph No. 72, DHHS Publication No. (ADM) 86-1473, pp. 172–184). Washington, D.C.: Superintendent of Documents, U.S. Government Printing Office.

Sells, S. B., & Simpson, D. D. (1979). Evaluation of treatment outcome for youths in the Drug Abuse Reporting Program (DARP): A follow-up study. In G. M. Beschner & A. S. Friedman (eds.), *Youth drug abuse: Problems, issues and treatments* (pp. 571–628). Lexington, Mass.: Lexington Books.

Shoemaker, R. H., & Sherry, P. (1991). Posttreatment factors influencing outcome of adolescent chemical dependency treatment. *Journal of Adolescent Chemical Dependency, 2,* 89–105.

Spear, S. F., & Akers, R. L. (1988). Social learning variables and the risk of habitual smoking among adolescents: The Muscatine Study. *American Journal of Preventive Medicine, 4,* 336–348.

Spear, S. F., Ciesla, J. R., & Skala, S. Y. (1999). Relapse patterns among adolescents treated for chemical dependency. *Substance Use & Misuse, 34,* 1795–1815.

Spear, S. F., & Skala, S. Y. (1995). Posttreatment services for chemically dependent adolescents. In E. Rahdert & D. Czechowicz (eds.), *Adolescent drug abuse: Clinical assessment and therapeutic interventions.* (National Institute on Drug Abuse Research Monograph No. 156, NIH Publication No. 95-3908, pp. 341–364). Rockville, Md.: U.S. Department of Health and Human Services, Public Health Service, National Institutes of Health.

Spear, S. F., & Skala, S. Y. (1998). Adolescents in treatment for chemical dependency: Profiles associated with a history of physical and sexual abuse. *Alcohol Treatment Quarterly, 16,* 31–43.

III

The Search for Interventions

ELEVEN

CASE MANAGEMENT IN SUBSTANCE ABUSE TREATMENT: PERSPECTIVES, IMPACT, AND USE

Harvey A. Siegal, Richard C. Rapp, Li Li, & Pranjit Saha

Case management is seen as a useful intervention for persons with substance abuse problems. It is assumed that the specific activities that compose case management help substance abusers access needed community services and enhance the quality and prolong the duration of their participation in treatment. This enhancement can lead to improved treatment outcomes like diminished likelihood of relapse. Case management has also been used in substance abuse treatment to offer social skills training and affect an increased level of coordination between substance abuse treatment and collateral services such as housing and vocational programs.

During the past twenty years several practitioners have written about the conceptual and practical aspects of using case management with substance abusers. Two in particular (Graham & Birchmore Timney, 1990; Willenbring, Ridgely, Stinchfield, & Rose, 1991) anticipated the burgeoning use of case management with this population. Today's use of case management for substance abusers evolved from its use with community-living people suffering from chronic mental illness. Currently, case management is used in substance abuse treatment settings representing different treatment modalities and diverse populations of chemically dependent people.

This research was supported by NIDA Grant #DA06944. Corresponding author: Harvey A. Siegal, Ph.D., Professor and Director, Substance Abuse Intervention Programs, Wright State University, School of Medicine, P.O. Box 927, Dayton, OH 45401-0927.

This chapter begins with a selected review of the empirical research examining the value of case management. More specifically, our focus is on the retention of clients in treatment and those enhancements that have been shown to improve treatment outcomes. We conclude our review with a summary of the findings from an eight-year project that has implemented strengths-based case management with crack cocaine users. Last, we discuss issues to be considered in the future of case management interventions for substance abusers.

CASE MANAGEMENT AND SUBSTANCE ABUSE TREATMENT

Those working with substance abusers have always provided "case management" services. They have helped substance abusers find housing and perhaps meals, spiritual guidance, and, when desired, treatment. As case management became professionalized, specific stages and activities were identified, including engagement in treatment, needs assessment, planning, accessing resources, monitoring, coordinating and advocacy, and disengagement from treatment (Ballew & Mink, 1996). In other case management models, intake, assessment, goal setting, resource identification and intervention planning, counseling and therapy, linking clients to formal and informal networks, monitoring reassessment and outcome evaluation, advocacy, and interorganizational coordination and agency access as the components of the intervention (Rothman, 1994) were articulated.

Support for the use of case management with substance abusers developed from the appreciation that substance abusers have significant problems in addition to using drugs (Oppenheimer, Sheehan, & Taylor, 1988; Westermeyer, 1989). Currently, people in substance abuse treatment generally have few resources, are addicted to several different drugs simultaneously, and are frequently involved with the criminal justice system. Case management, regardless of which specific model is used, has the potential to assist people who need help in obtaining resources that can support autonomous, stable living (Willenbring et al., 1991).

Today, case management is achieving the same acceptance in substance abuse treatment that the 1963 Federal Community Mental Health Center Act provided for mental health services. It is one of eight (counseling) skills identified by the National Association of Alcoholism and Drug Abuse Counselors (National Association of Alcoholism and Drug Abuse Counselors, 1986) and one of five performance domains developed in the Role Delineation Study (National Certification Reciprocity Consortium/Alcohol and

Other Drug Abuse, 1993). Case management functions — engagement; assessment; planning, goal-setting, implementation; linking, monitoring, advocacy; and disengagement — are incorporated within the referral and service coordination practice dimensions of the Addiction Counseling Competencies (California Addiction Technology Transfer Center, 1997). This document has been endorsed by the National Association of Addiction and Drug Abuse Counselors (NAADAC), the International Certification Reciprocity Consortium (ICRC), the International Coalition for Addiction Studies Education (INCASE), and the American Academy of Health Care Providers in the Addictive Disorders.

CASE MANAGEMENT AND SUBSTANCE ABUSE TREATMENT: EMPIRICAL RESULTS

This section summarizes the results of studies that have generated information on the role of case management in substance abuse treatment. We have organized it by setting and the nature of the population treated.

CASE MANAGEMENT DELIVERED IN CRIMINAL JUSTICE SETTINGS

One of the first widespread implementations of case management with substance abuse clients was provided through the Treatment Alternatives to Street Crimes (TASC) program, now Treatment Accountability for Safer Communities. As a central element of TASC, case management is designed to achieve both criminal justice and treatment-related objectives, the latter represented by efforts to coordinate the overall linkage between court system and treatment provider; eliminate programmatic and client barriers to treatment; orient clients to the treatment system; expand access to complementary social services; make referrals and coordinate services for individual offenders; monitor progress; and advocate for patients (Cook, 1992).

Two significant issues surround any assessment of case management's contribution to treatment-related outcomes. First is the expectation placed on case management to achieve criminal justice or control-related objectives rather than treatment objectives. Control activities frequently assigned to case management include supervision, the monitoring of abstinence through urinalysis, and compliance with therapeutic activities. How case management is ultimately practiced in this setting is determined by how closely, or distantly, the case management component is affiliated with either the criminal justice system or treatment program(s) (Cook, 1992). This variability establishes a powerful confound in any evaluation of case management in a criminal justice setting. Because of it, it is difficult to assess whether improvement is due to the case management or the result of the threat of court-imposed sanctions.

Variability in implementation also leads to a second problem in evaluating case management. The intervention is currently implemented in more than two hundred TASC settings with design and implementation affected not only by control-treatment issues but also by such other factors as the availability of needed services in a given community, staff to offender/client ratios, the model of case management implemented, and numerous other system-wide considerations. These same difficulties operate each time case management is implemented—therefore, it is very difficult, perhaps even impossible, to make any sweeping generalizations about the efficacy of case management or even its efficacy in TASC programs.

Results of a large scale non-TASC study involving almost 1,400 arrestees in Washington, D.C., and Portland, Oregon, addressed one of the key difficulties mentioned above—that is, uncertainty over the differential effects of coercion and case management (Rhodes & Gross, 1996). Although all clients were involved in the criminal justice system, there was, according to the authors of the study, no implied or overt pressure on clients to participate in case management services. Intensive case management provided for six months was compared to two other treatment interventions to test its relative value in reducing sexual- and injection-related risk behaviors implicated in the transmission of HIV, drug use, rearrest, and improving usage of substance abuse treatment. Although gains related to reducing HIV-risk behaviors were minimal, significant changes were attributed to case management in other outcomes.

The proportion of participants reporting heavy drug use declined dramatically in the case management group as it did in all three treatments in both sites. There were also substantial increases in the proportion reporting participation in drug treatment programs. In addition, in Washington, D.C., a significantly smaller proportion of those assigned to case management reported heavy drug use during the three months before both the three- and six-month interviews, and a significantly greater proportion reported participation in drug treatment programs in the three months before the three-month interview. In Portland, a significantly smaller proportion of those assigned to case management reported heavy drug use during the three months before the three-month interview, but there was no significant difference among the three treatments in the incidence of heavy drug use before the six-month interview, or any difference in reported participation in drug treatment programs during the three months before either the three- or six-month interview.

Participants in this study—many of whom were under criminal justice supervision for some part of the six-month follow-up period, although not by staff at the study sites—reported dramatic reductions in illegal activity from the rearrest period. For the three-month period just before the six-month interview, case management participants in both sites reported significantly less criminal behavior than other participants. Time spent in jail (in D.C. only) was significantly lower for case management participants than for other participants. In Portland, time spent in jail was lower for case management participants for the three-month period before the six-month interview, based on a comparison of case management outcomes with the two other interventions combined. In Washington, D.C., the reported reduction in criminal involvement was corroborated by correctional records showing that the case management participants were significantly less likely to be rearrested than were other participants. Another study provided support for case management's value with nonincarcerated offenders, finding lower rearrest rates and cost-effectiveness when compared to incarceration (Van Stelle, Mauser, & Moberg, 1994).

The use of case management with incarcerated offenders may be less viable. In a study of parolees released from the Delaware correctional system, researchers found no overall effect of assignment to Assertive Case Management (ACT) on behaviors including drug use, high-risk sexual behavior, and recidivism to rearrest and incarceration (Martin & Scarpitti, 1993). At the same time, positive effects were found for offenders who did become involved in the ACT program. The positive effects on drug severity of case management for this group were indirect, through such intermediate outcomes as retention in treatment, reduction in alcohol intoxication, value of individualized counseling, and improved self-esteem (Martin & Inciardi, 1996). Significant problems associated with implementing the intervention may have led to difficulties in engaging offenders in case management. Combining the roles of treatment counselor and case manager was cited as a problem in that it diluted both aspects of the program. Most notably, treatment and associated case management could not be required as a condition for early parole or as a condition of parole once the offender was released. Although these issues may have adversely affected the potential value of case management, they nonetheless raise questions about the viability of implementing case management in such a setting.

CASE MANAGEMENT AND DUALLY DIAGNOSED PERSONS

A significant body of literature exists that describes the implementation of case management with individuals who are "dually diagnosed" — that is, suffering from concurrent psychiatric and substance abuse disorders. In 1987 the National Institute of Mental Health funded ten demonstration projects targeted at young adults with coexisting mental health and substance use problems that used some form of case management (Teague, Schwab, & Drake, 1990). However, there is little empirical evidence for the success or failure of case management with this group. Although in many instances these studies reflect populations where the individuals are psychiatric patients first and substance abusers second, findings from these studies are still instructive. Given the significant coprevalence of substance abuse and psychiatric problems, it is likely that substance abuse treatment programs should anticipate the need to provide case management services for their patients with comorbid psychiatric illness (Sloan & Rowe, 1995).

Jerrell and colleagues (1994) have extensively examined the impact of case management in comparison to a behavioral coping skills model and participation in a twelve-step recovery model, considered to be a quasi-control condition. The case management utilized in this setting was a generalist model emphasizing support for clients in maintaining a drug-free environment and positive changes in living situation, employment, and social and family relations. Several findings from this study are noteworthy. First, when compared to the twelve-step recovery model, the case management intervention did have a positive impact in reducing the costs of three types of services — "mental health," "intensive," "supportive" treatment services — although the results were not always statistically significant. A subsequent study reported on the value of case management in improving psychosocial adjustment, psychiatric and substance abuse symptoms, and mental health services costs (Jerrell, 1996).

In an implementation of intensive case management, dually diagnosed clients showed a significant increase in the length of time they were maintained in the community compared to non–case-managed clients. This group also showed an increased use of community resources, although the reason for this finding may have been a matter of their longer time in the community and not the direct result of case management (Durell, Lechtenberg, Corse, & Frances, 1993). An evaluation of an intensive case management program for dually diagnosed homeless persons found that number of days homeless decreased 31% among case-managed clients, compared to a 6% decrease among control group clients (Brown, 1997).

ENGAGING HARD-TO-REACH POPULATIONS

Central to assessing case management's effectiveness with substance abuse clients have been efforts that sought to engage hard-to-reach populations like homeless persons. As the result of two National Institute on Alcoholism and Alcohol Abuse (NIAAA) and National Institute on Drug Abuse collaboratives in 1988 and 1990, several cities implemented some form of case management. In Philadelphia more than seven hundred homeless persons were recruited to participate in a project that randomly assigned subjects to one of three conditions: residential treatment focused heavily on recovery from addiction, shelter-based intensive case management program with peer case managers, and regular shelter services with case managers that had large caseloads (Stahler, Shipley, Bartelt, DuCette, & Shandler, 1995). The latter group was considered the control group for the purpose of this study. Although improvements were noted across all three groups, comparisons of the peer case management intervention with the control group was more ambiguous.

Addressing the issue of retention in treatment and case management, only 29% of the peer case managed group completed the prescribed program. Not surprisingly, this group did not show better outcomes on measures of substance use, housing stability, employment, or psychological status. Given the low completion rate for this group, many of the clients never received the case management intervention or were exposed only minimally. The authors attempted to account for this finding by comparing clients who never started treatment, those who started and then dropped out, and those who went straight through the program and graduated. These analyses found that those case-managed clients who graduated showed more improvement on alcohol use and housing stability than did clients in the comparison group; regression models failed to identify a subgroup of the peer case managed clients who performed better as a result of having received the case management intervention.

This study once again raises the issue of fidelity of implementation, but from a somewhat different perspective. As the peer counselors were "often themselves involved in the recovery process" (Stahler et al., 1995, p. 153), the question is raised as to whether those homeless individuals who completed treatment were actually exposed to the case management intervention. If because of their own needs for services the peer counselors were not able to fully implement the planned intervention, these findings may not represent a fair assessment of case management's value.

Case management alone and in combination with supported housing were both found to positively impact several areas among homeless individuals with substance abuse problems (Sosin, Bruni, & Reidy, 1995). The case management–only intervention provided a statistically significant but substantively moderate increase of 2.5 drug-free days and supported housing two days during the one year after the beginning of services. In comparison to a control condition, brokerage-style referral, the interventions also seemed to influence two mediating factors to substance use through increased willingness to talk to someone about problems or crises and decreased use of avoidance coping mechanisms. Residential stability was increased by nine days for case management and, surprisingly, six days for supported housing. An important context for this study is provided in the finding that the control group also made improvements in both substance use and residential stability. Although the authors do not detail specific reasons for this, it is possible that control group clients received case management, other supportive services, even supported housing, from agencies not involved in the study. Interestingly, the lack of case management effect evidenced in a Denver homeless study suggested that the lack of case management effect might be attributed to the availability of services to all clients—control and case managed alike—within the studied treatment program (Braucht, Reichardt, Geissler, Bormann, et al., 1995).

Orwin and colleagues (1994) conducted an analysis of three homeless demonstration projects—Boston, Louisville, Minneapolis—focusing on outcomes associated with case management. Outcome areas measured by the Addiction Severity Index (McLellan et al., 1992) and a treatment and housing readiness form included psychiatric functioning, physical health, employment status, relationships, stability of living situation, and substance use. Each of these areas of functioning was assessed by case managed clients' likelihood of improving (relative to non–case managed clients) and the magnitude of their improvement, again compared to non–case managed clients. Case management in Boston only was found to be associated with statistically significant, although not always substantively relevant, improvements. The data suggest that case-managed clients were more likely to improve on measures of housing permanence and housing independence. Clients' improvement on measures of alcohol and drug use as well as employment and economic security variables was equivocal, depending on whether it was assumed that clients who were lost to follow-up improved or not. If an assumption was made that these clients did not improve, analyses revealed a significant impact of case management.

An innovative application of case management was used to support the adoption of risk reduction practices among not-in-treatment injection drug users and crack cocaine users (Falck, Carlson, Price, & Turner, 1996). The rationale for integrating case management and risk reduction practices was predicated on the notion that a person's willingness to adopt a lower-risk lifestyle would be compromised by other problems that clients perceive to have greater salience and immediacy than contracting HIV (Carlson & Siegal, 1991). The authors described a serious inability to engage clients in the case management process. Of 105 clients randomly assigned to the case management intervention, 69 (65.7%) agreed to participate beyond the first office-based assessment session. Of these, 51 (48.7%) actually participated in at least one field-based session; only 38 (36.9%) participated in two or more sessions. In light of the minimal engagement obtained in this sample, it is not surprising that there were no significant differences between the case management and non–case management groups on measures of drug use, reduction in sex-risk behaviors, or utilization of social services. Many of the substance abusers in this study indicated that they were already aware of and had accessed social services, perhaps negating the need for case management assistance (Ashery, Carlson, Falck, & Siegal, 1995).

ENHANCING TREATMENT PARTICIPATION AND OUTCOME

Case management services are seen as useful for engaging and retaining substance abusers in treatment. Researchers have found a generally positive association between increased length of time in treatment and favorable outcomes (Brownell, Marlatt, Lichtenstein, & Wilson, 1986; Catalano, Howard, Hawkins, & Wells, 1988; Ito & Donovan, 1990; Walker, Donovan, Kivlahan, & O'Leary, 1983). Access to treatment was markedly improved by the presence of case managers who had funds with which to pay for treatment (Mejta, Bokos, Maslar, Mickenberg, & Senay, 1997). In this program intravenous drug users (IDUs) were identified at a central intake facility and randomly assigned to receive either case management services or a *standard treatment protocol*. Case-managed individuals were more likely to enter treatment than standard treatment individuals (97% vs. 53%), and they waited for treatment a much shorter period of time (16.8 days) than standard protocol individuals (101.7 days). In addition to the powerful influence of having funds with which to pay for treatment, case managers also advocated for clients, assisting them in negotiating the treatment system. This may have accounted in part for the eventual treatment retention rates that were also notably higher for case-managed clients. Other studies have associated the efforts of case managers, this time without access to funds, to improved enrollment rates in drug abuse treatment (Schlenger, Kroutil, & Roland, 1992).

One of the largest evaluations of case management's impact on clients receiving treatment for substance abuse problems was undertaken with more than 20,000 patients in publicly funded programs in Massachusetts (Schwartz, Baker, Mulvey, & Plough, 1997). A retrospective cohort design was used to study the effect of case management on clients discharged from short- and long-term residential treatment, outpatient treatment, and residential detoxification programs. Three intermediate outcome measures — staying in treatment long enough to reach a pre-established "long length of stay," transitioning to a more intense service within thirty days, being admitted to detox within thirty days of treatment discharge — were considered, each hypothesized to be related to more long-term treatment success. Although this study was not designed to follow these clients to assess eventual outcomes relative to sobriety and overall adjustment, case-managed clients had significantly better results across all three of these intermediate outcomes related to treatment attendance. Intensity of case management did not seem to provide any clear relation to these intermediate outcomes.

The impacts of three interventions that contain elements of case management were compared for their impact on substance abusers in Ontario, Canada. A central assessment and referral center (ARC), education of various professionals within the community concerning early identification and intervention, and actual case management provided through the ARC were assessed for their effects on retention and outcomes (Lightfoot et al., 1982). The full case-management intervention, compared to the other two interventions, was found to reduce attrition from treatment and improve both psychosocial and drug and alcohol outcomes. The greatest magnitude of improvement was noted among the most problematic clients.

STRENGTHS-BASED CASE MANAGEMENT

Two NIDA-funded companion projects, the Enhanced Treatment Project (ETP) and the Case Management Enhancements Project (CME), were designed to assess the impact that a strengths-based model of case management had on: (1) improving treatment retention among persons with substance abuse problems; and (2) improving treatment outcomes. Conducted by Wright State University and the Dayton Veterans Affairs Medical Center, the Enhanced Treatment Project and Case Management Enhancements were able to randomly assign veterans experiencing substance abuse problems to one of two treatments — traditional twelve-step, medical-model oriented treatment *or* traditional treatment and case management based on a strengths perspective (Siegal et al., 1995; Rapp, 1997). Besides substance abuse problems, these primarily crack- and cocaine-involved Vietnam-era males suffer from many of the problems that case management has traditionally been expected to address, including homelessness, lack of adequate employment, and uncoordinated involvement with numerous social service agencies.

The initial project (ETP) was designed to have case managers work with veterans immediately following their entry into primary substance abuse treatment. These contacts with 632 veterans were intended to promote a client's continued involvement in the early stages of treatment and establish a relationship between client and case manager that could then serve as the basis for work during the aftercare period. Case managers in the CME project work with clients in the latter stages of primary treatment and conduct their work with veterans from a community-based site rather than a medical center campus. Case management and aftercare services are highly integrated. The following findings provide results from the ETP and early findings from the CME in three areas: case management–mediated retention in treatment, outcomes associated with case management, and the characteristics of strengths-based case management that appear to impact on retention and outcomes.

STRENGTHS-BASED CASE MANAGEMENT: RETENTION AND OUTCOMES

One of the earliest findings from the ETP centered on clients' continued participation in case management activities into the aftercare period (Rapp, 1997). Case-managed clients demonstrated a pattern of selecting participation in case management services in the post-primary treatment (aftercare) period over participation in relapse prevention activities. Only 52% of clients in this group attended at least one session of aftercare following their discharge from primary treatment; in contrast, 66% of the clients in this group attended at least one session with their case manager after completion of primary treatment. The gap between attendance at relapse-prevention activities and case management activities grows significantly as time progresses; 35% of clients reported up to 20 weeks of contact with their case managers while only 11% of clients attended that amount of relapse prevention activities. A similar gap, up to 21%, between case management and relapse prevention attendance persisted until the end of the six-month follow-up period.

Coupled with this finding was the observation that in this particular treatment program inpatient completion rates approached 90% for both case-managed and non–case-managed clients alike. Together these findings suggest that the case manager's effort would be spent more productively in improving participation during the post-primary treatment period, encouraging participation in relapse-prevention activities and assisting veterans in reintegrating into the community. As a result, case management in the successor CME project was attached directly to the aftercare component in a community-based, as opposed to medical center–based, location.

A subsequent analysis attempted to determine what characteristics of the case management group may have led to the frequent selection of case management during the post-primary treatment period. To do this, cluster analytic techniques were used to describe the clients in the case-managed group and their use of services following primary treatment (Siegal, Rapp, Li, & Saha, 1997). Two variables, weeks in case management and weeks in aftercare treatment, were used to cluster the subjects. Descriptive comparisons among the clusters were conducted using such baseline measures as: (1) demographic characteristics such as age, marital status, ethnicity, gender, and educational level; (2) measures of psychosocial functioning, including drug use, employment status, and criminal justice involvement; and (3) scales measuring motivation for treatment. Psychiatric status was measured using the Global Severity Index (GSI) of the SCL-90 (Derogatis, 1977). Eight items from the Readiness for Treatment subscale of the Texas Christian University Self-Rating Form were used to compute a score that measured motivation for treatment; seven other questions were used to compute the Desire for Help subscale (Knight, Simpson, & Dansereau, 1994).

Clusters were also compared on nine indicators representing three dimensions of treatment outcomes: drug use, ongoing help to sustain abstinence, and improved social functioning. Cocaine and marijuana use were selected as measures of substance use, given their status as the two most abused (non-alcohol) drugs among subjects. Attendance at self-help group meetings was chosen as a "help" variable because it reflects a goal of treatment—namely, one that encourages clients to independently continue their recovery efforts. Two measures of social functioning chosen to compare the clusters were: (1) self-reports of illegal activities and incarceration, and (2) employment. Both recent—30 days—and more distal measures—six months in most cases—of the three dimensions were utilized.

The analysis revealed the presence of three distinct groups of clients: (1) those who quickly dropped out of post-primary treatment services, i.e., both aftercare and case management, (2) those who stayed in both aftercare and case management for most of the follow-up period, and (3) those who retained significantly longer contact with their case managers during the post-primary treatment period.

Three findings were of particular significance in addressing why some individuals elected to participate in case management and not relapse prevention activities during the post-primary treatment period. First, all three groups were remarkably similar at the time of admission to treatment on demographic characteristics, level of motivation, and the severity of substance abuse, psychiatric, and other problems. This suggests that the search for reasons for treatment retention differences were likely related to what happened *during* treatment and not on a priori differences in clients. Practically, this also suggests there are no obvious preexisting characteristics that would lead treatment programs to preselect clients as more or less appropriate for treatment. Second, our data suggest that had it not been for the case management enhancement an additional one-third of the overall sample — those who retained significantly longer contact with their case managers — would have dropped out after primary treatment. Last, at six months following entry into treatment, clients who retained contact with only case management services demonstrated outcomes generally as favorable as clients who remained with *both* case management and aftercare regimens. Although case management was implemented as an enhancement or adjunct to traditional aftercare services, this finding suggests that case management services may also be a useful *alternative* to traditional aftercare.

Multivariate analyses were conducted to explore further the relation between strengths-based case management, length of time in treatment, and drug use severity, a key outcome of substance abuse treatment (Rapp, Siegal, Li, & Saha, 1998). A standardized measure of post-primary treatment contact was created to represent the length of time subjects spent in services following their discharge from primary treatment. This variable was developed from subjects' self-reported contacts with either aftercare or case management during the six-month period following discharge from primary treatment. For clients who did not receive case management (NCM), the variable equaled the number of weeks they reported attending aftercare treatment. Because case-managed (CM) clients could participate in aftercare treatment, case management, or both, the variable was identified as the longer stay of either in aftercare or in case management. In both instances, the possible range for the measure was 0 to 30 weeks. Drug use severity, as measured by the Addiction Severity Index (ASI), was computed based on 13 questions that determine the frequency and consequences of recent (past 30 days) drug use (McLellan et al., 1992).

This analysis supported the earlier finding that case-managed clients on average stay longer in post-primary treatment services than non–case-managed clients. Although not evidencing a direct impact on drug use severity, case management affected that critical variable by facilitating longer post-primary treatment contact.

Beyond assisting individuals to reduce their drug involvement, a central goal of case management lies in helping individuals to become and remain employed (Siegal et al., 1996). In order to determine the impact of case management on employment, veterans entering substance abuse treatment were asked to indicate how interested they were in assistance with employment-related issues. The Patient Rating Scale from the ASI was used to allow clients to rate their interest in counseling for employment problems on a five-point scale. Those veterans from both case-managed and non–case-managed groups who indicated they were "extremely interested" in assistance with employment problems were selected for comparison. This grouping was used to eliminate clients who were already successfully employed and those who were not considering employment by virtue of a disability or other reason.

The "extremely interested" group consisted of 247 veterans who differed from veterans who were not extremely interested at intake in that they were more likely to be unemployed (81% vs. 64%) and less likely to be employed full-time (13% vs. 26%). In addition, those veterans who expressed extreme interest had worked fewer days in the past 30 days and had applied for twice as many jobs during the past year. Of these 247 veterans, 193 completed the six-month follow-up interview and were included in this analysis.

Among the 193 subjects expressing extreme interest in employment issues, significant differences were found between NCM and CM clients. Using ASI data, case management clients worked more days than the comparable group of NCM clients (15.6 days vs. 12.1 days). Beyond working more days, CM clients also reported fewer days of employment problems, feeling "less troubled" about their employment status and seeing "less need" for employment counseling. The latter two findings, less troubled about employment and less need for employment counseling/assistance, were based on client self-ratings on a patient self-rating scale of perceived need for assistance. The ASI severity ratings (an interviewer assigned rating of severity of employment problems) and composite scores focusing on functioning in the preceding 30 days also indicated greater average improvement for persons in the CM group with respect to employment.

STRENGTHS-BASED CASE MANAGEMENT AND RELAPSE PREVENTION

Data collected in the CME project also suggest some of the important elements of strengths-based case management. As in the earlier project, initial analyses focused on the issue of retention, defined as involvement in post-primary treatment or any scheduled treatment activities either at the medical center–based program or at the CME's community site. Data on aftercare attendance during the first month after discharge were collected at the 30-day follow-up interview, while data for the second and the third month were obtained through the 90-day follow-up. In a similar fashion, average contacts for aftercare, for both groups, were calculated for the first, second, and third months after discharge, respectively. These contacts included personal visits and telephone calls where aftercare issues were discussed.

Post-treatment contacts were reported by 68% of non–case-managed clients in the first month after discharge, then fell to 54.8% in the second month and 52.4% in the third month, while the contacts were reported by 93.5% of the case-managed clients consistently over the three-month period. During the first month after discharge the average post-treatment contacts by case-managed clients were 9.4, compared to the average contacts of 4.3 for the control group. A similar decline pattern was found for both groups over the three-month period. However, the average contacts in the third month after discharge reported by case-managed clients tripled the average number by the control group, 8.3 and 2.6, respectively.

A services utilization survey was administered to all CME participants as part of their six-month follow-up. Both CM and NCM clients were asked about the areas they had worked on with their aftercare counselors and, for case-managed clients, with their case managers as well. In addition, both groups were asked whether they believed the work had been beneficial and the degree to which they had been assisted in contacting needed resources. A list of nine topics that clients may have worked on with aftercare counselors or case managers included life skills, finance, leisure, relationship, living arrangement, occupation and education, health, internal resources, and recovery. Significant differences, based on chi-square tests, were found in every area mentioned; however, they were especially evident in the areas of occupation/education, recovery, and internal resources such as identifying and pursuing goals, identifying strengths, talents, and accomplishments.

Differences between the case-managed clients and the non–case-managed clients were also evident in terms of the degree to which aftercare counselors and case managers referred clients to needed services. Significant differences between the case-managed and non–case-managed subjects in reporting service referrals were found in clothing vouchers and housing assistance. Specifically, referrals for external services in these areas for case-managed clients were five or six times more than those referrals reported by non–case-managed clients. In general, the case-managed group reported more external service referrals than the control group in other areas including alcohol or drug (AOD) self-help groups, although the group differences in these areas were not statistically significant.

STRENGTHS SUMMARY

Several tentative conclusions can be drawn about strengths-based case management implemented with substance abusers. First, it seems that positive outcomes accrue to those clients who receive strengths-based case management, particularly in the areas of employment and drug use. The connection between case management and diminished drug use seems to occur because case managers keep clients involved in treatment services. Interestingly, case management was very effective in keeping clients involved with their case managers but only marginally effective in keeping them involved with their relapse counselor. Reasons for the longer involvement in the case management relationship may be related to case managers' willingness to meet clients in their homes, hangouts, and the like, as opposed to only in an office setting. In addition, clients had the opportunity to address recovery and multiple other life domains with their case manager. This "one-stop shopping" reflects a strengths perspective principal that encourages the case manager to be a central point in the client's search for resources. This is attractive to clients who typically have been involved with numerous, fragmented resources at any one time. Quite possibly clients may have found that a focus on strengths, and the opportunity to direct their own treatment in a highly individualized fashion, was more attractive than relapse prevention activities that focused on pathology.

DISCUSSION

These early findings provoke as many questions as they provide answers about the role of case management with substance abusers. Even the fairly consistent finding that case management has been associated with improving access and retention in treatment raises additional issues. This intermediate outcome appears to be extremely valuable in that it keeps individuals involved with treatment, thereby improving the opportunity for clients to become fully invested in treatment. The mechanism by which case management influences retention, however, is still not well-defined. Our own experiences suggest that the assertive outreach practiced by case managers, i.e., going to the client when the client doesn't come to the case manager, may be critical.

Efforts to document case management's role in improving treatment outcomes have produced mixed results. This may reflect unreal expectations of case management's direct effects on specific outcomes like drug use. In other words, it is probably unrealistic to expect an intervention that is designed to help patients identify and link with community resources to also impact directly on such a complex behavior as compulsive drug use. Confidence in case management may be warranted, as long as treatment professionals realize that case management's value in improving outcome may be the result of its role in retaining clients in treatment and that relations between case management and treatment outcomes are complex and, perhaps, indirect (Orwin et al., 1994; Rapp et al., 1998).

As with other populations establishing the efficacy, or lack of efficacy, of case management with substance abusers has been confounded by the same issues found in studying case management with other populations. These problems are conceptual, methodological, and technical in nature. One of the main conceptual problems involves the definition of case management itself. Although a rigorous standardized definition of the intervention would please evaluators, those responsible for developing and operating service programs might find such a definition counterproductive. They would argue that if case management is to be valuable in a wide variety of settings, it may well be that the intervention will have to be defined and described over and over again, specific to various settings. The challenge then will be to assess the fidelity with which the defined version of case management is implemented and then attempting to evaluate the model in terms of desired outcomes.

Additionally, there are methodological factors, several of them articulated by Orwin and colleagues (Orwin et al., 1994) in their analysis of NIAAA homeless projects, that should be addressed in any evaluation of case management. They include:

- Bias attributable to differential attrition between control and case-managed groups, i.e., case-managed clients who are doing less well may be easier to recontact at follow-up points than non–case-managed clients.

- Lack of sufficient intervention intensity and/or something other than case management really being implemented.
- A carry-over effect where non–case-managed clients actually receive some level of case management, either from staff delivering services to the control group or indirectly from case-managed clients.
- Contextual factors that are endemic to the network of services in a given community where these factors differentially affect the successful provision of case management services.

Technical problems that arise in evaluative research involve flaws in experimental design, lack of consensus on appropriate outcome criteria, measurement issues, low statistical power, and selection biases.

CONCLUSION

Case management resonates positively with substance abuse treatment services. Chemically dependent people are troubled people. Not only are they compulsive users of drugs, they find themselves — often directly because of their use — deeply enmeshed in problems that keep them from attaining and maintaining safe and stable housing, necessary health and mental care services, employment, job training/education, and the like. Case management can assist clients with treatment access and use these and other necessary services. Although the services themselves cannot bring about recovery, they can support the recovery process. Perhaps this occurs by binding the newly emerging identity of the "recovering person" with ties that will sustain this behavior and eschew the environment and interactions that would encourage relapse.

Perhaps the greatest motor that case management has is also its simplest. It seems to work because one person reaches out, sometimes repeatedly, to another. In this process, our clients either are held in treatment, which allows it to work, or maintain the appropriate post-primary treatment contacts that help avoid reuse of drugs.

The challenge for our field is now in the demonstration-evaluation arena. There is sufficient experience with case management to feel comfortable with its use as a treatment enhancement. We now need to design and implement demonstration projects that examine different models of the intervention with identifiable populations. The projects have to demonstrate first that the case management model has been implemented faithfully, and then appropriate methods used to both assess its impact vis-à-vis the project's goals and understand the process through which it affected its clients.

References

Ashery, R. S., Carlson, R. G., Falck, R. S., & Siegal, H. A. (1995). Injection drug users, crack-cocaine users and human service utilization: An exploratory study. *Social Work, 40*(1), 75–82.

Ballew, J. R., & Mink, G. (1996). *Case management in social work: Developing the professional skills needed for work with multiproblem clients.* Springfield, Ill.: Charles C. Thomas.

Braucht, G. N., Reichardt, C. S., Geissler, L. J., Bormann, C. A., et al. (1995). Effective services for homeless substance abusers. *Journal of Addictive Diseases, 14*(4), 87–109.

Brown, E. (1997). *Study shows that intensive, paired case management decreases number of homeless days for dually diagnosed homeless persons.* CSAT by fax, vol. 2. Rockville, Md.: Center for Substance Abuse Treatment and Center for Substance Abuse Research.

Brownell, K. D., Marlatt, G. A., Lichtenstein, E., & Wilson, G. T. (1986). Understanding and preventing relapse. *American Psychologist, 41*(7), 765–782.

California Addiction Technology Transfer Center. (1997). *Addiction counseling competencies: The knowledge, skills, and attitudes of professional practice.* La Jolla, Calif.: California Addiction Technology Transfer Center.

Carlson, R. G., & Siegal, H. A. (1991). The crack life: An ethnographic overview of crack use and sexual behaviors among African Americans in a midwest metropolitan city. *Journal of Psychoactive Drugs, 23,* 11–20.

Catalano, R. F., Howard, M. O., Hawkins, J. D., & Wells, E. A. (1988). Relapse in the addictions: Rates, determinants, and promising relapse prevention strategies. *Surgeon General's Report, The Health Consequences of Smoking: Nicotine Addiction,* Washington, D.C.: U.S. Government Printing Office, pp. 1–105.

Cook, F. (1992). TASC: Case management models linking criminal justice and treatment. In R. S. Ashery (ed.), *Progress and issues in case management.* Rockville, Md.: U.S. Department of Health and Human Services, pp. 368–382.

Derogatis, L. R. (1977). *SCL-90-R Administration and Scoring Procedures Manual.* Baltimore, Md.: Clinical Psychometrics Research.

Durell, J., Lechtenberg, B., Corse, S., & Frances, R. J. (1993). Intensive case management of persons with chronic mental illness who abuse substances. *Hospital & Community Psychiatry, 44*(5), 415–416.

Falck, R., Carlson, R. G., Price, S. K., & Turner, J. A. (1996). Case management to enhance HIV risk reduction among users of injection drugs and crack cocaine. In H. A.

Siegal & R. C. Rapp (eds.), *Case management and substance abuse treatment: Practice and experience* (pp. 91–104). New York: Springer.

Graham, K., & Birchmore Timney, C. (1990). Case management in addictions treatment. *Journal of Substance Abuse Treatment, 7,* 181–188.

Ito, J. R., & Donovan, D. (1990). Aftercare in alcoholism treatment: A review. In W. Miller & N. Heather (eds.), *Treating addictive behaviors: Processes of change.* New York: Plenum.

Jerrell, J. M. (1996). Toward cost-effective care for persons with dual diagnoses. *Journal of Mental Health Administration, 23*(3), 329–337.

Jerrell, J. M., Hu, T., & Ridgely, M. S. (1994). Cost-effectiveness of substance disorder interventions for people with severe mental illness. *Journal of Mental Health Administration, 21*(3), 283–297.

Knight, K., Simpson, D. D., & Dansereau, D. F. (1994). Knowledge mapping: A psychoeducational tool in drug abuse relapse prevention training. *Journal of Offender Rehabilitation, 20*(3/4), 187–205.

Lightfoot, L., Rosenbaum, P., Ogurzsoff, S., Laverty, G., Kusiar, S., Barry, K., & Reynolds, W. (1982). *Final report of the Kingston treatment programmed development research project.* Canada: Department of Health and Welfare, Health Promotion Directorate.

Martin, S. S., & Inciardi, J. A. (1996). *Case management outcomes for drug involved offenders.* American Society of Criminology Meetings, Chicago, Ill., November 22.

Martin, S., & Scarpitti, F. (1993). An intensive case management approach for paroled IV drug users. *Journal of Drug Issues, 23*(1), 81–96.

McLellan, A. T., Kushner, H., Metzger, D., Peters, R., Smith, I., Grissom, G., Pettinati, H., & Argeriou, M. (1992). The fifth edition of the Addiction Severity Index. *Journal of Substance Abuse Treatment, 9*(3), 199–213.

Mejta, C. L., Bokos, P. J., Maslar, E. M., Mickenberg, J. H., & Senay, E. C. (1997). The effectiveness of case management in working with intravenous drug users. In F. M. Tims, J. A. Inciardi, B. W. Fletcher, & A. M. Horton (eds.), *The effectiveness of innovative approaches in the treatment of drug abuse.* Westport, Conn.: Greenwood. pp. 101–114.

National Association of Alcoholism and Drug Abuse Counselors. (1986). *The eight counselor skill groups in the NAADAC certification commission oral exam.* Arlington, Va.: NAADAC certification commission.

National Certification Reciprocity Consortium/Alcohol and Other Drug Abuse. (1993). *Standards for certification.* Atkinson, N.H.

Oppenheimer, E., Sheehan, M., & Taylor, C. (1988). Letting the client speak: Drug misusers and the process of help seeking. *British Journal of Addiction, 83,* 635–647.

Orwin, R. G., Soinnefeld, L. J., Garrison-Mogren, R., & Smith, N. G. (1994). Pitfalls in evaluating the effectiveness of case management programs for homeless persons. *Evaluation Review, 18*(2), 153–207.

Rapp, R. C. (1997). The strengths perspective and persons with substance abuse problems. In D. Saleebey (ed.), *The strengths perspective in social work practice,* 2nd ed. New York: Longman.

Rapp, R. C., Siegal, H. A., Li, L., & Saha, P. (1998). Predicting post-primary treatment services and drug use outcome: A multivariate analysis. *American Journal of Drug and Alcohol Abuse.*

Rhodes, W., & Gross, M. (1996). *Case management reduces drug use and criminality among drug-involved arrestees: An experimental study of an HIV prevention intervention.* Final summary report presented to the National Institute of Justice and the National Institute on Drug Abuse. NIJ Research Report, Washington, D.C.: Office of Justice Programs.

Rothman, J. (1994). *Practice with highly vulnerable clients.* Englewood Cliffs, N.J.: Prentice Hall.

Schlenger, W. E., Kroutil, L. A., & Roland, E. J. (1992). Case management as a mechanism for linking drug abuse treatment and primary care: Preliminary evidence from the ADAMHA/HRSA linkage demonstration. In R. S. Ashley (ed.), *Progress and issues in case management.* NIDA Technical Review on Case Management. Rockville, Md.: U.S. Department of Health and Human Services.

Schwartz, M., Baker, G., Mulvey, K. P., & Plough, A. (1997). Improving publicly funded substance abuse treatment: The value of case management. *American Journal of Public Health, 87,* 1659–1664.

Siegal, H. A., Fisher, J. A., Rapp, R. C., Kelliher, C. W., Wagner, J. H., O'Brien, W. F., & Cole, P. A. (1996). Enhancing substance abuse treatment with case management: Its impact on employment. *Journal of Substance Abuse Treatment, 13*(2), 93–98.

Siegal, H. A., Rapp, R. C., Kelliher, C. W., Fisher, J. H., Wagner, J. H., & Cole, P. A. (1995). The strengths perspective of case management: A promising inpatient substance abuse treatment enhancement. *Journal of Psychoactive Drugs, 27*(1), 67–72.

Siegal, H. A., Rapp, R. C., Li, L., & Saha, P. (1997). Multidimensional relationships between pretreatment motivation and treatment outcomes. American Society of Criminology Annual Meeting, November 19–22, San Diego, California.

Sloan, K. L., & Rowe, G. (1995). Substance abuse and psychiatric illness: Psychosocial correlates. *American Journal on Addictions, 4*(1), 60–69.

Sosin, M. R., Bruni, M., & Reidy, M. (1995). Paths and impacts in the progressive independence model: A homelessness and substance abuse intervention in Chicago. *Journal of Addictive Diseases, 14*(4), 1–20.

Stahler, G. J., Shipley, T. F. J., Bartelt, D., DuCette, J. P., & Shandler, I. W. (1995). Evaluating alternative treatments for homeless substance-abusing men: Outcomes and predictors for success. *Journal of Addictive Diseases, 14*(4), 151–167.

Teague, G. B., Schwab, B., & Drake, R. E. (1990). *Evaluation of services for young adults with severe mental illness and substance use disorders.* Alexandria, Va.: National Association of State Mental Health Program Directors.

Van Stelle, K. R., Mauser, E., & Moberg, D. P. (1994). Recidivism to the criminal justice system of substance-abusing offenders diverted into treatment. *Crime and Delinquency, 40*(2), 175–196.

Walker, R. D., Donovan, D. M., Kivlahan, D. R., & O'Leary, M. R. (1983). Length of stay, neuropsychological performance, and aftercare: Influences on alcohol treatment outcome. *Journal of Consulting and Clinical Psychology, 51*(6), 900–911.

Westermeyer, J. (1989). Cross-cultural studies on alcoholism. In H. W. Goedde & D. P. Agarwal (eds.), *Alcoholism: biomedical and genetic aspects* (pp. 305–311). Elmsford, N.Y.: Pergamon.

Willenbring, M. L., Ridgely, M. S., Stinchfield, R., & Rose, M. (1991). *Application of case management in alcohol and drug dependence: Matching techniques and populations.* Rockville, Md.: U.S. Department of Health and Human Services.

TWELVE

SELF-HELP INITIATIVES TO REDUCE
THE RISK OF RELAPSE

Barry S. Brown, Timothy W. Kinlock, & David N. Nurco

Self-help initiatives are sufficiently wide-ranging to have penetrated both the popular and scientific press, and to have been endowed with the status of having become a "movement" (Gartner and Reissman, 1977). Thus, self-help strategies have been employed to support efforts at weight loss, recovery from a variety of dysfunctional family relationships (e.g., both having and being abusive parents, child loss, divorce), living with and recovering from a variety of diseases (e.g., cancer, AIDS, arthritis, psychiatric disorder) as well as recovery from an equally wide assortment of addictions (e.g., gambling, sex, alcohol, and various forms of illicit drug use). As suggested by these examples, self-help initiatives have been organized by and for those recovering from problems, those who must routinely cope with problems, and those who have been exposed to problems as the relatives or friends of others. As described by Katz and Bender (1976), self-help initiatives involve the joint efforts of individuals concerned with "satisfying a common need, overcoming a common handicap or life-disrupting problem, and bringing about desired social and/or personal change." Levy (1976) describes self-help efforts as having four possible foci: behavior change or control, coping with a stressful condition that is unavoidable, providing support to members at odds with the larger society by virtue of their lifestyle, and/or achiev-

This work was supported in part by NIDA Grant DA10180. The authors are grateful to Phil Stephenson and Thomas E. Hanlon for their important contributions to this chapter.

ing greater personal growth. All definitions, then, conceive of self-help as a strategy of individual strengthening to overcome adversity, to cope with adversity, or to change the conditions producing that adversity.

CHARACTERISTICS OF SELF-HELP PROGRAMS

Three characteristics can be seen as essential to self-help initiatives and as differentiating those initiatives from other behavior change forms. First, in spite of the term "self-help," these initiatives all involve the individual acting in collaboration with a group of similarly afflicted individuals. Somewhat paradoxically, these same initiatives are also described as mutual support programs. Thus, individuals meet on a regularly scheduled basis in groups that typically put a premium on maintaining individuals' anonymity while supporting each other's recovery or coping efforts. The only requirement for group participation is the sharing of a specific problem with other group members. For example, Narcotics Anonymous (NA, 1988) reports that "a meeting happens when two or more addicts gather to help each other stay clean."

Second, self-help initiatives have historically been distinctly, and indeed aggressively, nonprofessional. In fact, some self-help groups purposefully avoid all reliance on professionals, believing that professionals do not understand their particular problems or needs. Yet, many self-help groups have also forged strong collaborative alliances with professionals, and today other groups have been organized by or operated in conjunction with professional sponsorship.

For NA, however, self-help remains the involvement of individuals who share a common fate, work without title in support of each other's efforts, and draw strength both from the group and from a "higher power" (however that may be conceptualized) as well as from their own successes. That intervention is not seen as treatment; consequently, it does not require the involvement of a treatment professional. Indeed, in the workings of the group, every individual — regardless of background, education, or job status — is the equal of every other individual.

Third, the self-help initiative involves a loosely organized confederation of groups, all dealing with the same area of concern. Thus, groups may be organized nationwide or even worldwide around a single issue, e.g., alcohol abuse, with each individual group enjoying large autonomy in particular areas, e.g., developing a membership restricted to women or to nonsmokers — provided those groups adhere to certain inflexible standards, e.g., the maintenance of group members' anonymity and the refusal to engage in the promotion of products or of opinions on public issues. Thus, although a "headquarters" facility may exist, it acts to support local groups through the provision of media materials or to provide coordination of national or international meetings, but the central unit will not direct or monitor the functioning of local groups.

SELF-HELP AND SUBSTANCE ABUSE

Two concurrently occurring movements in human services can be seen as aiding the development of the self-help movement within the drug abuse framework and as being aided by that movement. First, the therapeutic community was emerging as a vital force in both mental health and drug abuse treatment. Jones (1957) described the therapeutic community as a mental health strategy in which the patients and staff of a residential treatment program work jointly to resolve problems within the community that both of them share. The therapeutic community, as first embodied in the Synanon program in 1958 as a primary treatment approach, championed the use of nonprofessional staff working in conjunction with drug abuse clients to permit gradually increasing maturity and responsibility taking by those clients. The mental health, and especially the drug abuse, therapeutic community programs can be seen as making use of mutual support efforts by and for clients and as emphasizing the work of nonprofessional and ex-client staff. The second and related movement in the human services paralleling self-help involved the emergence — or more likely, the recognition — of the therapeutic role played by paraprofessionals and, more particularly, their roles as change agents with regard to dysfunctional behaviors.

Thus, the therapeutic community movement gave status to the non-degreed service worker on the one hand, and to the individual with addiction experience on the other. The paraprofessional movement gave recognition to the nondegreed worker as a significant treatment agent. The view of ex-addict staff as having a significant role in drug abuse treatment can be seen as both supporting and being supported by 12-Step programming. In that sense, drug abuse treatment can be seen as reinforcing the ideas it had already adopted from the 12-Step movement. Thus, as reported by Gerstein and Harwood (1990), in its emphasis on fellowship, 12-Step programming exerted a major influence on the development of the long-term therapeutic community (TC), and an even larger influence on the development of 28-day residential programs that are, in fact, sometimes called 12-Step treatment.

Narcotics Anonymous, and its sister programs of Alcoholics Anonymous and Cocaine Anonymous, remain, however, the particular form of self-help initiatives most commonly associated by the general public with help-ing the substance abuser. As their primary purpose, 12-Step programs sup-port the individual's efforts to become and remain alcohol- and drug-free. Thus, the main goal for the 12-Step participant, as well as for the drug abuse treatment client, is drug and alcohol abstinence. Nonetheless, 12-Step pro-grams are distinguished from drug abuse treatment programs in several im-portant ways. For 12-Step programs, recovery from substance abuse is a con-tinuing process. Individuals in such programs regard every day as involving a struggle to remain free of illicit drug use. In contrast, drug abuse treatment strives to provide a cure for substance abuse during the course of a defined time period. Individuals who graduate or who are successfully discharged from treatment have become abstinent and have been prepared for changed life functioning without continued systematic support.

Moreover, most drug abuse treatment programs can be viewed as oper-ating in accordance with features consistent with the medical model. Ser-vices, designed to achieve cure, are offered to clients by professionals in office settings over a prescribed course. 12-Step programs are, however, de-cidedly nonmedical in both function and structure. Neither services nor patients/clients exist. Professionals, if present, are addressed by their first names and are the equal of all other self-help members in their capacities to advise or support others in their common struggle to overcome addiction. 12-Step programs meet in community settings willing and able to accommodate such groups, and in which the "host" agency expects no endorsement from the self-help group. Those settings may be the "group rooms" of treatment programs, church basements, community centers, or prison auditoriums.

It is interesting to note that, in spite of its rejection of professionalism and the medical model of treatment, the 12-Step movement embraces a view of addiction as disease. It is a disease that is a chronic condition that need not be inextricably associated with relapse. It is a disease that invades all aspects of the host individual's life, but that can be effectively combated one day at a time.

THE STRUCTURE AND FUNCTION OF NA

Although it is not the only self-help program dealing with drug use prob-lems, Narcotics Anonymous is clearly both the most ubiquitous and the most influential. Because of this, a detailed discussion of NA's structure and func-tioning is warranted.

For the individual member, the core of NA is the 12 Steps; for the individual group, the core of NA is the 12 Traditions. The 12 Steps provide a structure to the NA member's life. She or he is expected to "work" the Steps, which permit progression from the initial recognition of one's impotence in the face of one's addiction through personal commitment to change with the help of God (or of "a Power greater than ourselves") to an atonement to others for past offenses, and ultimately to a responsibility for positively influencing the lives of others. Progression through the Steps is critical to achieving and maintaining abstinence. The 12 Traditions provide the policy and regulations that are to govern each individual fellowship and guarantee the integrity of the whole. As described by NA (1988), they are the "guidelines that keep our Fellowship alive and free." The Traditions emphasize the responsibility of the Fellowship to the individual member, promising support and anonymity to all who "desire to stop using," while pledging autonomy to the local group except in matters having an impact on other groups or on the NA organization. Thus, the Traditions proscribe societal entanglements whether fiscal, political, or involving public relations.

The 12 Steps are described in the NA Basic Text as "the principles that made our recovery possible" (NA, 1988). The specific 12 Steps that build on each other and therefore are to be followed in sequence are as follows:

1 We admitted that we were powerless over our addiction, that our lives had become unmanageable.
2 We came to believe that a Power greater than ourselves could restore us to sanity.
3 We made a decision to turn our will and our lives over to the care of God as we understood Him.
4 We made a searching and fearless moral inventory of ourselves.
5 We admitted to God, to ourselves, and to another human being the exact nature of our wrongs.
6 We were entirely ready to have God remove all these defects of character.
7 We humbly asked Him to remove our shortcomings.
8 We made a list of all persons we had harmed, and became willing to make amends to them all.
9 We made direct amends to such people wherever possible, except when to do so would injure them or others.
10 We continued to take personal inventory and when we were wrong promptly admitted it.

11 We sought through prayer and meditation to improve our conscious contact with God as we understood Him, praying only for knowledge of His will for us and the power to carry that out.

12 Having had a spiritual awakening as a result of these steps, we tried to carry this message to addicts, and to practice these principles in our affairs.

Working the Steps is the responsibility of each individual NA member and much of it involves solitary activity. The individual studies the written materials that are made available to him or her through the Fellowship, assesses his or her functioning, prays for guidance and support, meditates, and strives to make each day an abstinent day. Nonetheless, what are best known to the public about the workings of NA are the group activities of the Fellowship. Meetings are held weekly, typically for periods of about an hour. Groups may be open or closed.

Perhaps the best-known and most common NA groups are the closed groups that encourage individuals to share their accomplishments, their fears, and their failures with peers who are uniquely qualified to provide support, advice, and understanding by virtue of sharing with each speaker a common history and an uncertain future. These closed groups are available only to individuals willing and able to describe themselves as "addicts," with that acknowledgment being the only requirement for entrance. Where those meetings involve exploration of issues important to recovery, one group member will have been chosen to preside over the discussion of a particular issue seen as significant to maintaining abstinence, e.g., relationships. Members share their life experiences, concerns, and ambitions relative to that topic. Also, in closed meetings, a member of that NA group or a guest from another group may present a discussion of his or her life — what it was like during their period of drug use, how NA came into their lives, and where they are now. The capacity to present one's experiences, particularly one's addiction, to the group, is seen as important and immensely positive, affording the individual a chance to admit to past failure while drawing strength from the group in its recognition of how far he or she has come. Open meetings permit nonaddict outsiders with a concern about friends or family members to attend and learn about the functioning of NA on condition only that the outsider participate when appropriate and respect the anonymity of group members.

At a meeting involving discussion of an issue relevant to members' maintaining abstinence, the leader will have been chosen by the group secretary to preside and guide the discussion. Leadership for group meetings will change from one week to the next. However, the secretary is likely to be "in office" for a period of one to six months on the basis of his or her election or appointment (DuPont and McGovern, 1994). In all meetings prior to group discussion or any other activity, the leader and all members typically recite the Serenity Prayer in unison, then an individual is called upon to read a selection from an NA publication. General announcements are made at the conclusion of the meeting or at a break during the meeting. In addition, opportunity will be provided to permit members to make a contribution to support the group's expenses. Frequently, time is also set aside to recognize individuals who have remained abstinent for defined periods (i.e., anniversary dates). At the meeting's end, members again recite the Serenity Prayer or the Lord's Prayer or some selected inspirational reading, usually while standing in a circle and holding hands. Upon leaving, members call encouragement to each other and urge one another to return.

New members are often encouraged to attend more than one meeting a week to support their efforts to maintain abstinence while also encouraging a special allegiance to the "home" group (DuPont, 1994). Indeed, a "90/90" prescription has been suggested such that new members attend 90 meetings in the first 90 days of activity. In this regard, it is noteworthy that the proliferation of NA makes attendance at several meetings, i.e., participation in several groups, feasible in a large number of communities. The significance of joint addiction to both alcohol and drugs has led to the suggestion that many substance users can benefit from attending both NA and AA meetings (Krupka and Blume, 1980; Nurco et al., 1983). In some instances, AA groups have permitted membership to individuals addicted to drugs but not to alcohol.

Although attendance at meetings forms the basis for most individuals' first contact with the NA Fellowship, it is seen as a less effective introduction to NA than being invited to join by an experienced member, with the opportunity that invitation provides for orientation and support. However, a survey of members found that only 29% were introduced to NA by an experienced member compared to 47% referred through treatment settings, and 24% by professionals associated with the criminal justice system, clergy, etc. (DuPont and McGovern, 1994). Where possible, new members may seek to attend meetings with people like themselves, e.g., professionals seeking groups attended by professionals (Ashery, 1979). As individuals become more comfortable with the Fellowship, and recognize the universality of its member-ship, they may become more comfortable with a wider range of options. Over time, and with sustained abstinence, individuals often reduce the frequency with which they attend groups, although it is recommended that individuals continue to attend two or more meetings a week, and leave themselves open to attend additional meetings if they feel their abstinence is threatened.

Although considerable public attention has focused on Fellowship meet-ings for their significance in supporting the individual's efforts to achieve and sustain abstinence, the importance of the NA sponsor appears to be less well appreciated. The Twelfth Step in NA calls upon members to work on behalf of other addicts in bringing them the NA message as well as practic-ing NA principles in all of their own community affairs. Often, Twelfth Step work involves outreach to the courts or other institutions seeing drug addicts (Nurco et al., 1983; DuPont and McGovern, 1994). In addition to that out-reach, working the Twelfth Step can involve sponsoring another NA member. Sponsors work with one, or several, new NA members by providing support, information, and advice in several areas: working the Steps, understanding the functioning of the Fellowship, understanding the process of recovery, and coping with sudden crises. Sponsors are expected to have achieved some un-defined period of sustained abstinence and must be the same sex as the indi-vidual being sponsored. Sponsors are available to their charges continuously (although members may have several sponsors sequentially) and the "Basic Text" of NA (NA, 1988) describes several accounts by members of instances in which sponsors dramatically extended themselves to provide the support essential to permitting those members to become and remain abstinent.

It is important to emphasize that neither sponsorship nor outreach is an act of simple altruism. "Twelfth Stepping" is not only a part of the respon-sibility of NA members to give back to others; it is also seen as supporting one's own efforts to maintain abstinence. In strengthening the capacity of others to achieve sustained abstinence, the NA member can view him- or herself as an individual capable of supporting others, thereby strengthen-ing his or her own sense of self and efforts to maintain abstinence. Riessman (1965) describes this as "helper-therapy." Simply stated, his principle asserts that "those who help are helped the most" (Gartner and Riessman, 1977). Similarly, Volkman and Cressey (1963) assert, "A group in which Criminal A joins with some noncriminal to change Criminal B, is probably most effec-tive in changing Criminal A, not B." Cressey (1965) referred to this process as "retroflexive reformation" and hypothesized that this could account for the success experienced by programs such as AA and Synanon.

NA AND DRUG ABUSE TREATMENT

NA views itself as neither a treatment alternative nor as an appendage to drug abuse treatment. Nonetheless, working with addict treatment clients is consistent with NA philosophy and does not violate NA tenets. Specifically, the NA Basic Text states that "Hospitals, drug recovery houses and parole offices are some of the facilities we deal with in carrying out the NA message . . . these organizations are sincere and we hold meetings in their establishments" (NA, 1988). NA can join forces with drug abuse treatment in terms of both providing additional supports to abstinence during the time the client is in treatment and/or providing aftercare for the client leaving treatment.

NA can be viewed as making possible the following resources that may be otherwise unavailable to the treatment client:

(1) NA provides a continuing peer group uniquely capable of supporting the individual's efforts to achieve and maintain abstinence. The importance of that new peer group can be seen from the finding that drug abuse clients typically have a preponderance of drug-abusing friends (Fraser and Hawkins, 1984). Moreover, the continuing availability of drug-abusing friends is associated with relapse to drug abuse posttreatment (Hawkins and Fraser, 1987; Waldorf et al., 1991) as well as to HIV risk-taking (Zapka et al., 1993). NA provides to the client a ready-made peer group that not only is invested in prosocial behaviors, but is aggressively antidrug. Moreover, these peers share both the client's struggle and the client's background of drug abuse. Thus, they share his or her failed efforts to break free of that dependence, as well as the family and community ostracism that has resulted from those failures. NA provides the support of a non–drug-using group that promises uncompromising acceptance—for as long as the client is willing to work the Steps toward continuing abstinence.

(2) Whereas treatment programs typically recognize the importance of aftercare, only a distinct minority have the resources to provide this service (Hubbard et al., 1989). NA provides aftercare that costs the program virtually nothing. Simply by making space available to NA groups and recommending NA participation, the treatment program assures itself of a posttreatment resource that clients can draw upon to continue the work of rehabilitation.

(3) NA helps the client to structure his or her free time. A particular issue for many clients, both during and after treatment, involves the use of leisure time. Thus, treatment efforts are likely to emphasize clients' acquisition of jobs, training, or schooling, but place far less emphasis on helping the client to structure, or develop strategies for structuring, their free time.

Nonetheless, involvement in prosocial leisure activities have been found to be associated with the prevention of relapse (Simpson et al., 1981). The NA group, with its evening meetings, provides activity during the client's non-work, nonschool time that permits — indeed encourages — abstinence. More-over, as noted above, in most communities, the client can attend several NA meetings a week as well as AA and/or CA meetings if those are relevant to his or her situation.

(4) NA also makes available to clients a unique individual in support of the client's efforts to maintain abstinence. The client's sponsor provides a com-plex blend of support, mentoring, and policing. The sponsor has been there, seen it all, and done most of it. The sponsor can thus provide understanding, assistance, advice and call a halt to "conning" or unproductive behaviors. Unlike the treatment counselor — even the formerly addicted counselor — the sponsor is available to the client at all times and in all places. It is not unheard of for clients to live for periods with their sponsors (NA, 1988). Sponsors do not concern themselves with maintaining an "appropriate distance" or with "tapering relationships" from their fellow NA members; they are available unconditionally for an unlimited period.

NA AND CRIMINAL JUSTICE PROGRAMMING

Whereas NA may ally itself with existing drug abuse treatment programs in a community, NA may be the only resource available in the correctional setting (Brown, 1992). A survey conducted by the U.S. General Accounting Office (1991) estimated that approximately 20% of more than 500,000 state inmates with drug abuse problems receive treatment. In a previous survey of the 50 state directors of correctional programs, it was reported that only 11% of inmates were enrolled in drug abuse treatment programs (Chaiken, 1989), which nonetheless represented a sharp increase from the 4% reported to be enrolled in an earlier survey (National Institute on Drug Abuse, 1981). The significance of the availability of NA resources in jails and prisons is height-ened when one considers that approximately 62% of those incarcerated have histories of frequent drug abuse (U.S. Department of Justice, 1993) and that there are more than one million prison and jail inmates nationwide (National Institute of Justice, 1996). In short, there is little reason to believe that exist-ing treatment resources can meet the needs of the correctional population. Moreover, the numbers of drug abusers being incarcerated are reported to be increasing as a consequence of changes in the law and its administration regarding drug abuse (Inciardi, 1996). The importance of an intervention that does not involve a demand for scarce human and material resources has obvious attraction and significance.

It is unclear to what extent NA is, in fact, in use in correctional settings. Moreover, where NA is available, its structure and functioning appear to differ from the structure and functioning of other NA groups. Institutional NA groups may rely on correctional staff rather than their own membership to obtain speakers and sponsors from the local community (Brown, 1995). The role of sponsor with an inmate in an institution must obviously differ from the role of sponsor with individuals in the community. Meetings may be required by correctional staff to remain open and accessible to the staff (DuPont and McGovern, 1994). Importantly, too, clients exiting correctional settings leave the NA groups with which they have become affiliated, i.e., there is no continuing home-base NA. It is unknown to what extent exiting clients seek out NA groups in their home communities. NA is intended to be a continuing resource available to individuals who must daily meet and conquer their addiction. Ideally, then, clients should have opportunity to be linked, or should have opportunity to link themselves, to NA groups in the communities to which they will be returning.

THE HISTORY OF SELF-HELP IN DRUG ABUSE

The first self-help approach specifically targeting drug abusers involved the establishment of an NA group in 1947 at the U.S. Public Health Services Hospital in Lexington, Kentucky (Ellison, 1954; Peyrot, 1985). The NA group at Lexington led to the development of an "officially organized" NA group in New York City (Nyswander, 1956) through the efforts of a Lexington graduate, Dan Carlson. This group was not an NA group in the strict sense because it did not adhere to the guiding principles of 12-Step programming, particularly with regard to that group's willingness to take money from sources outside NA and to lend its name to another organization (Peyrot, 1985). Most believe that the forerunner of NA, as we know it today, was founded in Sun Valley, California, in 1953 by AA members who did not see the AA fellowship as responding to the special concerns of drug abuse but did not feel that deviation from either the 12 Traditions or the 12 Steps was acceptable (Galanter et al., 1993; Nurco and Makofsky, 1981).

As described by Peyrot (1985), in separating itself from AA, NA placed an emphasis on a state, or condition, i.e., "addiction," rather than the specific underlying substance involved, i.e., "alcohol" or "narcotic drug." Beyond the difference in focus on problem behavior rather than on the substance abused, however, there are no meaningful differences between the philosophies and assumptions of AA and NA. The two programs also show common threads in their histories. Both found themselves either ignored or castigated in the professional literature (Murtagh and Harris, 1959). Both were first reported favorably in the popular press, and specifically in the *Saturday Evening Post,* Alexander reporting on AA (1941) and Ellison (1954) reporting on NA. And both grew dramatically in the communities toward which each was directed. NA moved gradually east, experiencing growth rates estimated to be between 30–50% per year (Wells, 1987; Narcotics Anonymous, 1989). By 1993 there were a reported 26,000 groups in 64 countries (DuPont and McGovern, 1994).

Just as NA grew out of a parent AA program, Cocaine Anonymous (CA), Marijuana Anonymous (MA), and Drugs Anonymous (DA) have their roots in NA (White and Madara, 1992; DuPont and McGovern, 1994). Although information is lacking on the numbers of all types of Fellowship programs, there are reported to be more than 1,500 CA groups in the United States (White and Madara, 1992).

Methadone Anonymous represents still another 12-Step initiative. Although many large-scale studies (Ball et al., 1988; Anglin and Hser, 1990; Ball and Ross, 1991; Hubbard et al., 1989; Nurco et al., 1994; Sells and Simpson, 1976) have documented the benefits of methadone treatment, including reductions in illicit drug use, crime, needle use and sharing—with attendant reduction in risk of HIV infection—as well as improvement in psychosocial functioning, there remains a persistent problem of secondary substance abuse (alcohol, cocaine, tranquilizers) among a sizable percentage of methadone clients. As an adjunct to formal treatment, Methadone Anonymous provides participants peer support in remaining abstinent from illicit drugs and alcohol. It also provides clients who elect to detoxify from methadone the peer support of others who have successfully done so. This has been a particular problem for methadone clients because they are terminated from treatment upon detoxification without access to others for support, advice, and/or guidance.

Methadone Anonymous was organized in 1991, under the sponsorship of the Man Alive treatment program in Baltimore, Maryland, as an alternative to NA. Methadone clients at Man Alive reported feeling unwelcome at NA meetings and in conflict with what they perceived to be NA's philosophy of total abstinence from all substances. As a result, Man Alive began sponsoring 12-Step meetings within the program, which rapidly became popular with their clients. In six years, Methadone Anonymous has grown to more than

458 chapters in all fifty United States, Mexico, Canada, England, and Ireland. There is no indication that Methadone Anonymous has been subjected to empirical study to evaluate its benefits as an adjunctive self-help treatment modality; but subjective reports and its rapid growth suggest that methadone treatment programs and their clients find the initiative worthwhile (personal communication with Gary Sweeney, Man Alive, Inc., May 1997).

Although 12-Step programs are the most well known and widely reported self-help approaches, other initiatives are in evidence. Rational Recovery (RR) was founded in 1986 as an alternative for recovering addicts who reject aspects of the 12-Step programs (Willis et al., 1992; Bishop, 1995). Specifically, Willis et al. identified that some recovering addicts reject such concepts as powerlessness, the role of victim implicit in the disease model, and the heavy reliance upon spirituality embodied in the 12-Step programs. Those who embrace RR believe it leads to "greater self-control rather than dependency on an external God for help" (Bishop 1995).

Founded in the systems of rational emotive therapy developed by Albert Ellis (Ellis and Harper, 1975; Ellis et al., 1988) and cognitive therapy developed by Beck (1993), RR teaches that addicts can end both their addiction and their *recovery* habit. RR draws from social-learning theory and teaches that addiction is an over-learned behavior that can be extinguished through a process of planned abstinence. A core concept of this approach is the Addictive Voice Recognition Technique (AVRT) (Trimpey, 1996). AVRT teaches the recovering addict to become aware of and listen to his or her self-talk (dysfunctional beliefs) that supports negative emotional states and addictive behavior. By replacing these dysfunctional beliefs with more rational beliefs, RR teaches that recovery once and forever is possible (not just a day at a time, as advocated by the 12-Step programs). Bishop (1995) lists the defining characteristics of RR:

1 People are largely responsible for their behaviors, including addictive behaviors.
2 A person can recover; that is, a person can gain control over his/her addictive behavior.
3 Lifetime membership is not required; many people can recover in a year or two.
4 Labeling of all kinds is discouraged; a person does not have to call him/herself an addict to begin to recover.
5 Addiction may or may not be a disease; however, a person has to find a way to cope and take responsibility for his/her life in any case.

6 The value of a person is not linked to his/her behavior, addictive or otherwise. A person will not be a better person if he/she gives up alcohol or some other addictive behavior; he/she may be a happier person, a person who has better relationships and can keep a job, but behavioral change does not affect the "goodness" of the self.

7 A person is not necessarily, ipso facto, "in denial" if he/she does not accept the basic AA tenets.

8 A person is not doomed to a life of addiction if he/she does not accept help from AA, a rehabilitation clinic, a hospital, and so on. People can recover on their own with or without the help of professionals and/or self-help groups.

The last characteristic clearly distinguishes RR from the 12-Step programs because it declares that the recovering addict, alone, can learn and benefit from RR independently of a support group. Group participation is encouraged so participants can help one another recognize and dispute the dysfunctional beliefs that have reinforced their addictive behavior. "War stories" or recapitulation of past mistakes and drug experiences are discouraged. Instead, RR focuses on the here and now. Further, there is a growing body of empirical evidence supporting the cognitive-behavioral techniques underpinning RR. Heather et al. (1991); Miller (1989); Miller et al. (1993); Monti (1990); and Oci et al. (1991) all report promising findings.

Another initiative employing self-help principles as a part of its strategy is represented by the work of Zackon, McAuliffe, and Ch'ien (1985) (herein cited as the McAuliffe team) in the United States and Hong Kong. Inspired by a large self-help movement in Hong Kong, the 1,000-member alumni association associated with the Society for the Aid and Rehabilitation of Drug Abusers (SARDA), the McAuliffe team tested the efficacy of a hybrid self-help/aftercare model, known as Recovery Training and Self-Help (RTSH) for heroin addicts. This model contained two components: (1) 23 structured and didactic recovery training sessions (e.g., Deaddiction and Craving, Your Dangerous Situations, Preparing for Stressful Situations, Assessing Your Social Life, Making a New Friend, Love and Intimate Relationships, and Looking Ahead: Plans, Goals, and Dreams), presented by a professional; and (2) 23 fellowship meetings, facilitated by either a group member or ex-addict peer, during which the recovery training material was discussed, peer support cultivated, and drug-free social activities organized. These groups targeted "people who are already clean, where the focus is on lifestyle change and dealing with the aftermath of addiction."

At the same time the McAuliffe team was developing RTSH, Nurco et al. (1981, 1983, 1991) were implementing the Clinically Guided Self-Help (CGSH) model for ex-narcotic addicts. Similar to RTSH, the focus of CGSH was not primary treatment; rather, the residual problems of addiction and lifestyle change were emphasized. Nurco and his associates found that even ex-addicts who had been drug free for many years could reinforce and sustain abstinence in CGSH groups that afforded opportunities for: (1) social and recreational activities, (2) peer support with residual treatment issues and/or unresolved personal problems (e.g., child rearing, family problems, self-esteem, unemployment and employment discrimination, and sexuality), and (3) community outreach and service as payback for the help they had received with their recovery and as social restitution for previous misdeeds. Nurco and his co-workers sponsored open-ended CGSH groups, in which participants set their goals. Professionals facilitated the CGSH process but only to the extent necessary to help the groups identify common goals and develop appropriate strategies for attaining them. Professionals acted as participant-observers to record and document the evolution of the CGSH groups.

The work of the McAuliffe and Nurco teams is significant because both demonstrated the efficacy of professionally sponsored and facilitated self-help/aftercare groups for ex-addicts. Additionally, the work of both teams is consistent with strategies for relapse prevention identified by Marlatt and Gordon (1985). All three draw upon social learning theory for their explanation of addiction, in opposition to the more popular disease model, and argue that, as a learned behavior, addiction can be extinguished and chances for relapse significantly reduced "through the application of self-management or self-control procedures" (Marlatt and Gordon, 1985). The work of the McAuliffe and Nurco teams differed to the extent that McAuliffe's Recovery Training model was didactic and time-limited, whereas Nurco et al. allowed their groups to develop spontaneously and no time limit was set for member participation.

Finally, DuPont and McGovern (1994), Molloy (1990), and O'Neill (1990) report on the Oxford Houses, a more recent self-help initiative. Oxford Houses afford ex-addicts a chance to support abstinence and efforts to re-establish community ties. Residents share expenses, routine household tasks, and decisions about new entrants. The literature indicates that the Oxford House movement incorporates 12-Step principles and members are often participants in 12-Step programs. However, the Oxford Houses are not formally associated with 12-Step programs and participation in them is not mandatory.

EVALUATING THE EFFECTIVENESS OF SELF-HELP PROGRAMS

Concerns about self-help, and specifically 12-Step programming, are often expressed in terms of a skepticism about the lack of empirical evidence for the effectiveness of such programs. In particular, concern is expressed about the absence of evaluation research and/or the difficulty of conducting those studies. 12-Step programming is seen as inhospitable to research because of (a) an insistence on anonymity, which obviously complicates the task of follow-up, and (b) an inability to refuse group membership to anyone, which makes random assignment of clients to intervention and control groups impossible. Moreover, similar to other faith-based interventions, NA is viewed by its adherents as working for any and all who are willing to let it work. That is, if the user is ready to accept NA, it will be successful; if the individual is not yet ready to accept NA, it will fail for that person and the fault is with the person, not with NA. Whereas the researcher is concerned with understanding to what extent NA is effective and with what individuals, the NA believer holds that NA is uniformly effective—with all those individuals willing to commit themselves to NA.

The difficulty and the importance of conducting careful study in association with 12-Step programs is a theme to which we will return frequently. One can conduct clinical trials with aftercare groups that are designed to resemble NA, for example, lacking "only" its spirituality, and make random assignment to an NA-like group joined to treatment and to a treatment-only group. The NA-like model is not NA, however, and clients in both the NA model and the treatment only groups are free to join NA during or after their time in treatment. That is, we can make assignment to groups, after which clients can make their own assignments.

The guarantee of anonymity afforded all NA members in community NA programs precludes a capacity to obtain a sample of new entrants to NA and to follow them over time to understand functioning over a set number of months and/or years from time of entrance into 12-Step, the research strategy customarily employed to understand the effectiveness of individual treatment modalities (Simpson and Sells, 1990; Hubbard et al., 1989). Consequently, some studies of AA have relied on 12-Step members who volunteered to participate in a follow-up evaluation (Tonigan et al., 1996). The use of volunteers is obviously far less than ideal. It is unclear to what extent volunteers represent the larger body of 12-Step members in terms of demographics, deviance, and background; however, it seems likely that the volunteers will be better motivated for recovery and more optimistic about their futures than those unwilling to volunteer themselves, i.e., to expose themselves to scrutiny regarding their capacities to maintain abstinence.

In a real sense, the 12-Step movement remains the cornerstone of self-help programming. More than that, however, the 12-Step movement appears to influence the lives of vast numbers of (former) drug users, while holding itself—and being held—at arm's length from drug abuse treatment. Thus, NA programming predates the development of all current treatment modalities; NA is the only organized system available to drug abusers that provides a lifetime support to abstinence; at any one time, NA may well have a larger population of drug abusers involved in its program than any other drug abuse recovery initiative; and NA is often unreported in major (and otherwise excellent) descriptions of drug abuse treatment (see, for example, Hubbard et al., 1989; Gerstein and Harwood, 1990). Nevertheless, it is obviously important to understand the effectiveness of a program that can be found in every community in the country (and in many parts of the world), that enrolls tens of thousands of drug abusers seeking abstinence from illicit drug use, and that maintains costs that make even efforts at voluntarism appear profligate. At the same time, that very lack of concern with finances, combined with its stature in the addict community and a philosophy that rejects publicity, make 12-Step programming unconcerned with proving its "worth" to a public it does not need. It can be argued, however, that if 12-Step programs can be shown as successful in the larger community, this may increase still further the willingness of clients to involve themselves in 12-Step programs, increase as well the willingness of family members and friends to support recovery efforts, and promote greater public concern for, and acceptance of, recovering people.

RESEARCH FINDINGS

In view of impediments to rigorous study, it is not surprising that there have been few systematic evaluations with regard to the effectiveness of self-help techniques in reducing illicit drug use and crime and promoting prosocial behavior. As Nurco et al. (1991) noted, it has been only recently that efforts have begun to conduct evaluations of the effectiveness of self-help programs. Thus, there is a lack of information regarding the relation of outcome to the structure, function, and operation of addict self-help groups. Moreover, much that has been written about self-help groups is descriptive and/or anecdotal in character and/or presented from a biased position. Among the few major self-help initiatives whose effectiveness has been carefully studied are those of McAuliffe and associates and Nurco and colleagues.

McAuliffe and associates randomly assigned 168 recovering heroin addicts to Recovery Training and Self-Help groups (RTSH) or to standard aftercare routinely provided by the treatment program (McAuliffe, 1990; McAuliffe et al., 1985 a,b). This study involved recovering addicts from both the United States (New England) and Hong Kong in a mix of relapse prevention skills training and mutual support self-help programming. The primary outcome measure in this research was relapse to heroin addiction at six months and at one year following randomization. Results for 138 subjects interviewed at this one-year point indicated that the RTSH group contained a significantly ($p < .05$) higher percentage of individuals who had abstained from heroin or who had rare "slips" (less than once a month) than the control group. In both New England and Hong Kong, subjects randomly assigned to RTSH were more likely than controls to have remained abstinent from heroin or have no more than "slips." In Hong Kong, this difference was statistically significant ($p < .05$) at six months and one year, whereas in the United States, this difference was significantly different ($p < .05$) at six months.

A second analysis concerning drug abuse involved group comparisons with regard to the number of days on which subjects used an illicit narcotic drug during the follow-up periods. Similar to the findings for categorized measures of illicit narcotic use, experimental subjects had significantly ($p < .01$) fewer days of illicit narcotic use at six- and twelve-month follow-up than controls. Also, as with the categorized measures, the results for continuous measures of illicit narcotic use showed similar patterns by site. In Hong Kong, experimental subjects reported significantly ($p < .05$) fewer days of illicit narcotic use than did control subjects at both follow-up points. In the United States, RTSH subjects reported significantly ($p < .01$) fewer narcotic use days than did controls at six months only.

There were some issues in the implementation of this study that may usefully be addressed in future research. First, a larger sample, in conjunction with an even higher rate of follow-up (the authors report a 71% follow-up rate across sites), may have yielded additional statistically significant differences in outcomes between experimental and control groups. Second, the study can be replicated with other client populations more typical of the narcotic addict population in the United States. Nearly all of the U.S. clients sampled by McAuliffe et al. were white (92%); the mean years of education completed was 12.9. In contrast, a considerable proportion of American narcotic addicts are black or Hispanic (Inciardi, 1986; Kinlock et al., 1998). Further, the mean years of education completed for most narcotic addicts of all ethnic groups in the United States was approximately 10–11 (Anglin and Hser, 1987; Anglin and Speckart, 1988; Inciardi, 1986; Inciardi and Pottieger, 1986; Nurco et al., 1988).

More recently, Nurco et al. (1995) evaluated the effect of a self-help program (CGSH) on locus-of-control beliefs. In this study, 50 heroin addicts attending a methadone maintenance clinic in New York City were randomly assigned to one of three groups. The experimental group received CGSH plus standard treatment (methadone maintenance plus individual counseling); one control group received standard treatment plus lectures on HIV/AIDS; and the second control group received standard treatment only. Results on 38 subjects reinterviewed 15 months after study entry indicated that the experimental group had demonstrated statistically significant ($p < .05$) changes in locus-of-control beliefs, from external to internal causation, i.e., assuming greater personal responsibility for drug dependence. In contrast, such changes were not indicated in either of the two control groups.

However, as in the research conducted by McAuliffe and colleagues, Nurco et al. (1995) noted some limitations in their study. First, random assignment was confounded by some subjects self-selecting at various points to groups other than those assigned. As noted by other researchers, client self-selection is a common problem in random assignment studies conducted on drug treatment programs (Hall, 1984; Friedman et al., 1987; Magura et al., 1991). Second, the number of outcome measures was limited. Also, the sample was small, composed of volunteers, and likely not representative of drug abuse clients.

One of the most extensive evaluations of 12-Step self-help residential program outcomes was conducted by Ouimette et al. (1997), which, although not a randomized trial, involved 3,018 male clients from 15 programs at the U.S. Department of Veterans Affairs Medical Centers. This research compared the effectiveness of (1) 12-Step, (2) cognitive-behavioral, and (3) combined 12-Step/cognitive behavioral approaches. These programs had a 21- to 28-day inpatient component with the expectation that clients would participate in aftercare in the community. Outcome measures included illicit drug and alcohol use, employment, psychological functioning, and contact with the criminal justice system.

Results at one-year follow-up indicated that although 12-Step clients were somewhat more likely to be abstinent, and clients in combined programs were least likely to be employed, the three programs were equally effective in reducing substance use and psychological symptoms, and in increasing the proportion of clients who avoided arrest and incarceration. Moreover, the finding of equal effectiveness was consistent across several treatment subgroups. Clients with only substance abuse diagnoses, those with concomitant psychiatric diagnoses, and those mandated to treatment showed similar improvements. Outcomes were entirely related to the clients' initial 21- to 28-day program status, however, and type and frequency of participation in aftercare in the intervening period was not considered.

As found for other modalities of drug abuse treatment (e.g., methadone maintenance, therapeutic communities, drug-free outpatient), length of time in self-help programs and/or frequency of meetings attended were positively associated with favorable outcome. Galanter et al. (1993) found that 73% of the RR members who had been attending for three months or more were abstinent. After six months of participation, 58% were abstinent. In contrast, of those who had participated for less than one month, 57% were still abusing. This suggested that continued attendance increases the proportion who opt for abstinence.

Further, Johnsen and Herringer (1993) reported a significant relation between frequency of attendance at NA and AA meetings and abstinence for drug abusers who had joined NA and/or AA after completing a 28-day treatment program. Data were obtained six months after completion of the 28-day program on 50 individuals of whom 70% were abusers of illicit drugs. In a subsequent study of 200 London NA members (100 men, 100 women), Christo and Sutton (1994) found that length of time in NA was significantly related to abstinence from illicit drugs. In this study, which primarily involved individuals who had been heroin addicts, length of time in NA was also significantly related to reduced anxiety and increased self-esteem.

Despite these favorable results, methodological concerns described earlier reduce our ability to draw firm conclusions from evaluations of NA. As was noted, rigorous experimental designs involving random assignment to NA and to other programs (or to control or no treatment conditions) is often not possible because drug abuse clients elect to receive treatment other than that to which they are assigned. Also, NA's concern with protecting member anonymity would make extremely difficult, if not preclude, the conducting of follow-up procedures designed to locate and assess the behavior of NA members. Furthermore, the NA dictum that an individual is continuously in recovery and therefore continuously in NA is an obvious impediment to conducting posttreatment evaluations of the effectiveness of NA.

Although residential programs employing 12-Step principles were found to reduce illicit drug use (e.g., Ouimette et al., 1997), still more favorable results might have been achieved if these programs served clients over a longer period. As extensive literature reviews (e.g., Anglin and Hser, 1990; Nurco

et al., 1994) have indicated, and as found for NA as well (Johnsen and Herringer, 1993; Christo and Sutton, 1994), the relation between length of time
in treatment and favorable outcome is one of the most consistently documented findings in drug abuse treatment evaluation research. In general,
findings of evaluations conducted on more traditional treatment modalities (e.g., methadone maintenance, therapeutic community, drug-free outpatient) have indicated that continuous participation in treatment for at least
three months is needed to effect reductions in the frequency of drug abuse
and criminal activity (Simpson, 1981; De Leon et al., 1980; Anglin and Hser,
1990; Nurco et al., 1994). Thus, the extent to which the favorable results of the
NA/12-Step evaluations cited above can be attributed to the mode of intervention or to the type of clients involved cannot be precisely determined.
Despite the extensiveness of the study by Ouimette et al., no information on
the drug abuse or criminal history of the clients was provided. Because all
subjects were veterans, it is possible that they may have been less deviant than
other drug abusers.

With regard to Cocaine Anonymous, one of the more rigorous evaluations
of this program involved a randomized clinical trial that examined the relative effectiveness of 12-Step and relapse prevention groups for cocaine abusers
(Wells et al., 1994). Clients in both groups reduced their cocaine, marijuana,
and alcohol use from pretreatment to posttreatment. Although no differences were found between treatment groups on posttreatment cocaine or
marijuana use, the 12-Step clients showed significantly greater increase in
alcohol use from 12 weeks' to 6-months' follow-up than did relapse prevention clients.

Results overall suggest that, at least for some heroin addicts who have successfully undergone standard drug abuse treatment, involvement in NA or
other self-help techniques may be helpful in achieving long-term recovery
from addiction. The relative contributions of self-help programming and
individual motivation are often unclear; however, studies have consistently
found that associating with addicts posttreatment is a major cause of relapse
to heroin and/or cocaine dependence and criminal activity (Leukefeld and
Tims, 1988; Maddux and Desmond, 1981; Nurco et al., 1991). Because self-help
groups and NA meetings offer many constructive alternatives to associating
with drug abusers, including positive peer support and non–drug-oriented
social and recreational activities, they have the potential for reducing relapse
and recidivism and increasing prosocial behavior (Brown, 1995; McAuliffe
et al., 1990–91; Nurco et al., 1994). That is, they require and merit great attention and study.

CONCLUSIONS

We have no ready solution to the difficulties involved in better integrating research and 12-Step programming, but we do have some cautions. In some real sense, the 12-Step movement calls into question not simply our capacity to evaluate that initiative but also our conception of the proper role and functioning of research in relation to treatment. It is our contention that evaluation research is a means toward achieving understanding. It is not an end in itself. Neither treatment programs nor the 12-Step initiatives can be compromised to meet the demands of research. It is the function of research to meet the demands of the intervention. The intervention must be permitted to retain its integrity or there is no good reason for its evaluation. In short, maintaining a vigorous research design is meaningful only if the intervention being evaluated is not changed in the effort to permit its study. This puts large responsibility on the researcher who must be creative within the boundaries of his or her own set of rules for conducting credible study. To ignore an intervention as influential as NA seems unconscionable; to conduct inadequate study seems pointless. And therein lies the dilemma.

Little wonder, then, that self-help initiatives hold a unique place in drug abuse treatment programming. An uncompromising insistence on anonymity has precluded the conduct of rigorous evaluation of self-help initiatives as they exist in their purest form, i.e., as 12-Step programs. Quite simply, it can be argued that 12-Step programs have no need for evaluation. Because they have no need for public funds, they have no need to prove themselves worthy of public funds. They involve no staff, no medications, no treatment setting; they involve only drug users helping drug users in a structured program of increasing responsibility taking and always with reliance on a "higher power." Nor has an absence of evaluation limited their appeal or reputation in the drug-using community. Consistent with their status as a quasi-religious movement, their ranks have been swelled through active proselytizing and through less formal communication by the core of believers.

Just as a near absence of evaluative study has not limited the dramatic growth of the NA, CA, and AA fellowships, that absence has not limited the capacity of the fellowships to influence the conduct of more traditional drug abuse treatment. Short-term residential facilities providing month-long treatment and long-term therapeutic community programs lasting six months to two years both place an emphasis on using the community of peers as change agent and acknowledge a debt to 12-Step programming, although both also make substantial use of professional staff. Outpatient programs involve 12-Step fellowships as aids to aftercare, have organized their own more largely secular fellowships, or have built self-help initiatives into the relapse prevention programs that have been developed for exiting clients. The programs that have been studied have been carefully evaluated and have typically been found to be associated with positive behavior change in treatment clients. Those findings, in conjunction with data suggesting a relation between length of time in 12-Step programming and positive outcomes, strongly support the utility of mutual self-help strategies for drug abuse treatment.

It is important to continue the work of developing strategies incorporating self-help principles and testing their effectiveness as adjuncts to existing drug abuse treatment. Indeed, the emphasis on managed care, and its translation into abbreviated care, should accelerate efforts to develop and test aftercare initiatives embracing self-help principles. However, it is equally important to recognize the significance of the 12-Step fellowships in terms of their potential for positively impacting the lives of tens of thousands of drug users worldwide, in spite of—and perhaps, in part, because of—an insistence by the fellowships that they relate to more formal drug abuse treatment on their own terms or not at all. Although academic descriptions of drug abuse interventions rarely give more than passing reference to fellowship initiatives, there is every reason to believe that such initiatives are a vigorous force in the community of drug users who need and desire behavioral change.

References

Alexander, J. (1941). Alcoholics Anonymous. *Saturday Evening Post, 213,* 9–11.

Anglin, M. D., & Hser, Y. (1987). Addicted women and crime. *Criminology,* 25, 359–397.

Anglin, M. D., & Hser, Y. (1990). Treatment of drug abuse. In M. Tonry & J. Q. Wilson (eds.), *Drugs and crime* [Crime and Justice: A Review of Research, Vol. 13] (pp. 393–460). Chicago: University of Chicago Press.

Anglin, M. D., & Speckart, G. (1988). Narcotics use and crime: A multisample, multimethod analysis. *Criminology, 26,* 197–233.

Ashery, R. S. (1979). *Self-help groups serving drug abusers.* In B. S. Brown (ed.), *Addicts and aftercare* (pp. 135–154). Beverly Hills: Sage.

Ball, J. C., Lange, W. R., Myers, E., & Friedman, S. R. (1988). Reducing the risk of AIDS through methadone maintenance treatment. *Journal of Health and Social Behavior,* 29, 214–226.

Ball, J. C., & Ross, A. (1991). *The effectiveness of methadone maintenance treatment: Patients, programs, services, and outcomes.* New York: Springer-Verlag.

Beck, A. T., Wright, F. D., Newman, C. F., & Liese, B. S. (1993). *Cognitive therapy of substance abuse.* New York: Guilford.

Bishop, F. M. (1995). Rational-emotive behavior therapy and two self-help alternatives to the 12-step model. In A. M. Washington (ed.). *Psychotherapy and substance abuse: A practitioner's handbook.* New York: Guilford.

Brown, B. S. (1992). Program models. In C. G. Leukefeld and F. M. Tims (eds.), *Drug Abuse Treatment in Prisons and Jails* (pp. 31–37). Washington, D.C.: U.S. Government Printing Office.

Brown, B. S. (1995). *Working with Narcotics Anonymous: Some questions and answers.* Rockville, Md.: Center for Substance Abuse Treatment.

Chaiken, M. R. (1989). *In-prison programs for drug-involved offenders.* Washington, D.C.: National Institute of Justice.

Christo, G., & Sutton, S. (1994). Anxiety and self-esteem as a function of abstinence time among recovering addicts attending Narcotics Anonymous. *British Journal of Clinical Psychology, 33,* 198–200.

Cressey, D. (1965). Social psychological foundations for using criminals in the rehabilitation of criminals. *Journal of Research on Crime and Delinquency, 2,* 49–59.

De Leon, G., Andrews, M., Wexler, H., et al. (1980). Therapeutic community dropouts: Criminal behavior five years after treatment. *American Journal of Drug and Alcohol Abuse, 6,* 253–271.

DuPont, R. L. (1994). The twelve step approach. In N. S. Miller (ed.), *Treating Coexisting Psychiatric and Addictive Disorders* (pp. 177–197). Center City, Minn.: Hazelden.

DuPont, R. L., & McGovern, J. P. (1994). *A bridge to recovery: An introduction to 12-step programs.* Washington, D.C.: American Psychiatric Association.

Ellis, A., & Harper, R. A. (1975). *A new guide to rational living.* Hollywood, Calif.: Wilshire.

Ellis, A., McInerney, J. F., DiGiuseppe, R., & Yeager, R. J. (1988). *Rational-emotive therapy with alcoholics and substance abusers.* Boston: Allyn and Bacon.

Ellison, J. (1954). These drug addicts cure one another. *Saturday Evening Post, 227,* 48–52.

Fraser, M. W., & Hawkins, J. D. (1984). The social networks of opioid users. *International Journal of the Addictions, 19,* 903–917.

Friedman, S. R., Des Jarlais, D. C., Sotheran, J. L., Garber, J., Cohen, H., & Smith, D. (1987). AIDS and self-organization among intravenous drug users. *International Journal of the Addictions, 22,* 201–219.

Galanter, M., Egelko, S., & Edwards, H. (1993). Rational recovery: Alternative to AA for addictions. *American Journal of Drug and Alcohol Abuse, 19,* 499–510.

Gartner, A., & Riessman, F. (1977). *Self-help in the human services.* San Francisco: Jossey-Bass.

Gerstein, D. R., & Harwood, H. J. (1990). *Treating drug problems: A study of the evolution, effectiveness, and financing of public and private drug treatment systems*, vol. 1. Washington, D.C.: National Academy Press.

Hall, S. M. (1984). Clinical trials in drug treatment: Methodology. In F. M. Tims & J. P. Ludford (eds.), *Drug abuse treatment evaluation: Strategies, progress, and prospects* [NIDA Research Monograph 51] (pp. 88–105). Rockville, Md.: National Institute on Drug Abuse.

Hawkins, J. D., & Fraser, M. W. (1987). The social networks of drug users before and after treatment. *International Journal of the Addictions, 22*, 343–356.

Heather, N., Miller, W. R., & Greeley, J. (eds.). (1991). *Self-control and the addictive behaviors*. New York: Macmillan.

Hubbard, R. L., Marsden, M. E., Rachal, J. V., Harwood, H. J., Cavanaugh, E. R., & Ginzburg, H. M. (1989). *Drug abuse treatment: A national study of effectiveness*. Chapel Hill, N.C.: University of North Carolina Press.

Inciardi, J. A. (1986). *The war on drugs: Heroin, cocaine, and public policy*. Palo Alto, Calif.: Mayfield.

Inciardi, J. A. (1996). HIV risk reduction and service delivery strategies in criminal justice settings. *Journal of Substance Abuse Treatment, 13*, 421–428.

Inciardi, J. A., & Pottieger, A. E. (1986). Drug use and crime among two cohorts of women narcotics users: An empirical assessment. *Journal of Drug Issues, 16*, 91–106.

Johnsen, E., & Herringer, L. (1993). A note on the utilization of common support activities and relapse following substance abuse treatment. *Journal of Psychology, 127*, 73–78.

Jones, M. (1957). The treatment of personality disorders in a therapeutic community. *Psychiatry, 20*, 211–220.

Katz, A. H., & Bender, E. I. (1976). *The strength in us: Self-help groups in the modern world*. New York: New View Points.

Kinlock, T., Hanlon, T., & Nurco, D. (1998). Heroin use in the United States: History and present developments. In J. A. Inciardi & L. Harrison (eds.), *Heroin in the age of crack-cocaine*. (pp. 1–30). Thousand Oaks, Calif.: Sage.

Krupka, L. F., & Blume, E. S. (1980). Alcoholics Anonymous in a therapeutic community. *Journal of Drug Education, 10*, 145–151.

Leukefeld, C. G., & Tims, F. M. (1988). An introduction to compulsory treatment for drug abuse: Clinical practice and research. In C. G. Leukefeld & F. M. Tims (eds.), *Compulsory treatment of drug abuse: Research and clinical practice* [NIDA Research Monograph 86] (pp. 1–7). Rockville, Md.: National Institute on Drug Abuse.

Levy, H. (1976). Self-help groups: Types and psychological processes. *Journal of Applied Behavioral Science, 12*, 310–322.

Maddux, J. F., & Desmond, D. P. (1981). *Careers of opioid users* [Praeger Studies on Issues and Research in Substance Abuse]. New York: Praeger.

Magura, S., Siddiqi, Q., Shapiro J., Grossman, J. I., Lipton, D. S., Marion, I. J., Weisenfeld, L., Amann, K., & Koger, J. (1991). Outcomes of an AIDS prevention program for methadone patients. *International Journal of the Addictions, 26,* 629–655.

Marlatt, G. A., & Gordon, J. R. (1985). *Relapse prevention: Maintenance strategies in the treatment of addictive behaviors.* New York: Guilford.

McAuliffe, W.E. (1990). A randomized controlled trial of Recovery Training and Self Help for opiate addicts in New England and Hong Kong. *Journal of Psychoactive Drugs, 22,* 197–209.

McAuliffe, W. E., Albert, J., & Cordill-London, G. (1990–91). Contributions to a social conditioning model of cocaine recovery. *International Journal of the Addictions, 25,* 1141–1177.

McAuliffe, W. E., Chien, J. M. N., Launer, E., Friedman, R., & Feldman, B. (1985a). The Harvard group aftercare program: Preliminary evaluation results and implementation issues. In R. Ashery (ed.), *Progress in the development of cost-effective treatment for drug abusers* (pp. 147–155). Washington, D.C.: National Institute on Drug Abuse.

McAuliffe, W. E., Chien, J. M. N., Zackon, F., Tang, W. C. Y., Friedman, R., Sun, F. K. C., Launer, E., & Loa, P. C. (1985b). Cross-cultural randomized trial of aftercare for treated addicts. In K. L. Stumpf, J. M. N. Chien, L. McQuarrie, W. Oram, I. Lam, & E. Lam (eds.), *Towards a coordinated approach: Current issues and future directions.* Hong Kong: Organizing Committee for the 2nd Pan Pacific Conference on Drugs and Alcohol.

Miller, W. R. (1989). Matching individuals with interventions. In R. K. Hester & W. R. Miller. (eds.) *Handbook of alcoholism treatment approaches.* New York: Pergamon.

Miller, W. R., Benefield, R. G., & Tonigan, J. S. (1993). Enhancing motivation for change in problem drinkers: A controlled comparison of two therapist styles. *Journal of Consulting and Clinical Psychology, 61,* 435–461.

Molloy, J. P. (1990). *Self-run, self-supported houses for more effective recovery from alcohol and drug addiction.* Washington, D.C.: Office of Treatment Improvement, U.S. Department of Health and Human Services.

Monti, P. M. (1990). Communication skills training: Communication skills training with family and cognitive behavioral mood management training for alcoholics. *Journal of Studies on Alcohol, 51,* 263–270.

Murtagh, J. M., & Harris, S. (1959). *Who live in shadow.* New York: McGraw-Hill.

Narcotics Anonymous (1988). *Narcotics Anonymous.* 5th edition (Basic Text). Van Nuys, California: Narcotics Anonymous World Service Office.

Narcotics Anonymous (1989). *A guide to public information.* Van Nuys, Calif.: Narcotics Anonymous World Service Office.

National Institute of Justice (1996). *Prisoners in 1995.* Washington, D.C.: U.S. Department of Justice.

National Institute on Drug Abuse. (1981). *Drug abuse treatment in prisons.* Rockville, Md: NIDA.

Nurco, D. N., Hanlon, T. E., & Kinlock, T. W. (1991). Recent research on the relationship between illicit drug use and crime. *Behavioral Sciences and the Law, 9,* 221–242.

Nurco, D. N., Hanlon, T. E., Kinlock, T. W., & Duszynski, K. R. (1988). Differential criminal patterns of narcotic addicts over an addiction career. *Criminology, 26,* 407–423.

Nurco, D. N., Kinlock, T. W., & Hanlon, T. E. (1994). The nature and status of drug abuse treatment. *Maryland Medical Journal, 43,* 51–57.

Nurco, D. N., & Makofsky, A. (1981). The self-help movement and Narcotics Anonymous. *American Journal of Drug and Alcohol Abuse, 8,* 139–151.

Nurco, D. N., Primm, B. J., Lerner, M., Stephenson, P., Brown, L. S., & Ajuluchukwu, D. (1995). Changes in locus-of-control attitudes about drug misuse in a self-help group in a methadone maintenance clinic. *International Journal of the Addictions, 30,* 765–778.

Nurco, D. N., Stephenson, P., & Hanlon, T. E. (1989, August). *Contemporary issues in drug abuse treatment linkage with self-help groups* [Paper presented at the National Institute on Drug Abuse on Improving Drug Abuse Treatment], Bethesda, Md.

Nurco, D. N., Stephenson, P., & Hanlon, T. E. (1991). Aftercare/relapse prevention and the self-help movement. *International Journal of the Addictions, 25,* 1179–1200.

Nurco, D. N., Stephenson, P., & Naesea, L. (1981). *Manual for setting up self-help groups of ex-narcotic addicts.* Washington, D.C.: U.S. Government Printing Office.

Nurco, D. N., Wegner, N., Stephenson, P., Makofsky, A. & Shaffer, J. W. (1983). *Ex-addicts' self-help groups: Potentials and pitfalls.* New York: Praeger.

Nyswander, M. (1956). *The drug addict as a patient.* New York: Grune and Stratton.

Oci, T. P. S., Lim, B., & Young, R. M. (1991). Cognitive processes and cognitive behavior therapy in the treatment of problem drinking. *Journal of Addictive Diseases, 10,* 63–80.

O'Neill, J. (1990). History of Oxford House, Inc. In S. Shaw & T. Borkman (eds.), *Social model alcohol recovery: An environmental approach* (pp. 103–117). Burbank, Calif.: Bridge Focus.

Ouimette, P. C., Finney, J. W., & Moos, R. H. (1997). Twelve-step and cognitive-behavioral treatment for substance abuse: A comparison of treatment effectiveness. *Journal of Consulting and Clinical Psychology, 65,* 230–240.

Peyrot, M. (1985). Narcotics Anonymous: Its history, structure, and approach. *International Journal of the Addictions, 20,* 1509–1522.

Riessman, F. (1965). The "helper-therapy" principle. *Social Work, 10,* 27–32.

Sells, S. B., & Simpson, D. D. (1976). *The effectiveness of drug abuse treatment*, vol. 3. Cambridge, Mass.: Balinger.

Simpson, D. D. (1981). Treatment for drug abuse: Follow-up outcomes and length of time spent. *Archives of General Psychiatry, 38,* 875–879.

Simpson, D. D., Crandall, R., Savage, L. J., & Pavia-Kreuger, E. (1981). Leisure of addicts at post-treatment followup. *Journal of Counseling Psychology, 28,* 36–39.

Simpson, D. D., & Sells, S. B. (1990). *Opioid addiction and treatment: A twelve-year-follow-up.* Malabar, Fla.: Krieger.

Tonigan, J. S., Radka, T., & Miller, W. R. (1996). Meta-analysis of the literature on Alcoholics Anonymous: Sample and study characteristics moderate findings. *Journal of Studies on Alcohol, 57,* 65–72.

Trimpey, J. (1996). *Rational recovery: The new cure for substance addiction.* New York: Simon and Shuster.

U.S. Department of Justice (1993). *Survey of State prison inmates.* Washington, D.C.

U.S. General Accounting Office (1991, September). *Drug treatment: Despite new strategy, few federal inmates receive treatment* [Report to the Committee on Government Operations, House of Representatives]. Washington, D.C.: Author.

Volkman, R., & Cressey, D. (1963). Differential association and the rehabilitation of drug addicts. *American Journal of Sociology, 69,* 129–142.

Waldorf, D., Reinarman, D., & Murphy, S. (1991). *Cocaine changes: The experience of using and quitting.* Philadelphia: Temple University Press.

Wells, B. (1987). Narcotics Anonymous (NA): The phenomenal growth of an important resource. *British Journal of Addiction, 82,* 581–582.

Wells, E. A., Peterson, P. L., Gainey, R. R., Hawkins, J. D., & Catalano, R. F. (1994). Outpatient treatment for cocaine abuse: A controlled comparison of relapse prevention and twelve-step approaches. *American Journal of Drug and Alcohol Abuse, 20,* 1–17.

White, B. J., & Madara, E. J. (1992). *The self-help sourcebook.* Denville, N.J.: American Self-Help Clearinghouse.

Willis, C., Gastfriend, D. R., & Meyer, S. (May 1992). *Rational recovery: A self-help alternative to Alcoholics Anonymous.* Paper presented at the 145th annual meeting of the American Psychiatric Association, Washington, D.C.

Zackon, F., McAuliffe, W. E., & Ch'ien, J. M. (1985). *Addict aftercare: Recovery training and self-help.* Washington, D.C.: National Institute on Drug Abuse, U.S. Department of Health and Human Services.

Zapka, J. G., Stoddard, A. M., & McCusker, J. (1993). Social network, support and influence: Relationships with drug use and protective AIDS behavior. *AIDS Education and Prevention, 5,* 352–366.

THIRTEEN

PHARMACOTHERAPIES USED IN COMMON SUBSTANCE USE DISORDERS

Carl Hart, Elinore F. McCance-Katz, & Thomas R. Kosten

This chapter provides an overview of the role of pharmacotherapies in preventing relapse and facilitating recovery from substance use disorders.[1] The problem of drug abuse and dependence has a long history and spans both licit and illicit drugs. Our discussion, however, focuses on alcohol, nicotine, cocaine, and opiates. These substances were selected because of their public health importance and because a large amount of research has been conducted regarding their use. The following discussion is prefaced with the proviso that the pharmacotherapies reviewed in this chapter should be utilized in conjunction with psychosocial therapies in order to maximize clinical benefits to the target population.

Currently, there are three basic pharmacotherapeutic approaches taken when treating substance use disorders following detoxification: *antagonism* of the abused substance to prevent the user from experiencing the reinforcing effects of the drug; *substitution* or maintenance agents for prevention of relapse; or the administration of a drug that is *pharmacologically incompatible* with the abused substance such that an aversive reaction occurs following ingestion of the abused drug. Naltrexone and naloxone are both examples of narcotic antagonists used to treat opiate-dependent individuals. These agents competitively bind to opiate receptors and selectively block the effects of heroin (or other opiate agonists), including euphoria and the development of physiological dependence that occurs from repeated use. Methadone, a long-acting μ-opiate agonist, has been used extensively as a substitute agent in heroin dependence. Similarly, nicotine gum and patches have been used to attenuate withdrawal symptoms and cravings in those attempting to quit the consumption of tobacco products. Treating alcoholics with disulfiram (Antabuse), which interferes with the normal function of the enzymes that participate in alcohol metabolism, is an example of an aversive therapy.

ALCOHOL PHARMACOTHERAPIES

It is estimated that more than 35 million American adults will meet diagnostic criteria for alcohol abuse or dependence disorder sometime in their lives (Helzer, Burnam, & McEvoy, 1991). Alcohol overindulgence is an age-old human problem and one that can be extremely costly to society, both in terms of dollars and wasted potential. Historically, the treatment of alcoholism has varied in accordance with the prevailing etiological perspective. Overindulgence has been ascribed to (1) the morally defective individual, (2) alcohol itself, or (3) alcoholism as an inherited disease. "Treatment" based on the idea that the alcoholic had a "moral defect" consisted of social ostracism, prison sentences, and/or other forms of punishment (Ray & Ksir, 1996). The attempt to prevent alcohol consumption by criminalizing its use during Prohibition serves as the most obvious example of treatment based on alcohol itself being considered the problem (Ray & Ksir, 1996). Physicians adhering to a disease model of alcoholism prescribed morphine, cocaine, or other drugs considered suitable substitutes for alcohol in the late nineteenth and early twentieth centuries (Ray & Ksir, 1996). Although the above represents three distinct ideologies and approaches to alcoholism treatment, it was not unusual for them to coexist. For instance, at the start of the twentieth century alcoholics were viewed by many as social outcasts who should be imprisoned. At the same time, the Prohibition movement was gaining momentum. Meanwhile, some physicians were prescribing morphine to alcoholics in an effort to treat their addiction to alcohol.

Although contemporary approaches to the treatment of alcohol abuse and dependence continue to vary, recent research revelations have helped shed light on more effective pharmacological interventions. Pharmacotherapies have become increasingly important in the treatment of alcoholism, in part because of the serious nature of acute alcohol withdrawal syndrome. This syndrome is typically characterized by tremors, tachycardia, hypertension, profuse sweating, insomnia, hallucinations, and seizures. Medical risks associated with alcohol withdrawal often require an inpatient medical setting. During detoxification, two of the central tasks for the clinician are to reduce autonomic hyperactivity and to prevent the development of seizures.

For several reasons, administration of tapering dosages of a benzodiazepine during alcohol detoxification is the standard approach to treatment. First, there is a high degree of cross-tolerance between alcohol and the benzodiazepines, particularly chlordiazepoxide and diazepam (Sellers, 1988). Because benzodiazepines can serve as substitutes for alcohol and generally have longer half-lives than alcohol, the withdrawal process can be safely completed. Benzodiazepines, by potentiating the inhibitory actions of γ-aminobutyric acid (GABA) on the central nervous system, significantly decrease the risk of seizures during detoxification. In addition, the increased autonomic arousal that occurs during alcohol withdrawal is analogous to the initiation of the "stress response," i.e., increased heart rate, blood pressure, respiration, and anxiety. This suggests that the mechanisms that mediate the stress response may also play a role in alcohol withdrawal symptoms. Because it is well documented that increased GABAergic transmission markedly diminishes the stress response (Chrousos & Gold, 1992), it is not surprising that benzodiazepines are also effective in attenuating the autonomic hyperactivity that accompanies the alcohol withdrawal process. Another reason benzodiazepines are commonly used during alcohol detoxification is for their anxiolytic properties. This issue is of particular importance in light of the finding that individuals who were diagnosed with comorbid disorders (alcohol dependence and anxiety disorders) were more likely to have an increased severity of alcohol withdrawal symptoms than those individuals who were not dually diagnosed (Johnston, Thevos, Randall, & Anton, 1991). Although benzodiazepines with intermediate half-lives like chlordiazepoxide and diazepam[2] are generally regarded as providing a more comfortable and safer withdrawal, it is recommended that patients with hepatic disease be detoxified with lorazepam or oxazepam because these drugs have no active metabolites requiring hepatic clearance. Lorazepam is also a good choice for detoxification of the patient suffering severe vomiting as it is well absorbed by the intramuscular route of administration. Individual variability notwithstanding, a benzodiazepine taper can typically be accomplished in three to five days.

A second approach used to attenuate alcohol withdrawal is the administration of adrenergic agents (ß-adrenergic blockers and α-adrenergic agonists). ß-adrenergic blockers, including atenolol and propranolol, and α-adrenergic agonists, such as clonidine and lofexidine, have been shown to be effective in reducing withdrawal symptoms of hypertension, tachycardia, and tremors (Romach & Sellers, 1991). Whether adrenergic agents are as effective as the benzodiazepines in assuaging these symptoms is an issue yet to be resolved. For example, Baumgartner and Rowen (1991) noted that transdermal clonidine was superior to chlordiazepoxide in reducing the physiological symptoms associated with alcohol withdrawal, while more recently Adinoff (1994) found the opposite effect with alprazolam and clonidine. What does seem clear, however, is that adrenergic agents are without effect on other alcohol withdrawal symptoms like anxiety, hallucinations, and seizures (Romach & Sellers, 1991).

A third strategy employed to detoxify alcoholics is the administration of anticonvulsant medications such as carbamazepine or valproate. In outpatient randomized clinical trials comparing carbamazepine to tapering dosages of benzodiazepines, carbamazepine was reported to be as effective in alleviating withdrawal symptoms when measured by the Clinical Institute Withdrawal Assessment Scale (Agricola, Mazzarino, Urani, Gallo, & Grossi, 1982; Malcolm, Ballenger, Sturgis, & Anton, 1989; Stuppaeck et al., 1992). Available research on the use of valproate suggests that it is a commensurate therapy for relieving alcohol withdrawal symptoms (Lambie, Johnson, Vijayasenan, & Whiteside, 1980; Hillbom et al., 1989; Roy-Byrne, Ward, Donnelly, 1989). Valproate has been reported to reduce the amount of other medications needed for the treatment of withdrawal, but a lack of statistical data analysis warrants caution in the interpretation of these results (Lambie et al., 1980). Given such an analysis, anticonvulsive medications may be promising alternatives to benzodiazepines because they appear to be as effective, less sedating, and less subject to abuse.

Other agents have been assessed for reduction of alcohol withdrawal symptoms, including GABAergic, dopaminergic, glutamatergic, and calcium channel blocking compounds. Of these agents, the GABAergic appear to be most encouraging. It has been reported that γ-hydroxybutyric acid (GABA metabolite) significantly suppressed and prevented the alcohol withdrawal syndrome in rats and humans (Fadda, Colombo, Mosca, Gessa, 1989; Di Bello, Gambassi, Mugnai, Masini, Mannaioni, 1995). GABA agonists have also been demonstrated to lessen alcohol withdrawal symptoms. In a double-blind study, Anton, Kranzler, McEvoy, Moak, and Bianca (1997) compared abecarnil (GABA agonist) to diazepam and found the drugs similar in their ability to decrease withdrawal symptoms.

Prior to 1990 the vast majority of alcohol medication research focused on withdrawal compounds. However, as our knowledge of underlying CNS mechanisms responsible for drug reward increased during the "Decade of the Brain," a shift in alcohol medication development research is underway. Since 1990 there has been a burgeoning interest in developing medications that will decrease the desire to drink in alcohol-dependent individuals. Neurochemical and neuroanatomical studies have provided a plethora of evidence that has implicated several neurotransmitters, including dopamine (DA), endorphins, and serotonin (5-HT), and various brain regions (the ventral tegmental area and nucleus accumbens) in mediating alcohol reward and craving (Chick et al., 1996). The recent Food and Drug Administration (FDA) approval of naltrexone for the treatment of alcoholism further highlights this point.

There are several lines of evidence favoring the employment of opiate antagonists in the treatment of alcoholism. Most importantly, researchers engaged in animal studies assessing the effectiveness of these compounds in attenuating alcohol intake have reported results that are promising for the treatment of human alcoholism (for a detailed review see Ulm, Volpicelli, & Volpicelli, 1995). In short, these studies indicated that when animals received pretreatment with naltrexone or naloxone they decreased their alcohol intake, independent of motor impairment. Moreover, it has been reported that consumption of alcohol by laboratory rats results in the activation of endogenous CNS opiate systems (Reid & Hunter, 1984). Presumably the increased activity in this system leads to a proclivity to ingest more alcohol. Hubbell, Abelson, Burkhardt, Herlands, and Reid (1988) reported that small doses of morphine increased alcohol self-administration in animals. These data taken together suggest that opiate receptor activity may modulate alcohol intake, and they also provide a solid basis for clinical research trials assessing the efficacy of opiate antagonists in the treatment of alcoholism.

Although several clinical studies have examined the efficacy of opiate antagonists in decreasing alcohol consumption, two are of particular importance. In a double-blind, placebo-controlled experiment, Volpicelli, Alterman, Hagashida, and O'Brien (1992) studied the effects of 50 mg/d naltrexone versus placebo over a 12-week treatment period. Naltrexone was found to significantly reduce alcohol craving, days of drinking per week, and the rate of relapse among those who drank. In a similarly designed study, O'Malley et al. (1992) found that naltrexone 50 mg/d markedly decreased alcohol craving, drinking, and alcohol-related problems compared to placebo. They further reported that patients who received both naltrexone and coping skills therapy were most successful in avoiding relapse to alcohol use. These findings have generated the most excitement in alcohol treatment research in some years. Moreover, naltrexone has been reported to be well tolerated and appears to have no abuse potential. Researchers are currently investigating the role that specific opiate receptor subtypes play in the alcohol abuse disorder. This line of inquiry should yield even more useful data.

Roughly two decades ago Ballenger, Goodwin, Major, and Brown (1979) observed significantly lower cerebrospinal fluid (CSF) levels of 5-hydroxy-indoleacetic acid (5-HIAA), the major metabolite of 5-HT, in alcohol-dependent patients. This finding suggested that some alcoholics had reduced 5-HT neurotransmission. Two years later, these findings were replicated and extended. Banki (1981) compared 36 alcoholic women's CSF 5-HIAA levels to those of 32 non–alcohol-dependent women and found significantly lower levels of the metabolite in the alcohol-dependent women. These studies provided the initial evidence for the 5-HT deficiency hypothesis of alcoholism, which states that alcoholism in some individuals may be the result of a neuro-chemical aberration creating a deficiency of 5-HT in the CNS (LeMarquand, Pihl, & Benkelfat, 1994). This abnormality is thought to increase vulnerability to alcohol disorders and other ailments.

A variety of pharmacotherapeutics that exert actions on brain 5-HT have been studied to determine their efficacy in alcoholism treatment. Unfortunately, the results from these experiments have been unimpressive. Of the serotoninergic agents, the serotonin-selective reuptake inhibitors (SSRI) have been the most extensively examined. More than a decade ago, Naranjo and coworkers began carrying out experiments studying the utility of SSRIs, including zimeldine,[3] citalopram, viqualine, and fluoxetine, and found only modest (approximately 17%) decreases in alcohol consumption (Naranjo et al., 1984, 1987; Naranjo, Kadlec, Sanhueza, Woodley-Remus, & Sellers, 1990; Naranjo, Poulos, Bremner, & Lanctot, 1992). More recent studies of fluoxetine 60 mg/d (Kranzler et al., 1995b) and citalopram 40 mg/d (Naranjo, Bremner, & Lanctot, 1995) revealed no significant effect of either drug in alcohol-dependent patients. The above data suggest that SSRIs are less effective pharmacotherapies for alcohol treatment than naltrexone.

Another 5-HT agonist that has been investigated for its potential therapeutic value in alcoholism is the anxiolytic buspirone (5-HT$_{1A}$ partial agonist). A few studies have reported success using buspirone in alcoholics with coexisting anxiety disorders. For example, Tollefson, Montague-Clouse, and Tollefson (1992) conducted a 24-week study in which alcoholics with co-morbid generalized anxiety disorder (as diagnosed by DSM-III-R) randomly received either buspirone or placebo, and they found that buspirone was superior to placebo in decreasing anxiety symptoms, alcohol use, and increasing treatment retention. A more recent double-blind, placebo-controlled study evaluated buspirone in the context of relapse prevention in anxious alcoholics following 12 weeks of treatment and at 6 months posttreatment (Kranzler et al., 1994). Buspirone-treated subjects were more likely to remain in treatment. Buspirone was also significantly more effective as an anxiolytic in patients with high pretreatment anxiety levels. Although buspirone did not significantly reduce frequency of alcohol consumption during the treatment period, patients who received buspirone had significantly fewer drinking days in the follow-up period. These studies indicate that buspirone might be beneficial to a subgroup of alcoholics, those with high levels of anxiety.

A series of experiments have been conducted employing the 5-HT$_3$ receptor antagonist ondansetron. The rationale for the use of this agent stems from the belief that 5-HT$_3$ receptor antagonists inhibit mesolimbic DA release[4] (Wozniak, Pert, & Linnoila, 1990), thereby decreasing the amount of alcohol reward experienced following drinking. Although this rationale appears straightforward, research findings regarding ondansetron's use are not. In one study, oral ondansetron was found to be superior to placebo in attenuating the desire to drink as measured by self-report (Johnson, Campling, Griffiths, & Cowen, 1993). However, Doty, Zacny, and de Wit (1994) found no difference between ondansetron and placebo on a variety of other subjective measures.

A new medication not yet available in the United States shows promise in the treatment of alcohol disorders. Acamprosate (calcium acetylhomotaurinate), an analogue of homocysteic acid has a structure similar to GABA and as such, has been reported to stimulate inhibitory GABA transmission and to antagonize excitatory amino acids (Zeise, Kasparov, Capogna, & Zieglgansberger, 1993). These properties have been postulated to be important to reduction in alcohol craving (Littleton, 1995). Unlike other drugs that enhance GABA activity (e.g., benzodiazepines and barbiturates), acamprosate has been reported to be devoid of abuse potential and has no hypnotic, muscle relaxant, or anxiolytic properties. Two placebo-controlled studies have reported on acamprosate in the treatment of alcoholism. In one study, 272 patients were randomized to 48 weeks of acamprosate or placebo and then followed for an additional 48 weeks without medication. Those who received acamprosate had a higher continuous abstinence rate during treatment and were significantly more likely to remain abstinent in the follow-up period (Sass, Soyka, Mann, & Zieglgansberger, 1996). The second study reported on 455 alcohol-dependent patients randomly assigned to acamprosate or placebo for 360 days. Acamprosate was well tolerated and was associated with longer duration of abstinence relative to placebo (Whitworth et al., 1996).

Nearly half a century ago Jacobsen and his collaborators serendipitously discovered that humans exposed to disulfiram while alcohol was present in the body experienced a characteristic unpleasant reaction, including facial flushing, accelerated pulse, throbbing headache, nausea, and vomiting (Hald, Jacobsen, & Larsen, 1948). These symptoms are thought to be the result of aldehyde dehydrogenase inhibition by disulfiram, partially because a similar reaction is reproduced by acetaldehyde infusion in humans (Asmussen, Hald, & Larsen, 1948). Since this initial observation, several studies have assessed disulfiram as a pharmacotherapeutic option in alcoholism treatment. In general, disulfiram has not been shown to be effective in achieving abstinence or delaying relapse (Fuller & Roth, 1979). However, for a select group of patients, those who are highly motivated, intelligent, not impulsive, and have no comorbid major psychiatric disorder, disulfiram in combination with psychosocial treatment may be effective (Fuller et al., 1986). Disulfiram illustrates how one person's toxicity can be another's therapy.

NICOTINE PHARMACOTHERAPIES

As new antismoking legislations are passed that restrict smoking in public places, and as the social acceptability of cigarette smoking is at an all-time low, nearly 50 million Americans persist undaunted in their tobacco smoking habit. As a result, in the United States alone there are approximately 1,200 deaths per day attributed to cigarette smoking and other forms of tobacco use (Bartecchi, MacKenzie, & Schrier, 1994). The fact that there are more than 400,000 deaths per year associated with tobacco intake has earned cigarette smoking and other forms of tobacco consumption the dubious distinction as the single most preventable cause of death in America. Perhaps even more interesting is that the number of deaths caused by tobacco use has surpassed deaths caused by all of the illicit drugs and alcohol combined (Bartecchi et al., 1994).

Why do people continue to consume tobacco products in light of the potential adverse effects to health and well-being? The answer to this question has been sought with tenacity by several groups of researchers for at least two decades. The 1988 U.S. Surgeon General report *Nicotine Addiction* concluded that tobacco use, especially cigarette smoking, is so robustly maintained because of the smoker's addiction to nicotine. Although it is true that nicotine is but one of more than 4,000 compounds found in tobacco smoke, the report cited numerous studies that illustrated that tobacco smoke inhalation was controlled by nicotine, independent of the other constituents found in tobacco smoke, including tar and carbon monoxide.

As with other often-abused drugs, nicotine dependence is contingent upon the rate and route of nicotine administration. Nicotine inhaled in tobacco smoke is thought to be the most addictive form of administration. Several seconds following inhalation, nicotine is rapidly absorbed in the pulmonary alveoli and carried to the heart and then to the brain and other organs. Rapid attainment of high nicotine brain levels results in relatively intense mesolimbic DA effects (as well as effects on other CNS structures) occurring in close temporal proximity to smoking. Because nicotine directly reinforces cigarette smoking with each inhalation, the behavior of smoking becomes more fortified. As reinforcement continues, the likelihood of future nicotine use increases. This makes it extremely difficult to quit the use of tobacco for many, so difficult that of the 34% of smokers who attempt to quit each year only 2.5% succeed (U.S. Public Health Service, 1988). In general, those who succeed report that several attempts were required over many years before they were able to permanently cease tobacco use. Mark Twain posthumously speaks to this issue, "To cease smoking is the easiest thing I ever did; I ought to know because I've done it a thousand times."

In recent years the foremost pharmacological treatment approach to nicotine use disorders has been nicotine replacement. Most smokers who attempt to quit relapse within the first week, at the time when peak withdrawal symptoms occur, such as anger, irritability, anxiety, depression, decreased concentration, and craving (Kottke, Brekke, Solberg, & Hughes, 1989). It is well documented that nicotine replacement is effective in relieving withdrawal symptoms, and the amount of relief is positively correlated with nicotine dose (U.S. Public Health Service, 1988). Nicotine replacement decreases withdrawal symptoms such that the smoker is allowed to focus more clearly on the necessary behaviors required for smoking cessation and results in less exposure to carcinogens found in cigarettes. The first nicotine medication, nicotine polacrilex (nicotine chewing gum) in the 2-mg form, was FDA-approved in 1984. Then, in 1992, the 4-mg form received FDA approval. Between 1991 and 1992, the FDA also approved four transdermal nicotine delivery systems (nicotine patches). More recently, some new nicotine delivery devices have been assessed for potential utility including a nasal spray, vapor inhaler, and lozenge. These nicotine formulations result in lower plasma nicotine levels achieved more slowly than those from cigarette smoking (Henningfield & Keenan, 1993). Based on the principle of behavioral reinforcement, this fact suggests that the above medications should have less abuse liability than cigarette smoking.

Chewing nicotine polacrilex provides systemic delivery of nicotine through buccal absorption. Typically, 50% of the nicotine contained in each piece of gum is absorbed, i.e., 1 or 2 mg with the 2 or 4 mg nicotine gums, respectively, over 20 to 30 minutes. However, absorption is decreased in an acidic environment. Hence, patients should be advised not to consume acidic beverages like coffee, juices, and soda, or foods that lower pH while using nicotine polacrilex (Henningfield, Stapleton, Benowitz, Grayson, & London, 1993). Dosing of nicotine polacrilex should be done 15 minutes before or after consumption of the above foods. Nicotine polacrilex appears to be effective at decreasing withdrawal symptoms and increasing cessation, but efficacy is dependent on psychosocial support (Hall, Hall, & Ginsberg, 1990; Schneider et al., 1983). Recent evidence also shows that scheduled dosing (i.e., one piece of gum/hour) is more effective than using the gum as needed for craving (Hughes, 1996). A 4-mg nicotine polacrilex gum has been proven more efficacious than the 2-mg nicotine dose in the treatment of highly dependent smokers who smoke in excess of 25 cigarettes daily (Sachs, 1995).

Transdermal nicotine is delivered through the skin in a controlled and continuous systemic fashion. Current standard transdermal medication delivers about 0.9 mg of nicotine per hour over a 24-hour period, but 16-hour patches are also available. Nicotine is absorbed slowly, with peak levels reached six to ten hours after application. These nicotine levels are about half those obtained through smoking. Following four to six weeks of treatment at the initial nicotine dose, a tapering schedule is usually implemented within two to four weeks of either 10 mg/16-hour or 14 mg/24-hour schedules. This, in turn, is followed by two to four weeks of the lowest nicotine dose, 5 mg delivered over 16 hours or 7 mg delivered over 24 hours. Abrupt cessation of patch use has not been associated with significant withdrawal; therefore, tapering may not be necessary (Fiore et al., 1994). Transdermal nicotine has been generally well tolerated, with the minor side effects of irritation at the application site, mild gastric disturbances, and abnormal sleep patterns sometimes reported. Abundant studies have been conducted with the nicotine patch. Meta-analyses summarizing the results of these have all concluded that the patch is an effective smoking cessation medication (Silagy, Mant, Fowler, & Lodge, 1994; Fiore, Smith, Jorenby, & Baker, 1994). The effectiveness of the patch appears to be less adjunctive therapy–dependent than is nicotine gum (Sonderskov, Olsen, Sabroe, Meillier, & Overvad, 1997; Jorenby et al., 1995).

Recently the FDA approved nicotine nasal spray as a prescription medication to aid adult smokers in their efforts to quit smoking. This product is a relatively rapid delivery system that delivers 0.5 mg of nicotine per pulse for absorption through the nasal mucosa (Sutherland et al., 1992). Of the currently available nicotine replacement therapies, the nasal spray most closely mimics cigarette smoking, due to the rapid absorption of nicotine from the nasal mucosa. In fact, Perkins et al. (1993) reported that the subjective effects following nasal nicotine were very similar to the effects produced by smoking. Not surprisingly, this product has a high abuse liability. Because of the abuse potential the FDA has recommended a treatment duration of three months with this product. Two randomized double-blind, placebo-controlled studies have examined the effectiveness of nicotine nasal spray on smoking cessation (Schneider et al., 1995; Hjalmarson, Franzon, Westin, & Wiklund, 1994). Both demonstrated a significant increase in abstinence in groups randomized to nicotine spray treatment at all follow-ups.

Another strategy used in nicotine replacement therapy involves combined administration of mecamylamine (a noncompetitive nicotinic receptor antagonist) and transdermal nicotine. The rationale for this approach is that mecamylamine would block any reinforcing effects of nicotine inhaled from cigarette smoke, while the patch would deliver an adequate amount of nicotine to relieve withdrawal symptoms. Results from at least two clinical studies employing mecamylamine-nicotine combinations are encouraging (Rose et al., 1994a; Rose et al., 1994b). The FDA is currently conducting clinical trials to investigate further the potential utility of this approach to nicotine-dependence treatment.

Non-nicotinic medications have also been investigated as potential aids in facilitating tobacco abstinence. The observation that failure in smoking cessation is predicted by a past history of depression and/or dysphoria prior to or at the onset of an attempt to quit smoking has led to some interest in the evaluation of various antidepressant agents. The results, however, have been inconclusive (Hughes, 1994; Humfleet, Hall, Reus, Munoz, & Triffleman, 1996). Clonidine, an α-agonist and antihypertensive agent, has also been assessed. In doses of 0.1–0.4 mg/day administered orally or transdermally for three to four weeks, it has been shown to reduce withdrawal symptoms and to ameliorate craving. However, side effects of sedation, postural hypotension, dizziness, and dry mouth may accompany this treatment (Gourlay & Benowitz, 1995). Clonidine treatment might be advised for those who do not want nicotine replacement therapy or who have failed other smoking cessation methods.

COCAINE PHARMACOTHERAPIES

The use of cocaine has an extensive history. Prior to being regarded as the nefarious rock, cocaine (as extracted from the shrub *erythroxylon coca*) enjoyed moments of high praise on the historical stage for at least 1,200 years. However, cocaine's euphoric, vasoconstricting, and local anesthetic effects were not widely appreciated until after 1860, when Albert Niemann chemically isolated it from the coca plant. With the invention of the hypodermic syringe in the late nineteenth century and as cocaine became more readily available, reports of cocaine abuse appeared. It has been estimated that at the turn of the century Americans consumed more than ten times the amount of cocaine used today, even though today's United States is roughly three times larger (Das, 1993). By 1910, President Theodore Roosevelt had officially declared cocaine "Public Enemy No. 1." After the passage of the Harrison Act (1914), which was intended to allow the federal government to regulate the prescription of narcotics by requiring physicians to register and pay an inexpensive tax, cocaine consumption substantially declined, and by the late 1950s cocaine abuse was described as a problem of the past. However, as the 1960s brought a shift to a less moralistic zeitgeist, cocaine use reemerged in the early 1970s.

More recent nationwide surveys conducted by the National Institute on Drug Abuse (NIDA) indicate that past-year and 30-day prevalence rates peaked in 1985 and have since steadily declined. Although the National Household prevalence rates appear to be on a downward trend, the number of reported emergency room admissions associated with cocaine use has dramatically increased. One possible explanation is that in the 1980s crack cocaine became more readily available. The rapid onset of smoked cocaine's effect may pose even greater potential cardiovascular risk than that of cocaine taken by nasal insufflation. In addition, the rapid onset and termination of smoked cocaine's effects increase the likelihood of chronic administration, which can produce a condition closely resembling paranoid schizophrenia. Both conditions could contribute to increases in emergency room visits associated with cocaine use.

The "dopamine depletion hypothesis," which states that during cocaine abstinence a hypodopaminergic state leads to dysphoria, craving, and subsequent drug use, has been the underlying rationale for much of the cocaine pharmacotherapy research to date. It is thought that by pharmacologically restoring and/or replenishing CNS DA levels the negative symptoms associated with cocaine abstinence would be assuaged, thereby decreasing subsequent cocaine use. Although the rationale for employing dopaminergic agents appears to be obvious, the plethora of research in this area has failed to produce an accepted effective pharmacotherapy. This is so, in part, because of severe adverse effects, including nausea, headaches, hypertension, tachycardia, and psychosislike symptoms experienced following the administration of dopaminergic agents.

Bromocriptine, a D_2 receptor agonist, has been assessed as a possible pharmacotherapy for cocaine abuse in several studies (Dackis, Gold, Sweeney, Byron, & Climko, 1987; Giannini, Baumgartel, & DiMarzio, 1987; Giannini, Folts, Feather, & Sullivan, 1989; Tennant & Sagherian, 1987; Kosten, Schumann, & Wright, 1988). Bromocriptine was generally reported to decrease craving and dysphoria during detoxification; however, significant adverse events, including syncopal episodes and high dropout rates, are likely to limit its clinical utility (Giannini et al., 1987; Tennant & Sagherian, 1987). Clinical trials with amantadine (DA indirect agonist) have yielded mixed results. One controlled trial reported no difference between amantadine and placebo (Weddington et al., 1991). Subsequently, Alterman et al. (1992) conducted a double-blind, placebo-controlled trial in which 42 patients enrolled in a day treatment program were randomized to amantadine 100 mg twice daily or placebo groups. In contrast, they concluded, based on urine toxicology screens, that those who had received amantadine were significantly more likely to be free of cocaine at the two-week and one-month follow-up visits. In a more recent study in which follow-up visits were conducted at two months, however, amantadine was found to be no more superior to placebo in treatment retention or in the number of benzoylecgonine (cocaine metabolite)-positive urine samples (Kampman et al., 1996).

The DA transporter inhibitor mazindol showed no significant efficacy curtailing cocaine craving or use, according to several studies (Diakogiannis, Steinberg, & Kosten, 1990; Kosten, Steinberg, & Diakogiannis, 1993; Preston, Sullivan, Berger, & Bigelow, 1993; Stine, Krystal, Kosten, & Charney, 1995). In a large multicenter study designed to assess the effectiveness of the antidepressant bupropion (dopaminergic and noradrenergic agonist) in cocaine dependence treatment, methadone-maintained patients showed little improvement (Margolin et al., 1995). Currently, bupropion is being studied in patients with primary cocaine dependence. Preliminary findings indicate bupropion 150 mg and 300 mg administered daily may decrease the positive subjective effects of cocaine use (Singha et al., 1998).

Other antidepressant compounds have also been evaluated as potential pharmacotherapies for cocaine use disorders. Justification for the exploration of these agents stemmed from the observation that some depressed abusers were self-medicating with cocaine. Thus, some speculated that if depressive symptoms in cocaine users were lessened with antidepressant medication, a resultant decrease in cocaine use might follow. Because findings from an earlier study indicated that desipramine, a tricyclic antidepressant, was effective in this capacity (Gawin & Kleber, 1984), several other investigations employing desipramine soon followed, but reported less encouraging results (Covi, Montoya, Hess, & Kreiter, 1994; Levin & Lehman, 1991; Kosten, Morgan, Falcione, & Schottenfeld, 1992; Arndt, Dorozynsky, Woody, McLellan, & O'Brien, 1992; Weddington et al., 1991).

Given that cocaine exerts inhibitory actions on the 5-HT transporter, some researchers reasoned that serotonergic agents may prove efficacious in the treatment of cocaine use disorders. In fact, findings from animal studies demonstrated that the reuptake inhibitor fluoxetine reduced cocaine self-administration (Richardson & Roberts, 1991; Carroll, Lac, Asencio, & Kragh, 1990). The above and a clinical study, which indicated that fluoxetine decreased subjective ratings of the positive mood associated with cocaine use (Walsh, Preston, Sullivan, Framme, & Bigelow, 1994), have led to larger clinical trials. Unfortunately, these later results suggested that fluoxetine was unsuccessful in the treatment of cocaine dependence (Grabowski et al., 1995; Batki, Washburn, Delucchi, & Jones, 1996).

MISCELLANEOUS AGENTS

Because cocaine dependence may be accompanied by abuse of other drugs like alcohol and/or opiates, and because their priming effects may serve for initiating cocaine use, agents that affect brain-endogenous opiate systems[5] have been investigated as potential therapies. Buprenorphine, an opiate agonist-antagonist, has been studied in this regard, but results are inconclusive. Several investigators found buprenorphine to be efficacious in decreasing cocaine and opiate abuse among patients who were both cocaine- and opiate-dependent (Kosten, Kleber, & Morgan, 1989; Gastfriend, Mendelson, Mello, Teoh, & Reif, 1993; Schottenfeld, Pakes, Ziedonis, & Kosten, 1993). Others reported less favorable results with buprenorphine therapy (Fudala, Johnson, & Jaffe, 1991; Oliveto, Kosten, Schottenfeld, Ziedonis, & Falcioni, 1994; Strain, Stitzer, Liebson, & Bigelow, 1994).

Examination of disulfiram therapy for cocaine-dependent individuals is based on the clinical observation that many cocaine abusers use alcohol and cocaine simultaneously. Some hypothesized that by preventing alcohol intake, it would no longer serve as a cue for cocaine consumption nor would it be used as an agent reported to potentiate cocaine euphoria or modulate unwanted stimulant effects of cocaine. Results from a few small studies exploring the utility of disulfiram revealed that both cocaine and alcohol use were reduced (Carroll, Ziedonis, O'Malley, McCance-Katz, & Rounsaville, 1993; Van Etten et al., 1994). McCance-Katz, Kosten, and Jatlow (1998) recently studied the interaction of cocaine and disulfiram. Treatment with disulfiram

250 mg daily significantly increased plasma cocaine concentrations. There were also significant increases in heart rate and blood pressure with the combination of cocaine and disulfiram relative to cocaine-alone administration. Nonsignificant increases in cocaine "high" and anxiety were observed when a moderate dose of intranasal cocaine (2 mg/kg) was administered following disulfiram 250 mg/d treatment. These findings indicate that although disulfiram treatment could produce an aversive reaction with cocaine use in some patients, disulfiram must be administered with caution given the significant pharmacokinetic interaction observed.

Initial findings from studies investigating carbamazepine, an anticonvulsant medication, in the treatment of cocaine disorders were encouraging. For example, Halikas, Kemp, Kuhn, Carlson, and Crea (1989) found that carbamazepine attenuated cocaine craving and reduced cocaine use. Subsequent experiments exploring carbamazepine treatments failed to replicate earlier results, however, thus casting doubt on its therapeutic value (Cornish et al., 1995; Kranzler, Bauer, Hersh, & Klinghoffer, 1995a).

Although it is early in the experimental process, two new strategies are potential options in the treatment of cocaine dependence. The exploration of the various subtypes of DA receptors have produced some interesting findings, suggesting that implementation of D_1 agonists may be a viable adjunctive pharmacotherapeutic approach in cocaine dependence (Self, Barnhart, Lehman, & Nestler, 1996). Another pharmacotherapy currently being investigated is cocaine immunization. In vaccinated individuals, cocaine's entry into the brain is considerably restricted, thereby preventing any of the psychoactive effects of the drug. Two recent animal studies reported that active immunization reduced brain cocaine levels following cocaine administration and suppressed cocaine-induced locomotion, stereotypy (Carrera et al., 1995), and self-administration (Fox et al., 1996). Human testing of cocaine vaccination is now underway. Yet this approach is not without a few shortcomings. Some researchers have raised concern about vaccinated individuals who might attempt to overcome the antibody effect by taking more cocaine, consequently overdosing. Future research should address such concerns.

OPIATE PHARMACOTHERAPIES

Addiction to opiate drugs, including opium, morphine, and heroin, is an age-old problem and one with an interesting history. With the 1821 publication of his article "The Confessions of an English Opium-Eater," Thomas De Quincey not only introduced the western world to the concept of opium addiction but also described in meticulous detail the effects that opium had on consciousness and feeling when he wrote: "Happiness might now be bought for a penny, and carried in the waistcoat pocket: portable ecstacies might be had corked up in a pint bottle; and peace of mind could be sent down in gallons by the coach mail." Although De Quincey's writings no doubt increased the popularity of opiate drugs in the United States, there is a consensus among historians that the development of the hypodermic syringe in 1853 and the advent of the three wars that followed (the American Civil War, 1861 to 1865; the Prussian-Austrian War, 1866; and the Franco-Prussian War, 1870) contributed even more significantly to the spread of opiate drug addiction. Opiates were commonly used by soldiers to lessen the pain of injuries. In fact, the number of veterans who were afflicted with opiate dependence was so high that the illness was commonly referred to as "soldier's disease" (Ray & Ksir, 1996). Isolated from the opium poppy in 1806 by the German Frederich Serturner and ten times more potent than opium, the opiate drug of choice in the United States during that time was morphine.

As more people, particularly those from the middle class, became "hooked" on morphine, the quest for suitable treatment began. Most infamously, in 1884 Sigmund Freud attempted to eradicate the morphine addiction of his friend Ernst von Fleischl with the use of cocaine. Fleischl, suffering severe thumb amputation pain, had been prescribed morphine and subsequently became addicted. Initially, Freud was encouraged by the results of the cocaine remedy with which he had treated Fleischl. In his paper "On Coca," Freud enthusiastically wrote, "Prof. Fleischl of Vienna confirms the fact that muriate of cocaine is invaluable, subcutaneously injected in morphinism (0.05–0.15 grm dissolved in water). A gradual withdrawal of morphine requires a gradual increase of cocaine, but a sudden abstinence from morphine, requires a subcutaneous injection of 0.1 grm of cocaine. Inebriate asylums can be entirely dispensed with; in 10 days a radical cure can be effected by an injection of 0.1 grm of cocaine 3 times a day. It is evident that there is a direct antagonism between morphine and cocaine." Such excitement over the curative properties of cocaine for morphine dependence proved to be ephemeral; less than a year later Fleischl had developed a severe dependence on cocaine.

OPIATE DETOXIFICATION

At the start of the twentieth century, anticholinergic medications, such as belladonna, were included in the physician's recommended arsenal to combat the opiate habit (Latimer & Goldberg, 1981). It was postulated that anticholinergics would produce a state of delirium for several days, after which the addict would emerge detoxified and cured from addiction without remembering the withdrawal process. Not too far removed from this reasoning are those current programs that offer "ultra-rapid anesthesia-assisted" opiate detoxification; the merits of which continue to be debated (Stephenson, 1997). A contemporary standard approach to opiate-induced overdose (coma and respiratory depression) includes the administration of the opiate antagonist naloxone. Because naloxone has a greater affinity for CNS opiate receptors than do most opiate agonists, including heroin, following its administration naloxone displaces the agonist from the receptors, thereby rapidly reversing the overdose. In suspected opiate overdose, naloxone may be administered intravenously or subcutaneously, at doses ranging from 0.4–0.8 mg. Naloxone treatment should reverse opiate toxicity within minutes of the injection. In patients who are opiate-dependent naloxone will precipitate opiate withdrawal.

Although opiate withdrawal is rarely life-threatening, such symptoms as nausea, vomiting, diarrhea, and myalgia, which accompany withdrawal, can be most unpleasant. Pharmacological agents are administered to minimize discomfort. The principles of detoxification are to substitute a longer-acting pharmacologically equivalent drug for the abused substance, stabilize the patient on that drug, and then gradually withdraw the substituted drug. Tapering doses of methadone are commonly used in this capacity, but concern about an associated protracted withdrawal syndrome has prompted the search for more efficient treatments. Accordingly, Gold, Redmond, and Kleber (1978) demonstrated that the severity of opiate withdrawal could be diminished with the α_2-adrenergic agonist clonidine. Studies using brain tissue have revealed that opiate and α_2-adrenergic receptors are co-localized in some brain regions, including the locus ceruleus. Morphine and clonidine were shown to produce similar neurophysiological effects on these norepinephrine-containing neurons in this region (Aghajanian, 1978). This evidence provides a further basis for the use of clonidine to reduce the severity and duration of opiate withdrawal. Using opiate antagonists (naloxone or naltrexone) to precipitate withdrawal while simultaneously treating patients with relatively high doses of clonidine has enabled opiate-dependent patients to become drug free in as little as three days, while also minimizing the antagonist-precipitated withdrawal symptoms (Charney et al., 1982; Kleber, Topazian, Gaspari, Riordan, & Kosten, 1987; Vining, Kosten, & Kleber, 1988). A recent report suggests that lofexidine, also an α_2-adrenergic agonist, may be equal to clonidine in alleviating opiate withdrawal, but with less adverse effects (hypotension and lethargy) (Kahn, Mumford, Rogers, & Beckford, 1997). Presumed advantages of α_2-adrenergic agonists are that they have no narcotic actions and are not addicting.

Buprenorphine, a partial opiate agonist at the μ receptor, has also been reported to attenuate opiate withdrawal (Kosten & Kleber, 1988; Cheskin, Fudala, & Johnson, 1994). In one study, heroin addicts and methadone-maintained patients were switched to buprenorphine for a month of stabilization at once-daily doses ranging from 2 to 8 mg sublingually (Kosten & Kleber, 1988). Buprenorphine was then abruptly terminated, and patients were given a high dose of intravenous naloxone (35 mg) to precipitate withdrawal. Buprenorphine withdrawal syndrome is relatively mild and can be treated with clonidine, if necessary. Following this precipitated withdrawal, the patient may be started on naltrexone the same day. A recent randomized trial comparing this procedure to standard clonidine detoxification showed greater success and fewer withdrawal symptoms using buprenorphine (Shi et al., 1993).

OPIATE MAINTENANCE MEDICATIONS

Although opiate detoxification is a critical initial step in the treatment of opiate dependence, opiate maintenance therapy remains the main pharmacological approach used. A primary goal of opiate maintenance therapy is to achieve a stable dose that reduces, or ideally, eliminates illicit opiate use and enables the patient to engage in a comprehensive program that promotes rehabilitation and eliminates abuse of other drugs (Ball & Ross, 1991; Senay & Uchtenhagen, 1990). Because treatment with opiate agonists produces dependence, it is critical to select patients who already have a history of prolonged dependence (greater than one year) and who demonstrate physiological dependence. Moreover, mortality and morbidity associated with illicit drug use, criminal activity by opiate addicts, and the transfer of HIV virus have all been demonstrated to be significantly reduced when opiate addicts are placed in maintenance therapy (Ball & Ross, 1991; Dole et al., 1969).

Currently, there are three maintenance pharmacotherapies that are FDA-approved in the United States — methadone, levo-alpha-acetylmethadol (LAAM), and naltrexone. Methadone is the most widely used form of opiate maintenance therapy. Because methadone is longer-acting than most opiate agonists, including heroin and morphine, it is admirably suited to saturate opiate receptors and thereby block the reinforcing effects of other opiate drugs. Abundant studies have demonstrated the efficacy of methadone treatment for decreasing the psychosocial consequences and medical morbidity associated with opiate dependence. Additionally, methadone continues to be important in decreasing the spread of HIV infection among injection drug users. The success of methadone spans a wide range of doses, and each patient's dose must be individually titrated. Methadone 40–60 mg daily will block opiate withdrawal symptoms, but doses of 70–80 mg daily are more often needed to relieve craving. Generally, doses greater than 60 mg daily are associated with better treatment retention and less illicit opiate use (Ball & Ross, 1991). Despite the relative success of methadone maintenance a significant number of patients continue illicit drug use. Further, the requirement that methadone be administered daily necessitates take-home doses over the weekend in some clinics, a potential source by which the drug could be illicitly marketed.

To address some of these concerns, the synthetic opiate agonist LAAM recently received FDA approval for opiate dependence treatment. This congener of methadone has a long terminal half-life of 92 hours, which permits three-times-per-week dosing. A multicenter trial compared LAAM (80 mg every other day) to two different doses of methadone (50 mg and 100 mg) over a 40-week study period (Ling, Charuvastra, Kaim, & Klett, 1976). During the first week of the study all participants received 30 mg per dose of their assigned medication. In subsequent weeks medication doses were increased by 10 mg until the targeted dose level was reached. Treatment retention was somewhat poorer with LAAM, perhaps due to dropout during the initial month of dosage stabilization. After 40 weeks, the LAAM group retention rate was 40%, whereas the two methadone groups retained 60% (50 mg) and 70% (100 mg) of patients. On the primary outcome measure, illicit opiate use as measured by urine samples, patients who received LAAM or methadone 100 mg had significantly better outcome than those who received methadone 50 mg. Thus, LAAM has shown good potential as an alternative to methadone, with the advantage of not requiring daily clinic visits of patients and reducing the potential for diversion.

The efficacy of naltrexone, an opioid antagonist administered as an oral preparation, in preventing opioid abuse has been evaluated in controlled trials. Following detoxification, opioid-dependent individuals were treated with naltrexone (50 mg daily, 3 doses/week) or matched placebo. Over the 12-week follow-up period there were fewer heroin-positive urines in the naltrexone group and more subjects randomized to naltrexone treatment remained opioid-free relative to those treated with placebo (Shufman et al., 1994). Another study examined the efficacy of naltrexone (350 mg weekly) in opioid-dependent patients who had been detoxified over a two-week period and who then initiated naltrexone treatment and were followed clinically for six months (San et al., 1991). Naltrexone treatment was not shown to be superior to placebo in terms of patient acceptance, drug use, medication compliance, or side effects, which highlights the need to select motivated patients for this form of maintenance treatment.

Naltrexone treatment is an option for patients who do not want to be maintained on opiate agonists (Kosten & Kleber, 1984). Naltrexone therapy should not begin until the patient is completely detoxified from opiates to avoid precipitating withdrawal; usually 7–14 days of abstinence is sufficient. Naltrexone can be administered at a dose of 50 mg daily, 100 mg every two days, or 150 mg every third day. Naltrexone should be administered for at least six months and discontinuation carefully planned with the patient. Naltrexone side effects are few, but hepatotoxicity has been reported, therefore, hepatic function should be determined prior to treatment and monitored at three-month intervals (Galloway & Hayner, 1993). A major problem with naltrexone has been a lack of patient compliance, which may be enhanced if medication administration can be observed by health care providers, or if available, family members or an employer (Galanter, 1993).

Although not yet FDA-approved as an opiate maintenance therapy, buprenorphine has been extensively evaluated in this capacity. Advantages of buprenorphine are as follows: because it is a μ-opiate agonist, its subjective effects are agonistlike (Jasinski, Pevnick, & Griffith, 1978); it lessens opiate withdrawal symptoms (Kosten & Kleber, 1988; Cheskin et al., 1994); and it blocks the effects of simultaneously administered opiate agonists (Jasinski et al., 1978). Yet, findings from experiments comparing buprenorphine to methadone have been inconclusive. Johnson, Fudala, and Jaffe (1992) reported that buprenorphine 8 mg/d was equivalent to methadone 65 mg/d, while superior to methadone 20 mg/d, in decreasing illicit opiate use and in treatment retention during their six-month trial. In another study, Kosten, Schottenfeld, Ziedonis, and Falcioni (1993) randomly assigned 125 opiate-dependent patients to either 2- or 6-mg buprenorphine groups or to 35- or 65-mg methadone groups. They noted that 6 mg buprenorphine was superior to 2 mg in reducing illicit opiate use, but the higher dosage did not improve treatment retention. Treatment retention was significantly better on methadone, and the methadone patients had significantly more opiate-free urines (51% vs. 26%). Abstinence for at least three weeks was also more common on methadone than on buprenorphine (65% vs. 27%). Thus, methadone was superior to these two buprenorphine dosages. These findings were recently bolstered by a clinical trial report that concluded that methadone 80 mg/d was superior to buprenorphine 8 mg/d (Ling et al., 1996). Other studies have suggested that treatment with higher doses of buprenorphine is superior to lower-dose treatment. In two outpatient dose-ranging studies (Bickel et al., 1989; Schottenfeld et al., 1993), opiate-free urines increased almost 90% at 12–16 mg of buprenorphine daily.

Buprenorphine appears to be a very promising treatment alternative for heroin addicts, particularly at dosages of 12 to 16 mg where its efficacy and acceptability to opiate addicts appears to be equivalent to methadone at standard therapeutic dosages of 65 mg daily. It is associated with good treatment retention, reduces illicit opiate abuse, and provides a rapid and relatively symptom-free detoxification to a drug-free state after sustained treatment.

In summary, the use of pharmacotherapies in preventing relapse and facilitating recovery from substance use disorders continues to be refined. There exists a general consensus regarding the utility of pharmacological treatments for alcohol, nicotine, and opiate use disorders. However, no pharmacological agent has been shown to be uniquely effective in treating cocaine dependence. As new approaches are explored this situation is expected to improve.

Notes

This research was supported by NIDA grants K02-DA00112 (TRK) and K20-DA00216 (EFM).

1. The term *substance use disorders,* as it is used here, encompasses the DSM-IV's definition of substance abuse and substance dependence.

2. Some physicians are reluctant to administer diazepam, as it has been reported to have euphoric effects in some patients.

3. Zimeldine was withdrawn from the market because some patients who were treated with the drug suffered severe side effects including Guillain-Barre syndrome (Editorial, 1984).

4. The mesolimbic DA pathway extends from the ventral tegmental area to the nucleus accumbens and is thought to be involved in positive reinforcement for drugs of abuse.

5. CNS endogenous opiates are thought to mediate some of the reinforcing effects of abused drugs, including heroin, alcohol, and cocaine.

References

Adinoff, B. (1994). Double-blind study of alprazolam, diazepam, clonidine, and placebo in the alcohol withdrawal syndrome: preliminary findings. *Alcoholism: Clinical and Experimental Research, 18,* 873–878.

Aghajanian, G. K. (1978). Tolerance of locus coeruleus neurones to morphine and suppression of withdrawal response by clonidine. *Nature, 276,* 186–188.

Agricola, R., Mazzarino, M., Urani, R., Gallo, V., & Grossi, E. (1982). Treatment of acute alcohol withdrawal syndrome with carbamazepine: a double-blind comparison with tiapride. *Journal of International Medical Research, 10,* 160–165.

Alterman, A. I., Droba, M., Antelo, R. E., Cornish, J. W., Sweeney, K. K., Parikh, G. A., & O'Brien, C. P. (1992). Amantadine may facilitate detoxification of cocaine addicts. *Drug and Alcohol Dependence, 31,* 19–29.

Anton, R., Kranzler, H. R., McEvoy, J. P., Moak, D. H., & Bianca, R. (1997). A double-blind comparison of abecarnil and diazepam in the treatment of uncomplicated alcohol withdrawal. *Psychopharmacology, 131,* 123–129.

Arndt, I. O., Dorozynsky, L., Woody, G. E., McLellan, A. T., & O'Brien, C. P. (1992). Desipramine treatment of cocaine dependence in methadone-maintained patients. *Archives of General Psychiatry, 49,* 888–893.

Asmussen, E., Hald, J., & Larsen, V. (1948). The pharmacological action of acetaldehyde on human organism. *Acta Pharmacology and Toxicology, 4,* 311–320.

Ball, J., & Ross, A. (1991). *The effectiveness of methadone maintenance treatment.* New York: Springer-Verlag.

Ballenger, J. C., Goodwin, F. K., Major, L. F., & Brown, G. L. (1979). Alcohol and central serotonin metabolism in man. *Archives of General Psychiatry, 36,* 224–227.

Banki, C. M. (1981). Factors influencing monoamine metabolites and tryptophan in patients with alcohol dependence. *Journal of Neural Transmission, 50,* 89–101.

Bartecchi, C. E., MacKenzie, T. D., Schrier, R. W. (1994). The human costs of tobacco use. *New England Journal of Medicine, 330,* 907–912.

Batki, S. L., Washburn, A. M., Delucchi, K., Jones, R. T. (1996). A controlled trial of fluoxetine in crack cocaine dependence. *Drug and Alcohol Dependence, 41,* 137–142.

Baumgartner, G. R., & Rowen, R. C. (1991). Transdermal clonidine versus chlordiazepoxide in alcohol withdrawal: A randomized, controlled clinical trial. *Southern Medical Journal, 84,* 312–321.

Bickel, W. K., Stitzer, M. L., Bigelow, G. E., Liebson, I. A., Jasinski, D. R., & Johnson, R. E. (1989). Buprenorphine: Dose-related blockade of opioid challenge effects in opioid-dependent humans. *Journal of Pharmacology and Experimental Therapeutics, 247,* 47–53.

Bruno, F. (1989). Buspirone in the treatment of alcoholic patients. *Psychopathology, 22* (suppl), 49–59.

Carrera, R. A., Ashley, J. A., Parsons, L. H., Wirsching, P., Koob, G. F., & Janda, K. D. (1995). Suppression of psychoactive effects of cocaine by active immunization. *Nature, 378,* 727–730.

Carroll, M., Lac, S., Asencio, M., & Kragh, R. (1990). Fluoxetine reduces intravenous cocaine self-administration in the rat. *Pharmacology Biochemistry and Behavior, 35,* 237–244.

Carroll, K. M., Rounsaville, B. J., Gordon, L. T., Nich, C., Jatlow, P., Bisighini, R. M., & Gawin, F. H. (1994). Psychotherapy and pharmacotherapy for ambulatory cocaine abusers. *Archives of General Psychiatry, 51,* 177–187.

Carroll, K., Ziedonis, D., O'Malley, S., McCance-Katz, E., & Rounsaville, B. (1993). Pharmacologic interventions for abusers of alcohol and cocaine: A pilot study of disulfiram versus naltrexone. *American Journal on Addictions, 2,* 77–79.

Charney, D. S., Riordan, C. E., Kleber, H. D., Murburg, M., Braverman, P., Sternberg, D. E., Heninger, G. R., & Redmond, D. E. (1982). Clonidine and naltrexone: A safe, effective and rapid treatment of abrupt withdrawal from methadone therapy. *Archives of General Psychiatry, 39,* 1327–1332.

Cheskin, L. J., Fudala, P. J., & Johnson, R. E. (1994). A controlled comparison of buprenorphine and clonidine for acute detoxification from opioids. *Drug and Alcohol Dependence, 36,* 115–121.

Chick, J., Erickson, C. K., & Amsterdam Consensus Conference Participants (1996). Conference summary: Consensus conference on alcohol dependence and the role of pharmacotherapy in its treatment. *Alcoholism Clinical and Experimental Research, 20,* 391–402.

Chrousos, G. P., & Gold, P. W. (1992) The concepts of stress and stress system disorders: Overview of physical and behavioral homeostasis. *Journal of the American Medical Association, 267,* 1244–1252.

Cornish, J. W., Maany, I., Fudala, P. J., Neal, S., Poole, S. A., Volpicelli, P., & O'Brien, C. P. (1995). Carbamazepine treatment for cocaine dependence. *Drug and Alcohol Dependence, 38,* 221–227.

Covi, L., Montoya, I. D., Hess, J., Kreiter, N. (1994). Double-blind comparison of desipramine and placebo for treatment of cocaine dependence. *Clin Pharmacol Ther, 55,* 132–138.

Dackis, C. A., Gold, M. S., Sweeney, D. R., Byron, J. P., & Climko, R. (1987). Single-dose bromocriptine reverses cocaine craving. *Psychiatry Research, 20,* 261–264.

Das, G. (1993). Cocaine abuse in North America: A milestone in history. *Journal of Clinical Pharmacology, 33,* 296–310.

De Quincey, T. (1907). Confessions of an English opium-eater. New York: E.P. Dutton.

Diakogiannis, I. A., Steinberg, M., & Kosten, T. R. (1990). Mazindol treatment of cocaine abuse. A double-blind investigation. *NIDA Research Monographs,* no. 105, 514.

Di Bello, M. G., Gambassi, F., Mugnai, L., Masini, E., & Mannaioni, P. F. (1995).

Gamma-hydroxybutyric acid induced suppression and prevention of alcohol withdrawal syndrome and relief of craving in alcohol dependent patients. *Alcologia, 7,* 111-118.

Dole, V. P., Robinson, J. W., Orraga, J., Towns, E., Searcy, P., & Caine, E. (1969). Methadone treatment of randomly selected criminal addicts. *New England Journal of Medicine, 280,* 1372-1375.

Doty, P., Zacny, J. P., & de Wit, H. (1994). Effects of ondansetron pretreatment on acute responses to ethanol in social drinkers. *Behavioral Pharmacology, 5,* 461-469.

Editorial (1984). When drug regulation fails. *Lancet, 1,* 718-719.

Fadda, F., Colombo, G., Mosca, E., Gessa, F. L. (1989). Suppression by gamma-hydroxybutyric acid of ethanol withdrawal syndrome in rats. *Alcohol and Alcoholism, 24,* 447-451.

Fiore, M. C., Smith, S. S., Jorenby, D. E., & Baker, T. B. (1994). The effectiveness of the nicotine patch for smoking cessation: A meta analysis. *Journal of the American Medical Association, 271,* 1940-1946.

Fox, B. S., Kantak, K. M., Edwards, M. A., Black, K. M., Bollinger, B. K., Botka, A. J., French, T. L., Thompson, T. L., Schad, V. C., Greenstein, J. L., Gefter, M. L., Exley, M. A., Swain, P. A., & Briner, T. J. (1996). Efficacy of a therapeutic cocaine vaccine in rodent models. *Nature Medicine, 2,* 1129-1132.

Freud, S. (1884). On Coca. *St. Louis Medical and Surgical Journal,* 502-505.

Fudala, P. J., Johnson, R. E., & Jaffe, J. H. (1991). Outpatient comparison of buprenorphine and methadone maintenance: II. Effects on cocaine usage, retention time in study and missed clinic visits. *NIDA Research Monograph,* no. 105, 587-588.

Fuller, R. F., Branchey, L., Brightwell, D. R., Derman, R. M., Emrick, C. D., Iber, F. L., James, K. E., Lacoursiere, R. B., Lee, K. K., & Lowenstam, I. (1986). Disulfiram treatment of alcoholism: A Veterans Administration cooperative study. *Journal of the American Medical Association, 256,* 1449-1455.

Fuller, R. F., & Roth, H. P. (1979). Disulfiram for the treatment of alcoholism: an evaluation in 128 men. *Annals of Internal Medicine, 90,* 901-904.

Galanter, M. (1993). Network therapy for addiction: A model for office practice. *American Journal of Psychiatry, 150,* 28-36.

Galloway, G. & Hayner, G. (1993) Haight-Ashbury free clinics' drug detoxification protocols, part 2: opioid blockade. *Journal of Psychoactive Drugs, 25,* 251-252.

Gastfriend, D. R., Mendelson, J. H., Mello, N. K., Teoh, S. K., & Reif, S. (1993). Buprenorphine pharmacotherapy for concurrent heroin and cocaine dependence. *American Journal of Addiction, 2,* 269-278.

Gawin, F. H., & Kleber, H. D. (1984). Cocaine abuse treatment: Open pilot trial with desipramine and lithium carbonate. *Archives of General Psychiatry, 41,* 903-909.

Gawin, F. H., Kleber, H. D., Byck, R., Rounsaville, B. J., Kosten, T. R., Jatlow, P. I., &

Morgan, C. (1989). Desipramine facilitation of initial cocaine abstinence. *Archives of General Psychiatry, 46,* 117–121.

Giannini, A. J., Baumgartel, P., & DiMarzio, L. R. (1987). Bromocriptine therapy in cocaine withdrawal. *Journal of Clinical Pharmacology, 27,* 267–270.

Giannini, A. J., Folts, D. J., Feather, J. N., & Sullivan, B. S. (1989). Bromocriptine and amantadine in cocaine detoxification. *Psychiatry Research, 29,* 11–16.

Gold, M. S., Redmond, D. E., & Kleber, H. D. (1978). Clonidine for opiate withdrawal. *Lancet, 1,* 929–930.

Gourlay, S. G., & Benowitz, N. L. (1995). Is clonidine an effective smoking cessation therapy? *Drugs, 50,* 197–207.

Grabowski, J., Rhoades, H., Elk, R., Schmitz, J., Davis, C., Creson, D., & Kirby, K. (1995). Fluoxetine is ineffective for treatment of cocaine dependence or concurrent opiate and cocaine dependence: two placebo-controlled, double-blind trials. *Journal of Clinical Psychopharmacology, 15,* 163–174.

Hald, J., Jacobsen, E., & Larsen, V. (1948). The sensitizing effect of tetraethylthiuram disulfide (Antabuse) to ethyl alcohol. *Acta Pharmacology and Toxicology, 4,* 285–296.

Halikas, J., Kemp, K., Kuhn, K., Carlson, G., & Crea F. (1989). Carbamazepine for cocaine addiction? [Letter to the editor]. *Lancet, 1,* p. 623–624.

Hall, S. M., Hall, R. G., & Ginsberg, D. (1990). Pharmacological and behavioral treatments for cigarette smoking. In: M. Hersen, R. M. Eisler, & P. M. Miller (Eds), *Progress in Behavior Modification, 25,* (87–118). Sage Publications, Newbury, Calif.

Helzer, J. E., Burnam, A., & McEvoy, L. T. (1991). Alcohol abuse and dependence. In L. N. Robins & D. A. Regier (eds.), *Psychiatric Disorders in America* (pp. 81–115). New York: Free Press.

Henningfield, J. E., & Keenan, R. M. (1993). Nicotine delivery kinetics and abuse liability. *Journal of Consulting and Clinical Psychology, 61,* 743–750.

Henningfield, J. E., Stapleton, J. M., Benowitz, N. L., Grayson, R. F., & London, E. D. (1993). Higher levels of nicotine in arterial than in venous blood after cigarette smoking. *Drug and Alcohol Dependence, 33,* 23–29.

Hillbom, M., Tokola, R., Kuusela, V., Karkkainen, P., Kalli-Lemma, L., Pilke, A., & Kaste, M. (1989). Prevention of alcohol withdrawal seizures with carbamazepine and valproic acid. *Alcohol, 6,* 223–226.

Hjalmarson, A., Franzon, M., Westin, A., Wiklund, O. (1994). Effect of nicotine nasal spray on smoking cessation: A randomized, placebo-controlled, double-blind study. *Archives of Internal Medicine, 154,* 2567–2572.

Hubbell, C. L., Abelson, M. L., Burkhardt, C. A., Herlands, S. E., & Reid, L. D. (1988). Constant infusions of morphine and intakes of sweetened ethanol solution among rats. *Alcohol, 5,* 409–415.

Hughes, J. R. (1994). Non-nicotine pharmacotherapies for smoking cessation. *Journal of Drug Development, 9*, 197–203.

Hughes, J. R. (1996). Treatment of nicotine dependence. In: C. R. Schuster, S. W. Gust, & M. J. Kuhar (eds.), *Pharmacological aspects of drug dependence: Toward an integrative neurobehavioral approach: Handbook of Experimental Psychology Series* (pp. 599–618). New York: Springer-Verlag.

Humfleet, G., Hall, S. M., Reus, V. I., Munoz, R. F., & Triffleman, E. (1996). The efficacy of nortriptylene as an adjunct to psychological treatment for smokers with and without depressive histories. *NIDA Research Monographs*, no. 162, 334.

Jasinski, D. R., Pevnick, J. S., & Griffith, J. D. (1978). Human pharmacology and abuse potential of the analgesic buprenorphine. *Archives of General Psychiatry, 35*, 510–516.

Johnson, B. A., Campling, G. M., Griffiths, P., & Cowen, P. J. (1993). Attenuation of some alcohol-induced mood changes and the desire to drink by 5-HT3 receptor blockade: A preliminary study in healthy male volunteers. *Psychopharmacology, 112*, 142–144.

Johnson, R. E., Fudala, P. J., & Jaffe, J. H. (1992). A controlled trial of buprenorphine for opioid dependence. *Journal of the American Medical Association, 267*, 2750–2755.

Johnston, A. L., Thevos, A. K., Randall, C. L., & Anton, R. F. (1991). Increased severity of alcohol withdrawal in-patient alcoholics with co-existing anxiety diagnosis. *British Journal of Addiction, 86*, 719–725.

Jorenby, D. E., Smith, S. S., Fiore, M. C., Hurt, R. D., Offord, K. P., Croghan, I. T., Hays, J. T., Lewis, S. F., & Baker, T. B. (1995). Varying nicotine patch dose and type of smoking cessation counseling. *Journal of the American Medical Association, 274*, 1347–1352.

Kahn, A., Mumford, J. P., Rogers, G. A., & Beckford, H. (1997). Double-blind study of lofexidine and clonidine in the detoxification of opiate addicts in hospital. *Drug and Alcohol Dependence, 44*, 57–61.

Kampman, K., Volpicelli, J. R., Alterman, A., Cornish, J., Weinrieb, R., Epperson, L., Sparkman, T., & O'Brien, C. P. (1996). Amantadine in the early treatment of cocaine dependence: a double-blind, placebo-controlled trial. *Drug and Alcohol Dependence, 41*, 25–33.

Kleber, H. D., Topazian, M., Gaspari, J., Riordan, C. E., & Kosten, T. (1987). Clonidine and naltrexone in the outpatient treatment of heroin withdrawal. *American Journal of Drug and Alcohol Abuse, 13*, 1–18.

Kosten, T. R., & Kleber, H. D. (1984). Strategies to improve compliance with narcotic antagonists. *American Journal of Drug and Alcohol Abuse, 10*, 249–266.

Kosten, T. R., & Kleber, H. D. (1988). Buprenorphine detoxification from opioid dependence: A pilot study. *Life Sciences, 42*, 635–641.

Kosten, T. R., Kleber, H. D., & Morgan, C. H. (1989). Treatment of cocaine abuse using buprenorphine. *Biological Psychiatry, 26,* 637–639.

Kosten, T. A., Kosten, T. R., Gawin, F. H., Gordon, L. T., Hogan, I. F., & Kleber, H. D. (1992). An open trial of sertraline for cocaine abuse. *American Journal on Addictions, 1,* 349–353.

Kosten, T. R., Morgan, C. M., Falcioni, J., & Schottenfeld, R. S. (1992). Pharmacotherapy for cocaine-abusing methadone-maintained patients using amantadine or desipramine. *Archives of General Psychiatry, 49,* 894–899.

Kosten, T. R., Schottenfeld, R. S., Ziedonis, D., & Falcioni, J. (1993). Buprenorphine vs. methadone maintenance for opioid dependence. *Journal of Nervous and Mental Disease, 181,* 358–364.

Kosten, T. R., Schumann, B., & Wright, D. (1988). Bromocriptine treatment of cocaine abuse in patients maintained on methadone. *American Journal of Psychiatry, 145,* 381–382.

Kosten, T. R., Steinberg, M., & Diakogiannis, I. (1993). Crossover trial of mazindol for cocaine dependence. *American Journal on Addictions, 2,* 161–164.

Kottke, T. E., Brekke, M. L., Solberg, L. I., & Hughes, J. R. (1989). A randomized trial to increase smoking intervention by physicians: doctors helping smokers, round 1. *Journal of the American Medical Association, 261,* 2101–2106.

Kranzler, H. R., Bauer, L. O., Hersh, D., & Klinghoffer, V. (1995a). Carbamazepine treatment of cocaine dependence-a placebo-controlled trial. *Drug and Alcohol Dependence, 38,* 203–211.

Kranzler, H. R., Burleson, J. A., Del Boca, F. K., Babor, T. F., Korner, P., Brown, J., & Bohn, M. J. (1994). Buspirone treatment of anxious alcoholics: a placebo-controlled trial. *Archives of General Psychiatry, 51,* 720–731.

Kranzler, H. R., Burleson, J. A., Korner, P., Del Boca, F. K., Bohn, M. J., Brown, J., & Liebowita, N. (1995b). Placebo-controlled trial of fluoxetine as an adjunct to relapse prevention in alcoholics. *American Journal of Psychiatry, 152,* 391–397.

Latimer, D., & Goldberg, J. (1981). *Flowers in the blood: The story of opium.* New York: Arno.

Lambie, D. G., Johnson, R. H., Vijayasenan, M. E., & Whiteside, E. A. (1980). Sodium valproate in the treatment of the alcohol withdrawal syndrome. *Australian and New Zealand Journal of Psychiatry, 14,* 213–215.

LeMarquand, D., Pihl, R. O., & Benkelfat, C. (1994). Serotonin and alcohol intake, abuse, and dependence: Clinical evidence. *Biological Psychiatry, 36,* 326–337.

Levin, F. R., & Lehman, A. F. (1991). Meta-analysis of desipramine as an adjunct in the treatment of cocaine addiction. *Journal of Clinical Psychopharmacology, 11,* 374–378.

Ling, W., Charuvastra, V. C., Kaim, S. C., Klett, C. J. (1976). Methadyl acetate and methadone as maintenance treatment for heroin addicts. *Archives of General Psychiatry, 33,* 709–712.

Ling, W., Wesson, D. R., Charuvastra, C., Klett, C. J. (1996). A controlled trial comparing buprenorphine and methadone maintenance in opioid dependence. *Arch Gen Psychiatry, 53,* 401–407.

Littleton, J. (1995). Acamprosate in alcohol dependence: how does it work? *Addiction, 90,* 1179–1188.

Malcolm, R., Ballenger, J. C., Sturgis, E. T., & Anton, R. (1989). Double-blind controlled trial comparing carbamazepine to oxazepam treatment of alcohol withdrawal. *American Journal of Psychiatry, 146,* 617–621.

Margolin, A., Kosten, T. R., Avants, S. K., Wilkins, J., Ling, W., Beckson, M., Arndt, I. O., Cornish, J., Ascher, J. A., & Li, S. H. (1995). A multicenter trial of bupropion for cocaine dependence in methadone-maintained patients. *Drug and Alcohol Dependence, 40,* 125–131.

McCance-Katz, E. F., Kosten, T. R., & Jatlow, P. (1998). Concurrent use of cocaine and alcohol is more potent and potentially more toxic than use of either alone—a multiple-dose study. *Biological Psychiatry, 44,* 250–259.

Naranjo, C. A., Bremner, K. E., & Lanctot, K. L. (1995). Effects of citalopram and a brief psychosocial intervention on alcohol intake, dependence and problems. *Addiction, 90,* 87–99.

Naranjo, C. A., Kadlec, K. E., Sanhueza, P., Woodley-Remus, D., & Sellers, E. M. (1990). Fluoxetine differentially alters alcohol intake and other consummatory behaviors in problem drinkers. *Clinical Pharmacology and Therapeutics, 47,* 490–498.

Naranjo, C. A., Poulos, C. X., Bremner, K. E., & Lanctot, K. L. (1992). Citalopram decreases desirability, liking, and consumption of alcohol in alcohol-dependent drinkers. *Clinical Pharmacology and Therapeutics, 51,* 729–739.

Naranjo, C. A., Sellers, E. M., Roach, C. A., Woodley, D. V., Sanchez-Craig, M., & Sykora, K. (1984). Zimeldine-induced variations in alcohol intake by nondepressed heavy drinkers. *Clinical Pharmacology and Therapeutics, 35,* 374–381.

Naranjo, C. A., Sellers, E. M., Sullivan, J. T., Woodley, D. V., Kadlec, K., & Sykora, K. (1987). The serotonin uptake inhibitor citalopram attenuates ethanol intake. *Clinical Pharmacology and Therapeutics,* 41, 266–274.

Oliveto, A. H., Kosten, T. R., Schottenfeld, R., Ziedonis, D., & Falcioni, J. (1994). A comparison of cocaine use in buprenorphine- and methadone-maintained cocaine users. *American Journal on Addictions, 3,* 43–48.

O'Malley, S. S., Jaffe, A. J., Chang, G., Schottenfeld, M. D., Meyer, R. E., & Rounsaville, B. J. (1992). Naltrexone and coping skills therapy for alcohol dependence: A controlled study. *Archives of General Psychiatry, 49,* 894–898.

Perkins, K. A., Grobe, J. E., Epstein, L. H., Caggiula, A., Stiller, R. L., & Jacob, R. G. (1993). Chronic and acute tolerance to subjective effects of nicotine. *Pharmacology, Biochemistry and Behavior, 45,* 375–381.

Preston, K. L., Sullivan, J. T., Berger, S. P., Bigelow, G. E. (1993). Effects of cocaine alone and in combination with mazindol in human cocaine abusers. *Journal of Pharmacology and Experimental Therapeutics, 267,* 849–868.

Ray, O., & Ksir, C. (1996). *Drugs, society, and behavior,* 7th ed. St. Louis, Mo.: Mosby.

Reid, L. D., & Hunter, G. A. (1984). Morphine and naloxone modulate intake of ethanol. *Alcohol, 1,* 33–37.

Richardson, N., & Roberts, D. (1991). Fluoxetine pretreatment reduces breaking points on a progressive ratio schedule reinforced by intravenous cocaine self-administration in the rat. *Life Sciences, 49,* 833–840.

Romach, M. K., & Sellers, E. M. (1991). Management of alcohol withdrawal syndrome. *Annual Review of Medicine, 42,* 323–340.

Rose, J. E., Behm, F. M., Westman, E. C., Levin, E. D., Stein, R. M., Lane, J. D., & Ripka, G. V. (1994a). Combined effects of nicotine and mecamylamine in attenuating smoking satisfaction. *Experimental and Clinical Psychopharmacology, 2,* 328–344.

Rose, J. E., Behm, F. M., Westman, E. C., Levin, E. D., Stein, R. M., & Ripka, G. V. (1994b). Mecamylamine combined with nicotine skin patch facilitates smoking cessation beyond nicotine patch treatment alone. *Clinical Pharmacology, 56,* 86–99.

Roy-Byrne, P. P., Ward, N. G., & Donnelly, P. J. (1989). Valproate in anxiety and withdrawal syndromes. *Journal of Clinical Psychiatry, 50* (suppl), 44–48.

Sachs, D. P. L. (1995). Effectiveness of the 4-mg dose of nicotine polacrilex for the initial treatment of high-dependent smokers. *Archives of Internal Medicine, 155,* 1973–1980.

San, L., Pomarol, G., Peri, J.M., Olle, J.M., Cami, J. (1991). Follow-up after a six-month maintenance period on naltrexone versus placebo in heroin addicts. *British Journal of Addiction, 86,* 983–990.

Sass, H., Soyka, M., Mann, K., & Zieglgansberger, W. (1996). Relapse prevention by acamprosate. *Archives of General Psychiatry, 53,* 673–680.

Schneider, N. G., Jarvik, M. E., Forsythe, A. B., Read, L. L., Elliott, M. L., & Schweiger, A. (1983). Nicotine gum in smoking cessation: a placebo-controlled, double-blind trial. *Addictive Behaviors, 8,* 253–261.

Schneider, N. G., Olmstead, R., Mody, F. R., Doan, K., Franzon, M., Jarvik, M. E., Steinberg, C. (1995). Efficacy of a nicotine nasal spray in smoking cessation: a placebo-controlled, double-blind trial. *Addiction, 90,* 1671–1682.

Schottenfeld, R. S., Pakes, J., Ziedonis, D. M., & Kosten, T. R. (1993). Buprenorphine: Dose related effects on cocaine and opiate use in cocaine-abusing opioid-dependent humans. *Biological Psychiatry, 34,* 66–74.

Self, D. W., Barnhart, W. J., Lehman, D. A., & Nestler, E. J. (1996). Opposite modulation of cocaine-seeking behavior by D1 and D2-like dopamine receptor agonists. *Science, 271,* 1586–1589.

Sellers, E. M. (1988). Alcohol, barbiturate and benzodiazepine withdrawal syndromes: Clinical management. *Canadian Medical Association Journal, 139,* 113–120.

Senay, E. C. & Uchtenhagen, A. (1990). Methadone in the treatment of opioid dependence: a review of the world literature. In: J. Westermeyer & A. Arif (eds.), *Methadone maintenance in the management of opioid dependence: An international review* (pp. 19–54). New York: Praeger.

Shi, J. M., O'Connor, P. G., Constantino, J. A., Carroll, K. M., Schottenfeld, R. S., & Rounsaville, B. J. (1993). Three methods of ambulatory opiate detoxification: Preliminary results of a randomized clinical trial. *NIDA Research Monographs,* no. 132, 309.

Shufman, E. N., Porat, S., Witzum, E., Gandacu, D., Bar-Hamburger, R. & , Ginath, Y. (1994). The efficacy of naltrexone in preventing reabuse of heroin after detoxification. *Biological Psychiatry, 35,* 935–945.

Silagy, C., Mant, D., Fowler, G., & Lodge, M. (1994). Meta-analysis on efficacy of nicotine replacement therapies in smoking cessation. *Lancet, 343,* 139–142.

Singha, A., Oliveto, A., McCance, E., Petrakis, I., Stine, S., & Kosten, T. R. (1998). Effects of cocaine prior to and during bupropion maintenance in cocaine abusers. *NIDA Research Monographs, 178,* 137.

Sonderskov, J., Olsen, J., Sabroe, S., Meillier, L., & Overvad, K. (1997). Nicotine patches in smoking cessation: a randomized trial among over-the-counter customers in Denmark. *American Journal of Epidemiology, 145,* 309–318.

Stephenson, J. (1997). Experts debate merits of 1-day opiate detoxification under anesthesia. *Journal of the American Medical Association, 277,* 363–364.

Stine, S. M., Krystal, J. H., Kosten, T. R., & Charney, D. S. (1995). Mazindol treatment for cocaine dependence. *Drug and Alcohol Dependence, 39,* 245–252.

Strain, E. C., Stitzer, M. L., Liebson, I. A., & Bigelow, G. E. (1994). Buprenorphine versus methadone in the treatment of opioid-dependent cocaine users. *Psychopharmacology, 116,* 401–406.

Stuppaeck, C. H., Pycha, R., Miller, C., Withworth, A. B., Oberbauer, H., & Fleischhacker, W. W. (1992). Carbamazepine versus oxazepam in the treatment of alcohol withdrawal: A double-blind study. *Alcohol and Alcoholism, 27,* 153–158.

Sutherland, G., Stapleton, J. A., Russell, M. A. H., Jarvis, M. J., Hajek, P. Belcher, M., & Feyerabend, C. (1992). Randomised controlled trial of nasal nicotine spray in smoking cessation. *Lancet, 340,* 324–329.

Tennant, F. S., & Sagherian, A. A. (1987). Double-blind comparison of amantadine and bromocriptine for ambulatory withdrawal from cocaine dependence. *Archives of Internal Medicine, 147,* 109–112.

Tollefson, G. D., Montague-Clouse, J., & Tollefson, S. L. (1992). Treatment of comorbid generalized anxiety in a recently detoxified alcohol population with a selective serotonergic drug (buspirone). *Journal of Clinical Psychopharmacology, 12,* 19–26.

Ulm, R. R., Volpicelli, J. R., & Volpicelli, L. A. (1995). Opiates and alcohol self-administration in animals. *Journal of Clin Psychiatry, 56,* suppl 7, 5–14.

United States Public Health Service (1988). *The health consequences of smoking: Nicotine addiction: A report of the surgeon general.* (DHHS Publication No. (CDC) 88-8406). Washington, D.C.: U.S. Government Printing Office.

Van Etten, M. L., Higgins, S. T., Budney, A. J., Bickel, W. K., Hughes, J. R., & Foerg, F. (1994). Disulfiram therapy in patients abusing cocaine and alcohol. *NIDA Research Monographs,* no. 141, 443.

Vining, E., Kosten, T. R., & Kleber, H. D. (1988). Clinical utility of rapid clonidine naltrexone detoxification for opioid abusers. *British Journal of Addiction, 83,* 567–575.

Volpicelli, J. R., Alterman, A. I., Hagashida, M., & O'Brien, C. P. (1992). Naltrexone in the treatment of alcohol dependence. *Archives of General Psychiatry, 49,* 867–880.

Walsh, S. L., Preston, K. L., Sullivan, J. T., Framme, R., & Bigelow, G. E. (1994). Fluoxetine alters the effects of intravenous cocaine in humans. *Journal of Clinical Psychopharmacology, 14,* 396–407.

Weddington, W. W., Brown, B. S., Haertzen, C. A., Hess, J. M. Mahaffey, J. R. Kolar, A. F., & Jaffe, J. H. (1991). Comparison of amantadine and desipramine combined with psychotherapy for treatment of cocaine dependence. *American Journal of Drug and Alcohol Abuse, 17,* 137–152.

Whitworth, A. B., Fischer, F., Lesch, O. M., Nimmerrrichter, A., Oberbauer, H., Platz, T., Potgieter, A., Walter, H., Fleischhacker, W. W., et al. (1996). Comparison of acamprosate and placebo in long-term treatment of alcohol dependence. *Lancet, 347,* 1438–1442.

Wozniak, K. M., Pert, A., & Linnoila, M. (1990). Antagonism of 5-HT$_3$ receptors attenuates the effects of ethanol on extracellular dopamine. *European Journal of Pharmacology, 187,* 287–289.

Zeise, M. L., Kasparov, S., Capogna, M., & Zieglgansberger, W. (1993). Acamprosate (calcium acetylhomotaurinate) decreases postsynaptic potentials in the rat neocortex: Possible involvement of excitatory amino acid receptors. *European Journal of Pharmacology, 231,* 47–52.

FOURTEEN

RELAPSE TO OPIOID AND COCAINE USE FOLLOWING METHADONE TREATMENT

Kirk M. Broome, D. Dwayne Simpson, & George W. Joe

The major outcome studies in the area of drug abuse treatment have established several facts about addiction and treatment. Treatment has a generally rehabilitative effect, with longer stays resulting in greater improvement, but some clients will return to use despite therapeutic intervention (Hubbard et al., 1989; Simpson, 1993, 1997; Simpson & Sells, 1982, 1990). The reality of relapse is frustrating for treatment providers. In the case of opioids, for example, approximately 60% of clients who used heavily before treatment relapse to some level of use in the year following treatment (Hubbard & Marsden, 1986; Simpson & Marsh, 1986). Evaluators and clinicians share a desire to reduce this rate.

Treatment outcome studies have identified several characteristics of likely relapsers. First, users of particular drugs or combinations of drugs were more likely to return to use. Clients addicted to heroin or who used multiple drugs relapsed in greater numbers (Hubbard & Marsden, 1986). Second, clients with poorer social adjustment (e.g., less employment and greater jail time)

This work was funded by the National Institute on Drug Abuse (Grant No. R01-DA06162). The interpretations and conclusions, however, do not necessarily represent the position of NIDA or the Department of Health and Human Services. Correspondence: Institute of Behavioral Research, Texas Christian University, TCU Box 298740, Fort Worth, TX 76129. More information (including data instruments that can be downloaded) is available on the Internet at *www.ibr.tcu.edu* and electronic mail can be sent to *ibr@tcu.edu*.

had higher risks of relapse (Simpson & Marsh, 1986). Importantly, clients who began treatment with better social adjustment as well as others who improved social functioning during treatment had more promising outcomes, pointing to the role of one's general social support network for sustained recovery.

These studies also have explored the complicated nature of the relapse and recovery constructs. In particular, relapse can be defined in several ways, so characterizing a relapse episode according to type of drug used and frequency of use simplifies the definition (Hubbard & Marsden, 1986; Simpson & Marsh, 1986). Resumed use of the same drug and shifting to a new drug (i.e., substitution) are qualitatively different aspects of returning to use. Likewise, posttreatment use that is less frequent than pretreatment use may be considered a step toward recovery.

Despite the improved understanding of relapse and recovery gained from these treatment evaluations, it is not clear that this information generalizes entirely to contemporary clients. The treatment system has continued to evolve and the major modalities have become increasingly diverse in clinical practice, funding sources, and clientele. Where earlier studies could safely draw conclusions about drug abusers in general, for example, current research results must often be qualified as applying specifically to methadone programs or therapeutic communities. We restrict our consideration of relapse and recovery in the present study to the contemporary outpatient methadone treatment (OMT) setting.

HISTORICAL CHANGES

Over the past thirty years, the clientele served by OMT clinics has changed, with cocaine users becoming increasingly common in this opioid-oriented modality. Figure 14.1 illustrates this shift. Among treatment admissions to the Drug Abuse Reporting Program (DARP), from 1969 to 1973 one-third of OMT clients used cocaine in the year before entering treatment, and only a trivial percentage indicated daily use (Simpson, Savage, Joe, Demaree, & Sells, 1976). By 1991 to 1993, the years of admission for the Drug Abuse Treatment Outcome Study (DATOS), two-thirds of OMT clients were reporting cocaine use and nearly one in four was a daily user (DATOS, 1995).

The emergence of cocaine has introduced an array of problems for methadone treatment providers. These clients undertake an especially difficult road to recovery because they typically confront problems with multiple drugs, a long history of dysfunction, and a pattern of failure in previous recovery attempts. Furthermore, the major therapeutic agent in the OMT regimen—

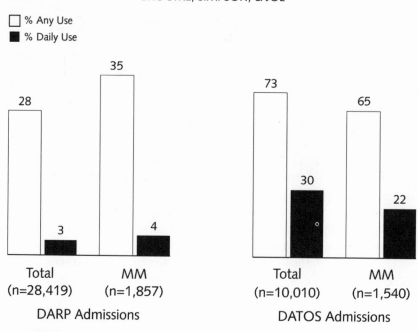

Fig. 14.1. Pretreatment cocaine use by clients admitted to DARP and DATOS.

the methadone compound—does not block the effects of cocaine (Avants, Margolin, & Kosten, 1994). Indeed there is some evidence suggesting that the action of methadone and cocaine in combination is similar to the "speedball" blend of heroin and cocaine (Condelli, Fairbank, Dennis, & Rachal, 1991), which is the primary drug problem for many of these clients. Consequently, treating cocaine abuse in OMT settings requires greater emphasis on counseling and other psychosocial components. The search continues for effective clinical protocols in this treatment area (Rawson, McCann, Hasson, & Ling, 1994). Cocaine abusers in OMT represent an extreme subpopulation whose needs may not be met adequately.

PROFILE OF THE COCAINE USER IN OMT

The behavior patterns of OMT clients who use cocaine as well as opioids are distinct from those of the more traditional opioid-only clients. These behaviors tend to be problematic for the client and inconsistent with the goals and strategies of OMT treatment.

Cocaine users in OMT usually have greater risk for HIV infection than their opioid-only counterparts. They use dirty or borrowed needles more frequently (Chaisson et al., 1989) and often report more preadmission sexual risk-taking as well (Broome, Joe, & Simpson, 1999). Especially troubling is the observation by Magura and colleagues (Magura, Kang, Shapiro, & O'Day, 1993) that nonusing women engaged in more risky sexual behavior during encounters with men who were using crack. OMT helps reduce risks of HIV infection by reducing behaviors that promote transmission (Ball, Lange, Myers, & Friedman, 1988). However, the risk-reduction benefits depend in part on level of reductions in drug use (Magura, Siddiqi, Freeman, & Lipton, 1991), so if clients continue to use cocaine, their HIV-risk benefits may be much more limited.

OMT clients with a cocaine problem are often criminally involved as well. In one sample of clients on steady maintenance doses, those who used cocaine were more likely than nonusers to commit property crimes or to be involved in drug dealing (Hunt, Spunt, Lipton, Goldsmith, & Strug, 1986). The more frequently these clients used cocaine, the more crimes they committed. For example, 79% of daily users had engaged in property crime during the two-week period prior to the interview (Hunt et al., 1986). Anecdotally, many clients admitted they were motivated toward crime to pay for cocaine; however, cocaine-using OMT clients also are characterized by other indicators of deviance, including hostility and antisocial personality (Broome, 1996; Ziedonis, 1992).

Unfortunately, response to the OMT treatment experience tends to be poorer among cocaine users. Such clients have a difficult time complying with program rules and policies. The primary goal for treatment is reduced drug use; clients sometimes successfully reduce or eliminate cocaine consumption during treatment (e.g., Hanbury, Sturiano, Cohen, Stimmel, & Aguillaume, 1986; Magura et al., 1991), but others continue taking the drug and a few initiate use of cocaine (Hanbury et al., 1986; Rawson et al., 1994). Half the sample interviewed by Hanbury and colleagues (1986) reported cocaine use during a six-month period of OMT, including 14% who had no pretreatment use. In-treatment users tend to drop out of OMT earlier (Broome, 1996; Lamb, Kirby, & Platt, 1996), and shorter stays mean both less opportunity to benefit from treatment and poorer long-term outcomes (e.g., Gerstein & Harwood, 1990).

In summary, cocaine users enter OMT with a broad range of problems and a clear need for assistance, but they are frequently unwilling or unable to cooperate with recovery efforts. Methadone medications during treatment address only part of their problems.

THE DATAR PROJECT

Our Drug Abuse Treatment for AIDS-Risk Reduction (DATAR—Phase 1) project was a multisite study of methadone treatment agencies. General goals were to improve therapeutic interventions for drug abusers and to better understand the treatment dynamics involved. This included enhanced strategies for engaging clients in treatment, reductions in early dropout, and improved the quality of care to reduce relapse rates and related HIV/AIDS risks (Simpson, Chatham, & Joe, 1993).

DATAR provided an opportunity to study cocaine users during and after OMT treatment. This contemporary treatment sample—admitted between 1990 and 1993—was monitored throughout their stay and followed one year after discharge, enabling us to reexamine what has been reported about cocaine users in previous studies of OMT programs. In particular, clients in this DATAR admission cohort comprised three groups with respect to cocaine use. The first, designated "Heavy" users, reported pretreatment use either daily or several times a week (36% of total sample). Next, the "Some" use group reported taking the drug no more than once each week (33%). The "None" group indicated no use of cocaine at treatment entry (31%). These groups represent the range of clients treated in OMT settings. Clients in the None group are more traditional opioid-only addicts, while the heavy cocaine use group represents the most extreme users, with addiction to both opioids and cocaine.

OBJECTIVES

In this study we address the impact of cocaine use among opioid addicts in two phases. First, we examine the relationship between pretreatment cocaine use and treatment engagement. The details of engagement (e.g., retention) indicate a client's commitment and in general reflect the "dose" of treatment received. With this information, we can evaluate whether the evolution of OMT in response to challenges like cocaine addiction has yielded progress in the capacity to treat these clients. Second, we consider drug use and other behaviors following treatment for these three groups. The long-term prognosis for cocaine users in a traditionally opioid-oriented program of care must be considered to determine the appropriateness of such clients for this modality. This information is also important to a broader understanding of relapse and recovery.

METHOD

ADMISSION SAMPLE

Daily opioid users ($N = 711$) admitted to three publicly funded methadone treatment programs during 1990 to 1993 were studied as part of a federally funded project for developing and evaluating therapeutic enhancement strategies (Simpson, Dansereau, & Joe, 1997). No-fee services were offered as an incentive to participate in the research, and written informed consent was obtained after treatment and data collection procedures had been fully explained. This cohort of admissions had the opportunity to stay in treatment provided through the project for at least a full year and was the focus of the 12-month posttreatment follow-up evaluation phase.

Average age of the clients was 37 years; 71% were male, and 43% were Mexican American, 36% Caucasian, and 16% African American. Almost half (44%) were married or living as married, and 62% had graduated from high school or received a GED. Only 57% had worked full-time or part-time during the 6 months before intake, and 34% had been arrested once or more during that time; 48% were legally involved (primarily parole) but less than 5% had been officially referred to treatment by legal authorities. After opioids, cocaine was the next most common drug used. Over two-thirds (69%) of the sample had used cocaine in the 6 months prior to treatment — 28% used it daily, 17% weekly, and 24% less than weekly (crack was used by only 13%).

At the end of the first year following admission, 25% of the sample was still in treatment (55% stayed less than 6 months, and 36% left within the first 90 days). By that time, almost half (46%) had terminated treatment "against medical advice" (AMA), 9% had transferred to other programs, 8% were discharged due to prolonged incarceration, 8% were terminated for noncompliance (such a violence or dealing drugs), and 4% were discharged for other reasons.

FOLLOW-UP SAMPLE

Clients were located and interviewed by trained follow-up workers approximately 12 months after official discharge from treatment. The interview was similar in structure and content to the one completed at intake and required approximately 80 minutes to complete. Respondents were paid $20 for finishing it, plus an additional $5 for a urine specimen. Teams of trained interviewers located 643 (90%) of the 711 former clients, but some could not be interviewed; for instance, 21 (3%) were deceased, 14 (2%) refused to be interviewed, and 3 (1%) were medically incapacitated. Another 36 (5%) had moved out of the targeted interviewing area (i.e., a radius of about one hundred miles around the city) and were inaccessible for personal interview, while 134 (19%) were in prison serving long-term sentences. Interviews were successfully completed for 435 clients, representing 61% of the 711 cases in the total sample. However, if the 194 persons who were unavailable for the follow-up study are omitted from the target sample—i.e., those who were deceased or medically incapacitated, had moved out of the area, or were in prison—then the 435 interviewed cases represent an 84% interview rate.

The high number of prison incarcerations at follow-up deserves special comment. First, the study was conducted during the years of a rapid statewide expansion of prison facilities in Texas, and as reported by Turner and Petersilia (1992), the state experienced an increasing rate of parole revocations. The majority of these revocations occurred in conjunction with legislative initiatives for "intensive supervision" and the simultaneous lengthening of prison terms due to truth-in-sentencing laws. We found, for instance, that 81% of our treatment clients who were imprisoned at follow-up had some form of legal involvement at the time of admission to treatment, including 63% who had been on parole. These rates were twice the levels observed for nonimprisoned clients who were located for follow-up and successfully interviewed. Former clients who were in prison, of course, could not be evaluated for drug use, criminal activities, and related outcome criteria during the follow-up period, so this subsample was not interviewed.

Concerns about potential sampling bias caused by these exclusions were addressed using a logistic regression analysis to compare the imprisoned and nonimprisoned subsamples. From the set of sociodemographic background, drug use, and criminal history variables examined, only the preadmission measure of current legal status (primarily parole) was a statistically significant predictor. There were no significant differences on the broader set of measures representing age, gender, race-ethnicity, marital status, education, criminal history, or drug use history. There also were no significant differences between them in causes of treatment discharge. Overall, we could find no evidence that systematic sampling bias occurred by excluding those imprisoned at the time of follow-up (see Hiller, Simpson, Broome, & Joe, 1997, for more information on this issue).

TREATMENT PROCEDURES

Counseling followed a brief therapy model with emphasis on problem solving, case management, and cognitively based enhancements of communications using a visual representation strategy (Dansereau, Dees, Greener, & Simpson, 1995; Dansereau, Joe, & Simpson, 1993). Clients were encouraged to attend at least one counseling session weekly, although program policy based on state guidelines required only one session per month. Attendance was influenced by client cooperation, counselor judgments of problems, therapeutic needs, and scheduling considerations. Methadone dosages averaged between 40 and 50 mg at the three treatment programs and ranged up to 90 mg per day. These levels fell below recommended therapeutic standards (Cooper, 1992), but they were nonetheless representative of national trends at the time of the study as indicated by survey findings that two-thirds of contemporary methadone programs in the United States provided average doses of 50 mg or less (D'Aunno & Vaughn, 1992).

MEASURES

A comprehensive set of intake, during-treatment, and follow-up data collection instruments was used to record information about client, counselor, and treatment process over time (Simpson, 1992). The intake and follow-up assessments each addressed sociodemographic characteristics, family background, peer relations, criminal history, health and psychological status, drug use history, and behavioral risks for HIV/AIDS. Both asked about total drug injection frequencies and 15 specific types of drug use (including alcohol) in the preceding 30 days and 6 months (with 9 frequency of use codes, ranging from "never used" to "4 or more times per day"). In addition, standardized seven-drug full-screen urinalyses (UAs) were performed on follow-up urine specimens using the enzyme multiplication immunoassay technique (EMIT). Test results for opioid and cocaine metabolites were reported as negative or positive, and reliability of self-reports at follow-up was supported by high agreements (above 80%) with UAs (Simpson, Joe, Dansereau, & Chatham, 1997).

In order to present the most accurate information possible with regard to drug use outcomes at follow-up, we combined self-report and urinalysis data for this study. That is, "daily use" of both opioids and cocaine was defined on the basis of (1) self-reported use of one or more times per day in the last 6 months before the interview, or (2) having a positive urinalysis for the drug at follow-up. Criminality measures were based on self-reports of involvement in illegal activities, arrests, and incarcerations in the last 6 months prior to intake and follow-up interviews. Information also was obtained via client self-report concerning full-time and part-time employment.

As described above, the sample was subdivided into three groups accord-

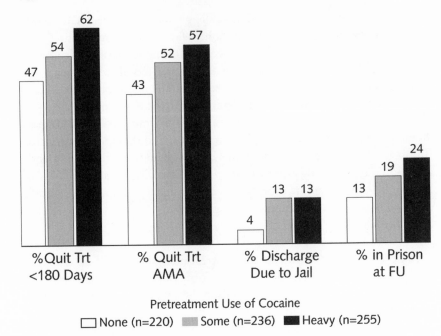

Fig. 14.2. MM treatment retention, discharge, and follow-up status.

ing to frequency of cocaine use. Thirty-six percent ($n = 255$) used cocaine daily or several times a week, 33% ($n = 236$) used cocaine less than weekly, 31% ($n = 220$) did not use cocaine. Outcomes are summarized within these groups.

RESULTS

TREATMENT ENGAGEMENT

Our first objective was to examine indicators of treatment engagement. Figure 14.2 summarizes some characteristics of treatment experiences: retention, conditions of discharge, and follow-up status. The Heavy group terminated earliest (χ^2 (2; $N = 711$) = 10.47, $p < .01$). Sixty-two percent of the Heavy group had less than 180 days of treatment, compared with 47% of None and 54% of Some clients. Consistent with their shorter stay, the Heavy cocaine users attended fewer counseling sessions (14) than the other two groups (20 each) during their course of treatment ($F(2,708) = 6.40$, $p < .002$).

Cocaine use also was related to type of discharge from treatment, as shown by the sets of bars in the center of figure 14.2. Heavy cocaine users were more

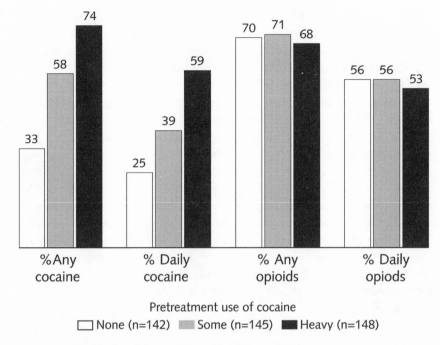

Fig. 14.3. Drug use in year following MM treatment.

likely to quit treatment AMA than the None group (χ^2 (2; N = 711) = 9.56, $p < .01$). Furthermore, 13% of both the Heavy and Some use groups were discharged from treatment due to long-term incarceration, compared with 4% of the None group (χ^2 (2; N = 711) = 13.19, $p < .001$). The cocaine users also were more likely to be in prison at the time of the 1-year follow-up (χ^2 (2; N = 711) = 8.27, $p < .02$).

These results reflect the difficulty of engaging cocaine-using clients in OMT treatment. Such clients typically experienced shorter, less productive treatment episodes that often concluded in a decision to leave or being sentenced to jail. Thus, the clients most in need of treatment received less of it, diminishing their prognosis for favorable outcomes following discharge.

POSTTREATMENT DRUG USE

Figure 14.3 shows rates of cocaine and opioid use after treatment for the follow-up interviewed sample. Continued or renewed use of opioids was common for all groups. For each, about 70% reported any use and just over half resumed daily use. However, the left portion of figure 14.3 shows there were substantial group differences in relapse rates for cocaine. The prevalence of any cocaine use followed an increasing pattern across the groups, with approximately one-third, one-half, and three-quarters reporting "any" use (χ^2 (2; $N = 435$) = 48.84, $p < .001$). There was a parallel trend for daily cocaine use (χ^2 (2; $N = 435$) = 32.63, $p < .001$).

These results also illuminate some important recovery trends. At intake, of course, virtually all clients were daily opioid users. One year after treatment, approximately 30% reported no opioid use, and an additional 15% had reduced their use below their previous daily levels. The Heavy cocaine group began treatment with levels of cocaine use comparable to opioid use in the sample. At follow-up, 26% of this group reported no cocaine use and 15% reported less than daily use—figures similar to those observed for opioids in the total sample. The pattern for the None and Some groups is more complex. Although these groups report lower cocaine prevalence at follow-up than the Heavy group—and 42% of Some clients reported abstention from the drug—many actually *increased* their use. By the Year 1 interview, one in four nonusers and more than one in three occasional users had become daily consumers of cocaine.

Logistic regression analytic models were used to relate the use of opioids and cocaine to treatment engagement measures and a set of background characteristics. The results are summarized in table 14.1. The one commonality between the models was the impact of longer treatment stays. Each additional month of treatment was associated with a 6–7% reduction in the likelihood of later use. For opioids, the only other significant predictor was pretreatment desire for help, a measure of treatment motivation (Simpson & Joe, 1993). The primary attribute distinguishing posttreatment cocaine users was pretreatment level of use. Cocaine use at follow-up was about three times more likely in the group with some use, and about five times more likely in the Heavy group. In addition, cocaine relapsers tended to be younger, female, and African American. These multivariate results suggest that understanding and anticipating relapse depend primarily on treatment duration and prior drug use. Clients with longer treatment were less likely to relapse; and as expected, those who did relapse tended to return to the same drugs they had used most heavily in the past.

OTHER OUTCOMES

Other outcomes at follow-up parallel the drug use differences observed between cocaine groups. The pattern of results in figure 14.4 points to the added difficulty that heavy cocaine use imposes on the opioid user seeking to recover. The group with no pretreatment cocaine use was less likely than the others to drink alcohol on a daily basis (χ^2 (2; $N = 435$) = 6.09, $p < .05$). In addition, reports of illegal activity increased across the groups (χ^2 (2; $N = 435$) = 7.45, $p < .05$). Finally, the heavy cocaine use group was the most likely to rely on welfare as their major financial support, and least likely to rely on a job (χ^2 (6; $N = 435$) = 14.36, $p < .05$). Overall, the posttreatment behavior of the heavy cocaine use group was not consistent with a successful and sustained recovery effort.

DISCUSSION

The traditional view of the cocaine-using OMT client as being difficult to treat is largely supported by the present findings. Our groups with pretreatment involvement in cocaine tended to drop out of treatment earlier, leave AMA or go directly to jail, and be in prison at follow-up. These are not the attributes of successful clients. Indeed, at the Year 1 follow-up the cocaine groups were more likely to be using cocaine or alcohol and to be engaging in criminal activity. Although many of these clients made some progress in reducing or eliminating cocaine use, overall evidence of improvement and social adjustment was much less encouraging.

Relapse patterns, however, are complex. In our multivariate models, no pretreatment variable was predictive of both opioid and cocaine use at follow-up. Pretreatment cocaine use was related to posttreatment cocaine use, but not to opioid use, and approximately half of the overall sample relapsed to daily opioid use. Typically, clients relapsed to their most preferred drugs. Hubbard and Marsden (1986) describe similar outcomes for clients in the Treatment Outcome Prospective Study (TOPS). They found that, among clients who relapse, it was typical for them to return to the same usage pattern exhibited before treatment. For example, 68% of relapsers in the heroin-only group resumed use of heroin only; in comparison, only 14% of relapsers in this group reported a posttreatment use pattern that included other narcotics. In our sample, all had used opioids daily before treatment, and opioids continued to be a problem. The heavy cocaine use group showed comparable rates of relapse to cocaine. In contrast, if clients in the group with no pretreatment cocaine use relapsed, they typically returned to opioids alone.

What is problematic for treatment planning is the large subgroup of clients in the groups with none or some use who either begin or increase their cocaine use following treatment. This is not an unusual finding. Hanbury et al. (1986) found OMT clients who first began cocaine use during treatment, and the TOPS findings (Hubbard & Marsden, 1986) suggest that opioid users

Table 14.1. Prediction summary for any use of opioids and any use of cocaine one year after MM treatment

PREDICTOR	OPIOIDS				COCAINE			
	R	B	OR	% CHANGE	R	B	OR	% CHANGE
Months in treatment	-.15**	-.08**		-7.4	-.17***	-.06**		-6.0
Heavy cocaine (intake)	-.03	-.23	.79		.27****	1.59****	4.89	
Some cocaine (intake)	.02	.11	1.12		.04	1.04****	2.83	
Desire for help (intake)	-.13**	-.47*		-37	-.06	-.25		-22
Age (intake)	.03	.00		.4	-.10*	-.03*		-3.4
Male	.02	-.14	.87		-.02	-.05*	.95	
Race ethnicity								
Black	.01	.33	1.39		.13**	.80*	2.23	

Mexican American	.10*	.41	1.51	.02	.33	1.39
White (reference)	−.08			−.15**		
Highest grade (intake)	−.13**	−.08	−7.2	−.06	−.04	−3.5
Marital status at intake						
Never married	−.04	−.24	.79	.04	.21	1.23
WSD marital status	.04	.10	1.10	.04	.21	1.24
Married (reference)	−.01			−.07		
Arrested in 6 mo (intake)	−.00	−.11	.89	.04	−.18	.83
Legal status (intake)	−.04	−.28	.75	.04	−.02	.98
Intercept	na	3.65		na	1.97	
Statistical test						
−2log likelihood	$\chi^2(13; N = 435) = 28.65$**			$\chi^2(13; N = 435) = 70.71$****		
Score	$\chi^2(13; N = 435) = 27.48$**			$\chi^2(13; N = 435) = 66.85$****		

*$p<.05$, **$p<.01$, ***$p<.001$, ****$p<.0001$

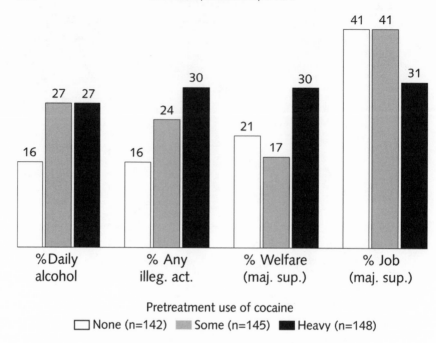

Pretreatment use of cocaine

☐ None (n=142) ▨ Some (n=145) ■ Heavy (n=148)

Fig. 14.4. Other outcomes in year following MM treatment.

are more likely to migrate to cocaine use following treatment than cocaine users are to move in the opposite direction. Overall, 36% of TOPS clients with occasional or no use of cocaine before treatment reported posttreatment use. Of course, both of these studies relied on data collected during the 1980s, a time when cocaine was still gaining prominence as a drug of abuse. Consequently, one interpretation of these findings might be that they do not reflect longitudinal changes for individual users, but instead reflect historical changes in drug availability and popularity. The pattern of opioid users changing to cocaine use appears in DATAR as well, based on data that are more contemporary and collected at a time when cocaine use was somewhat less prevalent (see Condelli et al., 1991). The consistency of this pattern of findings over time therefore reinforces the seriousness of the cocaine problem in treatment samples and indicates the need to address it.

TREATMENT INNOVATIONS

To improve treatment outcomes for cocaine users, it is important first to know more about relevant aspects of the therapeutic process. The DATAR project was designed for assessing and improving treatment services and experiences, and a number of findings are relevant here. As described in this study, clients with greater pretreatment cocaine use left treatment earlier and tended to either quit AMA or become incarcerated. They also attended fewer counseling sessions. Other DATAR studies have addressed these issues in the broader context of treatment process. The sequence of events seems to be as follows: although counseling can help reduce cocaine use, these clients attend fewer sessions and tend to continue using cocaine during the early phases of treatment (Joe, Dansereau, & Simpson, 1994; Simpson, Joe, Rowan-Szal, & Greener, 1995). Both low session attendance and continued drug use are associated with dropout (Simpson, Joe, Rowan-Szal, & Greener, 1997). Early dropouts, in turn, have poorer posttreatment outcomes (Simpson, Joe, & Rowan-Szal, 1997). Many of these findings have been replicated in other OMT programs (e.g., Broome, 1996).

This treatment process sequence implies that improving outcomes for cocaine users in OMT means first promoting participation in counseling efforts and reduction of cocaine use during treatment. Accomplishing these initial goals helps keep clients in programs and engage them in early recovery. As previously discussed, however, even these short-term goals are often difficult for OMT programs to achieve. The methadone compound clearly is not sufficient, so additional interventions are needed.

In a review of approaches for dealing with cocaine use among OMT clients, Rawson and colleagues (1994) describe a promising intervention protocol, including contingency management and relapse prevention. Contingency management (CM) techniques motivate clients to change their behavior through application of operant conditioning principles. Specifically, many successful CM interventions have employed contracts or agreements between client and staff stipulating benefits like methadone take-home privileges (Magura, Casriel, Goldsmith, Strug, & Lipton, 1988) or vouchers for retail goods (Rowan-Szal, Joe, Chatham, & Simpson, 1994; Rowan-Szal, Joe, Hiller, & Simpson, 1997; Silverman et al., 1993) in exchange for abstinence from cocaine. Clients rewarded in this fashion were more successful in reducing their cocaine use than clients under standard treatment conditions. Although some CM interventions rely on the use of negative consequences (e.g., methadone withdrawal) for continued use, this practice is inadvisable because it results in heavier dropout rates from treatment (Kolar, Brown, Weddington, & Ball, 1990; Rawson et al., 1994). The risk of return to opioid use and exposure to HIV make such an approach to treatment questionable.

The second intervention, relapse prevention (RP), focuses on maintaining behavior-change efforts. RP is designed to prevent a client's initial lapses and then, if a lapse should occur, prevent it from becoming a complete return to use (Marlatt & Gordon, 1985). Some specific skills involve identifying and avoiding potential relapse situations, developing new coping strategies and new behaviors, and increasing confidence for avoiding drugs and regaining abstinence should slips occur (Marlatt & Gordon, 1985; Rawson, Obert, McCann, & Marinelli-Casey, 1993a, 1993b). Cocaine-using OMT clients exposed to RP materials have shown greater reductions in use, relative to standard treatment (Magura et al., 1994). Clients who attended more of these specialized RP sessions showed even greater benefits (Rosenblum et al., 1995).

Initial trials suggest that CM and RP might be combined to produce an even better treatment tool (Rawson et al., 1994). In ongoing work with the DATAR project, we are evaluating an intervention of this type. A manual-driven cognitive-behavioral program known as Counseling on Cocaine Abuse (COCA) is being offered to improve client motivation to address their cocaine use as part of OMT, and to provide skills and guidance in dealing with cocaine triggers and cravings. The materials are organized into eight sessions to be used in an individual counseling format during the second and third months of treatment, an important time for improving therapeutic engagement. We are combining the COCA module with a voucher-based CM system in which clients can earn rewards for negative urine tests and for recovery-related behaviors, such as counseling session attendance and progress toward goals described in the treatment plan. Our earlier evaluations have shown that clients reinforced during the first three months of treatment attended more counseling sessions, were rated as more motivated by their counselors, and continued to give fewer cocaine-positive urine samples following the intervention (Rowan-Szal et al., 1997). Further study of these interventions seems warranted.

CONCLUSIONS

Cocaine users treated in OMT are highly resistant to change. We found in this study that many of these clients made substantial reductions in their cocaine use, but others did not. However, reductions in opioid use were comparable for clients in all three categories defined by pretreatment cocaine use. In terms of a broader set of compliance indicators and behavioral outcomes, those who used only opioids at intake outperformed the cocaine users. DATAR findings generally support the position of Rawson and colleagues (1994), who found that individuals dually addicted to opioids and cocaine are not wholly inappropriate candidates for OMT treatment, but they need supplemental interventions in order to benefit. Future work in this area should refine these interventions in an effort to further reduce rates of during- and posttreatment cocaine use.

In addition, the DATAR data support earlier relapse findings. When clients in our sample relapsed, they showed patterns of use and social functioning similar to those described in previous major outcome studies (Hubbard & Marsden, 1986; Simpson & Marsh, 1986). The consistency of these patterns over time indicates the continued need for systematic relapse prevention efforts.

References

Avants, S. K., Margolin, A., & Kosten, T. R. (1994). Cocaine abuse in methadone maintenance programs: Integrating pharmacotherapy with psychotherapeutic interventions. *Journal of Psychoactive Drugs, 26,* 137–146.

Ball, J. C., Lange, W. R., Myers, C. P., & Friedman, S. R. (1988). Reducing the risk of AIDS through methadone maintenance treatment. *Journal of Health and Social Behavior, 29,* 214–226.

Broome, K. M. (1996). *Antisocial personality and drug abuse treatment process.* Unpublished doctoral dissertation, Texas Christian University, Fort Worth.

Broome, K. M., Joe, G. W., & Simpson, D. D. (1999). HIV risk reduction in outpatient drug abuse treatment: Individual and geographic differences. *AIDS Education and Prevention, 11,* 293–306.

Chaisson, R. E., Bacchetti, P., Osmond, D., Brodie, B., Sande, M. A., & Moss, A. R. (1989). Cocaine use and HIV infection in intravenous drug users in San Francisco. *Journal of the American Medical Association, 264,* 561–565.

Condelli, W. S., Fairbank, J. A., Dennis, M. L., & Rachal, J. V. (1991). Cocaine use by clients in methadone programs: Significance, scope, and behavioral interventions. *Journal of Substance Abuse Treatment, 8,* 203–212.

Cooper, J. R. (1992). Ineffective use of psychoactive drugs: Methadone treatment is no exception. *Journal of the American Medical Association, 267,* 281–282.

Dansereau, D. F., Dees, S. M., Greener, J., & Simpson, D. D. (1995). Node-link mapping and the evaluation of drug abuse counseling sessions. *Psychology of Addictive Behaviors, 9,* 195–203.

Dansereau, D. F., Joe, G. W., & Simpson, D. D. (1993). Node-link mapping: A visual representation strategy for enhancing drug abuse counseling. *Journal of Counseling Psychology, 40,* 385–395.

DATOS (1995). *Drug Abuse Treatment Outcome Study (DATOS): Intake databook for outpatient methadone modality.* Raleigh, N.C.: NDRI-NC.

D'Aunno, T., & Vaughn, T. E. (1992). Variations in methadone treatment practices:

Results from a national study. *Journal of the American Medical Association, 267,* 253–258.

Gerstein, D. R., & Harwood, H. J. (eds.). (1990). *Treating drug problems.* Vol. 1. *A study of the evolution, effectiveness, and financing of public and private drug treatment systems* (Committee for the Substance Abuse Coverage Study Division of Health Care Services, Institute of Medicine). Washington, D.C.: National Academy Press.

Hanbury, R., Sturiano, V., Cohen, M., Stimmel, B., & Aguillame, C. (1986). Cocaine use in persons on methadone maintenance. *Advances in Alcohol and Substance Abuse, 6,* 97–106.

Hiller, M. L., Simpson, D. D., Broome, K. M., & Joe, G. W. (in press). Legal status at intake and posttreatment incarceration: 12-month follow-up of methadone treatment. *Journal of Maintenance in the Addictions.*

Hubbard, R. L., & Marsden, M. E. (1986). Relapse to use of heroin, cocaine, and other drugs in the first year after treatment. In F. Tims & C. Leukefeld (eds.), *Relapse and recovery in abuse* (NIDA Research Monograph Series 72, Publication No. ADM 86-1473, pp. 157–166). Washington, D.C.: U.S. Government Printing Office.

Hubbard, R. L., Marsden, M. E., Rachal, J. V., Harwood, H. J., Cavanaugh, E. R., & Ginzburg, H. M. (1989). *Drug abuse treatment: A national study of effectiveness.* Chapel Hill: University of North Carolina Press.

Hunt, D., Spunt, B., Lipton, D., Goldsmith, D., & Strug, D. (1986). The costly bonus: Cocaine related crime among methadone treatment clients. *Advances in Alcohol and Substance Abuse, 6,* 107–122.

Joe, G. W., Dansereau, D. F., & Simpson, D. D. (1994). Node-link mapping for counseling cocaine users in methadone treatment. *Journal of Substance Abuse, 6,* 393–406.

Kolar, T. A., Brown, B. S., Weddington, W. W., & Ball, J. C. (1990). A treatment in crisis: Cocaine use by clients in methadone maintenance. *Journal of Substance Abuse Treatment, 7,* 101–107.

Lamb, R. J., Kirby, K. C., & Platt, J. J. (1996). Treatment retention, occupational role, and cocaine use in methadone maintenance. *American Journal on Addictions, 5,* 12–17.

Magura, S., Casriel, C., Goldsmith, D. S., Strug, D. L., & Lipton, D. S. (1988). Contingency contracting with poly-drug abusing methadone patients. *Addictive Behaviors, 13,* 113–118.

Magura, S., Kang, S., Shapiro, J., & O'Day, J. (1993). HIV risk among women who are in jail. *Addiction, 88,* 1351–1360.

Magura, S., Rosenblum, A., Lovejoy, M., Foote, J., Handelsman, L., & Stimmel, B. (1994). Neurobehavioral treatment for cocaine-using methadone patients: A preliminary report. *Journal of Addictive Diseases, 13,* 143–160.

Magura, S., Siddiqi, Q., Freeman, & Lipton, D. S. (1991). Changes in cocaine use after entry to methadone treatment. *Journal of Addictive Behaviors, 10,* 31–45.

Marlatt, G. A., & Gordon, J. R. (eds.). (1985). *Relapse prevention.* New York: Guilford.

Rawson, R. A., McCann, M. J., Hasson, A. J., & Ling, W. (1994). Cocaine abuse among methadone maintenance patients: Are there effective treatment strategies? *Journal of Psychoactive Drugs, 26,* 129–136.

Rawson, R. A., Obert, J. L., McCann, M. J., & Marinelli-Casey, P. (1993a). Relapse prevention strategies in outpatient substance abuse treatment. *Psychology of Addictive Behaviors, 7,* 85–95.

Rawson, R. A., Obert, J. L., McCann, M. J., & Marinelli-Casey, P. (1993b). Use of relapse prevention strategies in the treatment of substance abuse disorders. *Journal of Psychoactive Drugs, 22,* 159–171.

Rosenblum, A., Magura, S., Foote, J., Palij, M., Handelsman, L., Lovejoy, M., & Stimmel, B. (1995). Treatment intensity and reduction in drug use for cocaine-using methadone patients: A dose-response relationship. *Journal of Psychoactive Drugs, 27,* 151–159.

Rowan-Szal, G. A., Joe, G. W., Chatham, L. R., & Simpson, D. D. (1994). A simple reinforcement system for methadone clients in a community-based treatment program. *Journal of Substance Abuse Treatment, 11,* 217–223.

Rowan-Szal, G. A., Joe, G. W., Hiller, M. L., & Simpson, D. D. (1997). Increasing early engagement in methadone treatment. *Journal of Maintenance in the Addictions, 1,* 49–61.

Silverman, K., Schuster, C. R., Brooner, R. K., Montoya, I. D., & Preston, K. L. (1993). *Contingency management of cocaine use in a methadone maintenance program.* Paper presentation at the annual meeting of the Association for the Advancement of Behavior Therapy, Atlanta, Ga.

Simpson, D. D. (1992). *TCU/DATAR forms manual: Drug abuse treatment for AIDS-risk reduction.* Fort Worth: Texas Christian University, Institute of Behavioral Research. (These data collections are available at the Web site *www.ibr.tcu.edu.*)

Simpson, D. D. (1993). Drug treatment evaluations research in the United States. *Psychology of Addictive Behaviors, 7,* 120–128.

Simpson, D. D. (1997). Effectiveness of drug abuse treatment: A review of research from field settings. In J. A. Egertson, D. M. Fox, & A. I. Leshner (eds.), *Treating drug abusers effectively* (pp. 41–73). Cambridge, Mass.: Blackwell.

Simpson, D. D., Chatham, L. R., & Joe, G. W. (1993). Cognitive enhancements to treatment in DATAR: Drug abuse treatment for AIDS-risk reduction. In J. A. Inciardi, F. M. Tims, & B. W. Fletcher (eds.), *Innovative approaches to the treatment of drug abuse.* Vol. 1. *Program models and strategies* (pp. 161–177). Westport, Conn.: Greenwood.

Simpson, D. D., Dansereau, D. F., & Joe, G. W. (1997). The DATAR project: Cognitive and behavioral enhancements to community-based treatments. In F. M. Tims, J. A. Inciardi, B. W. Fletcher, & Horton, A. M., Jr. (eds.), *Effectiveness of innovative approaches in the treatment of drug abuse* (pp. 182–203). Westport, Conn.: Greenwood.

Simpson, D. D., & Joe, G. W. (1993). Motivation as a predictor of early dropout from drug abuse treatment. *Psychotherapy, 30,* 357–368.

Simpson, D. D., Joe, G. W., Dansereau, D. F., & Chatham, L. R. (1997). Strategies for improving methadone treatment process and outcomes. *Journal of Drug Issues, 27,* 239–260.

Simpson, D. D., Joe, G. W., & Rowan-Szal, G. A. (1997). Drug abuse treatment and retention and process effects on follow-up outcomes. *Drug and Alcohol Dependence, 47,* 227–235.

Simpson, D. D., Joe, G. W., Rowan-Szal, G. A., & Greener, J. (1995). Client engagement and change during drug abuse treatment. *Journal of Substance Abuse, 7,* 117–134.

Simpson, D. D., Joe, G. W., Rowan-Szal, G. A., & Greener, J. (1997). Drug abuse treatment process components that improve retention. *Journal of Substance Abuse Treatment, 14,* 565–572.

Simpson, D. D., & Marsh, K. L. (1986). Relapse and recovery among heroin addicts 12 years after treatment. In F. Tims & C. Leukefeld (eds.), *Relapse and recovery in abuse* (NIDA Research Monograph Series 72, Publication No. ADM 86-1473, pp. 86–103). Washington, D.C.: U.S. Government Printing Office.

Simpson, D. D., Savage, L. J., Joe, G. W., Demaree, R. G., & Sells, S. B. (1976). *Statistics on characteristics of drug users in treatment during 1969–1974.* Fort Worth: Texas Christian University, Institute of Behavioral Research.

Simpson, D. D., & Sells, S. B. (1982). Effectiveness of treatment for drug abuse: An overview of the DARP research program. *Advances in Alcohol and Substance Abuse, 2,* 7–29.

Simpson, D. D., & Sells, S. B., eds. (1990). *Opioid addiction and treatment: A 12-year follow-up.* Malabar, Fl.: Krieger.

Turner, S., & Petersilia, J. (1992). Focusing on high-risk parolees: An experiment to reduce commitments to the Texas Department of Corrections. *Journal of Research in Crime and Delinquency, 29,* 34–61.

Ziedonis, D. M. (1992). Comorbid psychopathology and cocaine addiction. In T. R. Kosten & H. D. Kleber (eds.), *Clinician's guide to cocaine addiction* (pp. 335–358). New York: Guilford.

FIFTEEN

RELAPSE AMONG COCAINE ABUSERS: THEORETICAL, METHODOLOGICAL, AND TREATMENT CONSIDERATIONS

Damaris J. Rohsenow & Peter M. Monti

Cocaine abuse generates considerable concern because of its impact on medical and social problems, criminal activity, and overdose deaths, causing huge resulting costs to society (RAND 1992). The large-scale NIDA-sponsored Cocaine Treatment Outcome Study (CTOS) of results from treatment of cocaine abusers has found nationwide increases in abstinence from cocaine after treatment (Flynn et al., 1995), suggesting that various forms of treatment result in improvement. Because many cocaine abusers return to heavy use, however, improvements in prevention and treatment interventions remain important to develop.

Many general approaches to the treatment of substance abusers have been reviewed in other chapters and certainly apply to cocaine abuse, particularly as so many clients use multiple substances. The present chapter focuses specifically on treatment for cocaine abuse, reviewing approaches that have resulted in significant improvements in outcomes.

DEFINITION OF THE TOPIC

The role of all models of relapse is to be heuristic in stimulating research and in guiding treatment and prevention efforts. The social learning theory (SLT) perspective is one that integrates organismic and environmental factors into a dynamic model of the development and maintenance of substance abuse and of relapse (Abrams & Niaura 1987; Marlatt & Gordon 1985; Rohsenow, Niaura, Childress, Abrams, & Monti 1990; Wilson 1988). The social learning perspective is broad enough to allow inclusion of a number of different theoretical perspectives, including operant and respondent learning, cognitive processes, observational learning, genetic vulnerability, and neuroadaptational approaches to behavior. The model provides an ongoing integration of physiological, cognitive, biobehavioral, and sociocultural variables. Although this model has been most fully formulated for alcohol and tobacco abuse, the concepts apply equally well to cocaine abuse.

Many models focus on one or two types of processes to explain cocaine abuse and relapse processes. This may be a result of some insularity within disciplines, leading to a tendency to focus on only a few processes emphasized within the discipline. However, a wide variety of approaches to understanding relapse have merit. The growth of the science in our field may be best served by focusing on synthesis, emphasizing complementary aspects of the various models.

The general principles of social learning theory have been more fully delineated elsewhere (Bandura 1977) and the applications of social learning theory to substance abuse have been described elsewhere (e.g., Abrams & Niaura 1987; Marlatt & Gordon 1985; Rohsenow, Niaura, Childress, Abrams & Monti 1990; Wilson 1988). Therefore, we review these basic principles briefly here. The major emphasis in SLT is on cognitive information processing mechanisms involving an interaction between environmental variables and person variables. SLT proposes reciprocal associations among individuals, their behavior, and the environment. The primary types of variables involved in SLT models of substance abuse and relapse include person variables and environmental variables. Each of these aspects is described with examples below.

Person variables include one's history of actual consequences of cocaine use, beliefs and expectancies about the consequences of substance use, beliefs and expectancies about one's ability to stay sober (self-efficacy expectations), repertoire of coping skills that could be called on to prevent or avoid relapse, and genetic and other biologically based sources of vulnerability that may lead to increased susceptibility to relapse. *Actual consequences* of cocaine use involve a variety of positive and negative effects in addition to direct drug effects. The large number of negative effects (social, emotional, legal, financial, and health related) that result from cocaine use (Michalec et al. 1996) can provide incentive to stay sober. Proximal consequences are more powerful determinants of behavior than are distal consequences. Some of the categories of *expectancies* about the proximal effects of cocaine found by cocaine abusers include four positive ones (pleasurable stimulation, sexual enhancement, social enhancement, and pain reduction), one that can be either positive or negative (increased aggression), and two negative ones (increased tension and social withdrawal) (Rohsenow & Monti, 1993). *Self-efficacy* refers to the individual's confidence that he or she can avoid using substances in any particular high-risk situation. These self-efficacy expectations may derive in part from the individual's repertoire of skills and prior experiences with cessation attempts as well as being based on vicarious learning by observing the successes or failures of others who have gone through treatment. This may be one of the sources of strength in twelve-step and aftercare groups, which may provide an individual with frequent observation of others who have successfully maintained sobriety. *The repertoire of coping skills* that are most relevant includes both anticipatory coping to prevent a high-risk situation from occurring and immediate coping to cope with a high-risk situation once it has occurred (Rohsenow et al. in press; Shiffman 1984). Anticipatory responses include specific actions (e.g., moving from a bad neighborhood or changing a job) and global lifestyle changes (e.g., improving exercise and nutrition, joining sober social groups) designed to decrease both vulnerability and high-risk situations (Marlatt & Gordon 1985) as well as cognitive changes (e.g., planning ahead). For smokers, the use of any behavioral or coping response in a situation decreased the probability of relapse in a high-risk situation (Shiffman 1984). Although this may apply for cocaine abusers as well, it has not yet been investigated. *Biologically based sources of vulnerability* to relapse may include changes that result from prolonged drug use, including both tolerance and sensitization, and changes in kindling thresholds due to prolonged drug use. For example, Robinson and Berridge (1993) proposed that drug-induced sensitization-related neuroadaptations, especially to stimulants, can occur and can be long-lasting. Other vulnerabilities may precede and contribute to substance use, like depression (Brown et al. 1998), which may increase susceptibility to situations that increase negative mood, and genetically based differences in sensitivity.

Environmental variables include the people in the home environment whom the sober patient comes in contact with, cocaine use cues associated through conditioning with past use experiences, availability of cocaine, alternative positive sources of support, and community characteristics. *People in the environment* can affect relapse by being successful and unsuccessful role models (sober and relapsed cocaine abusers), by causing social pressure to use cocaine (e.g., offers) or to stay sober (e.g., sober spouse or children), or by providing reinforcement for either sobriety or relapse. *Cocaine use cues* include not only the sight and smell of cocaine but also environments associated with using (a neighborhood, a dealer's house) and other stimuli (a paycheck or ATM card are powerful cues) (Michalec et al. 1992). These cues may come to have effects through processes of respondent conditioning (Rohsenow et al. 1990). *Availability of cocaine* is determined by neighborhood, price, knowledge of dealers, and social network, and it usually changes little from before to after treatment. Some clients choose to restrict effective availability by having someone else manage their money for them to prevent their own access to funds. *Alternative sources of support* can derive from a number of positive influences. An intact family that is supportive of sobriety, a job that does not include substance abusers, and an aftercare or self-help group all provide sources of support that are likely to increase sobriety. *Community characteristics* can be strong determinants of the likelihood of using drugs and of the choice of drug of abuse (Chein et al. 1964). Therefore, the type of community the person returns to may be a strong determinant of the likelihood of relapse.

A model of processes involved in a relapse can be derived from SLT; one such version has been outlined by Marlatt and Gordon (1985). The SLT model of relapse focuses on proximal situational factors, "high-risk situations," that may precipitate a relapse in a cocaine abuser who is trying to stay sober. The model includes the following components: (1) Specific high-risk situations exist for each individual in which relapse is more likely to occur. These situations are based on the individual's past learning history (e.g., cocaine use cues) and personal vulnerabilities (e.g., a predisposition to depression). (2) The individual's reactions to the situation may include effective coping responses or failure to employ effective coping. These reactions are based on the individual's repertoire of coping responses, degree of motivation to stay sober, self-efficacy beliefs (confidence that she or he can carry out the coping behavior), and outcome expectancies (beliefs about the consequences of carrying out the coping). (3) The results of the individual's reactions to the situation have an effect on subsequent behavior. The individual's behavior and the results of this behavior may determine whether the person continues to resist temptation or continues into further use. Successful coping increases self-efficacy and makes it more likely that a coping attempt will be made in later high-risk situations. A weak or ineffective coping response may lead to a continuation of the threat of relapse and an undermining of self-efficacy, leading to increased likelihood of a relapse. (4) If an individual does slip or lapse (have a brief use of cocaine), he or she might make either a positive or negative response to this lapse. If the lapse is attributed to external, unstable, controllable and/or specific factors like the failure to anticipate the specific high-risk situation or excessive tiredness, the person might take steps to terminate the lapse episode, such as contacting an aftercare counselor or seeking some other sober support. If the lapse is attributed to internal, stable, and/or global factors that are seen as beyond an individual's control (such as "substance abuse is in my genes" or "once an addict, always an addict, so no point even trying"), the lapse may lead to a full relapse.

The advantage of the SLT model is that it suggests direct areas for intervening with cocaine abusers. Such areas include approaches designed to decrease vulnerabilities (e.g., through antidepressant medications), increase coping repertoires, heighten awareness of expectancies about cocaine's effects, find alternative sources for the positive expected effects, change actual reinforcement consequences of cocaine use, increase the repertoire of coping skills, increase self-efficacy about employing coping skills in high-risk situations, and decrease the power of conditioned responses to cocaine use cues to disrupt behavior. A number of these areas were incorporated into the treatments described below to increase the probability of successful outcomes.

Recently, an information-processing model of drug seeking has provided some new directions for research (Fiske et al. 1987; Tiffany, 1990). Although much of the model is focused on ongoing use, parts are relevant for predictions of relapse. According to this model, much drug seeking is under the control of automatic drug use action schemata outside a person's conscious awareness. That is, behaviors that are overlearned may be performed with a fair degree of automaticity (like lighting up a cigarette after a meal). These automatic processes are elicited by stimuli associated with past drug use and come into play when drug-seeking behavior is not blocked in any way. When drug seeking is blocked, either through barriers to availability or because of a deliberate attempt to resist using, then conscious processes (like urges and cravings) occur. Aspects of this model have received some support in our work with alcoholics, in which salivation in response to alcohol cues, as a marker of the automatic processes, has been shown to predict increased drinking during follow-up, and self-reported attention to the cues was associated with less drinking, probably because awareness can lead to mobilization of coping responses in a high-risk situation (Rohsenow et al. 1994). Additional support for the notion of automaticity has come from some of our more recent work with alcoholics who show changes in the prepulse inhibition of the startle reflex in response to alcohol cues (Monti, Rohsenow, & Hutchison, 1999). The implication is that cocaine relapses also may occur in high-risk situations in which cocaine is readily available without the person becoming conscious of a craving or aware of danger. One logical treatment implication is that approaches designed to increase attention to high-risk situations and awareness of danger would be of value in increasing the likelihood of using coping responses in high-risk situations.

PAST WORK

In general, no one form of treatment has emerged as the treatment of choice in reducing relapse for cocaine abusers, although increases in abstinence are found following a variety of treatment approaches (e.g., Hubbard et al. 1997). However, a number of promising behavioral interventions have emerged recently that may improve treatment outcomes. The approaches reviewed include pharmacotherapies, psychotherapeutic approaches that are not based on behavioral learning theories (which will be referred to as nonbehavioral psychotherapeutic approaches), and approaches based on the behavioral learning theories.

Medications development research has been a vigorous part of NIDA's portfolio, in an attempt to deal with some of the biochemical substrates of cocaine-seeking behavior. For example, dopaminergic pathways within the mesolimbic system involving the ventral tegmental area and pathways to the nucleus accumbens are associated with the reinforcing effects of cocaine ingestion (e.g., Wise 1988), suggesting that medications that affect this system might have utility. The principal types of medications that have been investigated to prevent cocaine relapse have included dopamine agonists (e.g., bromocriptine and amantadine), dopamine and 5HT antagonists (e.g., haloperidol and ondansetron), cocaine antagonists, and antidepressants (McCance 1997). Although some medications showed initial promise in initial trials, however, there are no medications currently with demonstrated efficacy for cocaine abusers (Rawson et al. 1991; McCance 1997). Even if an optimal medication is found, no one medication is likely to fill the needs of all patients; many may be unable to take a particular medication for medical reasons, and behavioral programs are likely to be needed both to encourage patients to continue using the medication and to teach the lifestyle changes that will be needed for patients to make lasting changes in their drug use behaviors.

Nonbehavioral psychotherapeutic approaches to cocaine relapse prevention have generally involved applying standard 28-day substance abuse programs or longer therapeutic community approaches to cocaine abuse, but most have not been systematically evaluated in controlled clinical trials (Rawson et al. 1991). A controlled study evaluating the effects of weekly outpatient supportive-expressive psychotherapy, group therapy, and family therapy failed to find lower rates of relapse in comparison with untreated cocaine abusers who had sought treatment (Kang et al. 1991). Interventions that are successful with opiate abusers would have potential application to cocaine abusers, but the nonbehaviorally based approaches with opiate abusers have mostly either failed to report follow-up data or failed to find differences in drug and alcohol use outcomes. For example, in a comparison of counseling with or without psychotherapy for opiate abusers, no differences were found during the six-month follow-up period in terms of drug or alcohol use outcomes (Woody et al. 1987).

Early behavioral approaches focused on simple contingent reinforcement methods. Contingency contracting focuses on changing some of the reinforcing consequences of cocaine use versus sobriety. Anker and Crowley (1982) provided one of the earliest examples of this approach with cocaine abusers. Contracts involved contingencies such as the therapist holding letters of notification of cocaine abuse or of resignation that the therapist could mail to legal agencies, employers, or professional licensing boards after a positive or missing urinalysis. Of those willing to participate, 30 out of 31 remained abstinent for the next three months. However, 52% approached for the study refused to participate because of the severity of the negative consequences that could result. Furthermore, more than half of the patients relapsed after the three-month contract was completed. Against the backdrop of the failures of many approaches in the past to affect substance use outcomes, demonstrating that a therapeutic approach results in any improvement in outcomes in controlled clinical trials would provide some guidance to clinicians. The current approaches that have demonstrated some effectiveness are reviewed below. It may be that there are other approaches in current clinical use that improve effectiveness, but without controlled clinical outcome data, this is not known.

MAJOR CONCEPTUAL ISSUES

A number of conceptual issues need to be considered when designing or evaluating the results of studies designed to improve treatment outcomes for cocaine abusers. These include issues of how to define relapse, how to define recovery, the use of continuous measures of outcome, methods of assessing outcome measures, the inclusion of non–drug-related criteria, and the impact of attrition or compliance on net effectiveness.

How to define relapse is one issue without a clearly agreed upon answer. Certainly, relapse is generally considered a dichotomous variable: one is either relapsed or not. The most stringent definition would be to count any cocaine use at all over the two years following treatment as a relapse. But, a person may slip and then return to abstinence or use only occasionally, and people with such great improvement should not be considered as having the same outcome as those who return to pretreatment levels of cocaine use. Some researchers distinguish between a lapse or "improvement," usually defined as some small number of days of use during the follow-up period, and a relapse, usually defined as a larger number of total days or the first occurrence of a certain number of consecutive days of cocaine use. Again, there are no agreed-upon criteria for these distinctions, but the distinctions usually seem to be clinically meaningful ones. Higgins et al. (1994b), for example, define "success" as ≥ 9 weeks of continuous abstinence out of a 12-week treatment trial, or ≥ 92% of the time abstinent during the same time period. One major problem with using only a dichotomous or trichotomous outcome criterion is the large loss of power to detect treatment differences. Categorical variables are much less sensitive to change than are continuous measures. As a result, a treatment study would need to be about twice as large to detect a same-sized treatment effect (Cohen 1992), leading to inaccurate conclusions that treatment has no significant effects on outcome.

How to define recovery is similarly unclear. Some of the terms that have been used imply a permanent state while others imply a temporary or fluctuating state (Maddox & Desmond 1986). The most stringent operational criteria have included three or five years of complete abstinence of the primary drug and no abuse of other drugs as the criterion for recovery (American Medical Association 1970; Bejerot 1975). A series of levels of degree of recovery have also been proposed, including such criteria as: Level 1—daily substitute medication for one month or longer, Level 2—abstinence from primary substance without substitute medication for one month or longer, Level 3—only occasional nonproblem use of any substance for a year or longer, Level 4—continuous voluntary abstinence from primary substance with only occasional use of other substances for a year or longer, Level 5— continuous voluntary abstinence from all substances except tobacco for a year or more (Maddux & Desmond 1986). Recovery can also be defined simply as no abuse of any drug during a specified period of time, with non-abusive occasional use allowed. "Short-term recovery" has been defined as no cocaine use for three consecutive weeks at the time of study termination (Carroll, Rounsaville and Gawin, 1991), a far less stringent criterion.

Continuous measures of substance use outcomes are increasingly being used. This approach has been used for studies of alcoholics for many years (e.g., Sobell, Sobell, & Ward 1980) to improve the power to detect improvements but has less frequently been used for studies of cocaine use outcomes. One rationale is that this method improves the power to detect improvements in substance use outcomes. This avoids the erroneous conclusion that the treatment program is having no effects on cocaine use outcomes if total abstinence during the follow-up period does not result. A second, related rationale is that improvement, or harm reduction (Marlatt, Somers, & Tapert 1993), is a valid and laudable outcome of treatment programs (even of abstinence-oriented programs). This recognizes that reductions in use reflect an important step in the right direction and can reduce medical, legal, and social consequences of use.

Some of the physiologically based continuous measures that have been used include number of cocaine positive urines (Carroll et al. 1993), amount of cocaine metabolite in the urine (Grabowski et al. 1993), number of weeks until first cocaine-positive urine, and number of weeks of cocaine-negative urines (Weddington et al. 1991). Some of the other continuous measures of cocaine use outcomes include number of days of cocaine use (Carroll et al. 1993; Rohsenow et al. in press), mean total grams of cocaine used (Carroll et al. 1993), the longest cocaine use binge (Monti et al. 1997), the longest continuous number of weeks of abstinence (Higgins and Budney 1993), and time to first use of cocaine (Monti et al. 1997).

The methods of assessing outcome measures also involve some controversy. It is obvious from the above list of outcome measures that not all studies rely solely on biochemical markers of cocaine use. Using urine drug screen data gathered several times per week has been the standard in many drug trials and, with the improvements in the accuracy of the urine drug screens, involves a fairly high degree of validity. There are some problems with using only this source of data, however. One is that this type of data is generally restricted to urines gathered during treatment as a part of treatment. This means that data cannot be gathered from those who drop out of treatment, although it would be erroneous to assume that these individuals are therefore using cocaine every day. Also, this type of data cannot be used to assess effects during a follow-up period after treatment is completed, yet it is crucial to know the effects of treatment on longer-term outcomes. Using this type of assessment during a posttreatment follow-up period would involve prohibitively high expense, require an improbable degree of compliance on the part of research participants, and could compromise the follow-up results by acting like a treatment for those who do comply. Analysis of amount of cocaine in hair samples is not yet an unbiased and valid alternative.

Self-report data are the other source of outcome information. Concerns about the lack of validity of self-report data come from experiences clinicians have had with cocaine abusers in treatment programs and in systems where legal consequences may occur. In these settings, however, there are negative consequences to reporting substance use, ranging from simple disapproval to legal sanctions. Sobell and Sobell (1986) have outlined the conditions under which alcohol abusers give valid self-reports, and these conditions should be used when conducting follow-up interviews with cocaine abusers as well. The conditions that increase the validity of self-reports include creating a set that encourages honest reporting, conducting interviews in a setting that is separate from treatment or legal personnel, ensuring the confidentiality of the reports from everyone but research personnel, ensuring a negative blood alcohol level at the time of interview, and having the participant agree in advance that the reports will be corroborated through urine screens on the interview day and/or collateral informant reports. As early as 1980, many studies had shown that drug abusers' self-reports are reliable and valid when conducted with assurances of confidentiality and a research set and setting (Callahan & Rawson 1980; Maisto & Cooper 1980). Furthermore, for evaluating between-groups treatment outcome questions, differential falsification of data as a function of treatment condition is unlikely so that valid differential treatment effects can be determined. Using a method that cues recall such as the Time Line Follow Back interview (Sobell et al. 1980) is likely to be even more accurate than global questions about the number of days used in the same period of time and has demonstrated reliability and validity (Fals-Stewart et al. 2000; Hersh et al. 1999). When asking questions about quantity of cocaine used, we find it useful to have prepackaged plastic bags of powdered sugar or rock candy of various weights (e.g., a gram and a quarter ounce) to aid memory.

The inclusion of non–drug-related outcome criteria is important for a complete picture of the degree of success of the recovery (Maisto & Cooper 1980). A person may be completely abstinent but unemployed, isolated, and in poor psychological and physical health. Therefore, evaluating the effects of treatment on emotional, vocational, legal, social, familial, and physical health measures is also important. The Addiction Severity Index Version 5 (ASI; McLellan et al. 1992), currently the most widely used measure for this purpose, has a new, more reliable set of scales for drug, alcohol, psychiatric, family, and legal problems (Alterman et al. 1998).

Compliance and attrition issues are also important aspects of outcome. If a form of treatment is effective for 90% of cocaine abusers who complete it, but 90% of patients drop out or fail to comply with the treatment, the treatment is actually beneficial for only 9% of patients.

CURRENT STATUS OF TREATMENT EFFECTIVENESS

Various of the determinants of relapse hypothesized by SLT are addressed by the more current behavioral treatments in particular. Whereas pharmaco-therapies are primarily designed to address aspects of biological vulnera-bility, the treatments discussed below focus on other aspects that may affect probability of relapse. Not all treatment studies are reviewed; instead, ex-amples of the more promising current approaches are described.

Contingency management approaches focus on changing the consequences of sobriety to make them more positive. Essentially, the interventions ar-range contingencies so that drug use will result in the loss of a positive re-inforcer, thus increasing the response cost for drug use. In a review of 13 controlled clinical trials of this approach, 11 (85%) resulted in significant treatment effects in reducing cocaine use (Higgins 1996). Two of these ap-proaches that have resulted in significant changes in cocaine use behaviors are described in more detail below.

Cocaine use among methadone-maintained substance abusers is a wide-spread problem. The group headed by Stitzer (Stitzer, Iguchi, & Felch 1992; Stitzer, Iguchi, Kidorf, & Bigelow 1993) relied on the fact that needing to report to the clinic every day to receive a supervised dose of methadone is somewhat aversive, thus, being allowed to have take-home doses of metha-done can be used to reinforce drug-free urines. Contingencies were used such that two weeks of drug-free urines (assessed three times per week) would earn the patient the first take-home methadone privilege, with up to three times per week of take-home doses being earned with increasing lengths of time drug free. A comparison condition receive noncontingent take-home privi-leges. About 30% of patients in each condition dropped out before the six-month trial was completed. However, more patients in the contingent condi-tion improved their rate of drug-free urines by 10% or more (32% of patients) than did patients in the noncontingent condition (12% of patients). When the contingency procedure was subsequently implemented clinic-wide, 24% of patients showed at least a 10% improvement in number of drug-free urines. Thus, this is a low-cost procedure that can be easily implemented to improve drug use during a period of treatment. No follow-up data were presented but improvement within an outpatient treatment period is a valuable accom-plishment in and of itself.

Higgins has applied a variety of positive reinforcers for abstinence in addi-tion to using behavioral analysis with cocaine abusers to effect improvement in outcomes. Four out of five of his controlled clinical trials of this approach resulted in significant decreases in cocaine use (Higgins 1996). In this approach, cocaine use is monitored through thrice-weekly urine screens, and continuous abstinence is reinforced by providing greater incentives for longer continuous periods of abstinence (Higgins & Budney 1993). During the first 12 weeks of treatment, the reinforcers are monetary values of vouchers that can be used to purchase a wide variety of retail items in the community, including ski-lift tickets, fishing licenses, meals at restaurants, camera equipment, etc. During the second 12 weeks, the amount of reinforcer is reduced so that each cocaine-free urine results in one state lottery ticket. In addition, to provide community reinforcement, each patient involved one sober significant other in the treatment. This person participated in reciprocal relationship counseling and was notified of each urinalysis result, with instructions to refrain from social activities with the patient if the urine was positive for cocaine. To build in a more healthy lifestyle, patients were taught to recognize antecedents and consequents of drug use, to restructure their activities to avoid antecedents and attain alternative positive reinforcers, and to learn problem-solving skills. Recreational activities were encouraged, and unemployed patients received employment counseling.

This approach has been compared to standard drug counseling with significantly greater treatment completion and greater lengths of continuous cocaine abstinence (Higgins et al. 1993b). The behavioral program has been compared with and without the voucher system, with twice as long continuous abstinence occurring in the group that received the vouchers (Higgins et al., 1994b). Of even greater interest is the fact that significant differences in drug use and in drug-related problems continued to be found during the 9 to 12 months after treatment and the voucher system were discontinued (Higgins et al. 1995, 2000). Thus, the rather artificially contrived greater initial abstinence may have allowed an opportunity for reinforcers in the environment and the skills training approach to make more lasting changes after the artificial reinforcer system was removed. Because participation by a significant other was the best predictor of abstinence (Higgins et al. 1994a), the change in social reinforcers could easily have lasted long after the end of treatment and helped to maintain the gains. Thus, this rather high cost system has excellent payoffs in terms of cocaine use outcomes. The next step needed may be a cost-benefits analysis of this approach.

Cue exposure with response prevention treatment (CET) is designed to decrease the power of stimuli that have been associated with cocaine use in the past (called cues) to elicit urges to use and other reactions that may increase the risk of relapse (Rohsenow et al. 1990, 1995b). This approach has produced beneficial results with alcoholics (Monti et al. 1993; Drummond & Glautier, 1994). The leading CET work with cocaine abusers is being done by a group headed by Childress (e.g., Childress et al. 1993). In this approach, patients are exposed to up to 15 one-hour sessions of videotaped and audio-taped stimuli based on the person's preferred route of administration (e.g., video of a user making a cocaine buy and trying it out, with facial reactions shown). Either passive exposure (patients are asked to simply focus on the materials) or an active cue exposure (patients are taught skills for coping with urges) is done. Passive cue exposure is designed to rely on extinction or habituation of elicited responses, and active cue exposure is designed to add coping skills training to the extinction or habituation. A controlled trial of the passive CET method with outpatients, added to either psychotherapy or drug counseling, found better treatment retention and more cocaine-free urines during treatment in the CET condition (Childress et al., 1993). Extinction was limited to the cues in the lab, however, so that patients still craved in response to other triggers in the environment, and reinstatement of craving and drug use occurred rapidly after one or two uses of cocaine. Although CET is designed to involve response prevention, cocaine is readily available among outpatients and extinction processes may not occur as a result. Another trial compared 12 weeks of active CET to a comparison condition (educational videotapes), with equivalent treatment retention found (about 70%) (Childress 1993). However, preliminary results are not yet available. Therefore, although a promising approach, CET has not yet received enough support to be recommended.

Aversive counterconditioning is designed to counteract the positive associations with cocaine by producing aversive conditioned reactions to the sight and smell of cocaine. These reactions are not intended to prevent cocaine use directly, but rather, if the aversion reduces craving in a treatment-motivated individual, this may assist in the person's recovery by reducing temptation while the individual is making lifestyle changes that may support recovery. Elkins and his research group have been creating aversion by chemically or hypnotically inducing nausea in cocaine abusers or by giving electric shocks while exposing them to cocaine use cues (Elkins 1993). The stimuli used are route-specific. These researchers have substances that look and smell like cocaine in powdered or rock crystal form that can be smoked or used intra-nasally and that simulate cocaine without having the positively reinforcing effects. In his study, all patients received milieu treatment with the study conditions added. The study used two control groups (milieu, and milieu plus eight sessions of relaxation training) and three experimental groups, each with 12 sessions (covert sensitization, emetic conditioning, and electric shock conditioning). The results of the six-month follow-up showed that emetic conditioning was superior to all other conditions, with 53% of patients completely abstinent in the emetic condition compared to 21% to 31% of patients abstinent in the other conditions (Elkins 1993). Thus, although some clinicians may be uncomfortable with using this approach, this relatively low-cost procedure can result in substantial improvement in outcomes.

Disulfiram (Antabuse) should have no direct effect on the pharmacologic effects of cocaine but may reduce the likelihood of cocaine use by making it impossible for the cocaine abuser to use alcohol in conjunction with the cocaine. About three-quarters of cocaine abusers are also diagnosed with alcohol abuse or dependence (Rohsenow et al. in press). Many report that they use alcohol after ingesting cocaine to take the edge off of the cocaine high. Therefore, if drinking is prevented, then the consequences of cocaine ingestion may be less positively reinforcing for some. Also, alcohol use may have become a conditioned stimulus associated with cocaine use, so disulfiram may reduce this source of risk for cocaine relapse.

Two studies found a beneficial effect of disulfiram on cocaine use outcomes. Carroll et al. (1993) compared naltrexone to disulfiram for 12 weeks for a small sample of outpatients with both cocaine and alcohol abuse and found fewer cocaine use days among those using disulfiram; however, attrition was substantial with only 54% completing the 12 weeks of disulfiram. With a similarly diagnosed small sample, Higgins et al. (1993a) found that on days when their patients were taking disulfiram they used cocaine significantly less frequently than on the days that they chose not to use it. However, compliance was again poor so that even those who agreed to take disulfiram failed to take it almost as often as they took it. Thus, although good results are found when cocaine abusers choose to comply with disulfiram, the results may be attributed to differences in preexisting levels of motivation for abstinence rather than to effects of the medication per se. Further studies are needed with larger samples and with better methods of enhancing compliance.

Cocaine-specific coping skills training (CSCST) is designed to address a number of the variables hypothesized to be associated with increased risk for relapse, including modifying the expected effects of cocaine, increasing the repertoire of effective coping skills, increasing self-efficacy about the patient's ability to apply the coping skills in high-risk situations, reducing the influence of negative social influences in the environment, increasing ability to resist social pressure to use, providing a means of coping with cocaine use cues, and decreasing the effective availability of cocaine through anticipatory coping (such as by reducing cash supplies). Coping skills training for relapse prevention is based on approaches originally found to be effective in improving treatment outcomes for alcoholics (e.g., Chaney et al. 1978; Monti, Abrams, Kadden, & Cooney, 1989; Monti et al. 1990). Many skills training programs are applied to mixed groups of alcoholics and substance abusers and may fail to adequately address the specific needs of cocaine abusers, such as cocaine-specific high-risk situations. Therefore, a coping skills training package was developed based on cocaine-specific high-risk situations.

High-risk situations were first identified through the use of a Cocaine High Risk Situations Survey administered to 179 cocaine users in treatment for substance abuse (Michalec et al. 1992). The survey identified a number of situations identified as frequently associated with cocaine use during times of ongoing use. The content area of these situations included negative emotional states (depression, anger, and frustration, primarily), external pressure to use, internal pressure to use (e.g., sudden urge), wanting to enhance positive affective states particularly in social situations, and cues such as a paycheck (endorsed by 74% of the patients). After the first treatment study (Monti et al. 1997) was completed, the situations in which cocaine abusers actually relapse were content analyzed so as to refine the focus of the treatment modules (Rohsenow et al. 1995a). The relapse situations with the highest frequency were explicit drug cues with other people present, alcohol use as a trigger for cocaine use, negative affect (almost always sadness or depression), testing control through attempted limited use of cocaine, and explicit drug cues without others present (primarily money as a trigger). The information from these two studies was used to develop the cocaine use triggers that were focused on in the CSCST sessions.

In a controlled clinical trial, CSCST was compared to an attention-placebo condition for 114 cocaine abusers when both were added to a two to three week substance abuse program at both a residential and a partial hospital program (Monti et al. 1997, Rohsenow et al. in press). Both treatments were manualized. The CSCST, conducted in individual sessions, involved functional analyses of the high-risk situations, with coping skills training focused on the individual's own antecedents and consequents of cocaine use. The treatment included modules on analyzing behavior chains, frustration, anger, other negative emotional states, assertiveness training, handling internal and external pressure to use, and enhancing positive moods. Both anticipatory and immediate coping skills were taught in each module. At three-month follow up, CSCST resulted in significantly fewer cocaine use days and the length of their longest cocaine use binge was significantly shorter than in the contrast condition, and the effects of this brief treatment lasted for six months. Thus, this relatively low-cost procedure results in significant improvements in cocaine use outcomes.

Relapse prevention training (RPT) for cocaine abusers, developed by Carroll's group, is quite similar in goals and methods to the CSCST approach described above. RPT uses cognitive-behavioral methods to help cocaine abusers learn to identify high-risk situations and to develop effective skills for coping with the situations and with urges to use. Outpatient cocaine abusers ($n = 42$) were assigned to 12 weekly sessions of either RPT or interpersonal psychotherapy (IPT) as their sole treatment, both administered with manuals (Carroll, Rounsaville, & Gawin 1991). Differences favoring RPT were not significant in the whole sample, possibly due to the small sample size. However, among the subgroup of 24 patients with more severe ASI drug index scores, those in RPT were significantly more likely to attain three consecutive weeks of abstinence (54% versus 9%), and to be classified as recovered at treatment termination (54% versus 0%). Those low in substance use severity did equally well regardless of treatment type. In a subsequent clinical trial investigating antidepressant medication for 110 outpatient cocaine abusers, patients were assigned to 12 weeks of either RPT or supportive clinical management (Carroll, Nich, & Rounsaville 1995). Medication had no significant effect. Among the 37 depressed cocaine abusers, however, those assigned to RPT had significantly better treatment retention and significantly longer periods of continuous abstinence than did those assigned to supportive clinical management.

In sum, approaches using coping skills training result in improved outcomes for cocaine abusers, both as an adjunct to an intensive inpatient or partial hospital program and when the skills training approach is the primary or sole treatment for outpatient cocaine abusers. The significant effects are found particularly for those with more severe substance abuse severity or with greater depression at start of treatment. Furthermore, use of more coping strategies predicted abstinence six months after treatment (Hall, Havassey, & Wasserman 1991), further supporting the value of the skills training approach.

CONCLUSIONS

Behavioral approaches to preventing relapse among cocaine abusers have shown considerable growth in recent years. A variety of innovative approaches have been developed, many of which have demonstrated improvements in treatment outcomes as reflected by a greater amount of time spent abstinent from cocaine. At the same time, the medications development portfolio at NIDA continues to thrive in the search for medications that may decrease the probability of relapse during treatment and early recovery, and thereby buy time for skills training and lifestyle changes to produce lasting effects on outcome. The most promising of the behavioral approaches are those that are solidly rooted in social leaning theory models of behavior. Two of the most effective types of approaches are contingency management approaches and cognitive-behavioral coping skills training approaches, each with several studies showing effectiveness.

FUTURE DIRECTIONS

One direction for the future is to continue to investigate additional promising treatment approaches derived from behavioral learning theories. The heuristic value of approaches based on SLT have been shown and should continue to produce benefits. Other variants being investigated include using empirical research on methods of effectively enhancing motivation (Miller 1991) to increase cocaine abusers' motivation to change prior to starting their skills training treatment (e.g., Monti, Rohsenow, & O'Leary 1997).

A second direction is the continued search for promising medications to reduce the probability of relapse. One advance in this direction is improvements in the theoretical and empirical foundations for this search (Grabowski & Johnson, 1993). It is important to consider whether the behavioral effect of the medication is reinforcement, extinction, or punishment because a medication that is effective in producing abstinence but that results in low rates of enrollment and/or low retention is of limited value ultimately (Grabowski & Johnson 1993). Any medication is likely to be best employed in combination with behavioral treatments designed to enhance medication compliance and to build alternative skills, lifestyle changes, or natural reinforcers that will help to maintain the gains after the medication is discontinued. For example, naltrexone works best for alcoholics when combined with a skills training approach (O'Malley et al. 1992), possibly because naltrexone reduces elicited reactions to alcohol stimuli (Monti et al. 1999) and thereby buys time for coping skills to have an effect.

A third direction is the integrated study of multiple addictions. The previously cited studies of disulfiram provide one example. Another example is finding that cocaine abusers with greater depression during treatment are more likely to relapse to alcohol use rather than cocaine use (Brown et al.

1998). Others might include the study, tracking, and targeting of comorbid nicotine addiction. Indeed, our laboratory has been in the forefront of alcohol-nicotine theoretical (Monti et al. 1995; Rohsenow et al. 1997) and treatment work (study in progress), and we have begun to study cocaine-nicotine interactions. It is only in the context of a complete behavioral analysis that includes evaluation across addictions that we are likely to increase our treatment effectiveness for substance abuse problems.

A final direction that would be of value would be to study the cost-effectiveness of approaches that have been found to have significant treatment effects. An approach that may seem expensive may be cost-effective in terms of the savings in future treatments and medical expenses, and demonstrating this would improve the acceptability of the approach to the treatment community.

References

Abrams, D. B., & Niaura, R. S. (1987). Social learning theory. In H. T. Blane & K. E. Leonard (eds.), *Psychological theories of drinking and alcoholism* (pp. 131–178). New York: Guilford.

American Medical Association Committee on Alcoholism and Drug Dependence. Recovery from drug dependence. (1970). *JAMA, 214,* 579.

Alterman, A. I., McDermott, P. A., Cook, T. G., Metzger, D., Rutherford, M. J., Cacciola, J. S., & Brown, L. S., Jr. (1998). New scales to assess change in the Addiction Severity Index for the opioid, cocaine, and alcohol dependent. *Psychology of Addictive Behaviors, 12,* 233–246.

Anker, A. L., & Crowley, T. J. (1982). Use of contingency contracts in specialty clinics for cocaine abuse. In L. Harris (ed.), *Committee on the Problems of Drug Dependence 1981, NIDA Research Monograph Series, 41,* 452–459.

Bandura, A. (1977). *Social learning theory.* Englewood Cliffs, N.J.: Prentice-Hall.

Bejerot, N. (1975). Evaluation of treatment of drug dependence: Premises and principles. In H. Bostrum, T. Larsson, and N. Ljungsted (eds.) *Drug dependence: Treatment and treatment evaluation.* Stockholm: Almqvist and Wiksell, 1975 (pp. 291–299).

Brown, R. A., Monti, P. M., Myers, M. G., Martin, R. A., Rivinus, T., Dubreuil, M. E., & Rohsenow, D. J. (1998). Depression among cocaine abusers in treatment: Relationships with cocaine and alcohol use and treatment outcome. *American Journal of Psychiatry, 155,* 220–225.

Callahan, E. J., and Rawson, R. A. (1980). Behavioral assessment and treatment evaluation of narcotic addiction. In Sobell, L. C., Sobell, M. B., & Ward, E. (1980). *Evaluating alcohol and drug abuse treatment effectiveness.* New York: Pergamon. (pp. 77–91).

Carroll, K. M., Nich, C., & Rounsaville, B. J. (1995). Differential symptom reduction in depressed cocaine abusers treated with psychotherapy and pharmacotherapy. *The Journal of Nervous and Mental Disease, 183,* 251–259.

Carroll, K. M., Rounsaville, B. J., & Gawin, F. H. (1991). A comparative trial of psychotherapies for ambulatory cocaine abusers: Relapse prevention and interpersonal psychotherapy. *American Journal of Drug and Alcohol Abuse, 17,* 229–247.

Carroll, K., Ziedonis, D., O'Malley, S., McCance-Katz, E., Gordon, L., & Rounsaville, B. (1993). Pharmacologic interventions for alcohol- and cocaine-abusing individuals: A pilot study of disulfiram vs. naltrexone. *American Journal on Addictions, 2,* 77–79.

Chaney, E. F., O'Leary, M. R., & Marlatt, G. A. (1978). Skill training with alcoholics. *Journal of Consulting and Clinical Psychology, 46,* 1092–1104.

Chein, L., Gerard, D., Lee, R., & Rosenfeld, E. (1964). *The road to H.* New York: Basic Books.

Childress, A. R. (1993). Using active strategies to cope with cocaine cue reactivity: Preliminary treatment outcomes. Paper presented at the NIDA Technical Review Meeting on *Treatment of Cocaine Dependence: Outcome Research.* Bethesda, Maryland, September.

Childress, A. R., Hole, A. V., Ehrman, R. N., Robbins, S. J., McLellan, A. T., and O'Brien, C. P. (1993). Cue reactivity and cue reactivity interventions in drug dependence. In L. S. Onken, J. D. Blaine and J. J. Boren (eds.), *Behavioral treatments for drug abuse and dependence.* NIDA Research Monograph 137 (pp. 73–95).

Cohen, J. (1992). A power primer. *Psychological Bulletin, 112,* 155–159.

Drummond, D. C., & Glautier, S. (1994). A controlled trial of cue exposure treatment in alcohol dependence. *Journal of Consulting and Clinical Psychology, 62,* 809–817.

Drummond, D. C., Tiffany, S. T., Glautier, S., & Remington, B. (1995). *Addictive behaviour: Cue exposure theory and practice.* New York: Wiley.

Elkins, R. (1993). Aversion therapy treatment of cocaine dependent individuals. Paper presented at the NIDA Technical Review Meeting on *Treatment of Cocaine Dependence: Outcome Research.* Bethesda, Maryland, September.

Fals-Stewart, W., O'Farrell, T. J., Freitas, T. T., McFarlin, S. K., & Rutigliano, P. (2000). The timeline followback reports of psychoactive substance use by drug-abusing patients: Psychometric properties. *Journal of Consulting and Clinical Psychology, 68,* 134–144.

Fiske, A. D., Ackerman, P. L., & Schneider, W. (1987). Automatic and controlled processing theory and its applications to human factors problems. In P. A. Hancock (ed.), *Human factors psychology* (pp. 159–197).

Flynn, P. M., Craddock, S. G., & Dunteman, G. H. (1995). *Cocaine treatment outcome study: Overview and findings.* Research Triangle Park, N.C.: Research Triangle Institute.

Grabowski, J., and Johnson, B. (1993). Medication adjuncts in cocaine dependence treatment: Conceptual framework and review of progress. Paper presented at NIDA Technical Review Meeting on *Treatment of cocaine dependence: Outcome research.* Bethesda, Maryland, September.

Grabowski, J., Rhoades, H., Elk, R., Schmitz, J., and Creson, D. (1993). Clinicside and individualized behavioral interventions in drug dependence treatment. In L. S. Onken, J. D. Blaine and J. J. Boren (eds.), *Behavioral treatments for drug abuse and dependence.* NIDA Research Monograph 137 (pp. 37–72).

Hall, S. M., Havassy, B. E., & Wasserman, D. A. (1991). Effects of commitment to abstinence, positive moods, stress, and coping on relapse to cocaine use. *Journal of Consulting and Clinical Psychology, 59,* 526–532.

Hersh, D., Mulgrew, C. L., Van Kirk, J., & Kranzler, H. R. (1999). The validity of self-reported cocaine use in two groups of cocaine abusers. *Journal of Consulting and Clinical Psychology, 67,* 37–42.

Higgins, S. T. (1996). Some potential contributions of reinforcement and consumer-demand theory to reducing cocaine use. *Addictive Behaviors, 21,* 803–816.

Higgins, S. T., and Budney, A. J. (1993). Treatment of cocaine dependence through principles of behavior analysis and behavioral pharmacology. In L. S. Onken, J. D. Blaine and J. J. Boren (eds.), *Behavioral treatments for drug abuse and dependence.* NIDA Research Monograph 137 (pp. 97–122).

Higgins, S. T., Budney, A. J., Bickel, W. K., & Badger, G. J. (1994a). Participation of significant others in outpatient behavioral treatment predicts greater cocaine abstinence. *American Journal of Drug and Alcohol Abuse, 20,* 47–56.

Higgins, S. T., Budney, A. J., Bickel, W. K., & Badger, G. J., Foerg, F., and Ogden, D. (1995). Outpatient behavioral treatment for cocaine dependence: One-year outcome. *Experimental and Clinical Psychopharmacology, 3,* 205–212.

Higgins, S. T., Budney, A. J., Bickel, W. K., Foerg, F., Donham, R., and Badger, G. J. (1994b). Incentives improve outcome in outpatient behavioral treatment of cocaine dependence. *Archives of General Psychiatry, 51,* 568–576.

Higgins, S. T., Budney, A. J., Bickel, W. K., Hughes, J. R., and Foerg, F. (1993a). Disulfiram therapy in patients abusing cocaine and alcohol. *American Journal of Psychiatry, 150,* 675–676.

Higgins, S. T., Budney, A. J., Bickel, W. K., Hughes, J. R., Foerg, F., and Badger, G. J. (1993b). Achieving cocaine abstinence with a behavioral approach. *American Journal of Psychiatry, 150,* 763–769.

Higgins, S. T., Wong, C. J., Badger, G. J., Haug Ogden, D. E., & Dantona, R. L. (2000). Contingent reinforcement increases cocaine abstinence during outpatient treatment and 1 year of follow-up. *Journal of Consulting and Clinical Psychology, 68,* 64–72.

Hubbard, R. L., Craddock, S. G., Flynn, P. M., Anderson, J., & Etheridge, R. M. (1997).

Overview of 1-year follow-up outcomes in the Drug Abuse Treatment Outcome Study (DATOS). *Psychology of Addictive Behaviors, 11,* 261–278.

Kang, S., Kleinman, P. H., Woody, G. E., Millman, R. B., Todd, T. C., Kemp, J., & Lipton, D. S. (1991). Outcomes for cocaine abusers after once-a-week psychosocial therapy. *American Journal of Psychiatry, 148,* 630–635.

Kraemer, H. C. (in press). You can't fix by analysis what you bungle by design. In F. M. Tims, J. D. Blaine, L. S. Onken, & B. Tai (eds.), *Treatment of cocaine abuse: Outcome research.* Monograph, National Institute on Drug Abuse.

Maddux, J. F., and Desmond, D. P. (1986). Relapse and recovery in substance abuse careers. In F. M. Tims and C. G. Leukefeld (eds.), *Relapse and recovery in drug abuse.* NIDA Research Monograph 72 (pp. 49–71).

Maisto, S. A., and Cooper, A. M. (1980). A historical perspective on alcohol and drug treatment outcome research. In Sobell, L. C., Sobell, M. B., & Ward, E. (1980). *Evaluating alcohol and drug abuse treatment effectiveness.* New York: Pergamon. (pp. 1–14).

Marlatt, G. A., & Gordon, J. R. (1985). *Relapse prevention.* New York: Guilford.

Marlatt, G. A., Somers, J. M., and Tapert, S. F. (1993). Harm reduction: Application to alcohol abuse problems. In L. S. Onken, J. D. Blaine and J. J. Boren (eds.), *Behavioral treatments for drug abuse and dependence.* NIDA Research Monograph 137 (pp. 147–166).

McCance, E. F. (1997). Overview of potential treatment medications for cocaine dependence. In B. Tai, N. Chang, & P. Bridge (eds.), *Medication development for the treatment of cocaine dependence: Issues in clinical efficacy trials.* NIDA Research Monograph 175 (pp. 36–72).

McLellan, A. T., Kushner, H., Metzger, D., Peters, R., Grisson, G., Pettinati, H., and Argeriou, M. (1992). The fifth edition of the addiction severity index. *Journal of Substance Abuse Treatment, 9,* 199–213.

Michalec, E. M., Rohsenow, D. J., Monti, P. M., Varney, S. M., Martin, R. A., Dey, A. N., Myers, M. G., & Sirota, A. D. (1996). A cocaine negative consequences checklist: Development and validation. *Journal of Substance Abuse, 8,* 181–193.

Michalec, E., Zwick, W. R., Monti, P. M., Rohsenow, D. J., Varney, S., Niaura, R. S., & Abrams, D. B. (1992). A cocaine high-risk situations questionnaire: Development and psychometric properties. *Journal of Substance Abuse, 4,* 377–391.

Miller, W. R. (1991). Emergent treatment concepts and techniques. *Annual Review of Addictions Research and Treatment,* 283–296.

Monti, P. M., Abrams, D. B., Binkoff, J. A., Zwick, W. R., Liepman, M. R., Nirenberg, T. D., and Rohsenow, D. R. (1990). Communication skills training, communication skills training with family, and cognitive behavioral mood management training for alcoholics. *Journal of Studies on Alcohol, 51,* 263–270.

Monti, P. M., Abrams, D. B., Kadden, R. M., & Cooney, N. L. (1989). *Treating alcohol dependence: A coping skills training guide.* New York: Guilford.

Monti, P. M., Rohsenow, D. J., Colby, S. M., & Abrams, D. B. (1995). Smoking among alcoholics during and after treatment: Implications for models, treatment strategies and policy. In J. B. Fertig & J. P. Allen (eds.), *Alcohol and tobacco: From basic science to clinical practice.* Research Monograph 30, National Institute on Alcohol Abuse and Alcoholism.

Monti, P. M., Rohsenow, D. J., & Hutchison, K. E. (in press). Toward biological, psycho-biological, and psychosocial models of alcohol craving. *Addiction.*

Monti, P. M., Rohsenow, D. J., Hutchison, K., Swift, R. M., Mueller, T. I., Colby, S. M., Brown, R. A., Gulliver, S. B., Gordon, A., & Abrams, D. B. (1999). Naltrexone's effect on cue-elicited craving among alcohols in treatment. *Alcoholism: Clinical and experimental research, 23,* 1386–1394.

Monti, P. M., Rohsenow, D. J., Michalec, E., Martin, R. A., & Abrams, D. B. (1997). Brief coping skills treatment for cocaine abuse: Substance use outcomes at 3 months. *Addiction, 92,* 1717–1728.

Monti, P. M., Rohsenow, D. J., & O'Leary, T. (1997, November). *Treating substance abusers with coping skills training and motivational interviewing.* Institute presented at the annual meeting of the Association for Advancement of Behavior Therapy, West Miami Beach, Florida.

Monti, P. M., Rohsenow, D. J., Rubonis, A., Niaura, R., Sirota, A., Colby, S., Goddard, P., & Abrams, D. B. (1993). Cue exposure with coping skills treatment for male alco-holics: A preliminary investigation. *Journal of Consulting and Clinical Psychology, 61,* 1011–1019.

O'Malley, S. S., Jaffe, A. J., Chang, G., Schottenfeld, R. S., Meyer, R. E., & Rounsaville, B. (1992). Naltrexone and coping skills therapy for alcohol dependence: A controlled study. *Archives of General Psychiatry, 49,* 881–887.

RAND Drug Policy Research Center. (1992). Cocaine: The first decade. *Drug Policy Research Center, 1*(1), 1–4.

Rawson, R. A., Obert, J. L., McCann, M. J., Castro, F. G., & Ling, W. (1991). Cocaine abuse treatment: A review of current strategies. *Journal of Substance Abuse, 3,* 457–491.

Robinson, T. E. & Berridge, K. C. (1993). The neural basis of drug craving: An incentive-sensitization theory of addiction. *Brain Research Reviews, 18,* 247–291.

Rohsenow, D. J., Martin, R. A., Colby, S. M., Myers, M. G., Carnevale, C. L., & Monti, P. M. (1995a, November). *Cocaine relapse situation categories.* Poster presented at the annual meeting of the Association for Advancement of Behavior Therapy, Washington, D.C.

Rohsenow, D. J., & Monti, P. M. (1993). *Cocaine specific assessments and their role in improving treatment.* Presented at The Future of VA Mental Health Research, Washington, D.C., November.

Rohsenow, D. J., Monti, P. M., & Abrams, D. B. (1995b). Cue exposure treatment for alcohol dependence. In D. C. Drummond, S. Glautier, B. Remington, & S. Tiffany (eds.), *Addiction: Cue exposure theory and practice.* London: Wiley & Sons.

Rohsenow, D. J., Monti, P. M., Martin, R. A., Michalec, E., & Abrams, D. B. (in press). Brief coping skills treatment for cocaine abuse: Twelve month substance use outcomes. *Journal of Consulting and Clinical Psychology.*

Rohsenow, D. J., Monti, P. M., Colby, S. M., Gulliver, S. B., Sirota, A. D., Niaura, R. S., & Abrams, D. B. (1997). Effects of alcohol cues on smoking urges and topography among alcoholic men. *Alcoholism: Clinical and Experimental Research, 21,* 101–107.

Rohsenow, D. J., Monti, P. M., Rubonis, A. V., Sirota, A. D., Niaura, R. S., Colby, S. M., Wunschel, S. M., & Abrams, D. B. (1994). Cue reactivity as a predictor of drinking among male alcoholics. *Journal of Consulting and Clinical Psychology, 62,* 620–626.

Rohsenow, D. J., Niaura, R. S., Childress, A. R., Abrams, D. B., & Monti, P. M. (1990). Cue reactivity in addictive behaviors: Theoretical and treatment implications. *International Journal of the Addictions, 25* (7A & 8A), 957–993.

Shiffman, S. (1984). Coping with temptations to smoke. *Journal of Consulting and Clinical Psychology, 52,* 261–267.

Sobell, M. B., Maisto, S. A., Sobell, L. C., Cooper, A. M., Cooper, T., and Sanders, B. (1980). In Sobell, L. C., Sobell, M. B., and Ward, E., *Evaluating alcohol and drug abuse treatment effectiveness.* New York: Pergamon (pp. 129–150).

Sobell, L. C., and Sobell, M. B. (1986). Can we do without alcohol abusers' self-reports? *Behavior Therapist, 7,* 141–146.

Sobell, L. C., Sobell, M. B., and Ward, E. (1980). *Evaluating alcohol and drug abuse treatment effectiveness.* New York: Pergamon.

Stitzer, M. L., Iguchi, M. Y., and Felch, L. J. (1992). Contingent take-home incentive: Effects on drug use of methadone-maintenance patients. *Journal of Consulting and Clinical Psychology, 60,* 927–934.

Stitzer, M. L., Iguchi, M. Y., Kidorf, M., & Bigelow, G. E. (1993). Contingency management in methadone treatment: The case of positive incentives. In L. S. Onken, J. D. Blaine and J. J. Boren (eds.), *Behavioral treatments for drug abuse and dependence.* NIDA Research Monograph 137 (pp. 19–36).

Tiffany, S. T. (1990). A cognitive model of drug urges and drug-use behavior: Role of automatic and nonautomatic processes. *Psychological Review, 97,* 147–168.

Weddington, W. W., Brown, B. S., Haertzen, C. A., Hess, J. M., Mahaffey, J. R., Kolar, A. F., and Jaffe, J. H. (1991). Comparison of amantadine and desipramine combined with psychotherapy for treatment of cocaine dependence. *American Journal of Drug and Alcohol Abuse, 17,* 137–152.

Wilson, G. T. (1988). Alcohol use and abuse: A social learning analysis. In D. A. Chaudron and D. Wilkinson (eds.), *Theories on alcoholism* (pp. 239–287). Toronto, Ontario, Canada: Addiction Research Foundation.

Wise, R. A. (1988). The neurobiology of craving: Implications for the understanding and treatment of addiction. *Journal of Abnormal Psychology, 97,* 118–132.

Woody, G. E., McLellan, A. T., Luborsky, L., & O'Brien, C. P. (1987). Twelve-month follow-up of psychotherapy for opiate dependence. *American Journal of Psychiatry, 144,* 590–596.

SIXTEEN

ARE MANAGED CARE AND RELAPSE PREVENTION COMPATIBLE?

Dennis McCarty & Shelley Steenrod

Programs and health plans that impose standardization, control, measurement, and accountability on the delivery of health care in order to balance the utilization of services with cost management while maintaining quality of care are frequently labeled "managed care" (Goldstein, 1989; Mechanic, Schlesinger, & McAlpine, 1995; Wells, Astrachan, Tischler, & Unutzer, 1995). Managed care initiatives achieve their goals using (a) utilization management through preauthorization, case management, and utilization review, (b) selective contracting with practitioners on the basis of price and/or quality, and (c) risk sharing and other financial incentives (Goplerud, 1995; Mechanic et al., 1995).

Organizations and individuals that deliver care often experience managed care as alterations in financial incentives, restrictions on the type or quantity of services that will be reimbursed, and more scrutiny on the services provided. Some critiques suggest that the modifications inhibit access, threaten quality care, and encourage practitioners to deliver suboptimal amounts and intensity of services in order to minimize the cost of care and maximize profits (Woolhandler & Himmelstein, 1995; Woolhandler & Himmelstein, 1996). As a result, clinicians and consumers may express negative views about managed care and suspect that it contributes to more rapid relapse and poor client outcomes.

The role of relapse prevention in a managed care environment, therefore, may not be readily apparent. Answers to the question asked in the chapter title (Are managed care and relapse prevention compatible?) require an understanding of managed care models, characteristic features of managed care, and current strategies for assessing the quality of care. Moreover, a review of the benefits included in model plans and the standards that purchasers establish for plan performance will help assess the current and potential relations between managed care and relapse prevention.

MANAGED CARE: HISTORY AND MODELS

Historically, managed care meant enrollment in a staff model health maintenance organization (HMO). Early HMOs evolved as alternatives to traditional indemnity health insurance and were designed to provide comprehensive prepaid health care including preventive and wellness services. The concept of prepaid health care has been generalized and now includes preferred provider organizations, point of service plans, and exclusive provider arrangements. Many of the primary care plans, however, limited benefits for substance abuse and mental health services to federally mandated minimums. As a result, relapse was common and consumers and employers were disappointed with the quantity and quality of the substance abuse services provided within the managed health care plan (Freeman & Trabin, 1994). Moreover, services were often expensive and expenditures grew rapidly. Employees with indemnity insurance often had generous inpatient benefits that were fully utilized, and the expense of care quickly became substantial; the cost of long-term psychotherapy was also difficult to manage (Freeman & Trabin, 1994).

Proactive purchasers, primarily employers with skilled work forces that were difficult to replace, began to demand better management of these benefits. The behavioral health capitation was separated from the capitation for primary care and awarded to managed behavioral health care organizations that specialized in the management of mental health and substance abuse services (Altman & Price, 1993; Bertlant, Trabin, & Anderson, 1994; Freeman & Trabin, 1994). Often, managed behavioral health care organizations grew out of employee assistance programs (Freeman & Trabin, 1994). These carve-outs were usually differentiated from general medical services, managed through a separate review process, and relied on a separate set of providers (Freeman & Trabin, 1994).

Although managed behavioral health carve-outs have been widely adopted, many are concerned that separation of primary care and behavioral health leads to uncoordinated care and some purchasers are reexamining carve-in models where mental health and substance abuse benefits are integrated with primary care (England & Vaccaro, 1991). Carve-in models may promote earlier identification of substance abuse problems through assessments during visits for primary care and better management of total health care expenditures.

Recovery from alcohol and drug dependence is often characterized by intermittent periods of renewed substance abuse (Institute of Medicine, 1990a; Institute of Medicine, 1990b). During these periods of relapse a primary goal is to re-engage the individual in the treatment process quickly. In theory, managed care plans have the flexibility to craft individualized treatment plans designed to provide the level and intensity of service that addresses the immediate needs and can incorporate sufficient continuing support to reduce future demands for acute care. The managed care organization has a corporate interest in providing sufficient treatment to prevent future episodes that require emergency or urgent care. Management strategies and the characteristic features of managed care, however, often neglect to maximize the potential value of relapse prevention.

MANAGED CARE: MAJOR ISSUES AND FEATURES

In both public and private service systems, the introduction of managed care may provide a rare opportunity to restructure the organization and financing of substance abuse treatment services. Well-designed and skillfully implemented managed care initiatives can be used to address many limitations in current systems of care and, arguably, increase access to care, enhance the quality and integration of services, and improve the management of costs (Boyle & Callahan, 1995; Kushner & Moss, 1995; Mechanic & Aiken, 1989; Mechanic et al., 1995). Alternatively, incentives in managed care plans may inhibit access to services to control costs (especially the most expensive and specialized levels of care), threaten quality of care if minimal services are provided, and enhance profit margins rather than the delivery of appropriate amounts and intensity of services (Mechanic & Aiken, 1989; Schlesinger, 1995; Schlesinger, Dorwart, & Epstein, 1996; Woolhandler & Himmelstein, 1995; Woolhandler & Himmelstein, 1996). Purchasers and consumers must work collaboratively to promote the positive potential in managed care and inhibit undesired consequences (Institute of Medicine, 1997; The Mental Health Program of the Carter Center, 1995). Typically, managed care plans use three sets of strategies to reduce cost and enhance outcomes: utilization management, selective contracting, and risk sharing.

UTILIZATION MANAGEMENT

The Institute of Medicine (1989) defined utilization management as "a set of techniques used . . . to manage health care costs by influencing patient care decision-making through case-by-case assessments of the appropriateness of care prior to its provision" (p. 17). Utilization management techniques include preauthorization of care, concurrent review, and retrospective review (Hodgkin, 1992). Prior review is the most common form of utilization management and includes requirements for reviews and approval before admission, at admission, during continuing care, and for discharge planning (Institute of Medicine, 1989). Managed care organizations use utilization management and treatment guidelines to ensure that appropriate levels and intensity of care are provided and to reduce expenditures on unnecessary services (Institute of Medicine, 1989; Institute of Medicine, 1992; Institute of Medicine, 1997). The American Society of Addiction Medicine's publication on patient placement criteria attempts to standardize the criteria for admission to different levels of care for substance abuse treatment (American Society of Addiction Medicine, 1991). Currently, however, universal patient placement criteria have not been adopted (Gartner & Mee-Lee, 1995) and each managed care company tends to use its own standards. The lack of uniform, explicit, and widely accepted criteria for assigning and monitoring substance abuse treatment may be problematic (Woodward, 1992) and may contribute to tension between practitioners and managed care entities over the appropriate level and intensity of care. The absence of standards, however, also reflects a paucity of documentation on more effective and less effective clinical interventions. There is little consensus on the duration and intensity of care required for specific levels in impairment. Current standards, therefore, should establish treatment expectations and assure that no one receives too little care. Willingness to meet standards is one factor in provider selection.

SELECTIVE PROVIDER ARRANGEMENTS

Another strategy that managed care organizations use to control costs and standardize services is to limit the number of providers in the service network. Participants may be selected because they agree to discounted payments or because they meet specific quality standards. In primary health care, provider-selection models include health maintenance organizations (HMOs), preferred provider organizations (PPOs), and exclusive provider arrangements (EPOs). Panel construction must also balance administrative ease with patient needs. Limited membership facilitates cost management and quality control. But the selection process may also inhibit the formation of a panel sufficiently broad to meet the diversity of patient needs. It is critical to incorporate providers to address appropriately needs for culturally specific and gender-specific services (Institute of Medicine, 1997). As managed care expands to include mental health and substance abuse services, the agencies that provide alcohol and drug treatment services may compete to join managed care networks (Murphy, 1995). Network membership is limited to participating organizations, and networks often enter into risk-sharing contracts that individual members are unable to assume.

Risk-sharing arrangements are one reason that many remain skeptical about the potential for any health plan to provide quality care, especially for complex and chronic conditions. A primary concern is the incentive inherent in prepaid health care for plans and practitioners to deliver less care in order to maximize their personal and corporate profits (e.g., Woolhandler & Himmelstein, 1995; Woolhandler & Himmelstein, 1996). Thus, cost management and financing are a third facet of managed care that must be examined.

RISK SHARING

Cost management is a key to managed care. Managed care plans often use prepayments and capitation to create financial incentives and control the cost of health care (Institute of Medicine, 1997). Capitation includes financial risk—if the cost of care is greater than the total payments the health plan incurs a loss; alternatively, profits accrue if the cost of care is less than the fees collected. Purchasers can increase or decrease the amount of financial risk the managed care organization assumes and reduce the incentives for undertreatment (Frank, McGuire, & Newhouse, 1995). Frank et al. (1995) promote the use of "soft" capitation where risk is shared between the purchaser and the managed care organization. Shared risk creates a potential for the purchaser to benefit from the savings achieved through managed care. If they choose to do so, purchasers can reinvest "savings" into additional benefits and expanded eligibility for services. Conversely, potential losses are capped so the managed care organization can manage care with less fear about the consequences of high-cost cases. Safeguards must also be introduced to monitor subcapitation carefully. Practitioners and community providers may enter into risk-sharing arrangements with managed care plans and accept a portion of the capitation (a subcapitation) and assume the financial risk if the cost of care exceeds the subcapitation. Each reduction of a capitation payment reduces the available funds and increases the potential for undertreatment.

Despite potential problems, prepayment for services through the use of capitation and case rates may permit service providers to be more creative and flexible in the services delivered. Instead of being locked into a specified set of limited benefits, providers can innovate and use traditional and nontraditional strategies to improve outcomes. Thus, prepayment not only creates the potential for entrepreneurial incentives but may also facilitate creative care strategies and has a potential to contribute to more effective care.

Behavioral health problems, including substance abuse, however, are associated with social complications, a potential for chronicity, and stigma that complicate the management of substance abuse disorders and may require changes in managed care techniques (Mechanic et al., 1995). The extensive social costs and complications associated with alcohol and drug abuse mean that treatment authorization may be influenced by factors other than or in addition to clinical signs and symptoms (e.g., a lack of housing, court mandates, pregnancy, HIV illness). Chronic cases can lead to high utilization of expensive services, and strategies to manage these cases must be developed. Finally, the stigma and denial attached to alcohol and drug abuse means that individuals often fail to seek care and that health care practitioners may fail to identify substance abuse and not intervene when it is suspected. Thus, managed care plans are challenged to manage services in ways that promote access to care and facilitate long-term engagement in services. Managed care and relapse prevention are compatible if care is managed to promote recovery and inhibit relapse.

PERFORMANCE STANDARDS AND MEASURES FOR MANAGED CARE AND RELAPSE

Because of the potential flexibility associated with prepaid health care and persistent concerns that financial incentives encourage denial of care, purchasers and consumers seek assurances that health plans provide appropriate care. Increasingly, managed care companies use performance measures to document health outcomes and plan processes. The National Committee for Quality Assurance (NCQA), for example, worked with public and commercial purchasers to develop the Health Plan Employer Data and Information Set (HEDIS 3.0). Health plans with NCQA accreditation must collect and report the HEDIS performance measures so that consumers and purchasers can assess and compare health plans in eight areas: effectiveness, accessibility, satisfaction, cost, organizational stability, consumer information, utilization, and health plan descriptions (National Committee for Quality Assurance, 1996). These measures are motivated, in part, by a recognition that as the cost of health care increases purchasers and beneficiaries seek better values and must be able to compare health plans on quality as well as cost (England & Vaccaro, 1991; National Committee for Quality Assurance, 1996). One limitation inherent in performance standards is that health plans and service providers may overemphasize the facets of care that are measured and neglect other unmeasured aspects. It is important to continue to assess overall outcomes and assure that gains in one facet of care are not offset by decrements elsewhere.

Currently, both trade groups and purchasers are developing performance measures specific to their needs. The American Managed Behavioral Healthcare Association developed performance measures for behavioral health services (American Managed Behavioral Healthcare Association, 1995) and Digital Equipment Corporation operationalized HEDIS measures for its *HMO Performance Standards* (Digital Equipment Corporation, 1995). The measures that reflect relapse and relapse prevention, however, are limited and suggest more interest in avoiding the costs of hospitalization than in assuring stable recoveries.

The American Managed Behavioral Healthcare Association's Performance Measures for Managed Behavioral Healthcare Programs (PERMS 1.0) (American Managed Behavioral Healthcare Association, 1995), for example, addresses access to care with measures of services utilization and telephonic response times. Only one measure reflects relapse; the standard labeled "Treatment Failure—Substance Abuse" monitors readmissions to detoxification services within 90 days as a sign of system ineffectiveness. PERMS also assesses continuity of care following detoxification by monitoring follow-up status 30 days postdischarge: no follow-up, follow-up contact, follow-up contact plus readmission, and readmission without follow-up. If follow-up, however, is merely a telephone contact to assess current functioning, rather than an evaluation of how care is progressing, then opportunity to promote continuing care and prevent relapse may be lost.

It is perhaps ironic that the performance standards for Health Maintenance Organizations may provide the most direct attention to relatively long-term relapse prevention. The National Committee for Quality Assurance's latest set of performance measures covers all aspects of the services provided in HMOs and are required for accreditation (National Committee for Quality Assurance, 1996). Substance abuse services are addressed in a small set of measures including an assessment of "readmission for chemical dependency." Unlike the other standards reviewed, this measure is operationalized to assess readmissions within 90 days and 365 days of discharge from all acute treatment facilities including day treatment and outpatient services. The documentation suggests that readmission rates may reflect weak efforts at relapse prevention but then qualifies the observation with a note that "factors beyond the health plan's control can also contribute to relapse" (p. 59).

Both the PERMS and HEDIS measures, therefore, place little emphasis on relapse prevention. The potential, however, is present for health plans to aggressively monitor sobriety and prevent relapse.

MANAGED CARE IN PRACTICE: CURRENT STATUS

Managed care plans vary substantially in delivery models, the populations served, and the benefits provided. It is difficult, therefore, to characterize how all plans operate. Some are more effective treating addiction disorders and others have less obvious effectiveness. For all health care plans, however, the presence of social complications, stigma, and the potential for chronic relapse make substance abuse difficult to treat (Mechanic et al., 1995). Not only are individuals in need of care often reluctant to enter treatment, but health care practitioners may not be sensitive to the signs and symptoms of alcohol and drug dependence and abuse. As a result, health plans and their clinicians may either fail to assess the contribution of substance abuse to the presenting problems or be reluctant to intervene if a problem is apparent or suspected. It tends to be easier to inhibit the use of substance abuse treatment services than it is to promote access.

It is noteworthy, therefore, when a managed care plan demonstrates enhanced access to substance abuse treatment. Evaluation data analyzed after the first year of operation suggested that the Massachusetts Medicaid-managed behavioral health care program for mental health and substance abuse services increased access to most types of substance abuse treatment with no evidence of reductions in the quality of care (Callahan, Shepard, Beinecke, Larson, & Cavanaugh, 1995). Massachusetts Medicaid introduced the nation's first statewide managed behavioral health carve-out for mental health and substance abuse services for Medicaid recipients in 1992. When a primary care clinician program was developed to improve the coordination and delivery of primary care services for Medicaid recipients, program planners recognized that primary care clinicians rarely had specialized training in the assessment of behavioral health problems. Mental health and substance abuse services were separated from the primary care clinician program and placed under the control of a managed behavioral health care organization. An evaluation (Callahan et al., 1995) reported that admissions to substance abuse treatment services increased from 32 users per 1,000 Medicaid enrollees in fiscal year 1992 to 36 users per 1,000 during fiscal year 1993 — a 10 percent improvement. Services in detoxification centers increased 45 percent and there was a 20 percent increase in admissions to methadone medication and counseling services; a decline in admissions to acute care hospitals for detoxification was explained by the intentional diversion of the hospital admissions to nonhospital detoxification centers. Thirty-day readmission rates were stable, and consumer and provider interviews suggested few changes in the perceived quality of care. Finally, Callahan et al. (1995) reported that despite the increased access to care, Medicaid expenditures for substance abuse treatment declined 45 percent from $28.6 million to $15.8 million primarily because of the reduced use of acute care hospitals. The increase in access to services that provided alternatives to hospital care and reductions in expenditures for substance abuse treatment services continued during the second year of the managed care program (Frank, McGuire, Notman, & Woodward, 1996). Thus, the Massachusetts Medicaid behavioral health carve-out is an interesting example of a managed care initiative that appears to be well positioned to embrace relapse prevention.

A review of the current benefits, performance standards, and performance improvement standards established for the managed behavioral health care organization suggest, however, that relapse prevention is given little direct attention. The substance abuse treatment benefits included in the mental health and substance abuse program are summarized in table 16.1 (inpatient services), table 16.2 (diversionary services), and table 16.3 (outpatient services). The performance standards (see table 16.4) and performance improvement standards (table 16.5) are also outlined.

The authorized benefits reflect the purchaser's (the state Medicaid authority) intent to reduce the use of hospital level of services and divert consumers to less expensive settings (the use of freestanding detoxification centers, intensive outpatient and day treatment services, and post-detoxification short-term residential care). Support is also apparent for a strong continuum of outpatient services that includes a range of options designed to treat dependence on alcohol and other drugs. What is not apparent are specialized services designed to prevent or arrest relapse. Although many of the services can contribute to relapse prevention, the absence of attention to relapse prevention in the benefits package suggests that the purchaser and the managed behavioral health care organization treat addiction as an episodic disorder rather than an illness that requires chronic care strategies.

The contract performance standards and the performance improvement standards address short-term relapse in three ways. First, the contract in-

Table 16.1. Substance abuse treatment benefits included in the Massachusetts Medicaid managed behavioral health carve-out: Inpatient services

BENEFIT	EXPLANATION
Enhanced Level III De-toxification for Pregnant Women	Short-term medical treatment for substance abuse withdrawal including medical and social components to ensure quality substance abuse treatment and obstetrical care to pregnant women.
Inpatient Substance Abuse Services (Level IV)	Hospital services which provide a planned detoxification regimen of 24 hour medically directed evaluation, care and treatment in a medically managed inpatient setting
Level III Detoxification	Short-term medical treatment for substance use withdrawal, individual medical assessment, evaluation, intervention, substance abuse counseling and post-detoxification referrals. These services may be provided in licensed freestanding or hospital-based programs.

(Services and explanations as listed in the Massachusetts Medicaid contract for the Mental Health and Substance Abuse Program (MH/SAP) — Appendix C: Covered Services Under MH/SAP; explanations edited and abridged.)

cludes a performance standard that requires an outpatient visit within three days of a discharge from an inpatient facility. There is a clear expectation that inpatient services must be linked to outpatient services and an implicit assumption that the linkage will reduce rapid relapse. This assumption is stated explicitly in the contract's second performance standard — readmissions to inpatient facilities within seven days of discharge must not exceed 5 percent. Note, however, that the standard is not specific to substance abuse and it seems likely that the primary concern is psychiatric readmissions. The emphasis in the seven additional standards on operational issues — promptness of admission authorizations, claims processing, and report generation — suggests that the purchaser expects administrative efficiencies as well as clinical efficiency. Finally, a third facet of the contract standards are the two performance improvement standards. The improvement standard for continuing

Table 16.2. Substance abuse treatment benefits included in the Massachusetts Medicaid managed behavioral health carve-out: Diversionary services

BENEFIT	EXPLANATION
Day Treatment for Pregnant Women	A structured addiction treatment program consisting of group counseling for pregnant women five days per week. Groups include information about addiction and incorporate cognitive and behavioral approaches aimed at supporting abstinence and special treatment issues of women.
Residential Substance Abuse Treatment	Short-term twenty-four hour therapeutically planned treatment and learning situation for adults or adolescents which provides continuity of care after Level III Detoxification.
Structured Outpatient Addiction Program	Short-term clinically intensive structured day and/or evening substance abuse services. It can be a step-down service for individuals being discharged from Level III Detoxification or can be utilized by individuals whose symptoms indicate a need for structured outpatient treatment beyond the standard outpatient levels.

(Services and explanations as listed in the Massachusetts Medicaid contract for the Mental Health and Substance Abuse Program (MH/SAP) — Appendix C: Covered Services Under MH/SAP; explanations edited and abridged.)

care specifies that the percent of inpatient hospital discharges who complete at least one outpatient visit per month for four months following hospital discharge should improve by 10 percent from the prior year. Although this continuation in care could contribute substantially to relapse prevention, the emphasis is on hospital discharges. Most substance abuse detoxification does not occur in hospitals and, therefore, is not covered under this standard. The standard appears to be focused again primarily at psychiatric discharges.

In summary, the Massachusetts Medicaid behavioral health carve-out reflects one of the more sophisticated managed behavioral health care plans in the nation. The plan emphasizes access to care and recognizes that Medicaid beneficiaries often have complicated health conditions and require strong continuums of care. It is instructive that the relatively well-designed plan in-

Table 16.3. Substance abuse treatment benefits included in the Massachusetts Medicaid managed behavioral health carve-out: Outpatient services

BENEFIT	EXPLANATION
Acupuncture Detoxification	Insertion of metal needles through the skin to withdraw individuals from dependence on substances.
Intensive Outpatient for Pregnant Women	Group counseling aimed at supporting abstinence and addressing special treatment issues of women.
Methadone Maintenance	Administration of methadone with appropriate social and medical services; includes both dosing and counseling.
Couple Counseling	Rehabilitative counseling provided to a couple whose primary complaint is disruption of their relationship or family due to substance abuse.
Family Counseling	Rehabilitative counseling of more than one member of a family at the same time in the same session where the primary complaint is disruption of the family due to substance abuse.
Group Counseling	Rehabilitative counseling of a group of individuals having a primary complaint that is associated with substance abuse.
Individual Counseling	Rehabilitative counseling provided to an individual whose primary complaint is substance abuse.
Substance Abuse Case Consultation	A preplanned meeting between the substance abuse treatment provider and other providers of treatment concerning an individual for identification and planning for additional services, coordination of a treatment plan, progress review, and revision of a treatment plan.
Substance Abuse Family Consultation	A preplanned meeting with family members for treatment and/or discharge planning.
Substance Abuse Diagnostic Evaluation	A biopsychosocial assessment of an individual's physical, psychological, social, economic, educational, environmental, and vocational assets and disabilities for the purpose of designing a treatment plan.

Table 16.3. Continued

BENEFIT	EXPLANATION
Substance Abuse Medication Visit	An individual visit for psychopharmacological evaluation, prescription, review, and/or monitoring.

(Services and explanations as listed in the Massachusetts Medicaid contract for the Mental Health and Substance Abuse Program (MH/SAP) — Appendix C: Covered Services Under MH/SAP; explanations edited and abridged.)

cludes little direct attention to supporting relapse prevention efforts among men and women with some period of stable sobriety.

An informed purchaser of commercial health plans, Digital Equipment Corporation, also requires little direct attention to relapse prevention. Since 1991, Digital Equipment Corporation has been an assertive purchaser of health care and promulgated explicit performance standards for all health plans that contract with the company (Digital Equipment Corporation, 1995). The behavioral health standards prohibit benefit limits, allow direct access to behavioral health services, promote prompt access to care, assure sufficient numbers of mental health professionals, foster linkages to the Employee Assistance Program, require case management, stipulate outcome measurement, and set expectations for quality improvement efforts. Although a variety of specialized services are specified, relapse prevention is not mentioned directly. The case management functions "continue until the patient sustains a long term stable life function level" (p. 34) and, therefore, may play an important role in preventing relapse. But, again the lack of explicit attention to relapse prevention suggests that the potential value of preventing relapse may be underappreciated.

CONCLUSIONS AND FUTURE DIRECTIONS

Managed care plans are moving toward outcomes management and integrated delivery systems (England & Vaccaro, 1991; Freeman & Trabin, 1994; Kushner & Moss, 1995). Increased emphasis on morbidity and mortality as outcome indicators will encourage more attention to strategies that inhibit and prevent relapse among individuals with substance abuse disorders. In addition, increased integration with primary care may promote opportunities to identify alcohol and drug abuse earlier in the disease process and facilitate intervention prior to dependence. Thus, managed care organizations are likely to foster screening and assessment strategies and integration with pri-

Table 16.4. Contractor performance standards for the Massachusetts Medicaid managed behavioral health carve-out

STANDARD	EXPLANATION
Outpatient Visits	Discharges from inpatient hospitals, freestanding detoxification facilities, and acute residential treatment facilities shall be followed by an outpatient visit within three days of discharge.
Readmissions	Readmissions to inpatient facilities within seven days of discharge shall not exceed five percent.
Timeliness of Inpatient Admissions	Inpatient admissions shall be approved within a defined time period when the clinical assessment has been completed and medical necessity has been determined.
Referrals to the Department of Mental Health	Enrollees referred to DMH Continuing Care Services shall meet eligibility requirements; inappropriate referrals shall not exceed five percent.
Inpatient Prior Approvals	Prior approval decisions for inpatient services shall be completed within three hours of receiving assessment information.
Continuation of Care	Prior approval decisions for continuing care in inpatient settings shall be completed within 24 hours of receiving all necessary clinical information.
Prior Approval of Outpatient Services	Decisions on prior approval for admission and continuing care approvals shall be completed within 10 business days of receiving all necessary clinical information.
Claims Processing	Review, process, and remit a check for 95 percent of clean claims within 30 days of receiving the claims.
Report Submission	All required reports shall be submitted within 45 days of the end of the quarter.

(Performance standards and explanations as listed in the Massachusetts Medicaid contract for the Mental Health and Substance Abuse Program (MH/SAP) — Appendix A; explanations edited and abridged.)

Table 16.5. Contractor performance improvement bonuses for the
Massachusetts Medicaid managed behavioral health carve-out

PERFORMANCE IMPROVEMENT STANDARD	EXPLANATION
Continuing Care Rate	The percentage of individuals discharged from an inpatient hospital unit who attend a minimum of one outpatient appointment per month for four months shall be required to increase 10 percent relative to the prior comparison period.
Discharge Information	The percentage of inpatient hospital charts with evidence of completed discharge information at the time of discharge shall be required to increase by 7.5 percent relative to the prior comparison period.

(Performance improvement standards and explanations as listed in the Massachusetts Medicaid contract for the Mental Health and Substance Abuse Program (MH/SAP)—Appendix A; explanations edited and abridged.)

mary care as indirect strategies to prevent relapse and reduce the burden of substance abuse on the health plan.

Effective management of substance abuse disorders requires aggressive aftercare, comprehensive screening and assessment, and strong links with primary care. Untreated substance abuse leads to inefficient health care utilization and increases the cost of medical services because alcohol and drug-related morbidity are increased, unexpected medical complications are more common when individuals are receiving standard medical care, and traumatic head injury and spinal cord injury are more likely (Fuller, 1995). Although screening initiatives have demonstrated potential to identify high-risk drinkers and brief interventions have led to substantial reductions in alcohol use (WHO Brief Intervention Study Group, 1996), few health plans include an emphasis on systematic screening of their patient population. The Oregon Health Plan provides an interesting example of large-scale implementation of screening procedures. The HMOs that enroll Medicaid beneficiaries must complete annual substance abuse screens on each Medicaid member. A 10-item screen, based on observations (needle marks), physiological tests (liver function), and CAGE type items, is used during routine examinations, prenatal visits, and for cases where medical utilization is high. Purchasers of health care, therefore, can have a substantial influence on the effort a health plan makes to screen and assess substance abuse problems among enrollees. Similar procedures can be used to support recovery and interrupt relapse episodes.

Managed care organizations can also enhance the relation between primary care and specialty substance abuse treatment services (Larson, Samet, & McCarty, 1997). This relation is important not only for early identification and treatment of substance abusers but also for continuity of care and support during aftercare. Primary care providers, ideally, support patients during substance abuse treatment and provide follow-up and aftercare support during medical office visits. A patient who is relapsing is more likely to confide in a primary care provider who has knowledge and awareness of his substance abuse history than in one who does not. Likewise, a physician who is aware of a patient's substance abuse history is more likely to recognize signs of relapse and encourage the patient to reenter treatment. Primary care providers, as part of a patient's social support network, need to be included and involved in the treatment planning initiatives of their patients. Managed care organizations will be more effective at relapse prevention if they enhance communication between primary care and specialty substance abuse treatment providers.

Current systems of care for the treatment of alcohol and drug abuse and dependence reflect a tradition of insufficient coverage for substance abuse in commercial health plans, reliance on public systems to care for individuals with the greatest impairment, and multiple funding mechanisms (Institute of Medicine, 1997). A common result is uncoordinated services that tend to respond to dependence on alcohol and other drugs as an acute illness rather than a chronic relapsing disease. The introduction of managed care strategies offers unique opportunities to modify and improve the delivery of substance abuse treatment services. Our review suggests, however, that much remains to be accomplished and that relapse prevention receives little explicit attention in most managed care initiatives. The purchasers of health care must emphasize the value of relapse prevention. Health plans, for example, can be structured to include specific benefits for individuals in early recovery and promote active client involvement in relapse prevention. The contract with the managed care organization, moreover, could include financial incentives to enroll men and women completing a substance abuse treatment episode into the relapse prevention program. Public and private purchasers of behavioral healthcare and the managed care organizations that supervise substance abuse treatment must soon recognize that attention to relapse prevention is not only compatible with managed care but necessary if treatment outcomes are to be enhanced and if the morbidity and mortality associated with abuse and dependence on alcohol and other drugs are to be reduced.

Acknowledgments

Preparation of this paper was supported by grants from the National Institute on Drug Abuse (P50 DA10233) and the National Institute on Alcohol Abuse and Alcoholism (R01 AA11363). Thanks to Richard Frank for comments and suggestions.

References

Altman, L., & Price, W. (1993). Alcan Aluminum: Development of a mental health "carve-out." *New Directions for Mental Health Services, (59)*, 55–65.

American Managed Behavioral Healthcare Association (1995). *Performance Measures for Managed Behavioral Healthcare Programs (PERMS).* Washington, D.C.: American Managed Behavioral Healthcare Association.

American Society of Addiction Medicine (1991). *Patient Placement Criteria for the Treatment of Psychoactive Substance Use Disorders.* Washington, D.C.: American Society of Addiction Medicine.

Bertlant, J., Trabin, T., & Anderson, D. (1994). The value of mental health and chemical dependency benefits: More than meets the eye. In E. Sullivan (ed.), *Driving Down Health Care Costs: Strategies and Solutions.* Frederick, Md.: Panel Publishers.

Boyle, P. J., & Callahan, D. (1995). Managed care in mental health: The ethical issues. *Health Affairs, 14*(3), 7–22.

Callahan, J. J., Shepard, D. S., Beinecke, R. H., Larson, M. J., & Cavanaugh, D. (1995). Mental health/substance abuse treatment in managed care: The Massachusetts Medicaid experience. *Health Affairs, 14*(3), 173–184.

Digital Equipment Corporation (1995). *HMO Performance Standards.* Maynard, Mass.: Digital Equipment Corporation.

England, M. J., & Vaccaro, V. A. (1991). New systems to manage mental health care. *Health Affairs, 10*(4), 129–137.

Frank, R. G., McGuire, T. G., & Newhouse, J. P. (1995). Risk contracts in managed mental health care. *Health Affairs, 14*(3), 50–64.

Frank, R. G., McGuire, T. G., Notman, E. H., & Woodward, R. M. (1996). Developments in Medicaid managed behavioral health care, *Mental Health U.S.: 1996.* Rockville, Md.: Center for Mental Health Services.

Freeman, M. A., & Trabin, T. (1994). *Managed Behavioral Healthcare: History, Models, Key Issues, and Future Course.* Rockville, Md.: Center for Mental Health Services.

Fuller, M. (1995). More is less: Increasing access as a strategy for managing health care costs. *Psychiatric Services, 46*(10).

Gartner, L., & Mee-Lee, D. (1995). *The Role and Current Status of Patient Placement Criteria in the Treatment of Substance Use Disorders.* Rockville, Md.: Center for Substance Abuse Treatment.

Goldstein, L. (1989). Genuine managed care in psychiatry: A proposed practice model. *General Hospital Psychiatry, 2,* 271–277.

Goplerud, E. (1995). *Managed care for mental health and substance abuse services.* Rockville, Md.: Substance Abuse and Mental Health Services Administration.

Hodgkin, D. (1992). The impact of private utilization management on psychiatric care: A review of the literature. *Journal of Mental Health Administration, 19,* 143–157.

Institute of Medicine (1989). *Controlling Costs and Changing Patient Care? The Role for Utilization Management.* Washington, D.C.: National Academy Press.

Institute of Medicine (1990a). *Broadening the Base of Treatment for Alcohol Problems.* Washington, D.C.: National Academy Press.

Institute of Medicine (1990b). *Treating Drug Problems.* Washington, D.C.: National Academy Press.

Institute of Medicine (1992). *Guidelines for Clinical Practice: From Development to Use.* Washington, D.C.: National Academy Press.

Institute of Medicine (1997). *Managing Managed Care: Quality Improvement in Behavioral Health.* Washington, D.C.: National Academy Press.

Kushner, J. N., & Moss, S. (1995). *Purchasing Managed Care Services for Alcohol and Other Drug Treatment: Essential Elements and Policy Issues.* Rockville, Md.: Center for Substance Abuse Treatment.

Larson, M. J., Samet, J. M., & McCarty, D. (1997). Managed care of substance abuse disorders: Implications for generalist physicians. *Medical Clinics of North America, 81*(4), 1053–1069.

Mechanic, D., & Aiken, L. H. (1989). Capitation in mental health: Potentials and cautions. *New Directions in Mental Health,* (43), 5–18.

Mechanic, D., Schlesinger, M., & McAlpine, D. D. (1995). Management of mental health and substance abuse services: State of the art and early results. *The Milbank Quarterly, 73,* 19–55.

The Mental Health Program of the Carter Center. (1995). *Managing Care in the Public Interest: The Eleventh Annual Rosalynn Carter Symposium on Mental Health Policy.* Atlanta, Ga.: The Carter Center.

Murphy, A. M. (1995). *Formation of Networks, Corporate Affiliations and Joint Ventures Among Mental Health and Substance Abuse Treatment Organizations.* Rockville, Md.: Center for Mental Health Services.

National Committee for Quality Assurance (1996). *HEDIS 3.0 Draft: Health Plan Em-*

ployer Data and Information Set. Washington, D.C.: National Committee for Quality Assurance.

Schlesinger, M. (1995). Ethical issues in policy advocacy. *Health Affairs, 14*(3), 23–29.

Schlesinger, M., Dorwart, R. A., & Epstein, S. S. (1996). Managed care constraints on psychiatrists' hospital practices: Bargining Power and Professional Autonomy. *American Journal of Psychiatry, 153,* 256–260.

Wells, K. B., Astrachan, B. M., Tischler, G. L., & Unutzer, J. (1995). Issues and approaches in evaluating managed mental health care. *Milbank Quarterly, 73,* 57–75.

WHO Brief Intervention Study Group (1996). A cross-national trial of brief interventions with heavy drinkers. *American Journal of Public Health, 86,* 948–955.

Woodward, A. (1992). Managed care and case management of substance abuse treatment. In R. S. Ashery (Ed.), *Progress and issues in Case Management: NIDA Research Monograph 127* (Vol. DHHS Publication No. ADM 92-1946). Rockville, Md.: National Institute on Drug Abuse.

Woolhandler, S., & Himmelstein, D. U. (1995). Extreme risk—the new corporate proposition for physicians. *New England Journal of Medicine, 333,* 1706–1708.

Woolhandler, S., & Himmelstein, D. U. (1996). Annotation: Patients on the auction block. *American Journal of Public Health, 86,* 1699–1700.

IV

*Evaluating Our Understanding of Recovery
and Preventing Relapse*

SEVENTEEN

FUTURE DIRECTIONS IN SUBSTANCE ABUSE RELAPSE AND RECOVERY

Carl G. Leukefeld, Frank M. Tims, & Jerome J. Platt

Because substance abuse is a chronic and relapsing condition, this chapter explores future possibilities for substance abuse relapse and recovery initiatives with emphasis on practice and research. Relapse has been a consistent concern. Early relapse estimates (Wanberg and Horn, 1970) were that more than 90% of patients at twelve-month follow-up from alcohol treatment used substances, and almost half returned to pretreatment use. These findings highlight a reality that recovery is an ongoing process. In fact, relapse and recovery are practically and clinically intertwined.

There are a number of persistent questions related to relapse and recovery. As examples: Is recovery the absence of any substance use, as those involved in mutual self-help recovery groups stringently endorse? Does recovery include substituting one substance for another substance? Can a person in recovery use substances at decreased levels? Clearly, these and other definitional issues are not resolved. To complicate this issue further, practitioners and researchers alter definitions of relapse and recovery for different purposes, with obvious implications for both practice and research. Consequently, recovery in one program that does not pay attention to substituting one drug for another—such as alcohol in a pharmacotherapy program or continued use of alcohol in a methadone maintenance program—may not be recovery in an alcohol treatment program.

Relapse prevention is now part of many behavioral and other substance abuse treatment interventions. These relapse prevention strategies, focused on stressors and coping approaches for high-risk situations, are exemplified by the early work of Marlatt and Gordon (1985). Marlatt and Gordon identified the following eight categories of high drinking situations: unpleasant emotions, physical discomfort, pleasant emotions, testing personal control, urges and temptations, conflict with others, social pressure to drink, and pleasant times with others. Currently, a number of commonly used intervention programs—including those developed by Monti et al. (1989)—target these situations as part of a formalized curriculum used to teach recovery and related social skills in order to prevent relapse and enhance recovery.

Internal motivation and external motivation enhancements have also been used to prevent relapse, and consequently to enhance recovery. Internal motivation enhancements incorporate principles from change models (see Prochaska and DiClemente, 1992) that describe specific stages of change as integral parts of the change process. As Marlow et al. (this volume) as well as Farabee and Leukefeld (this volume) indicate, external motivation enhancements incorporate criminal justice status—probation, parole, or mandatory release—to increase the length of time a person remains in substance abuse treatment and to increase positive treatment outcomes that enhance recovery.

CONCEPTUAL FRAMEWORK

An organizing framework, referred to as the bio/psycho/social model, has been used traditionally by treatment practitioners. It is used here as a framework to present theoretical underpinnings for relapse and recovery. This framework could be practical for practitioners and useful for researchers. When complicated issues like relapse and recovery are simplified with a reductionistic approach like the one presented here, details are, of necessity, omitted and complications can result. Simplicity is not the goal, however; rather, utility is a goal, particularly for practitioners.

The bio/psycho/social framework is relevant for substance abuse relapse prevention and recovery with its strong roots in the alcohol field—most specifically alcohol treatment (Wallace, 1989). This framework is frequently used by clinicians to bridge the disease model of alcoholism and the 12-step or mutual self-help group approach—which includes Alcoholics Anonymous (AA) and Narcotics Anonymous (NA) (Godlaski, Leukefeld, and Cloud, 1997)—with behavioral and learning theory approaches developed by psychologists and social psychologists.

Practitioners and researchers can, and frequently do, approach drug and alcohol use very differently. These approaches or frameworks are often solidified by experiences and education that generally determine a person's approach to use, abuse, dependency, and addiction. Frameworks and models can be important to facilitate communication and establish commonalities to deliver efficient clinical services for clients/patients.

The following framework expands the bio/psycho/social approach with the addition of spirituality/"connectedness." This framework, or the bio/psycho/social/spiritual framework (Leukefeld and Leukefeld, 1999), incorporates pathways and includes behavior, attitudes, values, and knowledge—as possible outcomes—that have been related to alcohol and drug use/abuse as individual and environmental factors. These pathways could also be described as predisposing factors associated with nature/nurture. These four factors are overviewed as:

Biological, genetic, and disease factors related to heritability (Cloninger, 1981; Anthenelli and Schuckit, 1991) that are the foundation for the disease model. The disease model has been criticized largely because alcoholics and drug abusers refuse to take responsibility for their drinking and drugging behaviors because a disease cannot be "controlled." Physicians and many health care providers approach treatment interventions from a diagnosable biological/genetic perspective (Galanter and Kleber, 1994; Schuckit, 1995). The recovering community approaches drug and alcohol abuse as a chronic disease (see Alcoholics Anonymous, 1996; Narcotics Anonymous, 1987; and McCrady and Miller, 1993). There is also an expanding literature, supported by clinical experience, that indicates that gender as a basic biological factor should be taken into account for both theoretical considerations and practice interventions. This literature stresses the importance of gender differences in clinical interventions (Tannen, 1990).

Psychological and cognitive factors incorporate individual characteristics that can be assessed and are learned. In one approach, many of these variables have been described as "risk" and "protective" factors (Hawkins, Cattalano, and Miller 1992). Psychological theories incorporate drug and alcohol behaviors as learned behavior. Therefore, if behavior is learned, it can be "unlearned" with appropriate interventions. For example, slips and lapses could be a focus of interventions before full relapse (Gorsky and Miller, 1986; Marlatt and Gordon, 1985). Can slips and lapses (Marlatt & Gordon, 1985) be discussed openly as part of treatment, or is this kind of discussion taboo? How can treatment motivation (see DeLeon, this volume) be enhanced? Can ap-

proaches like motivational interviewing (Miller and Rollnick, 1991) be used
to reduce relapse?

Social and behavioral factors include environmental, cultural, familial, and
peer factors that have been related in the literature to social learning (Bandura, 1977). For example, contingency management and behavioral re-
inforcements to enhance treatment, particularly pharmacological treatment,
largely in methadone maintenance programs, have been the focus of research
and practice (see Stitzer and Kirby, 1991) and cocaine interventions (O'Brien,
Childress, McLellan, and Ehrman, 1993). Clinical data suggest that such social factors as employment and the availability of social supports (O'Brien,
Childress, and McLellan, 1991) as well as case management services (Siegal
et al., this volume) are related to treatment outcome and retention. Additional studies are examining craving and environmental cues.

Spiritual, relational, and connectedness factors incorporate anecdotal and
other information that spirituality (Benson, 1996) and religiosity (Gorsuch,
1995) are related to preventing relapse and enhancing recovery. Although
most of the literature consistently reports that spirituality is related to recovery, it is not without controversy. Controversy surrounds the relation between spirituality and health and healing (Tessman and Tessman, 1997). The
idea that religiosity is a protective factor in preventing drug use (Adlaf and
Smart, 1985; Jessor and Jessor, 1977) is also controversial for some. Many participants in mutual self-help groups, including AA and NA, attribute their
recovery to a spiritual connectedness and relationship to a higher power that
maintains their recovery and prevents relapse (see Alcoholics Anonymous,
1996; Narcotics Anonymous, 1987). Natural recovery has been defined as processes that individuals use to stop their own addictions without treatment.
Self-recoverers indicate that, among other things, they disliked the culture
associated with their addiction, they were able to establish emotionally meaningful ties with others, and they developed new relationships with established
natural groups and communities to stop using (Granfield and Cloud, 1996).

Frameworks and their underlying theories can be problematic, particularly within a changing managed health care environment. Different frameworks and treatment approaches, as well as interventions, can be contradic-
tory. These contradictions frequently present dilemmas for patients/clients
who are exposed to several models as they "progress" through different treatment programs and modalities into their own recovery.

FUTURE DIRECTIONS FOR RELAPSE AND RECOVERY

The current literature, which is supported anecdotally by clinical practitioners, presents the overall consensus that relapse is usual and relapse is part of the recovery process. However, the relapsing nature of substance abuse is not always understood by the general public and those beginning their own recovery process. Therefore, it is important to continuously educate patients/clients that substance abuse is a chronic and relapsing condition. *Relapse is common for most people as part of their recovery process.* In fact, this message is critical for the general public so that there is an understanding of the relapsing nature of substance abuse recovery. Unfortunately, many believe that relapse is not part of substance abuse, and they indicate that substance abuse treatment is not effective when slips, lapses, and relapse occur. This issue should be an integral part of the treatment process for family members and significant others. That is to say that "cures" for substance abuse and dependency may not be possible, but recovery is ongoing.

FUTURE DIRECTIONS FOR RESEARCH AND PRACTICE

PRETREATMENT/BEFORE TREATMENT

Pretreatment can include activities to motivate and encourage individuals to enter and remain in treatment, more commonly used in behavioral treatments rather than pharmacological treatments. Pretreatment activities can range from a series of "warm-up sessions" to motivate clients/patients to participate in subsequent treatment to the use of external factors such as community and family sanctions to encourage substance abusers to enter treatment. Using a stages-of-change approach (see Prochaska and DiClemente, 1982), pretreatment involves the "get ready" stage of preparing for treatment. There is a growing literature related to before-treatment activities, but it remains limited and usually unrelated to better understanding of relapse and recovery.

Before-treatment approaches have been examined to decrease relapse. For example, Crowley (1984) successfully used written behavioral contracts with sanctions for failing to stay abstinent. Sanctions agreed upon in a written contract before treatment included job loss, loss of professional license, or disclosure of use to a probation or parole officer. Treatment matching before treatment has also been found to reduce relapse and to enhance retention in treatment (McLellan and Alterman, 1991). Treatment matching is expected to receive additional emphasis within a managed care environment. Matching clinicians to client/patient before-treatment is an additional area that has been examined to increase treatment retention and enhance recovery (see, for example, McCaul and Svikis, 1991).

Criminal justice authority, mandatory treatment, and civil commitment generally have a history of enhancing treatment retention and reducing relapse (Marlow, this volume; Leukefeld and Tims, 1988). Drug courts are now growing in popularity as a way of using criminal justice authority — judicial authority — as external motivation to decrease substance use and enhance recovery. Evaluations should provide additional information about this external approach to motivation. Developing and examining creative pretreatment and before-treatment approaches are "ripe" areas for creative research and practice. For example, treatment readiness is an area that has received limited research and practice attention to enhance recovery (see, for example, DeLeon, Melnick, and Tims, this volume).

TREATMENT/INTERVENTIONS

Most current discussions about substance abuse treatment either are introduced with managed care principals or their focus is almost exclusively on managed care. These discussions incorporate the idea that, within a managed care environment, treatment is limited and must be brief. However, effective substance abuse treatment is associated with longer stays in treatment. In spite of this contradiction, McCarty and Steenrod (this volume) indicate that managed care organizations should recognize that relapse prevention is necessary to enhance treatment outcomes and reduce associated morbidity and mortality. This provides opportunities for both practitioners and researchers (see, for example, Miller, Zweben, DiClimente, and Rycharik, 1995). Anglin and Fiorentine (this volume) suggest that a careers framework could be useful for consolidating findings and suggesting research directions.

Preventing relapse and enhancing recovery have received attention from a number of different points of view. But the most commonly used approach is to teach patients/clients to deal with slips and lapses that do not always lead to relapse (Gorski and Miller, 1985; Marlatt and Gordon, 1985). Other behavioral approaches, like incentives, have been used to decrease cocaine use (Higgins et al., 1994).

From the behavioral practitioner point of view, there is interest in preventing relapse. Enhancing patient/client motivation so clients/patients can engage in substance abuse treatment and consequently remain in treatment is receiving attention (see, for example, DeLeon, Melnick, and Tims, this volume). Early research on treatment motivation and clinical applications was developed by Miller (1985) and Miller and Rollnick (1991). With this approach, motivational interviewing is part of a therapeutic process that a clinician uses to "motivate" the client/patient to engage in self-change. In fact, each client/patient is responsible for his or her own change.

Pharmacotherapies keep patients/clients in treatment and consequently reduce relapse. Methadone maintenance has been successfully used as a pharmacotherapy treatment and to retain opioid users in treatment (Ball and Ross, 1991; Kree, 1992). Naltrexone has been reported to reduce relapse in alcohol dependency (Volpicelli et al., 1992). However, pharmacotherapies are not considered to be the magic bullet for everyone, and developing a pharmacotherapy for cocaine is still in process (Hart, McCance, and Kosten, this volume). Hart, McCance, and Kosten (this volume) also indicate that there is general consensus about the utility of pharmacological treatments for alcohol with antabuse, tobacco with nicotine replacement therapy including patches/gum, and methadone for opiates. The use of pharmacotherapies to prevent relapse continues to be refined with opportunities for understanding relapse and behavioral stressors, among other things.

Treatment enhancements to increase treatment retention and reduce relapse have been used selectively (see Pickens, Leukefeld, and Schuster, 1991). For example, treatment enhancements can include activities specifically designed for the individual client/patient, or they can be part of substance abuse treatment programs that include vocational training, job readiness training, and parent training. Program treatment enhancements can include the use of community referrals to enhance treatment in such settings as mental health treatment, STD and HIV clinics, and family services. Developing treatment enhancements for adolescents to reduce relapse is a special area deserving attention (see Spear, Ciesla, Skala, and Kania, this volume).

A particular issue related to enhancing recovery and reducing relapse, about which there is a great deal to learn, is assessing and diagnosing substance abuse that coexists with psychiatric disorders—comorbidity (see Sinha and Schottenfeld, this volume). Because most substance abuse treatment takes place in outpatient settings, practitioners are aware of the need to tailor interventions to enhance recovery. Treatment enhancements, for example, could incorporate family, peer, and workplace activities to supplement therapies. Researchers have not taken advantage of outpatient behavioral treatment settings, however, as they have in the case for pharmacotherapy treatment, especially methadone treatment.

Developing behavioral and pharmacotherapy treatments and understanding relapse among cocaine and crack users are receiving attention (see Rohsennow and Monti, this volume). Understanding relapse among cocaine users, particularly users of crack cocaine, which presents specific problems with its intense addictive qualities, has also been the focus of research (see Broome, Simpson, and Joe, this volume).

AFTERCARE/FOLLOW-UP

Early periods after treatment are possibly the most critical for relapse. With that in mind, a group of researchers and practitioners (Leukefeld and Tims, 1989) recommended that clinicians make aftercare contacts with clients in the following schedule for those who successfully complete treatment:

- First week after treatment
- First month after treatment
- Third month after treatment
- First year after treatment

Although these recommendations were made more than a decade ago, there has been very little research to systematically examine the intensity and duration of contacts after treatment termination when used as recovery enhancements. This information could be important because treatment exposures are getting shorter with managed care and there is a need to do more with less.

Mutual self-help group involvement is recommended to maintain sobriety, and Alcoholics Anonymous (AA) is a most important part of recovery for many alcohol abusers (Godlaski, Leukefeld, and Cloud, 1997). In fact, anecdotal reports by many alcohol abusers in recovery attribute sobriety to AA and consider AA involvement to be the most important part of their recovery. As Brown, Kinlock, and Nurco (this volume) indicate, mutual self-help interventions have not been evaluated because of the anonymity associated with membership. One contribution researchers could make is to better examine the role of mutual self-help organization membership in treatment outcome studies. This could include asking about mutual self-help involvement and taking this involvement into account for treatment outcome studies.

RESEARCH OPPORTUNITIES

The following areas of study are suggested. These areas are revised and expanded from those presented by Leukefeld and Tims (1989) after considering updated information. Nevertheless, there are striking deficiencies that remain to be examined. The following areas are suggested:

- Developing pharmacotherapies that can be used to decrease cocaine use. Paralleling the development of pharmacotherapies is a need to develop behavioral strategies that can assure that newly developed medications are used consistently and appropriately.
- Additional studies, particularly laboratory studies, can be initiated to understand the physiological aspects of recovery.
- Experimental studies can assess the interaction of behavior and environmental stimuli on relapse and recovery. These kinds of studies could incorporate bio/psycho/social/spiritual variables as well as "partitioning variables" by study. With additional information needed for both males and females, it is suggested that gender-specific, as well as gender-common, studies be developed.
- Longitudinal studies can be developed to examine the natural history of addiction careers including drug runs/drug use, incarceration, treatment exposures, HIV/AIDS, perceived recovery, and slips/lapses/relapses.
- In light of the prevalence of HIV/AIDS among injectors and crack users, studies could examine relapse(s) that go beyond descriptions of who relapses and begin to identify circumstances, settings, conditions, and factors related to relapse. It should be noted that these factors could differ by gender, substance, drug use progression, and sexual behaviors.
- Clinical studies can examine brief versus long-term treatment to understand better the impact of shorter treatment in a managed care environment. These results could be contrasted with findings that the length of time in treatment is associated with successful outcomes, including decreased relapse. Additional clinical studies could also add to our understanding of treatment, family characteristics, the role of comorbidity, and the use of treatment matching to enhance recovery.
- Longitudinal staged clinical studies that incorporate treatment assignment could go a long way to understanding age and gender-specific interventions as well as the additive nature of treatment exposures over a recovery career.
- Studies can be developed that focus on better understanding natural recovery and the role of mutual self-help groups in recovery.
- Basic and applied studies can add to the understanding of the nature of craving and substance use relapse.
- Criteria for assessing the success or failure of substance abuse treatment can vary by patient/client, clinical setting, program, and the general public. The basic indicator of success is not using drugs. Other indicators of success commonly used are the number of arrests and criminal acts,

which are important for the criminal justice system, employment and/or school involvement, and lifestyle. There are other indicators that could be used to better understand relapse. These indicators include quality of life, addiction career changes, reduced drug runs, decreased criminal lifestyle, well-being, and productive lifestyle.

CONCLUDING REMARKS

Drug and alcohol abuse are chronic and relapsing disorders. Although research has consistently reported that the longer a person remains in treatment the less likely the person is to relapse, current managed care approaches are shorting treatments to control costs and potentially increase relapse rates. Perhaps managed care as well as additional research will help convince the general public about the chronic and relapsing nature of substance abuse.

There are challenges as well as opportunities for clinicians to incorporate relapse prevention into practice and for researchers to help better understand the variety of possibilities to enhance recovery. These opportunities are varied and cut across bio/psycho/social/spiritual areas of professional interest and commonly held opinions. Consequently, understanding behavioral and pharmacological actions will clearly continue to be areas of interest to understand recovery better in the future.

Acknowledgments

Preparation of this chapter was supported by grants from the National Institute on Drug Abuse DA10101 and DA11309.

References

Adalf, E., and Smart, R. (1985). Drug use and religious affiliation, feelings and behavior. *British Journal of the Addictions.* 80:163–171.

Alcoholics Anonymous. (1996). Croton Falls, N.Y.: The Anonymous Press.

Anthenelli, R. M., and Schuckit, M. A. (1991). Genetic studies of alcoholism (review). *International Journal of the Addictions.* 25(1):81–94.

Ball, J., and Ross, A. (1991). *The Effectiveness of Methadone Treatment.* New York: Springer-Verlag.

Bandura, A. (1977). *Social Learning Theory.* Englewood Cliffs, N.J.: Prentice Hall.

Benson, H., with Marg Stark Scriber (1997). *Timeless Healing: The Power and Biology of Belief.* New York: Simon and Schuster.

Cloninger, C. R., Bohman, M., and Sigvardson, S. (1981). Inheritance of alcohol abuse: Crossfostering analysis of adopted men. *Archives of General Psychiatry.* 39:861–868.

Crowley, T. J. (1984). Contingency contracting treatment of drug-abusing physicians, nurses and dentists. In J. Grabowski, M. L. Stitzer, and J. E. Henningfield (eds.), *Behavioral Intervention Techniques in Drug Abuse Treatment* Washington, D.C.: U.S. Government Printing Office. 68–83.

Galanter, M. and Kleber, H. D. (1994). *Textbook of Substance Abuse Treatment.* Washington, D.C.: American Psychiatric Press.

Godlaski, T. M., Leukefeld, C. G., and Cloud, R. (1997). Recovery: With and without self-help. *Substance Use and Misuse.* 32(5):621–627.

Gordon, R. S. (1989). An operational definition of disease prevention. *Public Health Reports.* 98:107–109.

Gorski, T. T., and Miller, W. R. (1986). *Staying Sober: A Guide for Relapse Prevention.* Independence, Mo.: Independence Press.

Granfield, R., and Cloud, W. (1996). The elephant that no one sees: Natural recovery among middle-class addicts. *Journal of Drug Issues.* 26(1):45–61.

Gorsuch, R. L. (1995). Religious aspects of substance abuse and recovery. *Journal of Social Issues.* 51(2):65–83.

Hart, C., McCance-Katz, and Kosten, (2001). Pharmacotherapies Used in Common Substance Abuse Disorders. In F. Tims, C. G. Leukefeld, and G. Platt (eds), *Relapse and Recovery Process in Addictions.* New Haven, Conn.: Yale University Press.

Hawkins, J. D., Catalano, R. F., and Miller, J. Y. (1992). Risk and protective factors for alcohol and other drug problems in adolescence and early adulthood: Implications for substance abuse prevention. *Psychological Bulletin.* 112(1):64–105.

Higgins, S. T., Budney, A. J., Bickel, W. K., Foerg, F. E., Donham, R., and Badger, G. J. (1994). Incentives improve outcome in outpatient behavioral treatment of cocaine dependence. *Archives of General Psychiatry.* 51:568–576.

Jessor, R., and Jessor S. L. (1977). *Problem Behavior and Psychosocial Development: A Longitudinal Study of Youth.* New York: Academic Press.

Kreek, M. J. (1992). Rationale for maintenance pharmacotherapy of opiate dependence. In C. P. O'Brien, and J. H. Jaffe (eds). *Addictive States.* New York: Basic Books.

Leukefeld, C. G., and Bukoski, W. J. (1991). Drug abuse prevention evaluation methodology: A bright future. *Journal of Drug Education.* 21(3):191–201.

Leukefeld, C. G., and Godlaski, T. (1997). Structured behavioral outpatient rural therapy: A treatment manual for substance use and dependence. Lexington, Ky.: Center on Drug and Alcohol Research.

Leukefeld, C. G., and Leukefeld, S. (1999). Primary socialization theory and a bio/psycho/spiritual practice model for substance use. *Substance Use and Misuse.* 34(7):983–991.

Leukefeld, C. G., and Tims, F. T. (1988). *Compulsory Treatment of Drug Abuse: Research and Clinical Practice.* Washington, D.C.: U.S. Government Printing Press.

Leukefeld, C. G., and Tims, F. M. (1989). Relapse and recovery in drug abuse: Research and practice. *International Journal of the Addictions,* 24(3):189–201.

Marlatt, G. A., and Gordon, J. R. (1985). *Relapse Prevention: Maintenance Strategies in the Treatment of Addictive Behavior.* New York: Guilford Press.

McCaul, M. E., and Svikis, D. S. (1991). Improving client compliance in outpatient treatment: Counselor-target interventions. In R. W. Pickens, C. G. Leukefeld, and C. R. Schuster (eds.). *Improving Drug Abuse Treatment.* Washington, D.C.: U.S. Government Printing Office, 204–217.

McCrady, B. S., and Miller, W. R. (1993). *Research on Alcoholics Anonymous: Opportunities and Alternatives.* New Brunswick, N.J.: Alcohol Research Documentation.

McLellan, A. T., and Alterman, A. I. (1991). Patient treatment matching: A conceptual and methodological review with suggestions for future research. In R. W. Pickens, C. G. Leukefeld, and C. R. Schuster (eds.). *Improving Drug Abuse Treatment.* Washington, D.C.: U.S. Government Printing Office, 114–135.

Miller, W. R. (1985). Motivation for treatment: A review with special emphasis on alcoholism. *Psychological Bulletin.* 98:84–107.

Miller, W. R., and Rollnick, S. (1991). *Motivational Interviewing.* New York: Guilford Press.

Miller, W. R., Zweben, A., DiClimente, C. C., and Rycharik, R. G. (1995). *Motivational Enhancement Therapy Manual.* Rockville, Md.: National Institute on Alcohol Abuse and Alcoholism.

Monti, P. M., Abrams, D. B., Kaden, R. M., and Cooney, N. L. (1989). *Treating Alcohol Dependence: A Coping Skills Training Guide.* New York: Guilford.

Narcotics Anonymous. (1987). Van Nuys, Calif.: World Service Office.

O'Brien, C. P., Childress, A. R., and McLellan, A. T. (1991). Conditioning factors may help to understand and prevent relapse in patients who are recovering from drug dependence. In R.W. Pickens, C.G. Leukefeld, and C. R. Schuster (eds.). *Improving Drug Abuse Treatment.* Washington, D.C.: U.S. Government Printing Office, 293–312.

O'Brien, C. P., Childress, A. R., McLellan, A. T., and Ehrman, R. (1993). Developing treatments that address classical conditioning. In F. T. Tims and C. G. Leukefeld (eds.). Cocaine Treatment: Research and Clinical Perspectives. Washington, D.C.: U.S. Government Printing Office, 71–91.

Pickens, R. W., Leukefeld, C. G., and Schuster, C. R. (1991). *Improving Drug Abuse Treatment.* Washington, D.C.: U.S. Government Printing Office.

Prochaska, J. O., & DiClemente, C. C. (1992). Stages of change in the modification of problem behaviors. *Progress in Behavior Modification* 28:183–218.

Schuckit, M. A. (1995). *Drug and Alcohol Abuse: A Clinical Guide to Diagnosis and Treatment.* New York: Plenum.

Stitzer, M. L., and Kirby, K. C. (1991). Reducing illicit drug use among methadone patients. In R. W. Pickens, C. G. Leukefeld, and C. R. Schuster (eds.). *Improving Drug Abuse Treatment.* Washington, D.C.: U.S. Government Printing Office, 178–203.

Tannen, D. (1990). *You Just Don't Understand: Women and Men in Conversation.* New York: William Morrow.

Tessman, I., and Tessman, J. (1997). Mind and body. *Science* 276: 369–370.

Volpicelli, J. R., Alterman, A. I., Hayashida, M., and O'Brien, C. P. (1992). Naltrexone in the treatment of alcohol dependence. *Archives of General Psychiatry* 46: 876–880.

Wallace, J. (1989). A biopsychosocial model of alcoholism. *Social Casework* 70(6):325–332.

Wanberg, K. W., and Horn, J. L. (1970). Alcoholism symptom patterns of men and women: A comparative study. *Quarterly Journal of Studies on Alcohol* 31:40–61.

INDEX

Note: page numbers in italics refer to figures or tables.